THE FEMINISM BOOK

THE FEMINISM BOOK

DK

DK LONDON

PROJECT EDITOR
Zoë Rutland

PROJECT ART EDITOR
Katie Cavanagh

SENIOR EDITOR
Camilla Hallinan

US EDITOR
Megan Douglass

ILLUSTRATIONS
James Graham

JACKET EDITOR
Emma Dawson

JACKET DESIGNER
Stephanie Cheng Hui Tan

JACKET DESIGN
DEVELOPMENT MANAGER
Sophia MTT

PRODUCER, PRE-PRODUCTION
Gillian Reid

PRODUCER
Mandy Inness

MANAGING EDITOR
Gareth Jones

SENIOR MANAGING ART EDITOR
Lee Griffiths

ASSOCIATE PUBLISHING DIRECTOR
Liz Wheeler

ART DIRECTOR
Karen Self

DESIGN DIRECTOR
Philip Ormerod

PUBLISHING DIRECTOR
Jonathan Metcalf

DK DELHI

SENIOR ART EDITOR
Mahua Sharma

ART EDITORS
Meenal Goel, Devika Khosla, Rupanki Kaushik,
Debjyoti Mukherjee

ASSISTANT ART EDITOR
Mridushmita Bose

SENIOR EDITOR
Anita Kakar

EDITOR
Arpita Dasgupta

ASSISTANT EDITOR
Aishvarya Misra

JACKET DESIGNERS
Suhita Dharamjit, Dhirendra Singh

JACKETS EDITORIAL COORDINATOR
Priyanka Sharma

SENIOR DTP DESIGNER
Harish Aggarwal

DTP DESIGNER
Sachin Gupta

PICTURE RESEARCHER
Vishal Ghavri

MANAGING JACKETS EDITOR
Saloni Singh

PICTURE RESEARCH MANAGER
Taiyaba Khatoon

PRE-PRODUCTION MANAGER
Balwant Singh

PRODUCTION MANAGER
Pankaj Sharma

SENIOR MANAGING EDITOR
Rohan Sinha

MANAGING ART EDITOR
Sudakshina Basu

original styling by
STUDIO 8

TOUCAN BOOKS

EDITORIAL DIRECTOR
Ellen Dupont

SENIOR DESIGNER
Thomas Keenes

SENIOR EDITOR
Dorothy Stannard

EDITORS
John Andrews, Victoria Heyworth-Dunne,
Sue George, Cathy Meeus, Constance Novis,
Rachel Warren-Chadd

EDITORIAL ASSISTANTS
Ameera Patel, Ella Whiddett

INDEXER
Marie Lorimer

PROOFREADER
Sophie Gillespie

ADDITIONAL TEXT
Elaine Aston, Hilary Bird, Shelley L. Birdsong,
Alexandra Black, Helen Douglas-Cooper, Rachel Engl,
Sue George, Emily Goddard, Marta Iñiguez de
Heredia, Harriet Marsden, Abigail Mitchell, Raana
Shah, Shan Vahidy, Rachel Warren-Chadd

First American Edition, 2019
Published in the United States by DK Publishing
345 Hudson Street, New York, New York 10014

Copyright © 2019 Dorling Kindersley Limited
DK, a Division of Penguin Random House LLC
19 20 21 22 23 10 9 8 7 6 5 4 3 2 1
001–311038–March/2019

A catalog record for this book
is available from the Library of Congress.
ISBN 978-1-4654-7956-3

Printed in Malaysia

A WORLD OF IDEAS:
SEE ALL THERE IS TO KNOW

www.dk.com

CONTRIBUTORS

HANNAH McCANN, CONSULTANT EDITOR

Dr. Hannah McCann is a lecturer in gender studies at the University of Melbourne. She researches the way women present their gender and how this is represented within feminist discussion and in a wide range of LGBTQ+ communities. Her research monograph "Queering Femininity: Sexuality, Feminism and the Politics of Presentation" was published in January 2018.

GEORGIE CARROLL

Georgie Carroll is a PhD candidate at the School of Oriental & African Studies in London, UK. She has studied issues of gender in Indian national soap opera and her current research on aesthetics and the environment in a South Asian context considers gendered landscapes and female sexuality.

BEVERLEY DUGUID

Beverley Duguid is a historian, author, and writer. Her PhD thesis covers women's varied responses to formal and informal empires in the Caribbean and Central America during the 19th century. She has also written on the growth of black British women's political and feminist consciousness in the 1980s.

KATHRYN GEHRED

Kathryn Gehred graduated from Sarah Lawrence College with an MA in women's history. She is currently Research Editor at the University of Virginia, where she works at the Martha Washington Papers Project.

LIANA KIRILLOVA

Liana Kirillova is a doctoral candidate in History from Southern Illinois University Carbondale (SIUC), specializing on the Youth Movement in the Soviet Union in the context of the Cold War and Soviet Internationalism.

ANN KRAMER

Ann Kramer studied women's history at the University of Sussex, UK. She has written extensively on women's political activity from Mary Wollstonecraft through to the present day, as well as writing about women's experiences in both world wars.

MARIAN SMITH HOLMES

Marian Smith Holmes is a journalist and a former associate editor at *Smithsonian* magazine. Based in Washington, D.C., she specializes in African American history and culture. She edited and contributed to *Dream a World Anew: The African American Experience and the Shaping of America*, published in 2016.

SHANNON WEBER

Shannon Weber is a US writer, researcher, and feminist scholar. She holds a PhD in feminist studies from the University of California, and has been published in numerous popular and academic magazines, journals, and books. She has taught at a variety of academic institutions including Tufts University and Brandeis University.

LUCY MANGAN, FOREWORD

Lucy Mangan is a columnist, television reviewer, and features writer. She was educated in Catford, London, and Cambridge. She studied English at the latter and then spent two years training as a lawyer, but left as soon as she qualified and went to work much more happily in a bookshop. She is now a columnist for *Stylist* magazine, a frequent writer for *The Guardian, The Telegraph,* and other publications. She is the author of five books, most recently *BOOKWORM: A Memoir of Childhood Reading,* published in 2018.

CONTENTS

THE PERSONAL IS POLITICAL
1945–1979

THE POLITICS OF DIFFERENCE
1980s

A NEW WAVE EMERGES
1990–2010

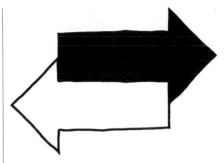

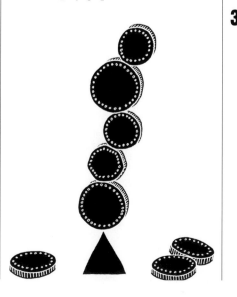

FOREWORD

Fresh out of university, I applied for a job in the city. The older of the two men who interviewed me looked at my resumé and, seeing that I had written about women's issues for the student paper, asked: "Are you a feminist, then?" I could practically see the thought cloud full of heavily dungareed women yomping around the streets with placards but I wanted a job, so I replied cautiously, "Well, I'm my idea of a feminist. I doubt whether I'm yours." He acknowledged my diplomacy with a nod but kept returning to the subject and—despite attempted intervention by his younger colleague—badgering me about it. In the end, in exasperation, I said, "Oh for God's sake! I shaved my legs for this interview, if that makes you feel any better!" His colleague froze but he laughed. I got the job.

All of which is by way of saying: it's a complicated business, feminism. Ignorance abounds, as do stereotypes, hostility, and simple confusion. The only way to dispel any and all of these is to provide greater information. To fill with facts the void that allows fears, doubts, and prejudices to rush in. Anything, from mastodons to global socio-political movements, become a whole lot less frightening when they step out of the shadows and you can see exactly what it is you are dealing with. This book illuminates feminism on all sides and beats back ignorance with every page.

The Feminism Book also performs a second vital function—to give women in particular a sense of their place in history, which is famously written by the victors. Female activists and their achievements have always been undercelebrated, underbroadcast, and underacknowledged. And when that happens, it becomes harder to build on what has gone before. The wheel has to be reinvented, which is exhausting even when you don't have to give birth to and raise the next generation at the same time.

Most of us are not taught the history of feminism in school. If we come to an awareness of the imbalance between the sexes, it is piecemeal. More often than not, for me, a tiny but outrageous snippet of news would catch my attention and lodge in my brain like a burr. When I was 10, for example, I learned that my friend's younger brother got more pocket money than she did. Why? Because he was a boy. My body practically jackknifed with the pain of the injustice. A few years later, I read in *Just Seventeen* magazine that Claudia Schiffer, the most super of the 1980s supermodels, was consumed with anxiety about her "uneven hairline." Somewhere deep within me I recognized that a world in which a young woman could feel like this was possibly not one that was fully arranged around women's comfort and convenience. Realizations come, large and small, over the years until the skewing of the world in favor of men eventually becomes too obvious to ignore. Then we start casting around for answers. Which is either electrolysis—or feminism.

But what is feminism? Can you be equal, but different? Can you be against the patriarchy but still like men? Should you fight every little thing or save your energy for the big ones? And did I disqualify myself from the sisterhood forever by shaving my legs for that interview?

How much better it would be to know what forms feminism has taken over the years, how it has evolved, its strengths and its blind spots. To know what fights have already been fought and won, or fought and need fighting again. To be able to look to your historical reserves, marshal your argument troops, and go into battle armed with the knowledge that you are not, and have never been, alone in it.

Herein lie mystics, writers, scientists, politicians, artists, and many more who offered new thoughts, new attitudes, new definitions, new rules, new priorities, new insights, then and now. What is feminism? It's in here.

Lucy Mangan

Lucy Mangan

INTRODU

For centuries, women have been speaking out about the inequalities they face as a result of their sex. However, "feminism" as a concept did not emerge until 1837, when Frenchman Charles Fourier first used the term *féminisme*. Its use caught on in Britain and the US during the ensuing decades, where it was used to describe a movement that aimed to achieve legal, economic, and social equality between the sexes, and to end sexism and the oppression of women by men.

As a consequence of differing aims and levels of inequality across the globe, various strands of what constitutes feminism exist. The evolving ideas and objectives of feminism have continued to shape societies ever since its conception, and as such, it stands as one of the most important movements of our time—inspiring, influencing, and even surprising vast populations as it continues to develop.

Paving the way

Male dominance is rooted in the system of patriarchy, which has underpinned most human societies for centuries. For whatever reasons patriarchy came into being, societies required more regulation as they became more complex, and men created institutions that reinforced their power and inflicted oppression on women. Male rule was imposed in every area of society—from government, law, and religion, to marriage and the home. Subordinate and powerless to this male rule, women were viewed as inferior to men in terms of their intellectual, social, and cultural status.

Evidence of women challenging the limitations imposed by patriarchy is sparse, mainly because men controlled the historical record. However, with the onset of the Enlightenment in the late 17th and early 18th centuries and the growing intellectual emphasis on individual liberty, pioneering women began

> 66
>
> I have never felt myself to be inferior … Nevertheless, 'being a woman' relegates every woman to secondary status.
> **Simone de Beauvoir**
>
> 99

to draw attention to the injustices they experienced. When revolutions broke out in the US (1775–1783) and France (1787–1799), many women campaigned for the new freedoms to be applied to women. While such campaigns were unsuccessful at the time, it was not long before more women took action.

The waves

Sociologists identify three main "waves," or time periods, of feminism, with some feminists hailing a fourth wave in the second decade of the 21st century. Each wave has been triggered by specific catalysts, although some view the metaphor as problematic, reducing each wave to a single goal when feminism is a constantly evolving movement with a wide spectrum of aims.

The goals of first-wave feminism dominated the feminist agenda in the US and Europe in the mid-19th century, and arose from the same libertarian principles as the drive to abolish slavery. Early feminists (mainly educated, white, middle-class women) demanded the vote, equal access to education, and equal rights in marriage. First-wave feminism lasted until around 1920, by which time most Western countries had granted women the right to vote.

With energy centered on the war effort during World War II (1939–1945), it was not until the 1960s that a second wave began to flourish, nonetheless influenced by writings that emerged during the war period. The slogan "the personal is political" encapsulated the thinking of this new wave. Women identified that the legal rights gained during the first wave had not led to any real improvement in their everyday lives, and they shifted their attention to reducing inequality in areas from the workplace to the family to speaking candidly about sexual "norms."

Spurred on by the revolutionary climate of the 1960s, the second wave has been identified with the fearless Women's Liberation Movement, which further sought to identify and to put an end to female oppression. While new courses in feminist theory at universities examined the roots of oppression and analyzed the shaping of ideas of gender, grassroots organizations sprang up to tackle injustices. Women wrenched back control of childbirth from the male-dominated medical profession, fought for the right to legal abortion, and stood up to physical assault.

The vitality of the second wave waned during the 1980s, weakened by factionalism and the increasingly conservative political climate. Yet the '80s saw an emergence of black feminism (also termed "womanism") and the idea of intersectionality—a recognition of the multiple barriers faced by women of color, which feminism, dominated by white, middle-class women, had failed to address. This concept, first put forward in 1989 by Kimberlé Crenshaw, resonated not only in the US and UK, but also across former colonial countries worldwide.

New concerns

When American feminist Rebecca Walker responded to the acquittal of an alleged rapist in the early 1990s, she vocalized the need for a third wave, arguing that women still needed liberation, and not just the equality that postfeminists thought had already been achieved. The third wave comprised diverse and often conflicting strands. Areas of division included attitudes toward "raunch culture" (overtly sexual behavior) as an expression of sexual freedom, the inclusion of trans women in the movement, and the debate over whether feminist goals can be achieved in a capitalist society. This rich exchange of ideas continued into the new millennium, aided by feminist blogs and social media.

> A woman must not accept; she must challenge.
> **Margaret Sanger**

Addressing issues from sexual harassment in the workplace to the gender pay gap, feminism is more relevant now than it ever has been.

This book

By no means an exhaustive collection of the inspiring figures who have advanced women's place in society, this book unpacks some of the most prominent ideas from the 1700s to the present day. Each entry focuses on a specific period of time, and centers around evocative quotes from those who spoke up either within, or about, these periods. *The Feminism Book* reflects how fundamental feminism is to understanding the way the world is organized today, and how far the movement still has left to go. ∎

THE BIR
FEMINIS
18TH—EARLY 19TH

In her book *Some Reflections on Marriage*, Englishwoman Mary Astell argues that God created men and women with **equally intelligent souls**.

In Britain, the Bluestockings Society, an informal **discussion group**, is formed for intellectual women and invited men.

1700

1750s

1734

1765

The Swedish Civil Code grants certain rights to women, notably forbidding men to sell their **wife's property** without her consent.

The **Daughters of Liberty** form in the US to protest against import duties and support American independence from Britain.

The word "feminism" did not gain currency until the 1890s, but individual women were expressing feminist views long before. By the early 1700s, women in different parts of the world were defining and examining the unequal status of women and beginning to question whether this was natural and inevitable. Exploring their situation through writing and discussion, women, individually or collectively, began to voice their objection to women's subservient position and to express their wish for greater rights and equality with men.

From weakness to strength

In the early 18th century, women were largely regarded as naturally inferior to men on an intellectual, social, and cultural level. This was a deep, long-held belief, reinforced by the teachings of the Christian Church, which defined women as the "weaker vessel." They were subject to their father's and, if married, their husband's control.

As the century wore on, social and technological changes began to have further profound influences on the lives of women. The growth of trade and industry created a burgeoning, aspirational middle class in which social roles were sharply defined by gender. The public sphere of work and politics was seen as uniquely male, while women were expected to remain in the private sphere of "home," a distinction that was to become increasingly entrenched.

Technology also transformed the printing industry, leading to an outpouring of journals, pamphlets, novels, and poetry, all spreading information and new ideas. These were absorbed by privileged, educated women, some of whom, despite social restrictions, turned to writing, expressing feminist views through the printed word.

Some of the earliest feminist writings came out of Sweden in the mid-18th century. There, a relatively liberal approach to women's legal rights enabled intellectuals such as the publisher and journalist Margareta Momma and the poet Hedvig Nordenflycht to develop feminist themes in print.

Britain, though less liberal than Sweden, had seen the expression of recognizably feminist theories by the start of the 1700s, notably through the work of Mary Astell. Arguing that God had made women just as rational as men,

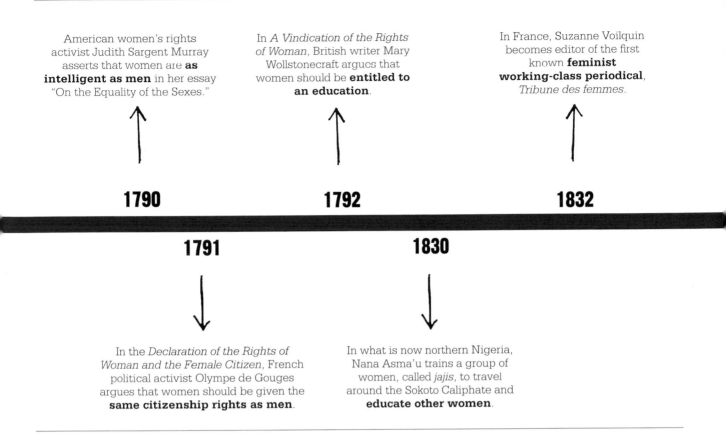

American women's rights activist Judith Sargent Murray asserts that women are **as intelligent as men** in her essay "On the Equality of the Sexes."

In *A Vindication of the Rights of Woman*, British writer Mary Wollstonecraft argues that women should be **entitled to an education**.

In France, Suzanne Voilquin becomes editor of the first known **feminist working-class periodical**, *Tribune des femmes*.

1790

1792

1832

1791

1830

In the *Declaration of the Rights of Woman and the Female Citizen*, French political activist Olympe de Gouges argues that women should be given the **same citizenship rights as men**.

In what is now northern Nigeria, Nana Asma'u trains a group of women, called *jajis*, to travel around the Sokoto Caliphate and **educate other women**.

she daringly stated that women's socially inferior role was neither God-given nor inevitable.

By around 1750, in Britain and other European countries, groups of intellectual women were coming together in literary "salons." In these forums, women discussed literature and shared ideas, carving out a space for female experience, the sharing of ideas, and the fostering of women writers and thinkers.

New ideas and revolution

Two particular intellectual, cultural, and political developments in Europe and America in the 18th century helped to galvanize the growth and spread of feminism: the Enlightenment and revolutions in America and France. Philosophers of the Enlightenment, such as the Frenchmen Jean-Jacques Rousseau

and Denis Diderot, challenged the tyranny of societies based on inherited privileges of kings, nobles, and churches. They argued for liberty, equality, and the "rights of man," which, particularly for Rousseau, excluded women.

Women were, however, actively involved in the revolutions that won America its independence from Britain in 1783 and convulsed France from 1789. Amid the rallying cries of liberty and citizens' rights, women also began to demand their own rights. In America, Abigail Adams, the wife of the second US president, called for the founding fathers to "remember the ladies" in the revolutionary changes, while in France playwright and activist Olympe de Gouges published *The Declaration of the Rights of Woman and the Female Citizen*, calling for

equal legal rights for women and men. Influenced by the French Revolution, the British writer Mary Wollstonecraft published *A Vindication of the Rights of Woman*, a landmark feminist treatise that identified domestic tyranny as the chief barrier preventing women from living independent lives and called for women to have access to education and work.

Although many of the most visible advocates of women's rights were from the privileged classes, by the early 19th century, working-class women in the US and the UK were becoming politically active, often within the newly forming labor movements. Feminist opinions were also being raised in parts of the Islamic world. Those voices would become much louder as the 19th century progressed. ∎

MEN ARE BORN FREE, WOMEN ARE BORN SLAVES

EARLY BRITISH FEMINISM

IN CONTEXT

PRIMARY QUOTE
Mary Astell, 1706

KEY FIGURE
Mary Astell

BEFORE
1405 In *The Book of the City of Ladies*, French writer Christine de Pizan creates a symbolic city of major historical female figures, highlighting women's importance to society.

1589 Englishwoman Jane Anger pens a defense of women and a critique of men in her pamphlet "Jane Anger: her Protection for Women".

AFTER
1792 In *A Vindication of the Rights of Woman*, Mary Wollstonecraft calls for women to cease depending on men.

1843 Scottish feminist Marion Reid writes *A Plea for Woman,* criticizing society's concept of "womanly behavior," which limits women's opportunities.

Nearly 200 years before "feminism" became a concept, some women began to challenge society's view that they should be subordinate. One of the most significant voices in Britain was that of Mary Astell. She argued in her writings that women were just as capable of clear and critical thought as men; their apparent inferiority was the result of male control and limited access to a sound education.

The weaker vessel?

The 17th century was a time of political upheaval, yet the English Civil War (1642–1651), followed by the restoration of the monarchy, had little impact on women. They were regarded as "the weaker vessel"— a view supported by the Christian Church and the Bible's assertion that Eve was created from Adam's rib. Their natural role was presumed to be only that of wife or mother.

There were exceptions. Certain nonconformist or dissenting sects, including the Anabaptists and Quakers, protested that women and men were equal before God. Not only could women attend their meetings, they could even preach. Women were also prominent in the

Margaret Cavendish declared that she wrote because women were denied so much else in public life. In 20 years, she published 23 works, including plays, essays, fiction, verse, and letters.

Levellers, an egalitarian political movement of the English Civil War, but were excluded from this group's call for wider suffrage.

Proto-feminists

Despite the barriers, a number of women turned to writing to challenge the view that the female sex was inferior. They included

See also: Early Scandinavian feminism 22–23 ▪ Enlightenment feminism 28–33 ▪ Emancipation from domesticity 34–35

Since GOD has given
Women as well as
Men Intelligent Souls,
how should they be
forbidden to
improve them?.
Mary Astell

Bathsua Makin, who wrote "An Essay to Revive the Ancient Education of Gentlewomen" (1673), and Margaret Cavendish, Duchess of Newcastle, who offered a forceful critique of women's place in society. In her *Philosophical and Physical Opinions* (1655), she complained that women were "kept like birds in cages," shut out of all power, and scorned by conceited men—a view met by harsh male criticism.

Born in 1640 of humble stock, traveller, spy, and writer Aphra Behn was said to be the first Englishwoman to earn her living from her pen. Her many plays mocked the male-dominated literary world and male behavior. Critics called them bawdy and accused her of plagiarism, but her popular works drew enthusiastic audiences.

A radical analysis

Against this background, writer Mary Astell explored and analyzed the contention that women, being "inferior," should be under the control of men. A devout Christian, she countered the Church's stance

Mary Astell

Born into an upper middle-class Anglican family in Newcastle upon Tyne in 1666, Mary Astell received little formal education. However, her uncle, Ralph Astell, educated her in classical philosophy. Following the death of her mother in 1688, Mary Astell moved to Chelsea, London, where she struggled financially as a writer but was encouraged by literary and intellectual women friends and patrons. William Sancroft, Archbishop of Canterbury,

was also a friend and gave her financial support. Her first book, *A Serious Proposal to the Ladies* established her as a significant thinker. In 1709 she withdrew from public life and founded a charity school for girls in Chelsea. She died in 1731 following a mastectomy to remove breast cancer.

Key works

1694 *A Serious Proposal to the Ladies*
1700 *Some Reflections on Marriage*

that women's secondary role was divinely ordained by arguing that God had created women with equally "intelligent souls" and the "faculty of Thinking." It was men who had made them subordinate. By denying women independent thought, men effectively kept them enslaved—an insult to God.

For Astell, a better education was the key to greater equality. In *A Serious Proposal to the Ladies* (1694), she urges women to learn to develop their intellect and skills, rather than constantly deferring to men. She even proposes setting up a type of secular nunnery or university where women can follow a "life of the mind." She accepts the need for marriage, although she herself did not marry, but, in *Some Reflections on Marriage* (1700), she warns women to avoid marriages based

on lust or money. Education, she believes, will help women choose wisely and avoid unhappiness.

Like her contemporaries, Astell was not an activist, but observed and wrote incisively about the situation of women around her, from what would now be described as a feminist perspective; her theories remain recognizable today. It would be nearly a century before other women took up the argument so publicly. ▪

Aphra Behn, here in a portrait by the 17th-century Dutch artist, Peter Lely, originally wrote to escape debt. Her writings made her a celebrity in her lifetime, and, at her death in 1689, she was buried in Westminster Abbey.

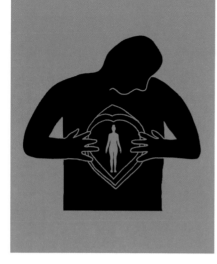

OUR BODY IS THE CLOTHES OF OUR SOUL

EARLY SCANDINAVIAN FEMINISM

IN CONTEXT

PRIMARY QUOTE
Sophia Elisabet Brenner, 1719

KEY FIGURES
Sophia Elisabet Brenner, Margareta Momma, Hedvig Nordenflycht, Catharina Ahlgren

BEFORE
1687 King Christian V of Denmark and Norway passes a law defining unmarried women as minors.

AFTER
1848 Swedish writer and feminist activist Sophie Sager prosecutes her landlord for rape in a landmark court case.

1871 The women's rights association Dansk Kvindesamfund (Danish Women's Society) is founded in Denmark by Matilde and Fredrik Bajer.

A t the beginning of Sweden's Age of Liberty (1718–1772), when power shifted from the monarchy to the government, there was increased political and philosophical debate, including calls for greater freedoms for women. This progressive milieu was reflected in the Civil Code of 1734, which gave women some property rights and the right to divorce on the grounds of adultery.

Early enlightenment
One of the first women to declare publicly that women deserved the same rights as men was Swedish writer Sophia Elisabet Brenner, an

Eighteenth-century Stockholm, seen in this painting by Elias Martin (1739–1818), was a place of growing civil rights and home to some of the world's first feminists.

educated aristocrat. In 1693, she published the poem "The justified defense of the female sex," asserting that women were intellectually equal to men, and in 1719, in a poem to Queen Ulrika Eleonora of Sweden, she argued that men and women were the same except for outward appearance.

In "Conversation between the Shades of Argus and an unknown Female" (1738–1739), journalist

See also: Early British feminism 20–21 ▪ Enlightenment feminism 28–33 ▪ The global suffrage movement 94–97

A forceful woman,
but full of talent.
Jonas Apelblad
Swedish travel writer describing
Catharina Ahlgren

Margareta Momma takes up the call for women to be educated and satirizes critics who deem women incapable of debate. Influenced by the European Enlightenment, and urging freedom of speech and religion, Momma also promoted the use of the Swedish language rather than aristocratic French to allow more people access to new ideas.

Intellectual recognition

Another writer and thinker, Hedvig Charlotta Nordenflycht made her literary debut with "The lament of the Swedish woman" (1742), a poem for the funeral of Queen Ulrika Eleonora, in which the poet speaks out for greater rights for her own sex.

Unlike Momma and many of her contemporaries, Nordenflycht published under her own name. Her career thrived and, in 1753, she was admitted to the Tankebyggarorden (Order of Thought Builders), a Stockholm literary group seeking to reform Swedish literature, of which she was the only female member. Nordenflycht hosted a salon in her home, attended by the best writers of the time, in order to exchange ideas. Defending the female intellect

in poems such as "The duty of women to use their wit" and refuting misogyny in "Defense of women" (1761), she claimed the right to be intellectually active.

The language of science

Catharina Ahlgren, a friend of Nordenflycht, published her first poem in 1764 for Queen Louisa Ulrika's birthday. Ahlgren was already known as a translator of English, French, and German works when, in 1772, under the pseudonym "Adelaide," she wrote rhetorical letters published in two series of popular Swedish-language journals.

Addressing men and women in the letters, Ahlgren argues for social activism, democracy, gender equality, and women's solidarity against male dominance, and expresses a belief that true love is only possible when a woman and a man treat one another as equals. Friendship is the most frequently aired subject in the "Adelaide" letters, but other topics include morality and advice to daughters. Ahlgren is also presumed to have been the author

Hedvig Nordenflycht was born in Stockholm in 1718. A poet, writer, and salon hostess, she was one of the first women whose opinions were taken seriously by the male establishment.

of the essay "Modern women Sophia and Belisinde discuss ideas." Here, she criticizes the teaching of French, the language of light romances, advocating instead that women study English, the language of science and learned discourse. ∎

Catharina Ahlgren

Born in 1734, Catharina Ahlgren served Sweden's queen, Louisa Ulrika, at court. The queen was an inveterate plotter and eventually dismissed Ahlgren from court because of an intrigue. Ahlgren subsequently made her living by writing, editing, printing, and managing a bookstore.

Ahlgren married and divorced twice and had four children. Later she moved to Finland where, in 1782, she

appeared in the city of Åbo (now Turku) as the editor of *The Art of Correct Pleasing*, one of the first Finnish newspapers. In 1796, she returned to Sweden to live with her youngest daughter, and died in around 1800.

Key works

1772 "A Correspondence between a Woman in Stockholm and a Country Woman"
1793 "Amiable Confrontations"

INJURED WOMAN! RISE, ASSERT THY RIGHT!

COLLECTIVE ACTION IN THE 18TH CENTURY

IN CONTEXT

PRIMARY QUOTE
**Anna Laetitia
Barbauld, 1792**

KEY FIGURE
Elizabeth Montagu

BEFORE
1620 Catherine de Vivonne
holds her first salons in Paris,
at the Hôtel de Rambouillot.

1670 Aphra Behn becomes the
first Englishwoman known to
have earned her living as a
writer after her play *The Forc'd
Marriage* is staged.

AFTER
1848 The first public gathering
devoted to American women's
rights takes place in Seneca
Falls, New York.

1856 The Langham Place
Circle meets for the first time in
London, UK, with a mission to
campaign for women's rights.

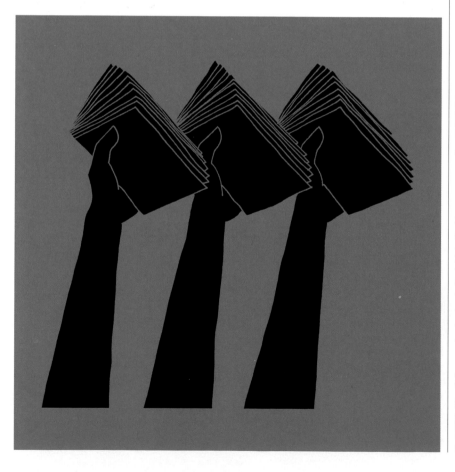

I n 18th-century Britain, as the
middle classes grew wealthier
and leisure time increased, an
ideology developed that promoted a
distinction between public and
private realms. Men, who were
busy exploiting the opportunities
offered by industrialization and
trade, occupied the "public realm"
where public opinion was formed,
while women "nurtured virtue"
within the "private realm," or home.

A woman's place

The publication of pamphlets,
magazines, and conduct books that
prescribed appropriate feminine
behavior proliferated throughout
this period and represented an

See also: Enlightenment feminism 28–33 ▪ Emancipation from domesticity 34–35 ▪ Working-class feminism 36–37 ▪ Rights for married women 72–75 ▪ Consciousness-raising 134–135 ▪ Radical feminism 137

> To despise riches, may, indeed, be philosophic, but to dispense them worthily, must surely be more beneficial to mankind.
> **Fanny Burney**

effort to encourage women to embrace this new private role, which was seen as a hallmark of elite status. These publications urged women to read "improving" books, especially the Bible and historical works. Novels, however, were actively discouraged, being described by Thomas Gisborne in his conduct book *An Enquiry into the Duties of the Female Sex* (1797) as "secretly corrupt." The entreaty to "improve" was designed to encourage women to keep high moral standards in the home, serve their husbands dutifully, and thus raise the virtue of society as a whole. Yet it also increased the number of educated women who strove to look beyond the narrow confines of domestic life. This was fueled by a surge in printed works that embraced not only the reading lists dictated by the conduct books, but also novels, newspapers, and journals. All this stimulated women's curiosity about the world, but they had limited means of influencing public debate because they were still confined to the private realm.

Meetings of minds

Some educated women found mutual support through "salons" where they could meet. These were spaces set up for debate by privileged women who saw private patronage and sociability as outlets for their intellectual capabilities and a way to influence society. The premier London salon was held in the Mayfair home of

Mary, Duchess of Gloucester (center), a prominent patron of the Bluestockings, introduces the poet and playwright Hannah More to an elite gathering.

Elizabeth Montagu, who had married into a rich family of coal mine and estate owners. Around 1750, she and a number of like-minded women, in particular the wealthy Irish intellectual »

English tea is served to a group conversing and listening to music in the Salon des Quatre Glaces at the Palais du Temple in Paris in 1764. The women outnumber the men and are relaxed in the mixed company.

The Salon

The word "salon" was first used in France in the 17th century, derived from the Italian *salone*, meaning "large hall." Catherine de Vivonne, the marquise de Rambouillet (1588–1665), was one of the first women to establish a salon, located at her Paris home in a room that became known as the *Chambre bleu* (Blue Room). Her success as a literary hostess inspired women to adopt roles of intellectual and social leadership as *salonnières*. Salons provided a respectable space in which women could exhibit their intellectual curiosity. At first, they featured discussions about literary works, then drew both men and women into discourse about political thought and scientific ideas.

Salons thrived across Europe throughout the 18th century, including the scientific salon hosted by Julie von Bondeli in Bern, Switzerland, and the literary salon of Henriette Herz, an emancipated Jewish woman, in Berlin, Germany.

Elizabeth Montagu

Known as the "Queen of the Blues," Elizabeth Montagu was a writer, social reformer, and literary critic, and the preeminent intellectual and artistic patron in 18th-century Britain. Born in 1718, as a child Elizabeth often visited Cambridge, where her step-grandfather, Conyers Middleton, was a university academic. Her marriage in 1742 to Robert Montagu, grandson of the 1st Earl of Sandwich, gave her the wealth and resources to support the work of English and Scottish writers. From 1750, she wintered in London, hosting intellectual parties and maintaining friendships with leading literary and political figures such as Samuel Johnson, Horace Walpole, and Edmund Burke. Montagu's salon in Mayfair thrived for 50 years until her death in 1800.

Key works

1760 Three anonymous sections in George Lyttleton's *Dialogues of the Dead*
1769 *An Essay on the Writings and Genius of Shakespeare*

Elizabeth Vesey, established the Blue Stockings Society. The name derived from the preference among men for blue worsted over black silk for daytime stockings. Its name symbolized a less formal occasion than a courtly gathering.

The Bluestockings brought together educated women, as well as selected men, to promote "rational conversation" that would engender moral improvement. Members generally met once a month, arriving in the late afternoon and sometimes staying until nearly midnight. Tea and lemonade were served rather than alcohol, and gambling, the usual diversion at social occasions, was banned. Between meetings, the Bluestockings were prolific letter writers. Elizabeth Montagu, for example, is known to have written some 8,000 letters.

Each of the regular hostesses had her own style. Elizabeth Vesey's gatherings, for example, were particularly informal, with chairs scattered around the room to encourage small discussion groups; Elizabeth Montagu, on the other hand, arranged her chairs in an arc, with herself at the center. Another hostess, Frances Boscawen held

The aims of the Bluestockings

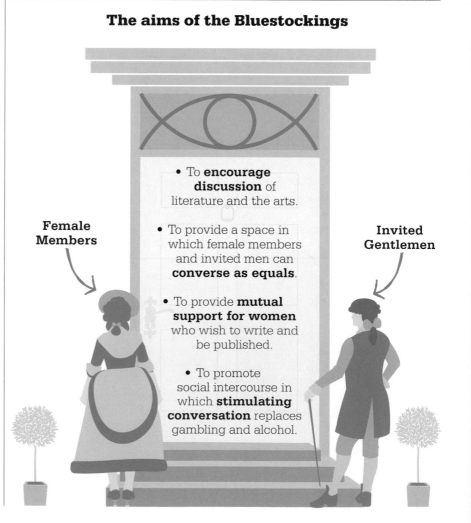

Female Members

- To **encourage discussion** of literature and the arts.

- To provide a space in which female members and invited men can **converse as equals**.

- To provide **mutual support for women** who wish to write and be published.

- To promote social intercourse in which **stimulating conversation** replaces gambling and alcohol.

Invited Gentlemen

gatherings at Hatchlands Park, her country house in Surrey as well as in her London home in Audley Street.

Literary aspirations

The Bluestockings supported the education of women and supported women such as Fanny Burney, Anna Laetitia Barbauld, Hannah More, and Sarah Scott (Elizabeth Montagu's sister) trying to make their way as writers. Called "amazons of the pen" by the author Samuel Johnson (another member of the society), these women challenged traditional notions about women and their intellectual capabilities by not only providing commentary on classic literary works but also writing their own poems, plays, and novels.

Elizabeth Montagu traveled to Paris to defend Shakespeare from attacks by the writer and philosopher Voltaire. Her *Essay on the Writings and Genius of Shakespeare*, initially published anonymously, was well received by critics and dented Voltaire's reputation when it was eventually translated into French. Another Bluestocking member, Elizabeth

Carter, was described by Samuel Johnson as the best scholar of classical Greek he had ever known. Over time, some Bluestocking members who were not financially independent even managed to earn a living from their work.

Rather than being seen as a threat to the established order of male superiority, the Bluestockings were praised as bastions of female virtue and intellect. In 1778, the artist Richard Samuel portrayed nine of the most eminent members as the classical nine muses and symbols of national pride. Yet behind this aura of learning and elegance was a desire for a more public place for women. Elizabeth Montagu, for example, had long been interested in the Scottish Enlightenment, which advocated a more prominent role for women.

Challenging men

Women were proving themselves the equals of men, perhaps where it mattered most, in the realm of ideas and intelligence. As they became more powerful, with some of them pursuing successful literary careers, the Bluestockings acquired

Upper-class women, including the Duchess of Devonshire, march in support of the radical politician Charles James Fox in 1784. By this time, women were making their voices heard.

a collective consciousness and a public voice. Within 50 years of the first Bluestocking meetings, educated women were transforming from figures of social stability and cohesion into rebels and radicals, brought into the open in an era of revolution in Europe and America. ∎

Our intellectual ore
must shine,
Not slumber idly in the mine.
Let education's moral mint
The noblest images imprint.
Hannah More
"The Bas Bleu" ("Blue Stockings")

The men are very
imprudent to endeavour
to make fools of those to
whom they so much
trust their honour,
happiness, and fortune.
Elizabeth Montagu

IT IS IN YOUR POWER
TO FREE YOURSELVES
ENLIGHTENMENT FEMINISM

IN CONTEXT

PRIMARY QUOTE
Olympe de Gouges, 1791

KEY FIGURES
**Olympe de Gouges,
Judith Sargent Murray**

BEFORE
1752 In London, women are
invited to attend a public
speaking event, "The Temple
of Taste," but are not allowed
to take part in the debates.

1762 French philosopher
Jean-Jacques Rousseau
publishes *Émile* in which he
argues that a woman's main
role is to be a wife and mother.

AFTER
1871 The Union des Femmes
(Union of Women) forms during
the Paris Commune in France.
It organizes working women to
take up arms for the revolution
and demands civic and legal
gender equality, right of
divorce, and equal pay.

The 18th-century intellectual movement known as the Enlightenment transformed Europe and North America. It emphasized reason and science over superstition and faith, and advanced new ideals about equality and freedom. Yet opinion was divided on whether notions of liberty and equal rights applied to women as well as men. The French thinker Jean-Jacques Rousseau, for example, deemed women to be weaker and less rational than men by nature, and therefore dependent on them. Others—including philosophers Denis Diderot, Marquis de Condorcet, Thomas Hobbes, and Jeremy Bentham—publicly acknowledged the intellectual capabilities of women and supported their goal of achieving gender equality.

Making their voices heard

On both sides of the Atlantic, women sought platforms from which they could actively engage in the intellectual discussions of the period and prove their equality with men. In London, public

We women have taken too
long to let our voices be heard.
Penelope Barker
Leader of the Edenton Tea Party,
North Carolina

debating societies, which were initially dominated by men, later hosted mixed-gender gatherings. In the 1780s, several women's debating societies flourished in London, including La Belle Assemblée, the Female Parliament, the Carlisle House Debates, and the Female Congress. Here, women could draw public

Enlightenment thinkers from across Europe met at the weekly Paris salon held by wealthy patron Madame Geoffrin, depicted here during a reading of a play by Voltaire in 1755.

See also: Early British feminism 20–21 ▪ Collective action in the 18th century 24–27 ▪ The birth of the suffrage movement 56–63 ▪ Marriage and work 70–71

attention to their demands for equality in education, in political rights, and in the right to carry out paid work.

Joining the revolution

In North America, and then in France, revolutionary movements challenged the established order, creating a political environment in which women could be actively involved. In the years leading up to the American Revolution (1775–1783), women began to take part in debates about the colonies' relationship with Britain.

When the Townshend Acts of 1767–1768 imposed import duties payable to the British Crown on tea and other commodities, American women organized boycotts against the consumption of British goods. Some gave up tea in favor of coffee or herbal brews; others showed their commitment to the non-importation movement and the national (Patriot) cause by making their own homespun cloth. Mass gatherings known as "spinning bees" to spin yarn were sponsored by the Daughters of Liberty—the first formal female association supporting American independence, which formed in 1765 in response to the taxation burden imposed on the colonies by Britain's Stamp Act of that year. Such initiatives encouraged women to join the revolutionary movement.

With the outbreak of war in 1775, women's participation increased. They took on roles outside the home, running businesses and making important family decisions, as their fathers and husbands were called up to serve in the army. Women also became politically active. In 1780, Esther Reed

"And women" is inserted into the statement from the 1776 American Declaration of Independence that "All men are created equal" in this 1915 cover image from *Life magazine*.

published the broadside, "The Sentiments of an American Woman," to boost female support for the Patriot cause. Her campaign raised $300,000. Together with Sarah Franklin Bache, daughter of Benjamin Franklin (one of the founding fathers of the US), Reed then launched the Ladies »

> " Remember all men would be tyrants if they could.
> **Abigail Adams**
> **Letter to her husband and statesman John Adams** "

Association of Philadelphia, the largest women's organization of the American Revolution; its members went door to door gathering money for the Patriot troops.

Some women stepped further into the male arena, playing an active military role. For example, Anna Smith Strong and Lydia Barrington Darragh served as Patriot spies, obtaining information on the British to give to General Washington. English spies included Ann Bates, who disguised herself as a peddler and infiltrated an American army camp. A few women even passed themselves off as men, so they could fight alongside other soldiers. Deborah Sampson, who loaded cannons, went on to receive a pension in recognition of her military service in Washington's army.

An ongoing fight for rights

From the outset, women played an active role during the French Revolution (1789–1799), which

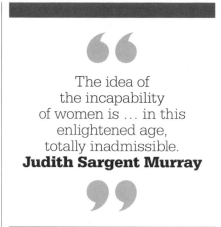

> The idea of the incapability of women is … in this enlightened age, totally inadmissible.
> **Judith Sargent Murray**

generated new demands for the advancement of women's rights. The thousands of working women who marched on the palace of Versailles demanding bread in October 1789 achieved what the storming of the Bastille on July 14 had not: their action effectively toppled the crumbling French monarchy. Yet when a group of these women submitted a six-page

petition proposing equal rights to the National Assembly that was now the governing body of France, the petition was never even discussed.

Frenchwomen persisted in the fight for equality as the revolution unfolded through the 1790s, taking part in public demonstrations, publishing newspapers, and creating their own political clubs when they were excluded from the male-dominated assemblies. The most notable of these was the Society of Revolutionary and Republican Women, founded in 1793, which promoted sexual equality and a political voice for women. Female clubs also addressed the issue of citizenship by claiming the title of *citoyenne* (female citizen) and therefore the rights and responsibilities that accompanied full citizenship in a republic.

Words as weapons

Amidst the din of war, key writers ensured that the discussion of women's rights was still heard. When the French revolutionary Declaration of Man and the Citizen in 1789 asserted the rights and liberty of all men, playwright and activist Olympe de Gouges penned her pamphlet *The Declaration of the Rights of Woman and the Female Citizen* (1791), asserting equal rights for women. In all her work, she articulated the values of the Enlightenment and how they could effect change in women's lives.

In America, the essayist and playwright Judith Sargent Murray challenged the widespread notion of women's inferiority in her

Liberty is portrayed as a woman in France, as in Eugène Delacroix's painting depicting the July Revolution of 1830. Yet Frenchwomen did not gain the vote until 1944.

The Enlightenment and feminism

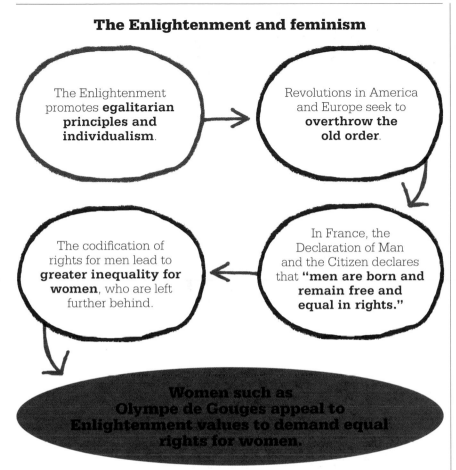

The Enlightenment promotes **egalitarian principles and individualism**.

Revolutions in America and Europe seek to **overthrow the old order**.

In France, the Declaration of Man and the Citizen declares that **"men are born and remain free and equal in rights."**

The codification of rights for men lead to **greater inequality for women**, who are left further behind.

Women such as Olympe de Gouges appeal to Enlightenment values to demand equal rights for women.

Olympe de Gouges

Born Marie Gouze in 1748, Olympe de Gouges overcame a questionable parentage as the illegitimate daughter of the Marquis de Pompignon, and then a marriage against her will at the age of 16, to fashion a place for herself among the French aristocracy. In the 1780s, she began writing plays and publishing political pamphlets that challenged male authority in society. She also addressed the evils of the slave trade.

With her "Declaration of the Rights of Woman and the Female Citizen," de Gouges was one of the first to make a persuasive argument in favor of full citizenship and equal rights for French women. During a bloody period of the French Revolution known as the Reign of Terror, de Gouges was arrested for criticizing the government and was executed by guillotine in 1793.

Key works

1788 "Letter to the people, or project for a patriotic fund"
1790 *The Necessity of Divorce*
1791 *The Declaration of the Rights of Woman and the Female Citizen*

landmark essay "On the Equality of Sexes," in which she argues that women would rival men's achievements if they were only permitted a similar education.

In Britain, Mary Wollstonecraft similarly stressed the importance of education in *A Vindication of the Rights of Woman* (1792). She contended that, from childhood, girls were taught to be subordinate and inculcated with the notion of their inherent inferiority to men—ideas Wollstonecraft vociferously challenged throughout her life.

Despite these clarion calls for equality, the legacy of the two revolutions would be somewhat mixed for women. Taking on male roles in time of war proved no guarantee of immediate gains in the gender equality battle. In France, the executions of three politically active women—de Gouges, Madame Roland, and Charlotte Corday (who had assassinated the Jacobin leader Jean-Paul Marat)—temporarily deterred French women from expressing political views.

However, the examples of politically active women, and the debates and writings about gender equality that began during the Enlightenment and proliferated through the two revolutions, are fundamental to modern feminist arguments, and helped women to gain momentum in the fight for equal rights. ■

I DO NOT WISH WOMEN TO HAVE POWER OVER MEN; BUT OVER THEMSELVES
EMANCIPATION FROM DOMESTICITY

IN CONTEXT

PRIMARY QUOTE
Mary Wollstonecraft, 1792

KEY FIGURE
Mary Wollstonecraft

BEFORE
1700 In *Some Reflections upon Marriage*, English philosopher Mary Astell queries why women are born slaves, while men are born free.

1790 British historian Catherine Macaulay writes *Letters on Education*. She argues that perceived female weaknesses are caused by an inferior education.

AFTER
1869 British philosopher John Stuart Mill publishes *The Subjection of Women*, whose powerful case for equal rights he developed with feminist Harriet Taylor Mill, his wife.

In 1792, with the publication of *A Vindication of the Rights of Woman,* Mary Wollstonecraft fired a powerful early salvo in the battle for female emancipation from domesticity. She wrote her feminist polemic in response to 18th-century Enlightenment thinkers, such as the philosopher Jean-Jacques Rousseau, who did not extend their ideas of liberalism to women. She criticizes the injustice and inconsistency of such men calling for freedom yet still subjugating women. She also rejects the contemporary perception that women were less rational. "Who made man the exclusive judge?" she demands. Women, she writes, might be weaker physically, but are just as capable of rational thought as men.

Men's playthings
Wollstonecraft maintains that women remained inferior because they were kept in the domestic sphere, forced to be men's "toys and playthings." Society taught them that looks, male opinion, and marriage were more important than intellectual and personal fulfilment. Sculpted by a gender stereotype that their mothers reinforced, girls were brought up to exploit their looks in order to find a man who would support and protect them.

Wollstonecraft was the first feminist to describe "marriage for support" as a form of prostitution—a shocking assertion for the time. A lack of means often compelled women to marry. Degraded by their dependency on male approval, they effectively became men's slaves. She felt that such a restricted life, limited by domestic trivia, could also wreak psychological damage.

To restore women's dignity, Wollstonecraft recommends "a revolution in female manners."

> 66
>
> She was created to be the toy of man, his rattle, and it must jingle in his ears whenever, dismissing reason, he chooses to be amused.
> **Mary Wollstonecraft**
>
> 99

See also: Enlightenment feminism 28–33 ▪ Female autonomy in a male-dominated world 40–41 ▪ Rights for married women 72–75 ▪ Wages for housework 147

She believed women and men should be educated equally, even suggesting a coeducational system. Women, she believed, should be in the public sphere and should be trained for work outside the home, in areas such as medicine, midwifery, and business. She urges an end to the social distinction between the sexes and calls for equal rights for women to enable them to take control of their lives.

Mixed reactions

Vindication was well received, particularly in intellectual circles. A hostile press, however, described Wollstonecraft as a "hyena in petticoats" for both her book and her unorthodox lifestyle. The book was not reprinted until the mid-19th century, when it was admired by figures such as British suffragist Millicent Fawcett and American activist Lucretia Mott. Wollstonecraft's advanced ideas would be echoed in the works of feminists from Barbara Bodichon to Simone de Beauvoir. ▪

Woman's work in the 18th century was invariably of a domestic nature. Laundresses might work outside the home, but they did long, backbreaking hours for little pay.

Mary Wollstonecraft

The Anglo-Irish feminist and radical Mary Wollstonecraft was born in London in 1759. Her father was a bully and a spendthrift. She was largely self-educated and started a school in North East London with a friend. When the school failed, she became governess to Lord Kingsborough's family, a position she hated.

By 1790, Wollstonecraft was working for a London publisher and was part of a group of radical thinkers that included Thomas Paine and William Godwin. In 1792, she went to Paris, where she met Gilbert Imlay with whom she had a daughter, Fanny. Imlay was unfaithful, and the affair ended. In 1797, Wollstonecraft married Godwin, but she died later that year, 10 days after giving birth to their daughter, Mary, who later, as Mary Shelley, would write the novel *Frankenstein*.

Key works

1787 *Thoughts on the Education of Daughters*
1790 *A Vindication of the Rights of Men*
1792 *A Vindication of the Rights of Woman*

WE CALL ON ALL WOMEN, WHATEVER THEIR RANK
WORKING-CLASS FEMINISM

IN CONTEXT

PRIMARY QUOTE
Suzanne Voilquin, 1832–1834

KEY FIGURE
Suzanne Voilquin

BEFORE
1791 In revolutionary France, Olympe de Gouges publishes *The Declaration of the Rights of Woman and the Female Citizen*, advocating women's equality with men.

1816 French aristocrat and political theorist Henri de Saint-Simon publishes *"l'Industrie,"* the first of several essays stating that human happiness lies in a productive society based on true equality and useful work.

AFTER
1870s French socialist and early leader of the French labor movement Jules Guesde tells French women that their rights are diversionary and will come as a matter of course once capitalism is dismantled.

Women (and men) are **divided** by status into the **"proletarian"** and the **"privileged."**

↓

But **oppression binds all women** from different backgrounds **together**.

↓

La tribune des femmes, **the first working-class feminist periodical, urged all women to contribute and help their progress.**

In many ways, industrialization increased the gulf between middle-class and working-class women. Both groups of women often felt oppressed, but while middle-class women—excluded from any economic function in the new industries—campaigned for better education, access to meaningful work, and the right to vote, working-class women—who contributed to the family income by working in the new mills and factories—were less audible and much more concerned with improving their pay and working conditions. Some working women looked to trade unionism; others were drawn to utopian movements such as Saint-Simonianism, which flourished in France in the first half of the 19th century. Inspired by the ideas of Henri de Saint-Simon, the movement advocated a "union of work" in which all classes cooperated to mutual and equal advantage in an increasingly technological and scientific world.

See also: Marxist feminism 52–55 ▪ Racism and class prejudice within feminism 202–205 ▪ Pink-collar feminism 228–229 ▪ The pay gap 318–319

Men! Be … no longer surprised by the disorder that reigns in your society. It is an energetic protest against what you have done alone.
Suzanne Voilquin

The Saint-Simonians promoted a communal lifestyle free of the tyranny of marriage, in which the feminine principles of peace and compassion would replace more aggressive masculine values. Satirical prints of the time depict male Saint-Simonians performing domestic chores and wearing corsets while their female counterparts take up what were considered male pursuits, such as hunting and making speeches.

A journal for women

Among those influenced by Saint-Simonianism was Suzanne Voilquin, a French embroiderer by trade who resolved to live as an independent woman after amicably separating from her husband. She wished to be both an example to others and an advocate for the Saint-Simonian cause, which she believed was urgent, especially in the wake of the July Revolution of 1830, which had done nothing to alter the fortunes of the working-classes. Voilquin herself had experienced hardship after the revolution, when a steep decline in the sale of luxury goods affected her work as an embroiderer and she endured a period of unemployment.

In 1832, Voilquin became editor of *La tribune des femmes*, a journal promoting Saint-Simonian values. Women of all classes were invited to contribute to the paper, though recruitment focused on working-class women. The writers published under their first names only, as a protest against having to take their husband's name. The journal advocated an alliance between "proletarian women" and "women of privilege" to create a *nouvelle femme* (new woman). "Each individual woman will place a stone from which the moral edifice of the future will be built," Voilquin said. *La tribune des femmes* was the first attempt to create a female consciousness. ▪

As countries industrialized, women and girls were increasingly employed outside the home. This 1898 photograph of a mill in Malaga, Spain, shows workers in the spooling room.

Suzanne Voilquin

The daughter of a hat-maker, Suzanne Voilquin was born in Paris in 1801. Her early life was comfortable, but she yearned for the education that her brothers had. When her father's bankruptcy led to hard times, Voilquin became an embroiderer.

In 1823, Voilquin married and joined the Saint-Simonian movement, an early type of utopian socialism. In 1832, after separating from her husband, she began to edit *La tribune des femmes*, the first known working-class feminist journal. She wrote about the unfairness of France's Civil Code, which did not include women in public affairs, and advocated women's education and economic self-sufficiency. In 1834, Voilquin answered the call to spread the word about Saint-Simonianism and traveled to Egypt, where she became a nurse. She later went to Russia and the US, but returned to France in 1860 and died in Paris in 1877.

Key works

1834 *My Law for the Future*
1866 *Memories of a Daughter of the People*

I TAUGHT THEM THE RELIGION OF GOD
EDUCATION FOR ISLAMIC WOMEN

IN CONTEXT

PRIMARY QUOTE
Nana Asma'u, 1858–1859

KEY FIGURE
Nana Asma'u

BEFORE
610 The Prophet Muhammad starts to receive revelations from God, which later form the Quran.

AFTER
1990s Shaykh Ibrahim Zakzaky establishes the Islamic Movement in Nigeria. It promotes female education.

2009 The Taliban carries out attacks on schools in the Swat Valley, Pakistan. Survivor Malala Yousafzai receives the Nobel Peace Prize in 2014 for advocating human rights, in particular for education for women and children.

2014 Boko Haram, a jihadist organization, kidnaps female students in the town of Chibok, western Nigeria.

E ducation is considered a duty for every Muslim. The Prophet Muhammad (571–632 CE) emphasized the need for learning, saying that a person seeking knowledge attains spiritual rewards equivalent to that person having fasted all day and kept a prayer vigil all night. Islamic teachings do not differentiate between religious and worldly knowledge: all learning is considered part of humanity.

In the Middle Ages, science thrived in Muslim lands. Scholars led the way in medicine, astronomy, and mathematics, calculating the Earth's circumference and laying down the principles of algebra.

> "
> Seeking knowledge is incumbent upon every Muslim, male and female.
> **Prophet Muhammad**
> "

In the early days of Islam (7th–8th century), women played an important role in spreading knowledge. Shia sources record how Fatima, the Prophet's daughter, and her daughter Zaynab were impeccably versed in the Quran and Hadith (a record of the sayings and deeds of the Prophet) and taught women in Medina. The Prophet himself told the city's women to learn from Fatima. Zaynab's nephew, Ali ibn al-Husayn (659–713 CE), thought by members of the Shia branch of Islam to be the divinely appointed Imam (leader), called his aunt "the scholar without a teacher," implying she had imbibed knowledge from the environment in which she lived.

Learned women
By the 11th century, Muslim women no longer had access to the same level of education as men. This was partly due to patriarchy, which assumed men would take on more public roles and therefore need a higher level of education. However, privileged women sometimes used their wealth and connections to overcome these barriers and fund women's education. Fatima al-Fihri founded

See also: Early Arab Feminism 104–105 ▪ Feminist theology 124–125 ▪ Patriarchy as social control 144–145 ▪ Anticolonialism 218–219 ▪ Modern Islamic feminism 284–285

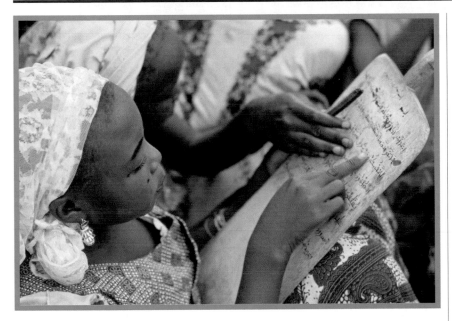

A young Nigerian girl learns the Quran using a *lawh* (a wooden tablet). To this day, in many Muslim countries a solid grounding in the Quran forms the basis of early education.

If girls aren't given opportunities to study and learn—it's basically live burial.
Shayk Mohammed Akram Nadwi
Islamic scholar

the University of Karaouine, in Tunisia, in 859 CE. Ibn Asakir (1105–1176), a Sunni scholar who traveled across the Muslim world, studied the Hadith with hundreds of teachers, including 80 women. Hajji Koka counseled the Indian Mughal emperor Jahangir (1569–1627) and used her wealth to fund educational endowments for women.

One of the most remarkable women in the 19th century was Nana Asma'u of the Sokoto

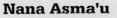

One child, one teacher, one book, one pen can change the world.
Malala Yousafzai

caliphate in what is now Nigeria, in West Africa. She rose to prominence not just because she was the caliph's daughter but also on account of her wisdom. Believing that education for girls needed to be institutionalized and standardized, she trained a network of women teachers known as *jajis*, who then traveled through the empire, enabling women to be taught in their own homes.

Nana's legacy lives on in Nigeria, in spite of efforts by the militant jihadists to disrupt girls' education: countless schools and women's organizations in Nigeria today are named after her, and her contributions have been enshrined in Nigerian history and culture. She is a reminder of the importance of education for all in Islam. ▪

Nana Asma'u

Born in northern Nigeria in 1793, Nana Asma'u was the daughter of Usman dan Fodio, the founder of the Sokoto caliphate (1809–1903) in West Africa. Like her father, Nana was a scholar of Quranic studies. She was also fluent in four languages; she used the medium of poetry to teach the principles of the caliphate.

When Nana's brother Mohammed Bello became the second Sokoto caliph, Nana was his close adviser. Her greatest legacy, however, was in producing an education system for women. When she died in 1864, she left a large legacy of writings—poetic, political, theological, and educational—in Arabic, Fula, Hausa, and Tamacheq Tuareg.

Key work

1997 *The Collected Works of Nana Asma'u Daughter of Usman dan Fodiyo (1793–1864)*

EVERY PATH LAID OPEN TO WOMAN AS FREELY AS TO MAN

FEMALE AUTONOMY IN A MALE-DOMINATED WORLD

IN CONTEXT

PRIMARY QUOTE
Margaret Fuller, 1845

KEY FIGURES
**Frances (Fanny) Wright,
Harriet Martineau,
Margaret Fuller**

BEFORE
1810 Sweden grants women
the right to work in all
guild professions, trades,
and handicrafts.

1811 In Austria, married
women are permitted financial
independence and the right to
choose a profession.

AFTER
1848 Three US states (New
York, Pennsylvania, and Rhode
Island) grant new property acts
that give women control of
what they own.

1870 The Married Women's
Property Act allows married
British women to have money
and inherit property.

As the Industrial Revolution
(1760–1840) gathered pace
in the early 19th century,
women began to examine their
status in societies that increasingly
emphasized the importance of
performing productive labor. French
philosopher and utopian socialist
Charles Fourier, who coined the
term *féminisme*, advocated a new
world order that was based on
cooperative autonomy for men and
women alike. He believed that all
work should be open to women,
according to their individual skills,
interests, and aptitudes, and that
their contribution—free from
patriarchal oppression—was vital for
a harmonious, productive society.
His views spread from Europe to the
US, where, in the 1840s and '50s,
supporters of his ideas created a
number of utopian communities in
which men and women lived and
worked cooperatively.

Thinkers and writers

Frances (Fanny) Wright, a Scottish-
born feminist, freethinker, and
abolitionist living in America,
advocated Fourier's beliefs. In a
series of letters published as *Views
of Society and Manners in America*
in 1821, she asserts that American

Educated women had few ways to
earn a good living. From the 1870s, the
introduction of typewriters—such as
this one, made by Scholes & Glidden—
led to opportunities for office work.

women were "assuming their place
as thinking beings" but were
hampered by their lack of financial
and legal rights. She spent time in
the utopian community of New
Harmony, Indiana, founded by the
Welsh social reformer Robert Owen,
a follower of Fourier, and became the
first woman in America to edit a
journal, *The New Harmony Gazette*.
In 1829, she moved to New York,

See also: Enlightenment feminism 28–33 ▪ Marriage and work 70–71 ▪ Rights for married women 72–75 ▪ Intellectual freedom 106–107

The extension of women's rights is the basic principle of all social progress.
Charles Fourier

where she broke the taboo on female public speaking and gave lectures calling for the emancipation of slaves and women, legal rights for wives, liberal divorce laws, and the introduction of birth control.

British writer Harriet Martineau tackled social, economic, and political issues that were more usually discussed by men. She rose to prominence with *Illustrations of Political Economy* (1832), 25 fictional "portraits" describing the impact of economic conditions on ordinary people at different levels of society. Martineau traveled to the US in 1834–1836, to examine its professed democratic principles, and then published her findings in *Society in America* in 1837. One chapter, "The Political Non-existence of Woman," notes that women receive "indulgence rather than justice" and calls for women to be better educated so they can exist without the financial support and control of men.

A few years later, the American journalist Margaret Fuller added her voice to these feminist writers with the book *Woman in the Nineteenth Century*, published in 1845. The book envisages a new awakening, in which independent women would build a better society on an equal footing with men. While accepting physical differences between the sexes, Fuller rejects defined attributes for each gender, writing, "There is no wholly masculine man, no purely feminine woman," a remark that was well ahead of her time.

Lasting influence

Such women inspired the fight for female emancipation in the US and Europe, and in the second half of the 19th century, a new wave of female campaigners would make their voices heard—a force that governments were eventually compelled to recognize. While these voices were generally from the middle-classes, the huge growth in business enterprises and bureaucracy fueled a demand for literate women from the working and lower middle classes to become stenographers, copyists, and bookkeepers—roles previously filled by men. However, any personal autonomy and satisfaction that such employment might have brought was reduced by its low pay and low status—women's work was still seen as secondary to men's. ∎

There exists in the minds of men a tone of feeling toward women as toward slaves.
Margaret Fuller

Harriet Martineau

Born in Norwich, UK, in 1802, the daughter of a cloth merchant, Harriet Martineau received a good education, but was confined to the domestic sphere by her mother's strict views on traditional gender roles. After her father's death in 1826, Martineau broke with convention to earn a living as a journalist, despite having been deaf since the age of 12.

The notable success of Martineau's *Illustrations of Political Economy* enabled her to move to London in 1832, where she met influential thinkers such as John Stuart Mill. After traveling to America and the Middle East, Martineau returned home and continued writing. Publishing more than 50 books and 2,000 articles, she campaigned for women's education, civil liberties, and suffrage all her life. She died in 1876 at a house she had designed and built in the Lake District.

Key works

1832 *Illustrations of Political Economy*
1836 *Philosophical Essays*
1837 *Society in America*
1848 *Household Education*

THE STRU
FOR EQUA
1840–1944

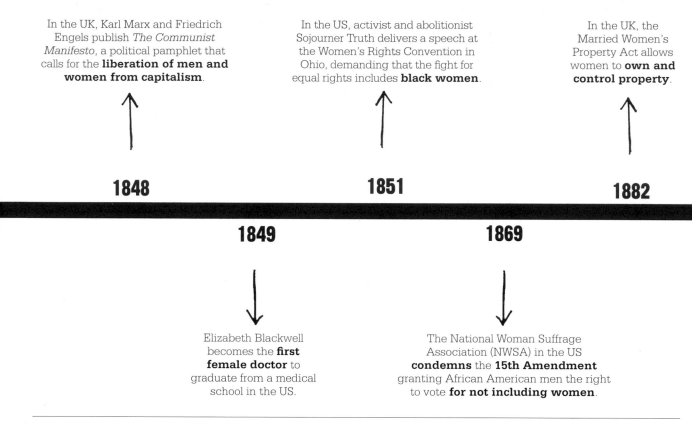

In the UK, Karl Marx and Friedrich Engels publish *The Communist Manifesto*, a political pamphlet that calls for the **liberation of men and women from capitalism**.

In the US, activist and abolitionist Sojourner Truth delivers a speech at the Women's Rights Convention in Ohio, demanding that the fight for equal rights includes **black women**.

In the UK, the Married Women's Property Act allows women to **own and control property**.

1848

1851

1882

1849

1869

Elizabeth Blackwell becomes the **first female doctor** to graduate from a medical school in the US.

The National Woman Suffrage Association (NWSA) in the US **condemns** the **15th Amendment** granting African American men the right to vote **for not including women**.

Feminist history often describes the period from the mid-19th century to the early 20th century as that of "first-wave" feminism. During this time, a definite women's movement emerged as feminists worldwide analyzed aspects of their lives and aimed to change the institutions that oppressed them. Gradually women began to get together to demand equal rights—in law, education, employment, and politics. From about the 1840s in the US, and then in Britain, women's demands for rights were channeled into what became a broad-based and sometimes divided campaign to win the vote. However, feminism was never one unified movement. Different political approaches caused the emergence of a variety of often conflicting strands.

First-wave feminists campaigned on many fronts. In Britain, activists Caroline Norton and Barbara Bodichon orchestrated attacks on laws that kept women, particularly married women, in a subordinate role. Their efforts resulted in the Matrimonial Causes Act of 1857—which forced men to prove a wife's adultery in court and allowed women to cite a husband's cruelty or desertion—followed by two married women's property acts, the second of which, in 1882, enabled married women to own property.

Breaking out of the home

Women also challenged the social restrictions that kept them in the domestic sphere of home and family. English feminists Harriet Taylor Mill and Elizabeth Blackwell argued that women should have the same access as men to university training, the professions, and paid employment, and threw their energies into opening up greater opportunities for women.

The writings of the German political theorists Karl Marx and Friedrich Engels were an influence on socialist feminists, such as Clara Zetkin in Germany and Alexandra Kollontai in Russia. They viewed women's oppression as a class issue, arguing that the development of the family as an economic unit fundamental to capitalism forced women into a subordinate role and that only a socialist revolution would free them.

While middle-class women in Western countries protested against lives of enforced idleness, working-class women in mills and factories had different concerns.

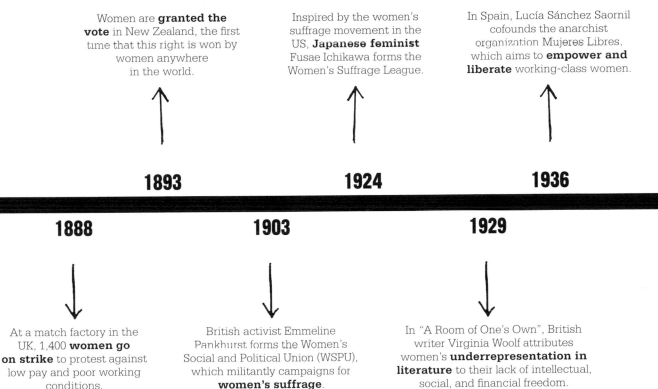

Women are **granted the vote** in New Zealand, the first time that this right is won by women anywhere in the world.

Inspired by the women's suffrage movement in the US, **Japanese feminist** Fusae Ichikawa forms the Women's Suffrage League.

In Spain, Lucía Sánchez Saornil cofounds the anarchist organization Mujeres Libres, which aims to **empower and liberate** working-class women.

1893   **1924**   **1936**

1888   **1903**   **1929**

At a match factory in the UK, 1,400 **women go on strike** to protest against low pay and poor working conditions.

British activist Emmeline Pankhurst forms the Women's Social and Political Union (WSPU), which militantly campaigns for **women's suffrage**.

In "A Room of One's Own", British writer Virginia Woolf attributes women's **underrepresentation in literature** to their lack of intellectual, social, and financial freedom.

They had always contributed to the family income, but industrialization had pulled them out of home-based activities into outside work with no protection from exploitation. Facing opposition from male trade unions, who saw women's work as a threat to their livelihoods, working-class women in the US and Britain took action, going on strike and forming women-only trade unions.

Race, sex, and the vote

Issues of race permeated first-wave feminism from the 19th century onward. Black feminists, such as the activist and former slave Sojourner Truth, experienced a double oppression on both gender and ethnic grounds. The abolitionist cause brought white and black women together, but divisions emerged during the latter part of the century, particularly during the fight for the vote, when, in the US, women's suffrage was postponed in favor of votes for black men.

Despite the social taboos against women talking about sex, some pioneering feminists in Britain, Sweden, and elsewhere highlighted sex and reproduction as key areas in which women had little control. In Britain and the US, feminist campaigners argued against male control of women's reproductive rights and fought for access to birth control. Even more radical were those, such as the English social reformer Josephine Butler, who identified a sexual double standard within society, whereby sexual activity was condoned in men but not in women, highlighted by society's ambiguous attitude to prostitution.

From around the middle of the first-wave period, feminists in Britain and the US came together in a mass movement to achieve suffrage, or the right to vote. Strategies for achieving this right varied enormously, and in Britain the struggle became increasingly bitter and violent. Despite divisions among feminists, the campaign for suffrage dominated much of their activity up to World War I (1914–1918) and in its immediate aftermath.

By the 1920s, feminist ideas and campaigns had emerged in many countries across the world, including Japan, where feminists such as Fusae Ichikawa argued for a woman's right to be involved in politics. In the Arab world, too, particularly Egypt, Huda Sharaawi and other feminists had set up the first feminist organizations. ■

WHEN YOU SELL YOUR LABOR, YOU SELL YOURSELF

UNIONIZATION

IN CONTEXT

PRIMARY QUOTE
Lowell Mill Girls, 1841

KEY ORGANIZATIONS
**Lowell Mill Girls,
the Match Girls**

BEFORE
Mid-1700s British inventions such as the spinning jenny, the water-frame, and improvements to the steam engine lead to the automation of heavy work.

1833 In the UK, the first Factory Act provides some legal protection to children working in factories.

AFTER
1888 American activist and suffragist Leonora O'Reilly begins a female chapter of the Knights of Labor, a national labor federation.

1903 Mary Harris Jones leads a parade of child workers from Philadelphia to New York to protest against child labor.

The Industrial Revolution fundamentally shifted the way people worked and lived. Mechanization made mass-production of goods possible, and companies began to hire large numbers of unskilled workers to tend to the machines, including women and children. As this work was usually repetitive and unskilled, bosses paid very low wages. Individual craftspeople could not compete with the low cost of industrially made goods, and for many people, selling their labor for a wage soon became the only option for finding employment.

Jobs for women
Women had traditionally done repetitive and tedious work in the home and on the land, and old notions of "women's work" dictated which jobs were open to women in the industrial economy. They took on a large proportion of low-paid clerical, retail, and factory work. As women typically sewed and mended clothing at home, textile factories usually hired largely female workforces. Leadership roles were rarely available to women, unmarried women were assumed

I will speak of the small to the great, and of the feeble to the strong.
Annie Besant

to be working only until they found a husband, and companies paid women a fraction of what male laborers received.

In the early 1800s, a textile mill in Lowell, Massachusetts, sent recruiters to small farms to hire young women workers. Most of New England's economy was agrarian at this time, and quite a few farming families sent their daughters off to earn extra money in the factories. The mill owners promised to fulfil a paternal role in these young women's lives by sending them to church and giving them a moral education. In reality, the factory's conditions

Sarah Bagley

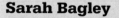

Born in Rockingham County, New England, in 1806, Sarah Bagley moved to Lowell, Massachusetts, in 1836 to work in one of the town's many textile mills. Over the course of a decade, Bagley noticed how the mill workers' pay and their quality of life remained the same even when production in the mills increased.

A strong personality and a charismatic speaker, Bagley and 12 other "Mill Girls" started the Lowell Female Labor Reform Association (LFLRA) in January 1845, and in May 1846 purchased a worker's newspaper, *The Voice*

of Industry, to share their ideas. The LFLRA joined a growing group of labor organizations in the US that were demanding fair wages and a 10-hour working day. The first union of women workers in the US, it grew to 600 branches.

In later life, Bagley practiced homeopathic medicine with her husband in New York City. She died in Philadelphia in 1899.

Key work

1846–1848 *The Voice of Industry*

See also: Collective action in the 18th century 24–27 ▪ Working-class feminism 36–37 ▪ Marxist feminism 52–55 ▪ Women's union organizing 160–161 ▪ Anticapitalist feminism 300–301

Hurdles to female unionization

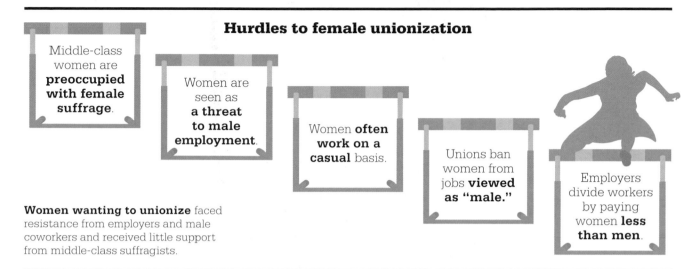

Middle-class women are **preoccupied with female suffrage**.

Women are seen as **a threat to male employment**.

Women **often work on a casual** basis.

Unions ban women from jobs **viewed as "male."**

Employers divide workers by paying women **less than men**.

Women wanting to unionize faced resistance from employers and male coworkers and received little support from middle-class suffragists.

were exploitative; women's wages at Lowell were about $4 per week in 1845 (around $100 today), and managers often lengthened the working day or demanded higher productivity with no change in pay. The average length of the working day was 13 hours.

Collective action

Women began to organize and unionize (make demands as a group rather than as individuals) early on in the industrial revolution, calling for better pay and fairer treatment from their employers. As early as 1828, the "Lowell Mill Girls," effectively the first female union in the US, took to the streets with banners and signs to protest against their employer's restrictive rules. In 1836, 1,500 female workers walked out in a full strike, bringing production to a halt.

The backlash against Lowell's strikers, who were portrayed as ungrateful and immoral by their employers, was fierce. Nonetheless, the Mill Girls came to be well known as a powerful union. In 1866, the year after the 13th

Amendment to the US Constitution ended slavery in the US, a group of formerly enslaved washerwomen formed the first labor union in the state of Mississippi. On June 20, they sent a resolution to the mayor of Jackson, the state capital, demanding a uniform wage for their labor. They also requested that any woman found working for less should be fined. A few days later, a group of formerly enslaved men, inspired by the women, held a meeting in Jackson's Baptist church to discuss striking for better wages.

Further strikes ensued. In the town of Lynn, Massachusetts, on July 28, 1869, a group of women shoeworkers created their own trade union. Calling themselves the "Daughters of St. Crispin" after their male counterparts, the "Knights of St. Crispin" (Crispin being the patron saint of cobblers), the female union grew rapidly, with lodges forming in Massachusetts, California, Illinois, Maine, New Hampshire, New York, Ohio, and Pennsylvania, and became the first national women's labor union in »

A monthly magazine, the *Lowell Offering*, published for the workers at Lowell Mill, idealized the life of the mill girls. The reality was rather different, with long hours and low pay.

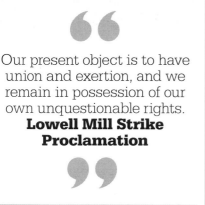

> Our present object is to have union and exertion, and we remain in possession of our own unquestionable rights.
> **Lowell Mill Strike Proclamation**

the US. In 1870, the Daughters of St. Crispin demanded equal pay with men for equal labor. They organized two strikes in 1872: the first, in Stoneham, Massachusetts, was unsuccessful, but the second, in Lynn, won higher wages for female workers. In 1874, the Daughters of St. Crispin went on to demand a 10-hour working day for women and children in manufacturing jobs.

Socialist links

In Britain and mainland Europe, industrialization advanced at an even faster pace than in the US.

Britain's 1847 Factory Act limited the work day to 10 hours a day for women and teenagers, but factory owners and large companies continued to pay low wages for work in unsafe conditions. A vast, impoverished workforce that had migrated to the cities from the countryside provided a large, desperate workforce. If a worker quit her job or fell ill, it was easy to find a replacement.

Philosophers and political theorists such as Karl Marx and Friedrich Engels wrote about the unfair exploitation of labor and suggested socialist alternatives to the capitalist system. The role of women, however, did not play a central part in the writings of Marx or Engels. Instead, women activists such as British suffragists Emma Paterson and Clementina Black based their politics on their own experiences of labor and class relations. In 1872, at the age of 19, Paterson became assistant secretary to the Workmen's Club and Institute Union, and two years later founded the Women's Protective and Provident League, with the specific goal of getting more women involved in trade union organizing. It was made up of mostly middle- and upper-class people with socialist views.

Clementina Black, a middle-class Englishwoman who was a family friend of Karl Marx, took a different approach. At first, she focused on using women's power as consumers to bring about social change. She worked on creating a consumers' league, which advocated buying only from industries that paid their workers fair wages. In 1886, Black became a member of Emma Paterson's Women's League, working as secretary to the organization.

Militant action

In 1888, Clementina Black became involved in the Match Girls' strike in London's East End. Its success convinced her that more militant, direct action was the best way to effect social change. In 1889, she helped found the Women's Trade Union Association, and in 1894, became editor of *Women's Industrial News*, the journal of the Women's Industrial Council (WIC), which published investigations into the quality of life and the working conditions of women laborers.

The strike in 1888 was not the match girls' first protest. In 1871, they marched against a proposed tax on matches.

The Match Girls' Strike

In July 1888, 1,400 women and girls walked out of the Bryant & May match factory in London, in what came to be known as the Match Girls' Strike. British socialist Annie Besant used her newspaper, *The Link*, to publicize the 14-hour workday, toxic materials, and the unfair difference between shareholder profits and the poverty wages paid to employees.

Workers complained of fines that cut into their wages, and of unfair dismissals. They also suffered breathing difficulties and other health problems because of the phosphorus fumes in the factory.

Bryant & May attempted to crack down on public criticism by making their workers sign a written denial of any ill-treatment. This, combined with another unfair dismissal, set off the strike. The public sided with the workers, and Bryant & May relented. The success of the match girls inspired a wave of similar strikes in the UK and boosted the rise of trade unionism.

> Never be deceived that the rich will allow you to vote away their wealth.
> **Lucy Parsons**

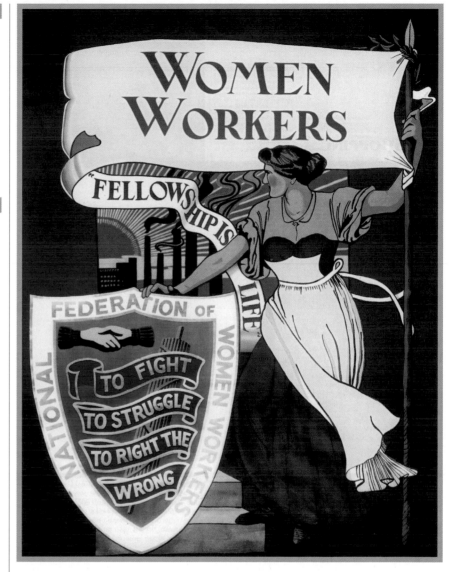

In the US, African American socialist and anarchist Lucy Parsons helped to found the International Working People's Association (IWPA) in Chicago in 1881. After moving with her husband to Chicago from Texas in 1873, she had opened a dress shop and hosted meetings of the International Ladies Garment Workers Union (ILGWU). She also wrote articles for *The Socialist* and *The Alarm*, two radical IWPA newspapers that were published in the city.

In 1886, Parsons helped to organize a May Day protest in which more than 80,000 workers in Chicago and some 350,000 workers across the US walked out on their jobs in a general strike to fight for an eight-hour work day. The strike became violent on May 3 after police fired into a crowd of protesters in Chicago. When one police officer was killed, retribution was swift and harsh. Despite not being at the meeting, Parsons' husband was hunted down, arrested, found guilty of the murder, and then executed.

Parsons continued with her activist work. She was the only female speaker at the inaugural meeting of the Industrial Workers of the World, an international labor organization founded in Chicago in 1905, and she traveled the world to lecture on socialist causes.

The labor abuses associated with industrialization were experienced by men and women, but most labor unions were still open only to men at the beginning of the 20th century. Women workers were generally forced to organize their own unions to address their specific concerns. These struggles were eventually taken up by the suffrage and women's movements. Women's unions helped to secure the eight-hour work day as standard (by 1940 in the US), end some of the worst workplace abuses of child labor, and achieve a better wage for women. ∎

The National Federation of Women Workers (NFWW) fought for a minimum wage in Britain and exposed the evils of sweatshop labor's long hours, poor conditions, and low pay. Founded in 1906, it had 20,000 members by 1914.

A MERE INSTRUMENT OF PRODUCTION

MARXIST FEMINISM

IN CONTEXT

PRIMARY QUOTE
**Karl Marx and
Friedrich Engels, 1848**

KEY FIGURES
**Karl Marx, Friedrich
Engels, Rosa Luxemburg,
Clara Zetkin, Alexandra
Kollontai**

BEFORE
1770s Scottish economist
Adam Smith's work largely
ignores the role of women in
the economy.

1821 German philosopher
George Wilhelm Friedrich
Hegel claims that women do
not belong in public spheres.

AFTER
1972 Marxist feminists launch
the Wages for Housework
Campaign in Italy.

2012 In the US, women's
unpaid domestic work is said
to raise GDP by 25.7 percent.

In *The Communist Manifesto*
of 1848, German philosophers
and revolutionary political
theorists Karl Marx and Friedrich
Engels claim that capitalism
oppresses women, treating them as
subordinate, second-class citizens
in both the family and society.
Marxist feminism adapts this theory
to seek women's emancipation
through the dismantling of the
capitalist system.

Marx's later writings primarily
focused on economic and social
inequalities between classes, and
paid little attention to the issue of
male domination, but he returned
to the subject of female oppression
at the end of his life, producing

See also: Unionization 46–51 ▪ Socialization of childcare 81 ▪ Anarcha-feminism 108–109 ▪ Radical feminism 137 ▪ Family structures 138–139 ▪ Wages for housework 147 ▪ Gross domestic product 217

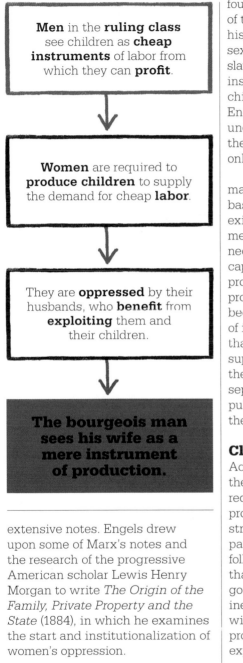

Men in the **ruling class** see children as **cheap instruments** of labor from which they can **profit**.

↓

Women are required to **produce children** to supply the demand for cheap **labor**.

↓

They are **oppressed** by their husbands, who **benefit** from **exploiting** them and their children.

↓

The bourgeois man sees his wife as a mere instrument of production.

extensive notes. Engels drew upon some of Marx's notes and the research of the progressive American scholar Lewis Henry Morgan to write *The Origin of the Family, Private Property and the State* (1884), in which he examines the start and institutionalization of women's oppression.

Women's servitude

Engels asserts that the violence and oppression that women suffer were rooted in the family at its very foundation. He describes the rise of the nuclear family as the "world historical defeat of the female sex" in which the woman was the slave of her husband and a mere instrument for the production of children. To ensure her fidelity, Engels writes, "she is delivered unconditionally into the power of the husband; if he kills her, he is only exercising his rights."

Classical Marxist writings maintain that, while the gender-based division of labor has always existed, the work performed by men and women is equally necessary. Only with the rise of capitalism, the advent of surplus product, and the accumulation of property did the human race become interested in the concept of inheritance. Engels maintains that the right of inheritance was supported by the idea of morality, the monogamous family, and the separation between private and public spheres, which then led to the control of female sexuality.

Class struggle

According to classical Marxist theory, women's emancipation required their inclusion in social production, and therefore women's struggle became an important part of the class struggle. The followers of Marxism believed that women shared the same goals as workers, and that gender inequality would disappear with the elimination of private property, since the reason for any exploitation would no longer exist.

Marxist feminists believed that in capitalist society women were a "reserve army of labor," called on when the need arose, such as during war, and excluded when that need

Karl Marx (left) and Friedrich Engels (right) met when Engels began writing for *Rheinische Zeitung*, a journal edited by Marx. When Marx's views led to his expulsion from Germany, the pair moved to Belgium and later England.

disappeared. Arguing that the patriarchy and male domination existed before the emergence of private property and class divisions, Marxist feminists identified capitalism and patriarchy as the dual systems that underpinned the oppression of women.

A joint struggle

Between the deaths of Marx (1883) and Engels (1895) and World War I (1914–1918), female socialist and communist theorists further elaborated on issues of women's empowerment and universal suffrage. Rosa Luxemburg and Clara Zetkin in Germany, and Alexandra Kollontai in Russia, leading theorists of the international communist movement, rejected the idea that because of their gender women did not belong in the socialist leadership. **»**

Clara Zetkin

Born in Saxony, Germany, in 1857, Clara Zetkin was an activist in the international communist movement and advocated suffrage and the reform of labor legislation for women. She helped make the Social Democratic Women's Movement in Germany one of the strongest in Europe. She edited its newspaper *Die Gleichheit* (*Equality*) from 1892 to 1917, and led the Women's Office of the Social Democratic Party in 1907.

Zetkin refused to support Germany's war effort during World War I and later urged workers to unite against fascism. When Adolf Hitler came to power in 1933, she fled to the Soviet Union. She died in Arkhangelskoye, near Moscow, later that year.

Key works

1906 "Social-Democracy and Woman Suffrage"
1914 "The Duty of Working Women in War-Time"
1925 "Lenin on the Women's Question"

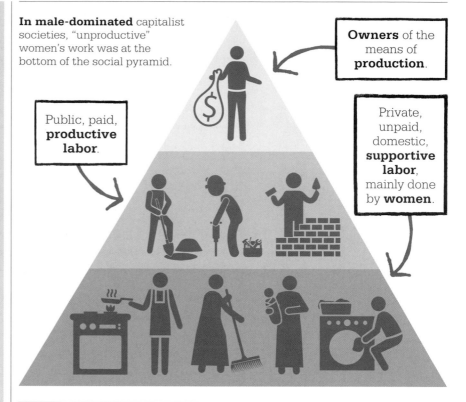

In male-dominated capitalist societies, "unproductive" women's work was at the bottom of the social pyramid.

Owners of the means of production.

Public, paid, productive labor.

Private, unpaid, domestic, supportive labor, mainly done by women.

Following their own principles, they brought the issue of women's rights to the fore in the fight for workers' emancipation.

The women's question

While the empowerment of women was not the chief focus of Rosa Luxemburg's writing, she believed that revolution was key to their emancipation and that women had the right to work outside the family. Highlighting the hypocrisy of preachings on gender equality by Christianity and by scholars from the bourgeois ruling class, she stated that capitalist society lacked any genuine equality for women and that only with the victory of a proletarian (working-class) revolution would women be liberated from household enslavement. In her 1912 speech "Women's Suffrage and Class Struggle," delivered at the Social Democratic Women's Rally in Stuttgart, Germany, she maintained that "socialism has brought about the spiritual rebirth of the mass of proletarian women," adding wryly, "and in the process has doubtless made [women] competent as productive workers for capital."

Luxemburg criticized the bourgeois women's movement. She described bourgeois wives as "parasites on society" and "beasts of burden for the family," and argued that only through the class struggle could "women become human beings." She maintained that the bourgeois woman had no real interest in pursuing political rights because she did not exercise any economic function in society and enjoyed the "ready-made fruits of class domination." For Luxemburg, the struggle for women's suffrage was not simply a mission for women, but the common goal of all workers.

She also saw women's suffrage as a necessary step in educating the proletariat and leading them forward in their struggle against capitalism.

Along with other socialist women, in particular her friend and confidante Clara Zetkin, who also dismissed liberal feminism as bourgeois, Luxemburg was involved in numerous campaigns that strengthened the solidarity of women. Many leftist female leaders met at international congresses to exchange their experiences and ideas, and established international women's organizations.

During World War I, Luxemburg and Zetkin participated in the antiwar campaign of the largest socialist newspaper for women, *Die Gleichheit* (*Equality*), urging readers to oppose militarism. Jailed in 1915 for expressing antiwar views, Luxemburg went on to found the Spartacus League with Zetkin in 1916; this underground Marxist group opposed German imperialism and sought to provoke revolution.

A new idea of woman

Revolutionary movements in Russia in the early 1900s spurred on the development of Marxist feminism.

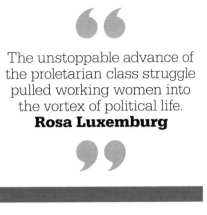

The unstoppable advance of the proletarian class struggle pulled working women into the vortex of political life.
Rosa Luxemburg

Alexandra Kollontai, a prominent communist revolutionary, placed female emancipation and gender equality at the center of the international socialist agenda. From 1905, she was active in promoting Marxist ideas among Russia's female workers. Kollontai demanded the radical break-up of traditional family relations, insisting that when a woman was economically dependent on a man and did not directly participate in public and industrial life, she could not be free.

Kollontai's 1918 article "The New Woman" proclaims that women would have to emerge from the subservient role imposed by patriarchal traditions and cultivate qualities traditionally associated with men. The new woman would conquer their emotions and develop strong self-discipline. She would demand a man's respect and not ask for his material support. Her interests would not be limited to home, family, and love, and she would not hide her sexuality.

In *Society and Motherhood* (1916), Kollontai analyzes factory work and states that hard labor turned motherhood into a burden, leading to health and social issues for women and children. Advocating improved working conditions and state recognition of the value of motherhood through the provision of national insurance, she claims that the health of a working woman and her child, as well as childcare while the mother worked, should be the responsibility of the state.

Marxist feminists of the early 20th century influenced state policies of later communist governments around the world. Later, in the 1960s and '70s, radical feminist groups such as Wages for Housework were also inspired by their ideas. ∎

International Women's Day and its origins

Celebrated annually on March 8, International Women's Day is traced back to the US in 1907, when more than 15,000 female textile workers marched through New York City, demanding better working conditions and voting rights. In 1909, the Socialist Party of America declared a National Women's Day, celebrated until 1913 on the last Sunday of February.

In 1910, about 100 women from 17 countries attended the Second International Conference of Women in Copenhagen, Denmark, at which Clara Zetkin proposed the establishment of International Women's Day, on which women would highlight women's issues. The following year, more than one million women and men attended International Women's Day rallies worldwide. In Russia in 1917, women marked the day with a four-day strike for "peace and bread" that was a key event in the lead up to Russia's October Revolution that year.

Women from many countries attend the International Women's Day march in London on March 8, 2018. The day was adopted by the United Nations in 1975 and is a national holiday in some countries.

WE HOLD THESE TRUTHS TO BE SELF-EVIDENT: THAT ALL MEN AND WOMEN ARE CREATED EQUAL

THE BIRTH OF THE SUFFRAGE MOVEMENT

IN CONTEXT

PRIMARY QUOTE
Elizabeth Cady Stanton, 1848

KEY FIGURES
Elizabeth Cady Stanton, Lucretia Mott, Susan B. Anthony, Lucy Stone

BEFORE
1792 Mary Wollstonecraft's *A Vindication of the Rights of Woman* is published in the UK.

1837 In "Letters on the Equality of the Sexes," Sarah Grimké argues that women have the same responsibility as men to act for the good of humanity.

AFTER
1869 Wyoming becomes the first US territory to grant female suffrage.

1920 The 19th Amendment to the US constitution is ratified, giving all American women the right to vote.

On July 19, 1848, 300 women and men gathered at Seneca Falls, New York, for the first assembly of women's rights activists. It was a time of great social change, especially in Europe. Karl Marx and Friedrich Engels had just published *The Communist Manifesto* in London, England, and republican revolts, known as the 1848 Revolutions, had erupted in France, the Netherlands, and Germany. The impetus for the Seneca Falls Convention, however, came out of women's experience of the abolitionist movement and the shift from moral opposition to slavery to political activism against it.

Like minds

The organizers of the Seneca Falls Convention were Lucretia Mott and Elizabeth Cady Stanton, abolitionists who had met at the World Antislavery Convention in London in 1840, where they had been united in their outrage at the marginalization of female delegates.

By 1848, Stanton had moved to Seneca Falls, New York. When Mott contacted her there, the pair decided it was time to confront the lack of social, civil, and religious

Lucretia Mott (center) and a fellow campaigner are escorted through a crowd of angry male protestors trying to derail the historic Seneca Falls Convention of 1848.

rights for women and organized a convention in the town. With only a few days' notice, they and other women, including the orator and abolitionist Lucy Stone, drew up "The Declaration of Sentiments and Resolutions," perhaps the single

---

Elizabeth Cady Stanton

Born in Johnstown, New York, in 1815, Elizabeth Cady Stanton claimed she received her first lesson in gender discrimination while studying in her father's law firm. Due to the laws at the time, a female client was denied a legal means to recover money that her husband had stolen.

A well-educated woman, Elizabeth married abolitionist and lawyer Henry Stanton in 1840, and the couple went on to have seven children. In later life, Elizabeth turned her attention to the representation of women in the Bible, arguing that organized religion had contributed to the subjugation of women. Such views, expressed in *The Woman's Bible*, published in 1895, were unpopular with both the Church and women's organizations. She continued writing well into old age, before dying of heart failure in 1902.

Key works

1881–1886 *The History of Woman Suffrage Volumes 1–3* (with Susan B. Anthony)
1892 *The Solitude of Self*
1895 *The Woman's Bible*

See also: Racial and gender equality 64–69 ▪ Rights for married women 72–75 ▪ Political equality in Britain 84–91 ▪ The global suffrage movement 94–97

most important document in the 19th-century American women's movement. They advertised the event in the *Seneca County Courier* and Mott, a well-known preacher, was the only listed speaker at the convention. Her husband, James, chaired the convention, and 40 men were among the 300 attendees. They included the noted abolitionist Frederick Douglass, who was invited to the convention by Elizabeth M'Clintock, Stanton's friend and fellow activist.

Constitutional precedent

Inspired by the US Declaration of Independence of 1776, "The Declaration of Sentiments and Resolutions" set out the ways in which the rights enshrined in the founding document of the US Constitution were denied to women. Stanton read out a list of 16 injustices, including the fact that women had no right to vote, limited property rights, and restricted access to advanced education and most occupations.

> ❝
> The history of mankind is a history of repeated injuries and usurpations on the part of man toward woman.
> **Elizabeth Cady Stanton**
> ❞

Women's rights were taken away not just by marriage, she said, but by all of the ways in which they had been deprived of responsibility and made dependent upon men. If these rights were to be given to women, Stanton argued, they could protect themselves and realize their potential as moral and spiritual leaders.

The "sentiments" were followed by 12 "resolutions," which the attendees were asked to adopt.

Eleven of these were passed unanimously, including resolutions for equal rights in marriage, religion, education, and employment. However, the one for women's suffrage was given less support—especially from the men at the convention—and was only adopted when Douglass, who advocated female suffrage in his newspaper *The North Star,* defended it from the floor. After his intervention, 100 people signed the resolution. »

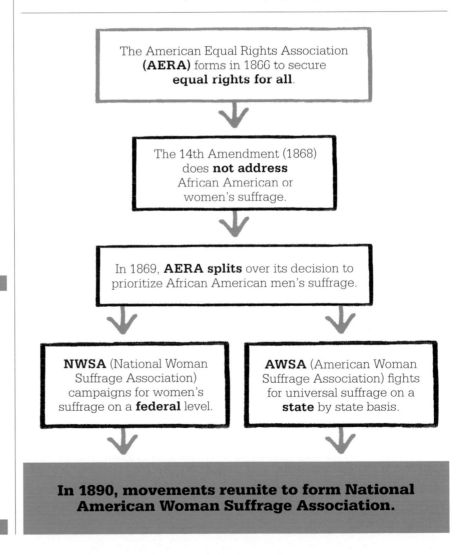

The American Equal Rights Association **(AERA)** forms in 1866 to secure **equal rights for all**.

The 14th Amendment (1868) does **not address** African American or women's suffrage.

In 1869, **AERA splits** over its decision to prioritize African American men's suffrage.

NWSA (National Woman Suffrage Association) campaigns for women's suffrage on a **federal** level.

AWSA (American Woman Suffrage Association) fights for universal suffrage on a **state** by state basis.

In 1890, movements reunite to form National American Woman Suffrage Association.

STRIVE TO EXCEL.

Factory workers make hoop skirts at Thomson's in London in the 1860s. As the industrial revolution took hold, the case for women keeping their own earnings became undeniable.

Two years later, in 1850, the first National Women's Rights Conference was held at Worcester, Massachusetts. Organized by Lucy Stone, it attracted 1,000 participants from 11 states. Further conferences took place through the 1850s, both nationally and locally.

Property matters

In 1851, Stanton was introduced to Susan B. Anthony by Amelia Bloomer, a campaigner against tight corsetry and other restrictive garments worn by women. Stanton and Anthony's complementary personalities and skills—Stanton was lively and talkative while Anthony was quiet and serious, with a good grasp of statistics—made them a powerful force for change. "In writing we did better work together than either did alone," said Stanton. Anthony, a schoolteacher from a family of Quakers and abolitionists in Rochester, New York, called for equal opportunities in education, and for schools and colleges to admit women and former slaves. She was also a labor activist and a temperance activist, but as a woman she was not allowed to speak at rallies for either cause.

Anthony organized her first women's rights conference in Syracuse in 1852 and campaigned for property rights for women in New York State from 1853. For many women, especially working women, property rights were more important than suffrage, which was only envisaged for well-off white women. While New York's Married Women's Property Act of 1848 had given married women the right to keep inherited money, earnings through employment remained the property of a woman's husband.

Anthony and Stanton worked together on Stanton's 1854 address to the New York State Legislature, in which Stanton listed all of the rights denied to women and asked that they be granted. This was delivered at the same time as a petition with 6,000 signatures to extend the 1848 Married Women's Property Act. A motion was defeated in 1854, but the lobbying continued until it was passed in 1860. The new act gave women the right to keep their own earnings and made them joint guardians with their husband over their children. A wife could also take out contracts independently from her husband,

who would not be bound by them, and as widows, they gained the same property rights as men.

Feminists who came from less wealthy backgrounds fought in different ways. Lucy Stone, a farmer's daughter, worked as a housekeeper in order to fund her teacher training. She had been reluctant to marry, as this would have meant the removal of all her rights, but in 1855 she married Henry Blackwell. At their wedding, they read a statement of protest, saying they did not accept the lack of rights for married women as they conferred "an injurious and unnatural superiority" on the husband. In 1858, Stone refused to pay her taxes, on the grounds of no taxation without representation. The government seized and sold her household goods as a result.

Amending the Constitution

During the American Civil War (1861–1865), abolitionism eclipsed campaigns for women's rights. Stanton and Anthony formed the Women's National Loyal League in

> " Our doctrine is that 'right is of no sex.'
> **Frederick Douglass** "

> The mass speak through us … the laboring women demanding remuneration for their toil.
> **Elizabeth Cady Stanton**

1863 to support the constitutional amendment to end slavery. Their petitions received around 400,000 signatures in 15 months. When Abraham Lincoln passed the 13th Amendment abolishing slavery in 1865, Stanton and Anthony believed, erroneously, that the Republicans would also address the issue of women suffrage at this point.

In 1866, the two women set up the American Equal Rights Association (AERA), aimed at securing rights for all people, regardless of race, color, or sex. Its first chair was Lucretia Mott. Stanton, Anthony, and Stone campaigned for female and African-American suffrage during a referendum held in Kansas in 1867. Their failure led to a split in the suffrage movement, with some prioritizing suffrage for African-American men over that of women. Anthony was outraged: "I will cut off this right arm of mine before I will ever work for or demand the ballot for the Negro and not the woman."

In 1868, Stanton and Anthony published *The Revolution* newspaper in Rochester, with the masthead: "Men, their rights, and nothing more; women, their rights, and nothing less." Funded by the racist entrepreneur George Train, it included writings from Stanton that set the rights of educated white women against those of uneducated black southern men.

The 14th Amendment—ratified in 1868—delivered citizenship and equal rights under the law to men who had been enslaved. Stanton and Anthony petitioned against its exclusion of women, but they were unsuccessful. Stone, however, supported the amendment as being a step toward universal suffrage.

In 1869, AERA split into the American Woman Suffrage Association (AWSA) and the »

A cartoon of 1869 entitled *The Age of Brass or the Triumph of Woman's Rights* captures the perceived threat to traditional gender roles that female suffrage evoked.

THE AWAKENING

A torch-bearing woman awakens American women as she strides across the US in an illustration that accompanied a rousing poem by suffragist Alice Duer Miller in 1915.

National Woman Suffrage Association (NWSA), founded by Anthony and Stanton in New York. The NWSA had only women members, and also advocated divorce reform and equal pay. The 15th Amendment, which said that the "right to vote shall not be denied or abridged by the United States or by any State on the grounds of race, color, or previous condition of servitude" was passed in 1870. Campaigners had thought gender would also be included but this did not happen. Anthony and Stanton denounced the 15th Amendment. However, the Boston-based American Woman Suffrage Association, supported by Stone, accepted the 15th Amendment as a step in the right direction.

Political pressure

Legal struggles for female suffrage continued through the 1870s. Anthony enlisted lawyers to argue that the 14th Amendment required states to permit women to vote. The Supreme Court disagreed. In 1872, Anthony, her three sisters, and other women were arrested for voting in Rochester, New York. Refusing to pay bail, she hoped the case would go to the Supreme Court, but because her lawyer paid it, she was not imprisoned, which prevented her from appealing.

Anthony also went on speaking tours. In 1877, she gathered petitions with 10,000 signatures from 26 US states, but Congress ignored them. In 1878, she tried to get a constitutional amendment introduced by Senator Sargent of California. This was rejected by the Senate but was reintroduced again and again over the next 18 years. The NWSA mainly gained

> That power is the ballot, the symbol of freedom and equality.
> **Susan B. Anthony**

support from upstate New York and the Midwest. They argued for changing the law at a federal level, while the AWSA argued for changing it state by state. As an organization, the AWSA was more conservative, working on suffrage and no other issues that could distract from that. Gradually, their persistence paid off. Women in Wyoming gained the vote in 1869, Utah in 1870, and Washington in 1883. Colorado followed in 1893, and Idaho in 1896.

In 1890, the two suffrage movements came together to form the National American Woman Suffrage Association (NAWSA). Anthony still campaigned for the federal vote, while other women sought state-by-state reform.

Work counts

American suffrage organizations continued to be led by "elite women" until the 1890s. It was widely thought that politics should be left to educated women, and working-class women should defer to their judgement. Younger women, including Stanton's daughter Harriot Stanton Blatch, emphasized the role of work,

> ❝
> The world has never yet seen a truly great and virtuous nation because in the degradation of woman the very fountains of life are poisoned at their source.
> **Lucretia Mott**
> ❞

paid or unpaid, in marking out a woman for leadership. Yet the focus remained on educated women rather than their working-class counterparts, who were in the workforce and often being exploited.

Inspiring the world

American women's early striving for suffrage had a worldwide impact. Inspired by the Seneca Falls Convention, French women began to campaign for reform: in 1848, when France became the first country to introduce universal male suffrage, one woman tried to vote and another put herself forward for political office, for which they were both imprisoned. British women were also inspired by the US campaigns. Women's suffrage societies proliferated in Britain in the 1870s, and thousands of signatures were added to petitions presented to parliament. Even so, the extensions to male suffrage during the 1880s were not applied to women.

Canadian women also gained support from American activists. They argued that an extension to suffrage would benefit the country, and the home and family, as well as individual women. The debates in the Canadian parliament centered on the rights of white, English-speaking Canadians, but some people also advocated the rights of indigenous women, as long as they were educated.

Suffrage was an issue over which women battled for many years; the first countries to give women the vote were New Zealand in 1893 and Australia in 1902 (though not until 1962 for Aboriginal women). American women gained the vote at a federal level in 1920. ∎

The International Council of Women

In addition to working to secure suffrage for American women, Susan B. Anthony and Elizabeth Cady Stanton were founding members of the International Council of Women, which held its first meeting in Washington, D.C., in April 1888. The event marked the 40th anniversary of the Seneca Falls Convention.

Initially the organization did not advocate women's suffrage for fear of alienating some of its more conservative members, but this changed from 1899 when it began to campaign on a wide range of issues such as health, peace, education, and equality. A feminist agenda was never adopted, however, and in 1902 a splinter group broke off to form the International Woman Suffrage Alliance to pursue a more radical agenda.

Originally representing nine countries, the membership has expanded to more than 70 and is now headquartered in Paris. It acts as a consultant on women's issues for the United Nations.

Delegates wave their national flags at a meeting of the International Council of Women in Berlin in 1929. By this time, membership had expanded beyond Europe, North America, and the British colonies.

I HAVE AS MUCH MUSCLE AS ANY MAN

RACIAL AND GENDER EQUALITY

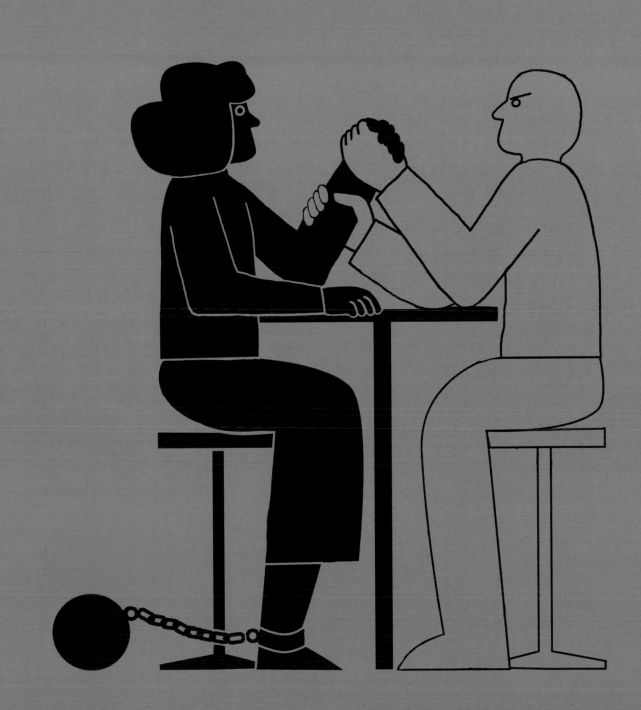

IN CONTEXT

PRIMARY QUOTE
Sojourner Truth, 1851

KEY FIGURES
**Sojourner Truth,
Elizabeth Cady Stanton,
Susan B. Anthony,
Frederick Douglass**

BEFORE
1768 Phillis Wheatley, an enslaved African in Boston, Massachusetts, writes a plea for freedom in the form of a poem that she addresses to King George III of Great Britain.

1848 Black abolitionist Frederick Douglass speaks at a women's rights convention to win delegates' approval for the first formal demand for women's right to vote.

AFTER
1863 Abolitionists Susan B. Anthony and Elizabeth Cady Stanton gather 400,000 signatures in support of the 13th Amendment to abolish slavery in the US.

1869 In protest against the exclusion of women in the 15th Amendment, which grants black men the right to vote, Anthony and Stanton sever ties with abolitionists and form the National Woman Suffrage Association to win suffrage for women.

In early 19th-century America, the idea of equal rights for women was just a vague concept talked about in a few enlightened circles. The pervasive thinking of the time, held by the majority of women as well as men, was that God had created women as subordinates to men. This belief was drawn from selected passages in the Bible, just as contorted interpretations of the Bible were widely used to declare black people inherently inferior to whites.

British teacher Mary Wollstonecraft's *A Vindication of the Rights of Woman* of 1792, which argues that women were as intellectually capable as men and deserving of the same human rights, had gone out of print in the US by 1820. The revolutionary climate in which it was written had given way to reactionary forces and there were fears the book would undermine the status quo in American homes. Similarly, when women in New Jersey, the only one of the former Thirteen Colonies that had granted female suffrage, suddenly lost their right to vote in 1807 (a party political move by New Jersey

This antislavery image accompanied a poem in the abolitionist newspaper *The Liberator*, published in 1832. It was designed to appeal to the sympathies of white female readers.

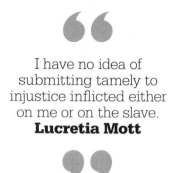

I have no idea of submitting tamely to injustice inflicted either on me or on the slave.
Lucretia Mott

Federalists to damage the Republican vote), the decision went unchallenged.

Such retrogressive steps were not confined to the US. France, for example, repealed its equal inheritance rights legislation for women in 1804, less than 15 years after its passage. A feminist awakening, however, was on the horizon in the US, encouraged by the abolitionist movement.

Roused to action

Moves to free enslaved black people dated back many years, with the first antislavery society originating in Philadelphia in 1775. After the American Revolution (1775–1783), northern states gradually emancipated their slaves. Southern states, however, developed a large-scale farming economy based on cotton and tobacco crops that relied on slave labor to turn a profit. As the South's chattel labor system became more entrenched, the number of abolitionists proliferated, many inspired by the religious revival known as the Second Great Awakening, which denounced slavery as immoral. By 1830, abolitionists, which had thousands of white women in their ranks, were gathering momentum

See also: Marxist feminism 52–55 ▪ The birth of the suffrage movement 56–63 ▪ The global suffrage movement 94–97 ▪ Racism and class prejudice within feminism 202–205 ▪ Black feminism and womanism 208–215

Women participate at what is thought to be a rally of the American Anti-Slavery Society in 1840, by which time women were taking a more forceful role in the organization.

in their efforts to eradicate slavery. Educated free black women such as Frances Harper and Sarah Remond joined the cause as well as escaped slaves Harriet Tubman and Sojourner Truth. Just days after the founding of the male-led American Anti-Slavery Society in 1833, a group of women organized the Philadelphia Female Anti-Slavery Society, which welcomed both black and white women.

Like their male counterparts, women mobilized and traveled the antislavery lecture circuit, speaking daily for months on end and at times being the target of jeering and mob violence. Women excelled at raising money to aid fugitive slaves and sometimes acted as conductors on the dangerous Underground Railroad, a network of secret routes used to take slaves from the South to the North. They circulated petitions and wrote hundreds of letters and editorials against slavery. Women such as Lucy Stone, Elizabeth Cady Stanton, Lucretia Mott, and sisters Sarah and Angelina Grimké emerged as leaders and organizers in the abolitionist movement.

Shared causes
Experiences in the antislavery struggle laid the groundwork for feminism early on and symbiotically linked the two movements. Reform-minded women could not long ignore the suppression of their own rights »

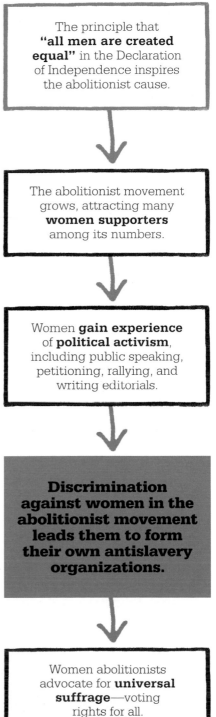

The principle that **"all men are created equal"** in the Declaration of Independence inspires the abolitionist cause.

The abolitionist movement grows, attracting many **women supporters** among its numbers.

Women **gain experience** of **political activism**, including public speaking, petitioning, rallying, and writing editorials.

Discrimination against women in the abolitionist movement leads them to form their own antislavery organizations.

Women abolitionists advocate for **universal suffrage**—voting rights for all.

as they pressed for freedom for enslaved African Americans. For several decades, the campaigns of the two causes would overlap.

At the World Anti-Slavery Convention in London, UK, in 1840, female delegates from the US were barred from speaking on the grounds that they were "constitutionally unfit" for business matters. This early effort to silence women eventually led to the first official women's conference at Seneca Falls, New York, in 1848, organized by Lucretia Mott and her fellow abolitionist Elizabeth Cady Stanton. Many male abolitionists also attended this meeting, including the activist Charles Remond, a free African American.

The 1850 National Women's Rights Convention in Worcester, Massachusetts, reiterated the demand for women's suffrage and called for a woman's right to hold office and for equality under the law "without distinction of sex or color," a further merging of the two causes. By this time, the noted black female abolitionist Sojourner Truth, an uneducated former slave, had joined the lecture circuit promoting female suffrage, and made a memorable women's equality speech at the 1851 Women's Rights Convention in Akron, Ohio. When antislavery and women's rights conventions converged in New York City in 1853, the roster of speakers was identical for both causes.

Eclipsed by civil war

The crisis over slavery continued to intensify, finally plunging the nation into civil war in 1861. Uncertain whether Abraham Lincoln, the newly elected president, would compromise on slavery to preserve the Union, abolitionists rallied all their forces to lobby for full emancipation. Work on women's

Uncle Tom's Cabin

The antislavery novel *Uncle Tom's Cabin* by Harriet Beecher Stowe was an extraordinary intervention by a woman in the mid-19th century. In the novel, Stowe takes an important public issue and dramatizes it for a private audience, a large proportion of whom were women. Writing to an editor, Stowe said, "I feel now that the time has come when even a woman or a child who can speak a word for freedom and humanity is bound to speak."

The novel, which was initially published in 41 installments in an antislavery newspaper in 1851, helped build popular opinion against slavery. Abraham Lincoln is said to have remarked that the Civil War could be attributed to the antislavery sentiments that were expressed in the book, purportedly calling Stowe "the little woman who started this war." In the south of the United States, possession or even knowledge of the book was considered dangerous.

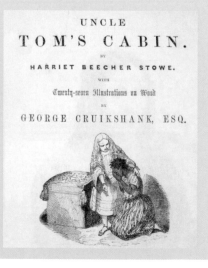

rights issues was suspended for the duration of the war. After the Emancipation Proclamation in 1863, antislavery women, worried that the proclamation might be overturned, petitioned for a constitutional amendment to secure black people's freedom. Elizabeth Cady Stanton and Susan B. Anthony organized the Women's National Loyal League to collect 400,000 signatures in support of the 13th Amendment, which abolished slavery in the US. With this in place, some antislavery organizations dissolved, but others vowed to put "the ballot in the hand of the freedman."

Perceiving an opportunity to gain the vote for women as well as blacks, Anthony accelerated women's activism through a new organization called the American Equal Rights Association, formed in 1866, which advocated universal suffrage. Longtime abolitionist and women's rights supporter Wendell Phillips, among others, objected. "This hour belongs to the Negro," he said, putting aside the goal of women's suffrage until a future time. Activism and resources would go toward guaranteeing

The mission of the Radical Anti-Slavery Movement is not to the African slave alone, but to the slaves of custom, creed, and sex, as well.
Elizabeth Cady Stanton

I do not see how anyone can pretend that there is the same urgency in giving the ballot to women as to the Negro.
Frederick Douglass

voting rights for black men through the 15th Amendment ratified in 1870. Douglass, who had been a supporter of women's suffrage for more than 20 years, defended this strategy. Because of racism, he argued, ensuring the ballot for black men was "a question of life and death."

Left behind

Relations between the abolitionist and women's movements soon turned acrimonious. Stanton was especially vocal and caustic, even racist, in her anger against old abolitionist allies. She fumed in public and in print about "ignorant negroes and foreigners," "the lower orders of … unlettered manhood" getting the vote before "the higher orders of womanhood." Stanton and Anthony opposed ratification of the 15th Amendment. The rift between the two movements divided women into two camps: those who supported the 15th Amendment and those who did not. As a result, two organizations emerged to take up the fight for female suffrage— the National Woman Suffrage Association (NWSA) and the American Woman Suffrage Association (AWSA). The battle raged for almost another 50 years. ∎

Sojourner Truth

Born into slavery in the state of New York around 1797, Sojourner Truth became a key figure in the abolitionist and women's rights movements. Named Isabella Baumfree by her slave owner, she fled her master in 1826 after a profound religious experience. Inspired by her faith, she became a traveling preacher.

In 1843, Baumfree changed her name to Sojourner Truth and joined an egalitarian commune in Massachusetts that was devoted to the abolition of slavery. Truth met leading abolitionists, including William Lloyd Garrison, Frederick Douglass, and David Ruggles, who sparked her passion to speak out against slavery and women's inequality. At approximately 6 ft (1.8 m) tall, with a commanding presence, she delivered powerful oratory laced with sarcasm. In her speech at an 1851 women's rights convention in Ohio, she declared herself equal to men in strength and intellect, setting her course as a major symbol of antislavery feminism. She campaigned well into old age and died in 1883, aged around 86.

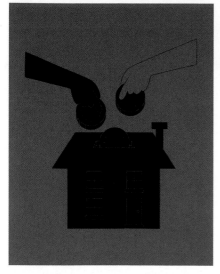

A WOMAN WHO CONTRIBUTES CANNOT BE TREATED CONTEMPTUOUSLY
MARRIAGE AND WORK

IN CONTEXT

PRIMARY QUOTE
Harriet Taylor Mill, 1851

KEY FIGURE
Harriet Taylor Mill

BEFORE
1825 In Britain, Anna Wheeler and William Thompson publish their appeal for women to be freed from political, civil, and domestic slavery.

1838 Harriet Martineau writes *On Marriage* about the inequities married women have to suffer.

AFTER
1859 Britain's Society for Promoting the Employment of Women is established.

1860 The Victoria Press is founded in London, producing the *English Women's Journal.*

1870 The Married Women's Property Act gives women in England and Wales more financial independence.

In 1851, inspired by the first women's rights conventions in the US, British women's rights activist Harriet Taylor Mill wrote her powerful essay, "The Enfranchisement of Women," calling for equality with men "in all rights, political, civil, and social" and insisting on a right to work outside the home. She was a prominent voice in an increasing volume of such protests in the US and Britain.

Wife and mother

In mid-19th-century Britain, most middle-class married women conformed to the domestic role of wife and mother that Victorian social convention idealized and imposed on them. They were not permitted an education equal to that of men, which limited career aspirations. In the lower classes, most wives had to run the home, raise a family, and work for meager wages in agriculture, industry, and trade; when pregnant, they often

Women would play valuable roles in society as educational and work opportunities expanded, but as this 1912 suffrage poster wryly illustrates, only men could vote, even those who were drunkards and wastrels.

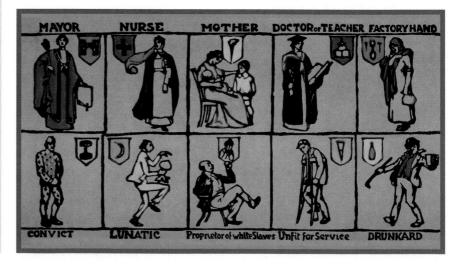

See also: Emancipation from domesticity 34–35 ▪ Marxist feminism 52–55 ▪ Family structures 138–139 ▪ Wages for housework 147

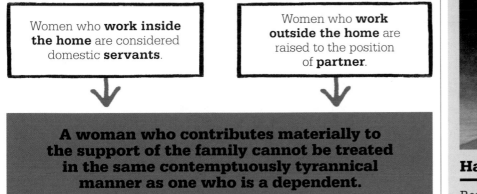

Women who **work inside the home** are considered domestic **servants**.

Women who **work outside the home** are raised to the position of **partner**.

A woman who contributes materially to the support of the family cannot be treated in the same contemptuously tyrannical manner as one who is a dependent.

worked up to the point of giving birth. Women in all classes had no rights to keep what they earned; on marriage, all their money and property passed to their husband. The situation was similar in the US and most of Europe.

Protesting feminists included the Irish-born writer Anna Wheeler, who left her husband and earned a living as a translator and writer. She advocated equal political rights and equal access to education for women, convinced that gender equality could never exist while women were excluded from socially productive work. British writer and social theorist Harriet Martineau deplored the fact that wives were treated as inferior, despite the mutual interest both partners had in building a successful marriage.

A turning point

The companion and future wife of the economist and philosopher John Stuart Mill, Harriet Taylor Mill drew attention to the prejudice that excluded women from almost all work that required either thinking or training. She pointed out that a well-educated wife who could contribute to the family income

would win more respect from her husband and be treated as a partner. She argued that this would benefit not only women but society as a whole; women who failed to engage with society could hinder their family's moral development.

Taylor Mill did not live to see the changes she called for, but her writings fueled the call for better women's education and training on both sides of the Atlantic. In 1870, married women in Britain won the right to keep any money earned, yet a century would pass before equal pay was written into UK law. ▪

Nothing but the power of the purse—in default of the stick—can permanently and thoroughly secure authority.
Frances Power Cobbe
Women's suffrage campaigner

Harriet Taylor Mill

Born in London in 1807, Taylor Mill came from a comfortable and traditional background. For all her radical views, she was upset by the scandal created when she separated from her husband John Taylor to be with John Stuart Mill, who treated her respectfully, as an intellectual equal. Social ostracism did not deter her from the relationship, and she married Mill when Taylor died.

Harriet published little under her own name; her newspaper articles, several about domestic violence, were published anonymously. Mill stated that much of what was published under his name should be considered her work as much as his. A significant influence on Mill's treatise *The Subjection of Women* (1869), she also contributed to *Principles of Political Economy* (1848) and *On Liberty* (1859), which was dedicated to her. She died in 1858.

Key works

1848 "On the Probable Future of the Laboring Classes"
1851 "The Enfranchisement of Women"

MARRIAGE MAKES A MIGHTY LEGAL DIFFERENCE TO WOMEN

RIGHTS FOR MARRIED WOMEN

I n England during the 1800s, as in the US, a married woman was the property of her husband, according to common law. Known as "coverture," this subordinate status had been the case since the Norman invasion of Britain in the 11th century. From the 1850s, two women, Caroline Norton and Barbara Leigh Smith Bodichon campaigned to overturn the law.

Legal status

Under the legal doctrine of coverture, a husband could "discipline" his wife physically and lock her up to ensure she complied with his domestic

See also: Emancipation from domesticity 34–35 ▪ Marriage and work 70–71 ▪ The problem with no name 118–123 ▪ Family structures 138–139 ▪ Protection from domestic violence 162–163

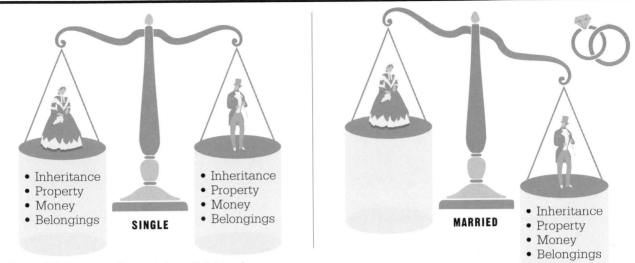

The Law of Coverture dictated that all rights of a woman pass to her husband on marriage, as well as her property, money, belongings, and any inheritance she was entitled to.

and sexual needs. Men were the sole guardians of the couple's children and could punish them, take them from their mother, and send them away to be looked after by someone else. They also had rights to their wives' property. On marriage, the couple became one person in law, and the wife lost the rights she had as a single woman. Her husband became responsible for her acts, and she lived under his protection or cover.

The richest families ensured that their female members were able to retain their capital through equity law. Prenuptial settlements ensured the woman's capital was held in trust for the duration of the marriage and that all interest belonged to the wife. However, this arrangement was costly and so only open to the very well off.

Divorce required a private act of parliament involving three separate lawsuits and was therefore unusual. Only four women instituted divorce proceedings against their husbands

between 1765 and 1857, and for women, only gross cruelty, incest, or bigamy were grounds for divorce. Legal separation was possible but costly. Even if a couple separated, any money a wife then earned belonged to her husband, although in theory he was obliged to carry on supporting her financially. A husband could also sue men they suspected of having sexual relations with his wife for having "criminal conversation" with her.

Marital cruelty

The first challenges to the law of coverture came from Caroline Norton, a woman from an upper middle-class family, with many political, artistic, and social contacts, who earned money as a writer and magazine editor. In

1835, her husband George Norton beat her so badly that she suffered a miscarriage and fled to her mother's home. She returned to find George had ended their marriage, barred her from the house, and taken her three sons away, the youngest of whom »

Caroline Norton was a social reformer and writer, who campaigned intensively during the mid-19th century for the protection of women after suffering at the hands of her violent husband.

Barbara Leigh Smith Bodichon

The illegitimate daughter of milliner Anne Longden and radical MP Benjamin Leigh Smith, Barbara Leigh Smith was born in Sussex, UK, in 1827. When her mother died, Barbara lived with her father's family. Unusually, the girls were educated to the same standard as the boys. An advocate for girls' education all her life, at 21 she used her inheritance to create a school for girls and later founded Girton—the first women's college at Cambridge.

Leigh Smith married Dr. Eugene Bodichon in 1857. Their marriage was unconventional: they lived together in Algiers, Algeria, for half the year, where he pursued his interest in anthropology, while she spent the other six months alone in London, working as an artist. Leigh Smith died in Sussex in 1891.

Key works

1854 "A Brief Summary in Plain Language of the most Important Laws concerning Women"
1857 *Women and Work*

was aged only two. George sued the prime minister Lord Melbourne for "criminal conversation" with his wife, and although the court found Melbourne innocent, Caroline's reputation was ruined. George sent the children to live with relatives, with very limited contact with their mother. Six years later, the youngest son died in an accident, which Caroline put down to neglect.

Meanwhile, Caroline remained financially tied to her husband. He took all her money, both earned and inherited, and the allowance he was obliged to pay her often went unpaid. In social circles, her situation was widely considered a huge injustice.

Protection of women

In 1837, Caroline began a campaign to change the law around custody of children, so that nonadulterous mothers would have custody of children under seven and access to older children. She wrote several polemical pamphlets, which she circulated privately, highlighting the fact that a mother could not sue for custody because she had no legal existence. The MP Thomas Talfourd agreed to introduce a bill in parliament, but the House of Lords rejected it by two votes. Caroline Norton responded with her pamphlet "A Plain Letter to the Lord Chancellor on the Law of Custody of Infants" (1839), which she sent to every MP, asking for their help and protection. This led to the Custody of Infants Act later that year, but it was too late for Norton, whose husband had moved their children to Scotland by then, where the act did not apply.

In 1854, Norton wrote "English Laws for Women" to advocate for reform. A further pamphlet a year later, "A Letter to the Queen on Lord Chancellor Cranworth's Marriage and Divorce Bill," detailed the injustices she had experienced at the hands of her husband and the legal system. The pamphlet

The Victoria Press in London, England, was set up by Emily Faithfull in 1860 to promote the employment of women. It printed *The English Women's Journal*, Britain's first feminist publication.

A woman takes the stand in a divorce court in the 1870s. Held only in the High Court, divorce proceedings were extremely costly and therefore reserved for the rich.

compared the situation of ordinary women with that of Queen Victoria, who was respected by all. Norton argued that Cranworth's 1854 Divorce Bill did not take women's rights in divorce seriously enough.

In all her writings, Norton asked for sympathy and protection rather than any equality with men, which she called "absurd." She stressed the prevailing view of the time: that men have a "sacred duty" to protect women.

Ladies of Langham Place

"English Laws for Women" inspired women's rights activist Barbara Leigh Smith Bodichon to advocate the education of girls. In 1854, she wrote "A Brief Summary in Plain Language of the most Important Laws concerning women." Unlike Norton's work, this pamphlet was not a polemic but a description of how various laws affected women. It laid out all the rights that women did not have.

During the late 1850s, Leigh Smith helped to found the Ladies of Langham Place, the first feminist

> **"**
> An English wife has no legal right even to her clothes.
> **Caroline Norton**
> **"**

activist group in the UK. Its middle-class and well-educated members set up petitions to reform the laws for married women. In 1856, petitions with more than 26,000 signatures were delivered to the House of Commons; signatories included the writers Elizabeth Gaskell and Elizabeth Barrett Browning. Partly as a result of Norton and Leigh Smith's lobbying, the Matrimonial Causes Act was passed in 1857. This led to the establishment of Britain's first divorce court, the first step in the dismantling of "coverture." However, married women were still unable to own their own property.

Leigh Smith's 1857 book *Women and Work* argues that married women's economic dependence on their husbands was degrading, and that they should be free to earn their own money. Along with her friend Bessie Rayner Parkes, Leigh Smith founded and published *The*

English Woman's Journal. Between 1858 and 1864, it advocated the improvement of women's education both to make them better wives, mothers, and governesses, and also to enable them to take up independent employment.

In 1859, the Ladies moved to 19 Langham Place, the London premises of *The English Woman's Journal.* The building had a dining club, library, and coffee shop. From 1866, the Ladies of Langham Place began to fight for female suffrage. Their campaigns led to the Married Women's Property Act in 1870, which gave women the right to keep their own earnings, personal property, income from some rents and investments, and bequests below £200. Although this gave married women some security, they still had fewer rights than single women, a situation that did not change until an extension of the act in 1882. ■

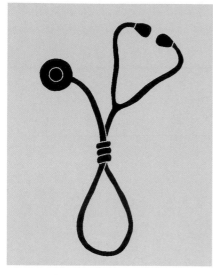

I FELT MORE DETERMINED THAN EVER TO BECOME A PHYSICIAN

BETTER MEDICAL TREATMENT FOR WOMEN

IN CONTEXT

PRIMARY QUOTE
Elizabeth Blackwell, 1895

KEY FIGURES
**Elizabeth Blackwell,
Sophia Jex-Blake,
Elizabeth Garrett Anderson**

BEFORE
1540 In Britain, the Charter
of the Company of Barber
Surgeons, forerunner of the
Royal College of Surgeons,
explicitly forbids women from
becoming surgeons.

1858 The Medical Act, UK,
bans women from becoming
medical students.

AFTER
1876 A new Medical Act
enables British medical
authorities to grant licenses
to both women and men.

1892 The British Medical
Association accepts women
doctors as members.

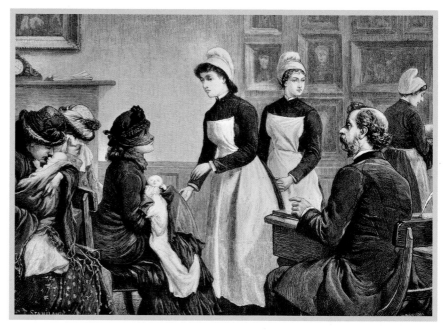

During the 19th century, medicine was a man's world despite women's long association with healing as herbalists, midwives, and nurses. Women were cared for by male doctors, who pronounced on all aspects of women's health, and the idea of having women doctors was considered preposterous. First-wave feminists demanded access to medical training and the right to practice medicine,

A nurse in a foundling hospital in the 19th century takes a baby from a mother who cannot look after her child. Women could take up nursing careers but men, as doctors, were in charge.

along with wider demands for university education and other professional work.

The fight to open the medical profession and training to women was long and hard. One woman who argued that women would be

See also: Birth control 98–103 ▪ Woman-centered healthcare 148–153 ▪ Achieving the right to legal abortion 156–159 ▪ Global access to education for girls 310–311

best treated by female doctors was Elizabeth Blackwell. Her example helped to open up the medical profession to women.

The fight to qualify

Reputedly influenced by a dying friend telling her that she was too embarrassed to consult male doctors, Blackwell became convinced that women would receive better health care from women. Initially repelled by the idea of studying the human body, yet determined to become a doctor, she approached various medical schools in Philadelphia, without success. The widespread view, as expressed in the British medical journal *The Lancet* in 1870, was that women were sexually, mentally, and constitutionally unfit for the onerous responsibilities of being a doctor. It was also feared that women doctors would undermine the high status and expertise of male physicians.

Eventually Blackwell gained a place to study medicine at Geneva Medical College in New York, and graduated in 1849, the first woman to earn a medical degree in the United States. As a doctor, she encountered opposition from male colleagues but also from women patients, who associated female doctors with back street (and often female) abortionists.

Traveling in Europe, Blackwell continued to study medicine and gain experience, but as a woman she was often prevented from visiting hospital wards. She went back to New York in 1857, and with her sister Emily and Dr. Marie Zakrzewska, opened the New York Infirmary for Women and Children in the slums. Despite much opposition, Blackwell succeeded in establishing the principle that women understood more about women's health than men did, and added a women's medical school to her New York hospital in 1868.

Training takes off

Blackwell had no doubt that society would eventually recognize the need for women physicians. Like other female medical pioneers, she was adamant that training should be equal for men and women, with no special concessions for women. Blackwell inspired two women in particular. Sophia Jex-Blake spearheaded a campaign that finally forced Edinburgh University to admit female medical students in 1870. Elizabeth Garrett Anderson sat in on lectures intended for male doctors, eventually passed her medical examinations through the Society of Apothecaries, and in 1872 set up the New Hospital for Women in London; the UK's first women's hospital, it was later renamed the Elizabeth Garrett Anderson Hospital. In 1874, with Jex-Blake and Garrett Anderson, Blackwell founded the London School of Medicine for Women. ▪

If society will not admit of woman's free development, then it must be remodeled.
Elizabeth Blackwell

Elizabeth Blackwell

Born in the city of Bristol, UK, in 1821, Elizabeth Blackwell immigrated with her family to the US in 1832. Following her father's death in 1838, she took up teaching to help support the family, and went on to qualify as a physician in 1849. While working in hospitals in Europe, she lost her sight in one eye following an infection. In 1856, while establishing her New York infirmary, she adopted an Irish orphan, Kitty Barry, who stayed with her all her life.

Returning to the UK in 1869, Blackwell continued to practice medicine but spent much of the next four decades campaigning for wide-ranging reforms in medicine, hygiene, sanitation, family planning, and women's suffrage. She retired to the seaside town of Hastings, and died there in 1910, after suffering a stroke.

Key works

1856 *An Appeal in Behalf of the Medical Education of Women*
1860 *Medicine as a Profession for Women*
1895 *Pioneer Work in Opening the Medical Profession to Women*

PEOPLE CONDONE IN MAN WHAT IS FIERCELY CONDEMNED IN WOMAN
SEXUAL DOUBLE STANDARDS

IN CONTEXT

PRIMARY QUOTE
Josephine Butler, 1879

KEY FIGURE
Josephine Butler

BEFORE
1738–1739 Swedish writer
Margareta Momma explores
the unequal status of women
in marriage in several essays.

1792 British feminist Mary
Wollstonecraft compares
marriage to legal prostitution
in *A Vindication of the Rights
of Woman.*

AFTER
1886 The UK's Contagious
Diseases Acts, permitting the
forcible examination of
prostitutes, are repealed.

1918 In Sweden, the Lex
Veneris Act abolishes state
control over prostitution.

2003 New Zealand is the first
country to decriminalize sex
work. It also provides rights and
protections for sex workers.

From the second half of the 19th century, a number of feminists in Britain and Sweden began to challenge what they saw as an unacceptable sexual double standard: society condoned sexual activity and promiscuity in men, while women were expected to be pure and remain virgins until they married. Underpinning this sexual double standard was society's highly ambiguous view of prostitution. Prostitutes were regarded as a

"social evil" to be shunned by all respectable women, but they were also considered an inevitable and essential consequence of a man's uncontrollable sexual urges. As feminists increasingly argued, this double standard divided women into "good" wives and "bad" women, and enabled men to control and oppress all women.

Punitive laws
In the 19th century, rapid population growth in Europe led to a dramatic increase in sexually transmitted diseases, particularly syphilis. A moral panic ensued, with the authorities blaming prostitutes for spreading venereal disease, especially in large urban areas such as London, where an 1835 report estimated some 80,000 women were working as prostitutes.

Punitive laws were introduced, ostensibly to prevent the spread of disease. In Sweden, by 1859 all prostitutes had to register at a

A French prostitute strikes a pose in a photograph taken at the turn of the 20th century. By the time of World War I, it was estimated that Paris alone had 5,000 licensed and 70,000 unlicensed prostitutes.

See also: Rights for married women 72–75 ▪ Sexual pleasure 126–127 ▪ Antipornography feminism 196–199 ▪ Sex positivity 234–237 ▪ Raunch culture 282–283 ▪ Bringing feminism online 294–297 ▪ Supporting sex workers 298

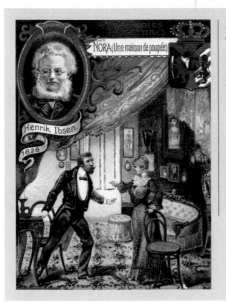

A Doll's House

In 1879, Norwegian playwright Henrick Ibsen's play *A Doll's House* premiered at the Royal Theater in Copenhagen. Set in a Norwegian town of the period, the play explores, through the experiences of the main character, Nora, the sexual double standard underpinning an apparently happy middle-class marriage. Unable to reconcile the infantilizing ideals of femininity and what it means to

Nora tells her shocked husband, Helmer, why she wants to leave him, from a series of French prints (c. 1900) on famous tragedies.

be fully adult, Nora finally refuses to play the part of a subordinate and obedient wife—her husband's "doll." In an explosive ending, she leaves her husband and children, slamming the door behind her.

This was a dramatic reflection of Ibsen's own belief that a woman was unable to be herself in a society where men set the rules and enforce those rules. Regarded as scandalous at the time because of its realistic depiction of the unequal relationship between husband and wife, the play remains a classic portrayal of women's oppression within marriage.

special bureau and undergo weekly medical examinations. In Britain, laws known as the Contagious Diseases Acts, passed between 1864 and 1867, stated that any woman suspected of being a "common" prostitute could be arrested and forcibly examined. If she refused, she could be sent to jail. If infected, she could be confined in a lock-up hospital for up to three months.

Rising to the challenge
In 1869, British feminist and social reformer Josephine Butler founded the Ladies' National Association (LNA) to campaign for the repeal of the CD Acts. Her argument was simple: the laws were unjust and exposed the sexual double standard. They punished the victims (women) of male exploitation, while leaving the perpetrators (men) untouched. Butler also drew attention to the class bias within the Acts, which protected upper- and middle-class

men, while targeting working-class women, and claimed that the CD Acts effectively created prostitutes as a "slave class" to please men.

Influenced by the LNA, the Svenska Federationen (Swedish Federation) was established in 1879 in Stockholm. Through public meetings and its newspaper *Sedlighetsvännen* (*Friend of Virtue*), it campaigned against the regulation of sex work, arguing that this stigmatized women.

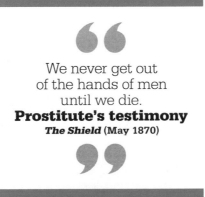

> We never get out of the hands of men until we die.
> **Prostitute's testimony**
> *The Shield* (May 1870)

The cultural debate over sexual morality spread through the rest of Scandinavia during the 1880s. It was led by writers such as Norway's Henrick Ibsen and Sweden's August Strindberg, who, in 1884, was charged with blasphemy for his portrayal of women as equal to men in his collection of short stories entitled *Getting Married*.

A safer future
It took courage for the LNA and the Swedish Federation to challenge the sexual double standard and the exploitation of prostitutes at a time when it was taboo for "respectable" women to discuss such matters. The LNA campaign also made important links between prostitution and economic conditions. These resurfaced during the 1970s, when prostitutes in Britain, France, and the US began to organize, demanding the right to be regarded as professional "sex workers." ▪

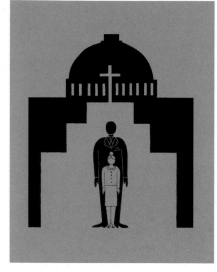

CHURCH AND STATE ASSUMED DIVINE RIGHT OF MAN OVER WOMAN
INSTITUTIONS AS OPPRESSORS

IN CONTEXT

PRIMARY QUOTE
Matilda Joslyn Gage, 1893

KEY FIGURE
Matilda Joslyn Gage

BEFORE
1777 New laws in every US state deny women the vote.

1871 Matilda Joslyn Gage and some 150 other women attempt to vote, but fail. They cite the 15th Amendment, which declares that neither the government nor state can deny US citizens the right to vote on the basis of "race, color, or previous condition of servitude."

AFTER
1920 The 19th Amendment gives American women the right to vote; American Indian suffrage follows in 1924.

1963 The Equal Pay Act promises equal pay to all workers, regardless of gender, race, or color.

I n 1852, aged 26, Matilda Joslyn Gage delivered her first public address, at the third National Woman's Rights Convention in Syracuse, New York. A highly educated suffragist, abolitionist, American Indian rights activist, free thinker, and writer, she spoke of the degradation felt by intelligent women subjected to the "tyrant rule" of men, and declared that the US government treated women with contempt.

Confronting the cause

Gage blamed both the state and the Church for women's subjugation, and in 1893 she set out her theories in *Woman, Church, and State*. She details Christianity's record of supporting female subjugation, controlling marriage as a male-dominated institution, persecuting women accused of witchcraft, and preaching women's inferiority from the pulpit. The Church, she notes, declared woman to have been made from man and under his command. Considering Eve, the first woman, to be the originator of

sin, the Church also held "as its chief tenet, a belief in the inherent wickedness of woman." Such convictions had reinforced the patriarchal values that deprived women of legal rights and exposed them to physical and sexual abuse.

A lifelong campaigner for equal rights in every aspect of life, Gage died in 1898; the inscription on her tombstone reads: "There is a word sweeter than Mother, Home or Heaven; that word is Liberty." ∎

> [Women] are … taught before marriage, to expect a support from their fathers, and after, from their husbands.
> **National Woman's Rights Convention**

See also: Early Arab feminism 104–105 ▪ The roots of oppression 114–117 ▪ Feminist theology 124–125 ▪ Patriarchy as social control 144–145

ALL WOMEN LANGUISHING IN FAMILY CHAINS

SOCIALIZATION OF CHILDCARE

IN CONTEXT

PRIMARY QUOTE
Alexandra Kollontai, 1909

KEY FIGURE
Alexandra Kollontai

BEFORE
1877 In Switzerland, working mothers are given the right to eight weeks' unpaid, job-protected maternity leave.

1883 Germany becomes the first country to give women paid maternity leave, for three weeks, providing they have paid national insurance.

AFTER
1917 The Bolshevik revolution overthrows Russia's Czarist rule and leads to the creation of the Soviet Union in 1922.

1936 The Soviet Union under Joseph Stalin, who was concerned by the falling birth rate, tightens laws on divorce and bans abortion unless the life of the woman is in danger.

Alexandra Kollontai was an early Russian advocate of a restructured, fairer society, in which Russia's women—especially working mothers—were supported by the state and had political and legal rights equal to those of men. Born in St. Petersburg in 1872, the daughter of a cavalry officer, she was well read, fluent in several languages, and had absorbed socialist and Marxist ideas in Europe after leaving a marriage in which she felt trapped.

Empowering women
A member of the Russian Social Democratic Labour Party from 1899, Kollontai urged women workers to join their male counterparts in the fight for political and economic emancipation. In 1909, she wrote *The Social Basis of the Woman Question*, proposing measures such as state-financed support for expectant and nursing mothers, and the socialization of domestic labor and childcare. Kollontai argues that by making childcare the responsibility of society rather

Kollontai meets homeless families in her capacity as People's Commissar for Social Welfare. She was the first and most prominent woman to hold office in the Bolshevik government of 1917–1918.

than the individual, women would be able to contribute politically and economically to the state.

In 1919, Kollontai established the Zhenotdel, the world's first government department devoted to women. New legislation led to paid maternity leave, maternity clinics, crèches, and homes for single mothers. By 1921, abortion was free at many hospitals, and a literacy program was underway. ∎

See also: Marxist feminism 52–55 ▪ The problem with no name 118–123 ▪ Family structures 138–139 ▪ Wages for housework 147

WOMAN WAS THE SUN. NOW SHE IS A SICKLY MOON
FEMINISM IN JAPAN

IN CONTEXT

PRIMARY QUOTE
Raicho Hiratsuka, 1911

KEY FIGURES
Raicho Hiratsuka,
Fusae Ichikawa

BEFORE
1729 Neo-Confucian philosopher Kaibara Ekiken writes *Onna daigaku* (*Greater Learning for Women*), in which he emphasizes the importance of women's moral training.

1887 Author, educator, and advocate of reform, Fukuzawa Yukichi writes *Donjo kosairon* (*The New Greater Learning for Women*), which sets forth new ideas on gender roles.

AFTER
1978 The Women's Studies Society of Japan is founded in Kyoto.

1985 Japan's government passes the Equal Employment Opportunities Bill.

The feminist movement in Japan emerged during the Meiji Restoration (1868–1912), which ended the military shogunate and brought Japan's feudal society into the modern age. Previously, women had not had any legal status, could not own property, and were inferior to men in all respects. With the restoration of imperial rule, Japan strove to catch up with the West in terms of technology, military, and law, to abolish feudal privileges, and to redress some of the inequality of the sexes, looking toward the ideas of the Enlightenment in Europe.

Lady writers

An interest in European literature provided the impetus for the Japanese feminist movement. In 1907, a group of women founded a literary society called Keishu Bungakukai (Lady Writers' Society), which organized meetings with well-known writers and professors of European literature. In 1911, Raicho Hiratsuka, a member of the society, founded a new women's group called Seitosha (Bluestockings), inspired by the 18th-century Blue Stockings, a discussion group founded by Elizabeth Montagu in London. Hiratsuka was herself a writer and her autobiography, *In the Beginning, Woman Was the Sun*, describes her rebellion against the social codes of the time, in which female compliance was paramount.

Among its activities, Seitosha published a magazine called *Seito* (Bluestocking) to promote creative writing among Japanese women and cultivate the image of the "new

---

Women were once the Sun. They were their **authentic** selves, with a strong sense of **self-worth** and **liberation** ...

↓

... but society forced them to **hide their potential**, depend on men, and **reflect men's brilliance**.

↓

Now women are a wan and sickly moon.

See also: Early British feminism 20–21 ▪ Early Scandinavian feminism 22–23 ▪ Collective action in the 18th century 24–27 ▪ Enlightenment feminism 28–33

woman". The Seitosha struggled against traditional, feudalistic attitudes and became subject to government censorship, accused of spreading "revolutionary ideas." In 1916, it was banned.

The NWA

Seitosha paved the way for a new organization, the Shin Fujin Kyokai (New Women's Association, or NWA), which campaigned for women's political rights from 1920. The NWA raised the issue of emancipation among Japanese intellectuals, both men and women, and promoted the ideal of the "new

Suffragettes in Tokyo in 1920 spread the word about the "new woman," who is eager to destroy traditions and laws established solely for the convenience of man.

woman" who tried to break Japan's feudal bonds and patriarchy. Under its leader Fusae Ichikawa, the NWA framed its claims in terms of women's traditional roles in the family, stressing that women would become better wives and mothers if they had a stake in determining the future of the country.

Japan's women gained full suffrage in 1945, soon after the end of World War II. It was believed that their sufferings in the war had earned them the right to vote. Yet women's needs were primarily seen in terms of better access to health and work, the elimination of poverty, and the protection of motherhood. Many women as well as men still saw the patriarchal system as the basis of law and order. The clash between traditional and modern values is still to be resolved. ▪

Fusae Ichikawa

Suffragist, feminist, and politician, Fusae Ichikawa was one of the most influential women in 20th-century Japan. Born in 1893, she worked as a journalist at the Nagoya Shimbun newspaper company and cofounded the Shin Fujin Kyokai (New Woman's Association) in 1920.

In 1921, she traveled to the US and met suffrage leader Alice Paul. Upon her return to Japan in 1924, she formed the Fujin Sanseiken Kakutokukisei Domeikai (Women's Suffrage League). After Japanese women gained the vote in 1945, Ichikawa formed the Shin Nihon Fujin Domei (New Japan Women's Union), which among other things campaigned to end the chronic food shortages of the postwar period. The government of the Allied Occupation banned her from public service but she returned to politics in 1953 and worked until the 1970s. She died in Tokyo in 1981.

Key works

1969 *Sengo fujikai no doko* (*Trends of Women's Circles in the Postwar Period*)
1972 *Watakushi no fujin undo* (*My Women's Movement*)

TAKE COURAGE, JOIN HANDS, STAND BESIDE US

POLITICAL EQUALITY IN BRITAIN

IN CONTEXT

PRIMARY QUOTE
Christabel Pankhurst, 1908

KEY FIGURES
**Millicent Fawcett,
Emmeline Pankhurst,
Sylvia Pankhurst,
Christabel Pankhurst,
Mary Leigh, Emily Davison**

BEFORE
1832 The Great Reform Act excludes women from voting in parliamentary elections.

1851 The Sheffield Female Political Association is formed, the first women's suffrage group in the UK.

AFTER
1918 Women of property and over the age of 30 are granted the vote. At the same time, male suffrage is extended to all males over 21.

1928 British women gain the same voting rights as men.

Of all the developments that advanced the cause of feminism in the 20th century, the suffragette movement can be singled out for its effective use of political violence in helping to secure voting rights for women in Great Britain and Ireland. Led by Emmeline Pankhurst and her daughters, the suffragettes gripped the public's attention because the women involved—mostly middle and upper class—were prepared to risk arrest, injury, and even death for their cause.

The suffragettes stood for two principles. One was that women should have the right to vote in public elections on the same terms as men—a proposal advocated by the women's suffrage movement that had emerged in the mid-19th century. The second was that any action justified achieving this end, a precept embodied in the mantra of "deeds not words." It was the adoption of militant protest tactics that set the suffragettes apart from the suffragists, who used strictly peaceful means to achieve their goals.

Campaigning for the right of women to vote was not a new phenomenon—women's suffrage had been on the agenda in several nations since the early to mid-19th century, and in Sweden from the 18th century. In the US, the topic of women's suffrage emerged around the same time as calls for the abolition of slavery began to gather strength in the 1840s. In the UK, the first women's suffrage petition had been presented to parliament by women's rights activist Mary Smith in 1832. There was some progress toward the goal of extending the vote to women but it was slow.

Gaining momentum

In 1867, John Stuart Mill, MP for the City of Westminster, proposed a bill to the British parliament that would have given women the same political rights as men. Soundly defeated, the failed bill was the catalyst for the formation of suffrage societies around the country, 17 of which amalgamated in 1897 as the National Union of Women's Suffrage Societies (NUWSS). By pooling resources and acting with a united front, the suffragists hoped to gain momentum for what they called "The Cause"—political equality for women, which was most clearly symbolized in the vote.

Within a few years, Millicent Fawcett, the wife and daughter of prominent political radicals, had taken on the role of leader and spokesperson. The suffragists had a middle-class focus, and this was reflected in their aims—to secure the vote for women who owned

Suffragettes march in support of fellow activists released from Holloway prison in August 1908. The women had been jailed for throwing stones at the prime minister's windows.

See also: The birth of the suffrage movement 56–63 ▪ The global suffrage movement 94–97

Suffragists v. Suffragettes

Suffragists, led by **Millicent Fawcett** …

Suffragettes, led by **Emmeline Pankhurst** …

… form the **National Union of Women's Suffrage Societies (NUWSS)**.

… form the **Women's Social and Political Union (WSPU)**.

Almost all members are **middle or upper class**.

Some members seek to appeal to the **working-class**.

They advocate a **nonconfrontational approach** through peaceful petitioning and public meetings.

They emphasize **"deeds not words"** and advocate **militant actions** to gain publicity.

> The difference between a Suffragist and a Suffragette … the Suffragist just wants the vote, while the Suffragette means to get it.
> **The Suffragette**
> (1914)

property. Their activities were legal and constitutional, and included writing letters to MPs and holding rallies and marches.

A different strategy
Like Fawcett, fellow suffragist Emmeline Pankhurst was middle class, but where Fawcett could be considered liberal-conservative,

Pankhurst was socialist, and her strategy for achieving political equality for women was very different. Where Fawcett's suffragists pursued peaceful means, Pankhurst advocated militant action. Despite being an active member of the NUWSS, in 1903 Pankhurst was compelled to form her own breakaway group, the

Women's Social and Political Union (WSPU), when her local branch of the Independent Labour Party repeatedly refused to put the vote for women on its agenda. This breakaway was significant, since the party had worked alongside the NUWSS in investigating social inequality and proposing reforms to the British parliament.

Emmeline Pankhurst's daughters Sylvia, Christabel, and Adela were also founding members of the WSPU. Eventually the family members would fall out over Sylvia's increasing conviction that working-class women should be included in the union's agenda, but for the first years of the WSPU the family was united in its efforts. Mrs. Pankhurst, as Emmeline became known in the media, had been active in the cause of women's suffrage since 1880 and over the course of more than 20 years had come to the conclusion that votes for women would never be won through conventional political channels. A radical approach was needed that »

> I had to get a close-hand view of the misery and unhappiness of a man-made world, before I could … successfully revolt against it.
> **Emmeline Pankhurst**

would force the government to pay attention and take the vote for women seriously. Drawing on the militant tactics of Russian revolutionaries, Pankhurst and her band of followers devised a strategy of civil disobedience and terrorism aimed at compelling parliament to pass legislation that would give women electoral voting rights.

This extremism highlighted the difference between Fawcett's suffragists of the NUWSS and the Pankhurst-led suffragettes of the WSPU. In fact, the WSPU stood in direct opposition to the NUWSS, which it refused to join. The term suffragettes was adopted by the WSPU in 1906, after the name was coined in an article in the *Daily Mail* newspaper. The editor intentionally added the diminutive suffix "ettes" as an insult, implying that these women were merely an imitation of the real thing. The WSPU's clever response to the *Daily Mail*'s wit was to adopt the term as a badge of honor.

Inspiration and tactics

From a young age, Emmeline Pankhurst had heard stories about civil unrest in Russia as its citizens fought for freedom under the Czar. Her family had welcomed Russian exiles to gatherings at their home in London's Russell Square. Pankhurst almost certainly knew about the trial of Vera Zasulich, charged with attempting to assassinate Governor Trepov in St. Petersburg in 1878. Found not guilty, Zasulich had proudly declared that she was not a murderer; she was a terrorist. She was acting for the Russian anarchist group Narodnaya Volya (the People's Will), a political organization fighting for equality in Russian society. Women were active participants in the group's acts of political violence, including the assassination of the Czar.

Informed in part by these women who had risked everything in the quest for equality, Emmeline Pankhurst decided that the most effective way to gather support for the suffragette movement was through the publicity that would result from imprisonment. Arson, bombing, destruction of property, and the act of chaining themselves to public buildings were part of the suffragette's arsenal.

Breaking windows was introduced as a tactic in the summer of 1908. Suffragettes staged a march to Downing Street on June 30 and threw stones through the windows of the prime minister's residence. Among the 27 women arrested at the scene and incarcerated at Holloway Prison was former schoolteacher Mary Leigh, who had joined the WSPU in 1906. In October that year, Leigh was arrested again and sentenced to three months in prison for grabbing the bridle of a police horse during a demonstration outside the House of Commons.

Emmeline Pankhurst

Born in Manchester, England, in 1858, Emmeline Gouldern was raised in a family with radical views. In 1879, she married Richard Pankhurst, a lawyer and suffrage supporter who had written the UK's Married Women's Property Acts of 1870 and 1882. Among her achievements were the formation of the Women's Franchise League in 1889 and the Women's Social and Political Union (WSPU) in 1903. She was imprisoned seven times for civil disobedience yet she was fiercely patriotic and encouraged women's contribution to Britain's war effort from 1915. She later disowned her daughter Sylvia for her socialist and pacifist politics. In 1926, Emmeline joined the Conservative Party, and shortly before her death in 1928 she became its candidate for an East London constituency.

Key works

January 10, 1913 A letter to members of the WSPU outlining the case for militancy.
November 13, 1913 "Freedom or death" speech, delivered in Hartford, Connecticut.

JULY 6, 1910.]   PUNCH, OR THE LONDON CHARIVARI.   9

THE SUFFRAGETTE THAT KNEW JIU-JITSU.
THE ARREST.

A *Punch* cartoon from 1910 depicts the intimidation of London's policemen by a suffragette who has been taught jujitsu. Edith Garrud, a jujitsu expert, ran classes for fellow suffragettes and penned articles with self-defense tips in the WSPU newspaper.

Emmeline Pankhurst's daughter Christabel emerged as the suffragettes' creative strategist, orchestrating many of the events that garnered media attention. She organized a Women's Parliament in 1908, for example, and a massive rally of up to 500,000 women in London's Hyde Park. Her rationale was inspired in part by a comment made by Liberal MP Herbert Asquith, widely tipped to be the next prime minister, that if he could be convinced that women really wanted the vote, he would withdraw opposition to the move.

In 1910, when parliament was on the verge of granting women the vote in the form of the Conciliation Bill, Asquith, now prime minister, intervened to stop the bill before its second reading. Of the 300 or so women who subsequently marched on parliament to protest on November 18, 1910—what became known as Black Friday—119 were arrested, two women died, and many complained of being knocked down or assaulted by policemen or male hecklers.

From the start, the WSPU's acts of civil disobedience came with reports of manhandling, violence, and sexual indecency perpetrated by police and male members of the public. Black Friday now proved a turning point for the women of the WSPU, and they geared up to protect themselves. Some began wearing cardboard vests under their clothing to protect their ribs, but Emmeline Pankhurst proposed that the most effective means of self-defense was jujitsu, the martial art that was mandatory in police training. The popular media relished the vision of militant middle-class women practicing martial arts, and it was not long before the term "suffrajitsu" entered into common use. In a speech in 1913, Sylvia Pankhurst urged all suffragettes to learn self-defense.

Clashes with police intensified as the suffragettes ramped up their activities with midnight arson and bombing attacks on MPs' houses, churches, post offices, and railway stations. As a result, the women increasingly found themselves

behind bars. Music hall star Kitty Marion, a strident WSPU activist since joining in 1908, was arrested on several occasions for breaking windows and for arson attacks. She set fire to the houses of MPs who opposed women having the vote, including the home being built for David Lloyd George, then the Chancellor of the Exchequer.

Punishment
Pankhurst and her daughters Christabel and Sylvia were among the most arrested suffragettes. The women went on hunger strikes while in prison to highlight their protest, which prompted a controversial policy of force-feeding. The brutal practice of forcibly thrusting feeding tubes down the women's throats commonly resulted in internal injuries to the women, Emmeline included. Suffragettes were outraged by the treatment of their leader, »

> "I nor any of the women have … any recognized methods of getting redress … except the methods of revolution and violence.
> **Emmeline Pankhurst**

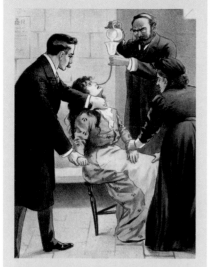

Force-feeding

One of the most controversial aspects of the government's handling of imprisoned suffragettes was the policy of force feeding, which was introduced to prevent the suffragettes from dying on hunger strike and becoming martyrs. Press reports stoked public disquiet over the practice. One account detailed the torment suffered by Kitty Marion, who was force fed more than 230 times.

Suffragette Mary Leigh's account of being force fed with a nasal tube that was "two yards long, with a funnel at the end and a glass junction in the middle to see if the liquid is passing" was published while she was still in prison. The resulting public uproar led to her release.

In response to the persistent hunger striking, parliament introduced the so-called Cat and Mouse Act in 1913. This legislation allowed the release of hunger strikers until they were well enough to be rearrested and returned to prison.

in particular, prompting one member, Mary Richardson, to slash *The Rokeby Venus*, a much-loved painting by Velázquez, on display at the National Gallery. She declared: "I have tried to destroy the picture of the most beautiful woman in mythological history as a protest against the Government for destroying Mrs. Pankhurst, who is the most beautiful character in modern history."

The members of the WSPU were determined to protect Emmeline Pankhurst from further arrests and imprisonment, and so Edith Garrud selected and trained a core group of around 30 women who became known as The Bodyguard. They accompanied Pankhurst to key appearances to prevent her being grabbed by police. Armed with clubs hidden in their dresses, the members of The Bodyguard were prepared to use any means to protect their leader, but they also employed decoys and other tricks to help her evade capture by the police.

One suffragette who captured the nation's attention in the most horrific way was Emily Davison. On June 13, 1913, she threw herself under the king's horse at the Epsom

> From the moment that women had consented to prison, hunger-strikes, and forcible feeding as the price of the vote, the vote really was theirs.
> **Christabel Pankhurst**

Emmeline Pankhurst is arrested during a demonstration that turned violent outside Buckingham Palace on May 21, 1914. Pankhurst had organized a march to petition George V to support female suffrage.

Derby, a horse race attended by the king himself. Davison's death, which some historians think may have been simply an attempt to seize the horse's bridle, and therefore accidental, was caught on newsreel cameras.

Male support

Despite their reputation for radicalism and their portrayal in the media as violent, the WSPU garnered support among some high profile male figures who were prepared to risk their reputations in order to further the goals of the WSPU. The Labour politicians Keir Hardie and George Lansbury spoke in the House of Commons to bolster the suffrage movement and went to WSPU rallies. The retailer Henry Gordon Selfridge flew the flag of the WSPU above his department store on Oxford Street in London, as a sign of solidarity.

Disarmed by war

What really swayed both the public and politicians in favor of the vote for women was the outbreak of World War I in 1914. With Britain engulfed in the war, the WSPU was forced to reconsider its militant stance. In support of the war, Emmeline Pankhurst suspended the activities of the WSPU. According to fellow suffragette Ethel Smyth, "Mrs. Pankhurst declared that it was not a question of Votes for Women, but of having any country left to vote in."

Emmeline Pankhurst argued that since peaceful argument for women's freedom was futile, the Union was better off diverting its energies into supporting the war effort. This decision proved a turning point that would eventually help the organization achieve its long-term goal of votes for women. As part of its effort to support the war, the WSPU renamed *The Suffragette* newspaper *Britannia* and worked alongside Lloyd George, who replaced Lord Asquith as prime minster in 1916, in support of the National Register. In preparation for national service, this listed the personal details of everybody in Britain, including women, many of whom worked in munitions factories during the war. The WSPU used the war to show that women were capable of contributing equally to society and had therefore earned the right to vote. Some members supported the White Feather Campaign, in which women gave white feathers symbolizing cowardice to men dressed in civilian clothes.

Votes at last

The suffragette war effort did not go unnoticed, and helped engender the support of those previously unmoved by the cause of women's suffrage. Even before the close of the war in November 1918, women were on the road to getting the national vote.

On February 6, 1918, the Representation of the People Act granted property-owning women

over the age of 30 the right to vote in Great Britain and Ireland. Around 8.4 million women, or 40 percent of the UK's female population, were now newly entitled to vote. This was a milestone in the fight for women's suffrage, yet it excluded women between the ages of 21 and 30, and those who did not own property, essentially working-class women.

Men also benefited from the act, which extended voting rights to males who did not own a property, typically from the working class, and those aged 21 and above, thus increasing inequality between the sexes. The 1918 Act took the total

Christabel Pankhurst casts her vote in a polling booth in 1910, in one of her many publicity stunts. Like her mother, she was a motivational leader and the WSPU's key strategist, who knew how to draw the attention of the press.

number of voters in the British electorate from 8 million to 21 million. It would take another 10 years before the Conservative government extended voting rights to all British women over the age of 21. The Equal Franchise Act of 1928, which almost doubled the number of women who could vote, became law a few weeks after Emmeline Pankhurst died on June 14. ∎

WE WAR AGAINST WAR
WOMEN UNITING FOR PEACE

The outbreak of World War I in 1914 caused a rift in the suffrage movement. Some women saw war as made solely by men and advocated pacifism; others argued that if violence was justifiable in the fight for sexual equality, the same was true in other kinds of conflict, such as war between nations. Women in the latter camp temporarily abandoned the fight for suffrage in order to prioritize the protection of their nation. Even the militant British suffragette leader Emmeline Pankhurst turned her attention to recruiting women for wartime roles, a course of action opposed by her daughter Sylvia, who articulated pacifist views in her newspaper, *The Woman's Dreadnought*. There were enough women like Sylvia to form an international alliance of women who envisaged pacifism and feminism coexisting hand in hand.

Shared cause

In April 1915, some 1,100 women converged on The Hague, in the Netherlands, for the first International Congress of Women to discuss what they could do to foster peace. Among them were American peace campaigner Jane Addams, Dutch physician Aletta Jacobs, German trade union activist Lida Gustava Heymann, and Hungarian journalist Rosika Schwimmer. Only 20 of the 180 British women planning to attend were issued passports as the rest were under surveillance for their antiwar stance.

Two main policies emerged at the conference. The first was the need to impress upon governments the suffering of women and children in war—a concern that could unite people across national

Can we believe that we are fitted to dominate all other peoples? We, with those serious social failings toward our own people, especially toward women.
Sylvia Pankhurst

See also: The birth of the suffrage movement 56–63 ▪ Ecofeminism 200–201 ▪ Women against nuclear weapons 206–207 ▪ Women in war zones 278–279

As the Mothers of the Race, it is your privilege to conserve life, and love, and beauty, all of which are destroyed by war.
Vida Goldstein

borders. The women linked universal social views about the sanctity of motherhood and the innocence of children with their call for peace. The second policy was women's suffrage: if women could vote, they would be able to influence international politics.

Within a few months, the Congress members sent delegates to both warring and neutral states, including the US. Although they had limited success, their case for mediation to end the war was at least voiced. The Hague meeting also led to the founding of the International Committee of Women for Permanent Peace (ICWPP), which in the space of a year expanded to 16 national chapters across Europe, North America, and Australia, and the Women's International League for Peace and Freedom (WILPF).

These peace organizations also alerted people to the dangers of an imperial power dragging a subject nation into war. In Australia, groups such as the Women's Peace Party and the Sisterhood of International Peace, led by Vida Goldstein and Eleanor Moore, helped to foster a vision of Australia as an independent nation. ▪

American delegates arrive on the MS *Noordaam* for the International Congress of Women at The Hague in 1915. Many women who had criticized the war were forbidden to attend the meeting by their governments.

Vida Goldstein

The daughter of a suffragist, Vida Goldstein was born in Portland, Australia, in 1869. Encouraged to think for herself, she was educated and widely read. She honed her interest in politics by sitting in on parliamentary sessions in her home state of Victoria.

By 1899, Vida had become the leader of the suffrage movement in Victoria and began publishing a journal called *The Australian Women's Sphere* to promote the cause. After Australian women were granted the national vote in 1902, she ran for parliament, and in 1903 became the first elected female official in the British Empire. In 1911, she visited Britain, where women flocked to hear her speak.

After the outbreak of World War I in 1914, Goldstein became an ardent pacifist. She never fulfilled her goal of becoming prime minister, but she continued to lobby for social reforms, including provision of birth control. She died at the age of 80 in 1949.

Key work

1900–1905 *The Australian Women's Sphere*

LET US HAVE THE RIGHTS WE DESERVE

THE GLOBAL SUFFRAGE MOVEMENT

IN CONTEXT

PRIMARY QUOTE
Alice Paul, 1923

KEY FIGURES
**Kate Sheppard,
Jessie Street, Alice Paul,
Clara Campoamor**

BEFORE
1793 In France, Olympe de
Gouges, author of *The
Declaration of the Rights
of Woman and the Female
Citizen*, is sent to the guillotine.

1862–1863 Swedish women
who pay taxes gain voting
rights in local elections.

1881 Female property owners
in Scotland are permitted to
vote in local elections.

AFTER
2015 Women in Saudi Arabia
vote in municipal elections for
the first time.

I n the late 19th century
and the first decades of the
20th century, women around
the world began lobbying their
governments for enfranchisement.
Their methods for achieving
this, and the arguments they
put forward, were not identical.
Women's suffrage organizations
were often affiliated to pressure
groups that had other agendas
such as racial equality or self-
determination. In New Zealand,
which would become the first self-
governing nation in the world
to give women, including Maori
women, parliamentary voting rights
in 1893, activist Kate Sheppard and
her peers were founding members of
the Women's Christian Temperance
Union (WCTU). They argued that

See also: The birth of the suffrage movement 56–63 ▪ Feminism in Japan 82–83 ▪ Political equality in Britain 84–91 ▪ Early Arab feminism 104–105

Indian suffragists were among the 60,000 women who joined the Women's Coronation Procession, a march for suffrage held in London before King George V's coronation in 1911. Women came from across the British Empire.

women needed political power in order to control the country's liquor laws and curtail men's drunken tyranny at home. The New Zealand women presented the government with suffrage petitions in 1891, 1892, and 1893. The final petition had nearly 32,000 signatures.

Mutual encouragement

Sheppard had taken inspiration from the American WCTU and British feminists of the time; in turn, her victory in New Zealand inspired suffragists in the US and the UK. Her visits to both countries, along with newspaper reports of her achievements, breathed new life into their suffrage movements, especially in Britain. International connections such as this were key to the global suffrage movement. When Finland won the vote for

women in 1906, as part of the socialist uprising against the Russian Empire, it was the result of mass demonstrations and the threat of a general strike, inspired in part by Russian revolutionaries. As one journal of the day declared, "We [women] have to shout to the world that we are demanding the right to vote and to stand for election, and that we are not going to settle for anything less. Now is not the time for compromises."

In Estonia, Latvia, and Lithuania, women's suffrage, granted in 1918, was also embedded in the nationalist struggle against the Russian Empire. In Ireland, female suffrage was linked to Irish independence from Britain.

The British suffragettes' willingness to die for their cause attracted many admirers around the world. In Australia, Jessie Street, who became a leading campaigner in the country's suffrage movement, had first become interested in suffrage while visiting relatives in the UK. The Quaker activist Alice Paul in »

Alice Paul

The daughter of a suffragist mother and a businessman, Alice Paul was born in Moorestown, New Jersey in 1885. After graduating from what is now Columbia University with a master's degree in sociology, she traveled to the UK in 1910 to study social work. There she met fellow American Lucy Stone and joined the suffrage movement. Returning to the US, Paul formed the National Women's Party to lobby Congress for constitutional reform. Her persistence led to the passing of the 19th Amendment in 1920, granting women suffrage at state and federal levels.

Paul spent the following years campaigning for equal rights in divorce, property, and employment. Although passed by 35 states in the 1970s, her Equal Rights Amendment was never ratified. Paul died in 1977, aged 92.

Key works

1923 *Equal Rights Amendment*
1976 *Conversations with Alice Paul: Woman Suffrage and the Equal Rights Amendment*

Clara Campoamor

Born in the Masalaña district of Madrid, Spain, in 1888, Clara Campoamor was shaped by her working-class roots. After the death of her father when she was 13, she left school to help her seamstress mother support the family. Within a few years she was working as a secretary for various organizations, including the liberal political newspaper *La Tribune*, where she began to take an interest in women's rights.

Motivated by a growing political fervor, she studied law at the University of Madrid, graduating at the age of 36 to become the first female lawyer in the Spanish Supreme Court. In 1931, she became a member of the National Constituent Assembly, formed to write the country's new constitution. She ensured that universal suffrage was included, though the Fascist dictator General Franco later cancelled this.

After the rise of Fascism, Campoamor fled Spain and went to live in exile. She was banned by Franco from ever returning to Spain and she died in Switzerland in 1972.

the US, frustrated by the slow progress of Congress to make suffrage a priority, formed the National Women's Party in 1913, inspired by the militant tactics of Britain's suffragettes. On the day before Woodrow Wilson's inauguration as president in March 1913, she organized a march of around 8,000 women, marking the start of a sustained campaign against Wilson's administration for blocking changes to the Constitution that would enfranchise women. She and a team of women picketed the White House for 18 months.

Paul's strategy eventually wore down Wilson's resistance, and by 1917 he started to support Paul's aims—the same year that the state of New York gave women the vote. On June 4, 1919, the 19th Amendment granted American women the right to vote at state and federal levels. It was a major milestone on the road to women's equality.

Local first

Up until World War I, only New Zealand, Australia (excluding indigenous women), Finland, Norway, and 11 US states had full voting rights for women. Despite pressure from suffragists, Britain was slow to grant women the vote other than in local elections. In line with the "separate spheres" tradition of gender relationships, it was considered acceptable for British women to vote on local issues such as education provision but not on national matters. The

The *Women Are Persons* monument in Ottawa, Canada, depicts The Famous Five, who overturned a rule preventing women from running for the Senate. The statue of one of them, Nelly McClung, holds up news of their victory.

governments of Sweden, Belgium, Denmark, and Romania also ascribed to this distinction.

World War I

For many countries, World War I was a turning point in the suffrage movement. The suffragettes, led by Emmeline Pankhurst, actively supported the British war effort, and hundreds of thousands of British women worked in munitions factories, overturning traditional arguments that women could not vote because they did not participate in war, the ultimate tool of government. British women's loyalty was rewarded with a partial concession in 1918, when property-owning women over the age of 30—around 40 percent of the adult female population—were enfranchised. It would be another decade before all adult women in Britain became eligible to vote.

Other countries prioritized working women who paid taxes, or more educated women. Such limitations were often supported by middle-class suffragists. In Canada, women had won the vote in 1918

Women's suffrage

Even after female suffrage was introduced, it was often restricted by class, age, race, or education. For example, in Britain, suffrage was initially limited to property-owning women over 30, and in Australia, Aboriginal women could not vote until 1967.

Date female suffrage at national level is introduced

- Pre-1914
- 1914–1920
- 1921–1945
- 1946–1970
- 1971 and later
- No national suffrage

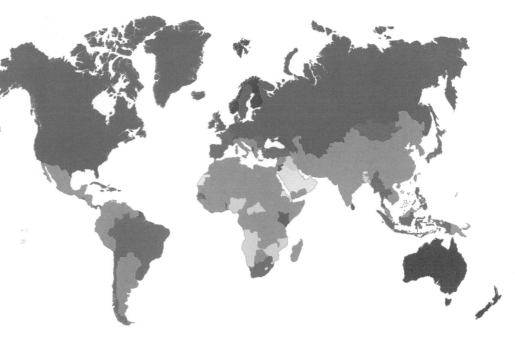

(excluding those in the province of Quebec), but their struggle was not over. Although they became eligible to run for election to the country's House of Commons in 1919, the Senate was still out of bounds, due to the wording of a law that deemed only "qualified persons" could be appointed. The Canadian government insisted that this meant men, not women. In 1929, five prominent women activists, known as "The Famous Five," successfully challenged this.

Late voters

Some countries were surprisingly slow in granting female suffrage. In France, the seat of revolution in 1789, women could not vote until 1944; in Belgium, it was 1948. Sometimes such delay was because the ruling parties feared the political alliances that enfranchised women might make.

> " This is an experiment so large and bold that it ought to be tried by some other country first.
> **Viscount Bryce**
> **British politician**

For example, communists, who wanted to limit the powers of the Church, thought women were more likely than men to support conservative Catholic values that opposed communism. At the same time, the Church in many Catholic countries was opposed to female

suffrage on the grounds that it would undermine marriage and the family, important pillars of the Church.

After World War II, few countries wishing to be seen as modern democracies could deny female suffrage, but delays in achieving democracy or independence slowed change in former colonies. Fascist dictatorships also hindered progress. Portuguese women, for example could not vote until 1975, the year after the Estado Novo dictatorship fell, and Spain did not gain full suffrage until after the death of Fascist dictator General Franco in 1976. Franco, who had reversed the progress on women's suffrage made by the lawyer and activist Clara Campoamor in 1931, had prohibited contraception, divorce, and abortion, and restricted women's access to employment and property. His death liberated Spanish women socially, economically, and politically. ∎

BIRTH CONTROL
IS THE FIRST STEP TOWARD
FREEDOM

BIRTH CONTROL

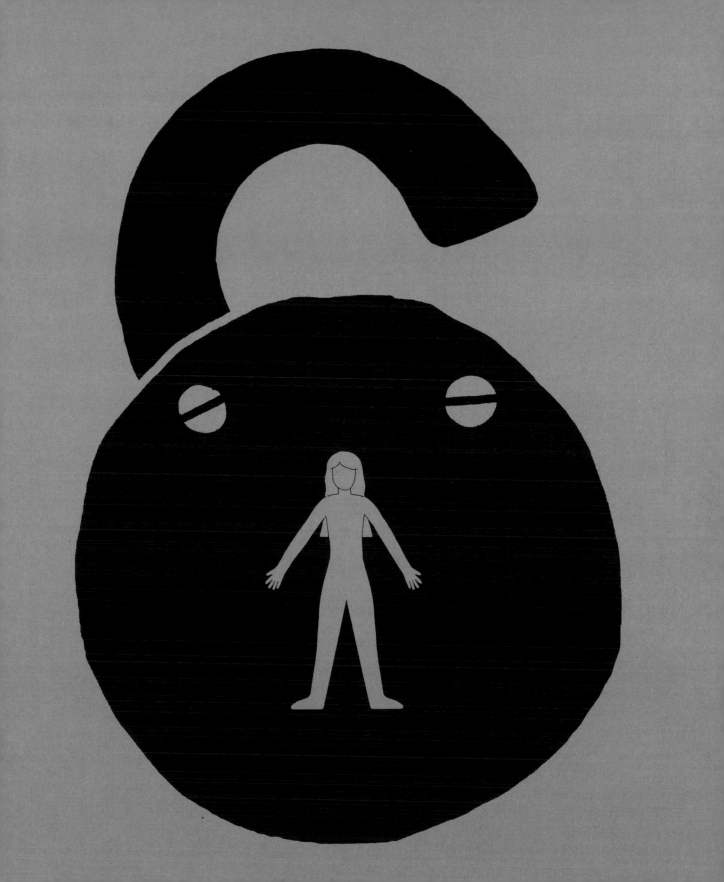

IN CONTEXT

PRIMARY QUOTE
Margaret Sanger, 1918

KEY FIGURES
**Margaret Sanger,
Marie Stopes**

BEFORE
1873 The Comstock Act in the US makes the distribution of birth control literature and the sale of contraceptives illegal as "articles of immoral use."

1877 Annie Besant and Charles Bradlaugh are put on trial in the UK for publishing *Fruits of Philosophy*, which advocates birth control.

AFTER
1965 The US Supreme Court gives married couples the right to use birth control, extending it to single people in 1972.

1970 In the UK, the Women's Liberation Movement calls for free abortion and contraception on demand.

Until the American socialist Margaret Sanger linked the emancipation of women with birth control in the first decade of the 20th century, many early American feminists, such as Charlotte Perkins Gilman and Lucy Stone, and Anglo-American Elizabeth Blackwell, were opposed to or suspicious of contraception. Far from seeing birth control as contributing to women's emancipation, they viewed it as a corrupting practice that would encourage women to be sexually active and allow men unlimited sexual freedom both in and outside marriage.

Calling for limits

Early feminists had recognized the need for women to limit the size of their families, but they believed that this should be achieved through voluntary motherhood—a wife's right to refuse a husband's sexual demands. A call for male abstinence was made by several feminists, including British activist Josephine Butler, who spearheaded a campaign against the Contagious Diseases Acts in the 1860s. These laws, which aimed to control venereal disease in the armed forces, authorized compulsory venereal

> Woman must have her freedom, the fundamental freedom of choosing whether or not she will be a mother.
> **Margaret Sanger**

checks on prostitutes. Effectively placing the blame for the spread of sexual diseases on women, they exposed the sexual hypocrisy of Victorian Britain.

One organization that actively advocated "family limitation" was the Malthusian League. Founded in 1877, it was named after the British economist Thomas Malthus, whose views on the need to control population growth were influential. Many radicals supported the League, which campaigned for contraception and family limitation as a solution to poverty and overpopulation. Conversely, some socialists opposed the League,

The history of contraception

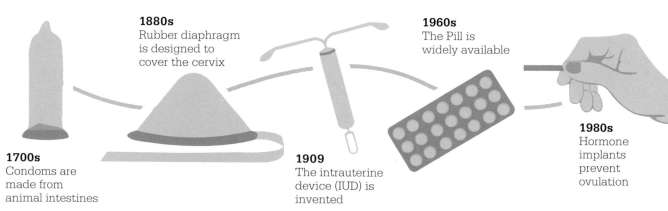

1880s
Rubber diaphragm is designed to cover the cervix

1960s
The Pill is widely available

1700s
Condoms are made from animal intestines

1909
The intrauterine device (IUD) is invented

1980s
Hormone implants prevent ovulation

See also: Sexual pleasure 126–127 ▪ The Pill 136 ▪ Woman-centered health care 148–153 ▪ The right to legal abortion 156–159

believing it was designed to limit the natural rights of the working classes while the bourgeoisie were allowed to multiply.

Gaining access

Contraception was rudimentary in the late 19th century. Commonly used methods included coitus interruptus, vaginal sponges soaked in quinine, injections of alum and water into the vagina, and sheaths. The Catholic and Protestant churches, and society at large, regarded contraception as dangerous, because it encouraged sexual relations outside marriage.

Despite public knowledge of contraception being limited, middle-class families managed to obtain information and buy contraceptives, disguising their purchases as "feminine hygiene." Working-class women, however, had little access to birth-control literature and could not afford contraceptives. Attempts to prevent pregnancies often involved unsuccessful and dangerous folk remedies. Many women tried to abort unwanted pregnancies themselves, or sought the help

of an abortionist, which was illegal. Other women were almost always pregnant or breastfeeding, with 12 or more children being common in a family.

Starting a movement

During the early years of the 20th century, radical feminists on both sides of the Atlantic began to change their views on sexuality and birth control, and the issue became an increasingly important one in the women's movement. Many of these women were also socialists and were influenced by the writings of British sex reformers such as Havelock Ellis and Edward Carpenter. In the US, supporters included feminists Crystal Eastman and Ida Rauh, and the anarchist Emma Goldman; living in New York's Greenwich Village in the second decade of the 20th century, these women advocated freer sexual relations, help for working mothers, and pregnancy prevention.

Margaret Sanger also lived in Greenwich Village at this time. Writing in *The Woman Rebel*, a radical magazine she founded, »

1990s
Hormone shots are introduced

2000s
Skin patches and gels become a popular alternative to the Pill

> No woman can call herself free who does not own and control her body.
> **Margaret Sanger**

Margaret Sanger

Birth control activist Margaret Sanger was born in New York in 1879, the sixth of 11 children in an Irish Catholic family. Her mother's death at the age of 49, after 18 pregnancies, had a profound influence on Sanger. She qualified as an obstetrics nurse, which confirmed her views on the impact multiple pregnancies had on women, especially the poor. Involved in radical politics, she joined the New York Socialist Party.

In 1916, Sanger opened a short-lived birth control clinic, and in 1921, she established the American Birth Control League. She went on to organize the first World Population Conference in Geneva, Switzerland, and in 1953 became president of the International Planned Parenthood Federation. Sanger died of heart failure in Tucson, Arizona, in 1966.

Key works

1914 *Family Limitation*
1916 *What Every Girl Should Know*
1931 *My Fight for Birth Control*

A nurse poses outside a Marie Stopes clinic in Bethnal Green, London, in 1928. These mobile clinics could be taken to where they were most needed, such as London's overpopulated East End.

in 1914, she included the term "birth control," the first known use of the phrase. Sanger—together with feminist and suffragist Marie Stopes in Britain—was pivotal in starting a birth control movement. Setting out to challenge the Comstock Law, under which dissemination of information about contraception was deemed immoral and illegal, she wrote explicit articles for women on sex

and contraception and embarked on speaking tours that were often attended by working-class women. In 1915, to escape prosecution, Sanger went to England, where a birth control movement was also underway. Sanger met activists such as Stella Browne and Alice Vickery, and also Marie Stopes, who went on to become the most influential figure in the British birth control movement. Sanger

explained her private and personal idea of what feminism should mean: that women should first free themselves from biological slavery, which was best achieved through birth control. Sanger's emphasis on the word "control" was significant because of her profound belief that women, not men, should govern their reproduction.

Marie Stopes approached women's need for contraception slightly differently. She had experienced a miserable and unconsummated marriage, which convinced her that sex education and birth control were essential if women were to achieve sexual fulfilment. In 1918, she published the book for which she is best known, *Married Love*, one of the very first books to explain sex and sexual pleasure openly and explicitly. The medical profession denounced this and her subsequent books for the "monstrous crime" of spreading knowledge about birth

A modern and humane civilization must control conception or sink into barbaric cruelty to individuals.
Marie Stopes

Politicizing birth control

Changes in government can affect the availability of birth control. In 2010, US President Barack Obama signed into law the Affordable Care Act, which stipulated that employers needed to provide health care, including contraceptives, for their employees. Four years later, following lobbying by the religious right, the US Supreme Court ruled that a Christian-owned company, Hobby Lobby, could claim exemption on grounds of religious belief. For

liberals, this set a precedent that was particularly harmful for low-paid employees.

Foreign aid for birth control programs in developing countries has often been contentious. In January 2017, for example, the Trump administration banned US government aid to developing countries that "actively promote" abortion. Many argue that such a policy will lead to illegal abortions and unwanted pregnancies.

control. However, five editions of *Married Love* were printed in the first year and Stopes received thousands of letters from women and men expressing gratitude and asking for advice.

A mainstream movement

On her return to the US in 1916, Margaret Sanger opened America's first birth control clinic in Brooklyn. She also promoted the newly developed Dutch cap, or diaphragm, which she brought back with her from Europe. The clinic was raided after only nine days, and Sanger, her staff, and her sister were arrested and jailed for 30 days for breaking the Comstock Law. The publicity kick-started a birth control movement that spread throughout the US and brought much-needed financial support. The movement achieved a major victory in 1918 when a New York court ruling allowed doctors to prescribe contraception.

In 1921, Marie Stopes opened the UK's first permanent birth control clinic, in London. Women obtained advice and were shown how to use a diaphragm. In both the US and the UK, the birth control movement gained ground, as the issue of contraception became one of women's welfare and not just feminism.

Detractors and accusers

Opposition to birth control continued, not least from the Catholic Church, but by the 1930s it was becoming socially acceptable, for married women at least (calls for single women to have access did not emerge until the late 1960s). In 1930, a Birth Control Conference was held in London and a few months later the British Ministry of Health ruled that local authorities could give contraceptive advice in mother and children's welfare centers.

Birth control campaigners, including Sanger and Stopes, were at times accused of eugenics (both had links with eugenics groups), yet their work also changed women's lives. Demands for reproductive rights reemerged with the rise of the Women's Liberation Movement in the 1960s and continue to resonate today. ■

This famous, head-turning poster published by Britain's Health Education Council in 1969 attempted to make men take more responsibility for contraception. At the time, the poster was considered shocking and even offensive.

Would you be more careful if it was you that got pregnant?

Contraception is one of the facts of life.
Anyone, married or single, can get free advice on contraception from their doctor or family planning clinic.
You can find your local clinic under Family Planning in the telephone directory or Yellow Pages.

The Health Education Council

MEN REFUSE TO SEE THE CAPABILITIES OF WOMEN
EARLY ARAB FEMINISM

eminism first reached the Arab world via colonialism. Exposure to European empires and post-Enlightenment thinking led Arab Muslims in colonized lands to ask how they had come to be ruled by foreigners and whether flaws in their culture had allowed colonialism to happen. Reformists blamed religion, arguing that literal interpretation of the Quran was incompatible with the modern age.

Remarkable women sometimes **rise to prominence** in society.

⬇

Men put these **women** on a **pedestal** and view them as **exceptional**.

⬇

This way, men can avoid recognizing the capabilities of all women.

This tension between tradition and modernity, and religion and secularism, was particularly marked in the field of women's rights. Capable women in the public sphere presented a paradox to patriarchal society. Although often respected and valued by men, they were looked upon as exceptions and not representative of a wider potential that could threaten the status quo.

Women of substance
In the first half of the 20th century, Egyptian feminist Huda al-Sharaawi became an activist during the fight against colonialism. After Egypt gained independence in 1922, she campaigned for women's rights and education. She set up a women's clinic in Cairo, with royal help, and moved in theological circles to advocate reforms in family law, especially a ban on polygamy. However, Sharaawi was shaped by her class and the period in which she lived. She was criticized for viewing the rich as guardians of the poor, and the working class as passive and unable to effect change.

After Sharaawi, feminism in the Arab world developed two strands: secular, inspired by Western ideas,

See also: Education for Islamic women 38–39 ▪ Anticolonialism 218–219 ▪ Postcolonial feminism 220–223 ▪ Modern Islamic feminism 284–285

> There appear to be two distinct voices within Islam, and two competing understandings of gender.
> **Leila Ahmed**
> **Professor of Islamic law and feminism**

and theological, which seeks to reveal the rights given to women by God that were later obscured or denied by men. In 1972, Nawal el-Saadawi, an Egyptian doctor and women's rights activist who draws on Marxist arguments, published *Woman and Sex*, which details all the ways in which Egyptian women were oppressed, including the practice of female genital mutilation in the country.

Egyptian women rally the crowds at a demonstration in support of the Egyptian Revolution of 1919. Opposing British occupation and demanding change, women activists described themselves as "Mothers of the Nation."

She founded the Arab Women's Solidarity Association in 1982, and was imprisoned many times during her life. Rejecting men's interpretation of Islam, she believed women's liberation lay outside Islamic theology.

Theological support

Other feminists in the Muslim world draw on theology to oppose women's cultural oppression. In Morocco, for example, Fatima Mernissi studied Hadith (records of the Prophet Muhammad's deeds and sayings) to show how passages used against women were often fabrications or drawn from weak sources. Mernissi carried out painstaking historical research to show their inaccuracy.

Likewise, theologians Asma Barlas, an American-Pakistani scholar, and Amina Wadud, an

African-American scholar, have produced interpretations of the Quran that challenge patriarchal readings. Both women believe that women's God-given rights have been eroded. In Malaysia, Wadud cofounded Sisters in Islam to tackle discriminatory laws and practices carried out in the name of Islam. Both theologians have shaped Arab feminist thinking, where the struggle for equality and plurality continues. ∎

Huda al-Sharaawi

Often described as Egypt's first feminist, Huda al-Sharaawi was born into a privileged family in Cairo in 1879. She was married by the age of 13, yet managed to further her studies and travel during a temporary separation from her husband.

Sharaawi later joined her husband as an anticolonial activist. After going to Europe in 1914, she returned to Egypt to mobilize women against British rule. In 1923, she founded the Egyptian Feminist Union.

After her husband's death, Sharaawi famously removed her face veil (but not her head scarf) for the first time in public at the International Woman Suffrage Alliance of 1923 in Rome.

Sharaawi also wrote poetry, and in 1925 began publishing a journal called *L'Egyptienne* (The Egyptian Woman). She died from a heart attack in 1947.

Key work

1986 *Harem Years: The Memoirs of an Egyptian Feminist (1879–1924)*

> I intend to start a revolution for the silent women.
> **Huda al-Sharaawi**

THERE IS NO GATE, NO LOCK, NO BOLT THAT YOU CAN SET UPON THE FREEDOM OF MY MIND
INTELLECTUAL FREEDOM

IN CONTEXT

PRIMARY QUOTE
Virginia Woolf, 1929

KEY FIGURE
Virginia Woolf

BEFORE
1854–1862 *The Angel in the House* by the English poet Coventry Patmore reinforces the image of wives as devoted, domestic, and submissive.

1892 Charlotte Perkins Gilman's *The Yellow Wallpaper* portrays a wife driven mad by her husband's suffocating care.

AFTER
1949 In *The Second Sex*, Simone de Beauvoir discusses women's treatment in history.

1977 Elaine Showalter's *A Literature of Their Own* analyzes the works of female novelists.

1986 Jane Spencer's *The Rise of the Woman Novelist* charts an earlier 18th-century tradition of female writers.

Women play tennis at Girton College, Cambridge, UK, in around 1900. Woolf's lectures at the women's colleges of Girton and Newnham helped inspire "A Room of One's Own."

In the early 20th century, the role of women was largely domestic, their education was often minimal, and most professions were closed to them. As a result, very few enjoyed intellectual freedom—the power to conceive, receive, and freely express ideas—which many feminists came to value above all else. The literary canon of the time was dominated by men, and female writers often published under "Anonymous" or male pseudonyms.

In her essay "A Room of One's Own" (1929), Virginia Woolf discusses the struggles women writers had faced to win the same success as their male counterparts. Acknowledging the achievements of novelists such as Jane Austen and George Eliot, Woolf describes how the confines of domesticity could hinder such work. Women often wrote in communal areas of the home, surrounded by distractions, and seldom had the financial independence necessary to break free. She conjures up Judith, a fictitious sister of William

See also: Collective action in the 18th century 24–27 ▪ Enlightenment feminism 28–33 ▪ Emancipation from domesticity 34–35

It would have been impossible … for any woman to have written the plays of Shakespeare in the age of Shakespeare.
Virginia Woolf

Shakespeare, and wonders what life would have been like for her. Had she been "as imaginative, as agog to see the world" as her brother, she would still have been expected to be content with being a wife and mother. Woolf imagines that, in despair, Judith kills herself, her genius unexpressed.

Other women writers had considered a similar scenario: (Stella) Miles Franklin's *My Brilliant Career* (1901) tells of Sybylla, a young Australian woman unable to follow her dream of writing as a result of family duties, poverty, and wider society's misogyny.

Space for creativity
Woolf proposes that women need "a room of their own" in order to exercise their creativity free from domestic chains. For Woolf, the financial independence required to achieve this was even more important than gaining the vote. Once women had the space to think, they could become more experimental and could develop a female language previously absent from literature.

Woolf suggests that female writers had to fight an internal battle against the Victorian ideals of womanhood, as epitomized by the perfect wife and mother in the popular narrative poem, *The Angel in the House*. In her 1931 essay "Professions for Women," she dubs that angel a "phantom" haunting the mind of women writers, which in order to write successfully, has to be excised: "Had I not killed her, she would have killed me."

A modernist legacy
Woolf's demand for intellectual freedom paved the way for the second wave of feminism in the mid-20th century. Her work would later inspire Elaine Showalter's theory of gynocritics, defined as "a female framework for the analysis of women's literature." Other feminists have used "A Room of One's Own" to criticize 20th-century feminism. Alice Walker, for example, observed that the lack of a room of one's own was the least of the impediments faced by women of color. ▪

Woolf's creative space was her writing lodge in the extensive garden of Monk's House, East Sussex, Virginia and Leonard's country home from 1919.

Virginia Woolf

Born in 1882 to a prominent family, Woolf would grow up well-connected, but received no formal education. During her adolescence, a series of family deaths strongly affected her mental health. She studied at King's College London, where she met radical feminists. She also joined the Bloomsbury Group, a circle of intellectuals, where she met Vita Sackville-West, her lifelong friend and lover, and Leonard Woolf, her husband.

In 1917, Virginia and Leonard set up the Hogarth Press, allowing her to publish her own work. She experimented with narrative prose styles, becoming a key figure in the modernist movement. She often raised feminist and social issues, using interior monologues and a multiplicity of viewpoints to discuss them. In 1941, deeply depressed, Woolf died by suicide.

Key works

1928 *Orlando*
1929 "A Room of One's Own"
1931 "Professions for Women"
1937 *The Years*
1938 *Three Guineas*

RESOLUTION LIES IN REVOLUTION
ANARCHA-FEMINISM

IN CONTEXT

PRIMARY QUOTE
**Lucía Sánchez
Saornil, 1935**

KEY FIGURES
**Emma Goldman,
Lucía Sánchez Saornil**

BEFORE
1881 French anarchist
feminist Louise Michel attends
the International Anarchist
Conference, London, and
visits Sylvia Pankhurst.

1896 *La Voz de la Mujer* (*The
Woman's Voice*) is launched in
Argentina; the newspaper's
motto is "Neither god, nor
boss, nor husband."

AFTER
1981 Female antinuclear
protesters establish a peace
camp at Greenham Common,
UK, active for 19 years.

2018 Feminist protesters
across Chile call for an end
to machismo culture and
its violence.

In 1897, an American journalist asked the young, politically active Emma Goldman what anarchy promised women. Goldman replied that it would bring "freedom, equality—everything that women don't have now." Goldman's feminist anarchism meant not only fighting the exploitative relations between bosses and their workers, or between governments, the military, and the civilian population, but also challenging the subjection that a capitalist patriarchy had historically imposed on women. She was a precursor of what is now called anarcha-feminism, whose ideas are rooted in the workers' movements of the late 19th and 20th centuries.

"Free Women" fight back

One of the most representative anarcha-feminist groups, Mujeres Libres (Free Women), was launched in Spain in 1936, at the start of the Spanish Civil War. Its founders— Lucía Sánchez Saornil, Mercedes Camposada, and Amparo Poch y Gascón— were members of the Confederación Nacional del Trabajo (CNT), an anarcho-syndicalist confederation of unions that joined forces with the Republicans against the Fascists led by General Franco. Like their fellow male anarchists, the women were fighting for a social revolution, but insisted that it could not be achieved while the CNT remained a largely male preserve. Mujeres Libres demanded that the CNT should swiftly address the "woman question" and male dominance within the anarchist movement,

Anarchist Emma Goldman was born in Lithuania. She defied society's conventions, writing and lecturing on controversial issues in the US and Europe all her life.

See also: Marxist feminism 52–55 ▪ Radical feminism 137 ▪ Wages for housework 147

The working classes confront the establishment in this 1933 anarchist poster. Anarchism gained momentum with the rise of the anarcho-syndicalist CNT, a confederation of labor unions.

which in every other way they supported. Although they were fighting for gender equality, Mujeres Libres rejected the "feminist" label; they thought the feminism of their time was too bourgeois in its values, promoting equality between men and women but failing to criticize capitalism and class divisions.

Within two years, membership of Mujeres Libres grew to 30,000. Its supporters traveled the country with two key strategies: *capacitación*—empowering women to realize their true potential—and *captación*—attracting women to join the anarchist fight against patriarchal capitalism, under which women would forever be enslaved. New education and training initiatives were launched, and day care centers were established to enable mothers to attend union meetings. At work, women were urged to fight against wage inequality. The aim was to prepare women to play a full part in a new society that was structured along gender and socially equal lines.

A battle postponed
The Nationalist victory that ended Spain's Civil War in 1939 and ushered in Franco's dictatorship dispelled Spanish women's immediate aspirations. The ideas of Mujeres Libres would, however, fuel second-wave feminism in the late 1960s and early '70s, as women began more forcefully and globally to challenge male dominance in all elements of society.

Anarcha-feminist activists continue to battle against the relationship between patriarchy, capitalism, militarism, and empire. It is this, they maintain, that perpetuates the continuing persecution of minorities, and the social inequalities that so many women in the world still face. ▪

Lucía Sánchez Saornil

Born in 1895 in Madrid, Lucía Sánchez Saornil was raised in poverty by her widowed father. Her poetry gained her a place at the Royal Academy of Arts of San Fernando. In 1931, she took part in a CNT strike, an event that sparked her political activism. She later cofounded Mujeres Libres to press for gender equality and a classless society. In 1937, while editing a journal in Valencia, she met her lifelong partner, América Barroso, and fled with her to Paris after General Franco's victory. They returned to Madrid in 1941, but had to keep their relationship secret. Sánchez Saornil continued to write poetry and work as an editor until her death from cancer in 1970.

Key works

1935 "The Question of Feminism"
1996 *Poesía*

> The love of liberty and the sense of human dignity are the basic elements of the Anarchist creed.
> **Federica Montseny**
> Spanish anarchist

THE PER
IS POLIT
1945–1979

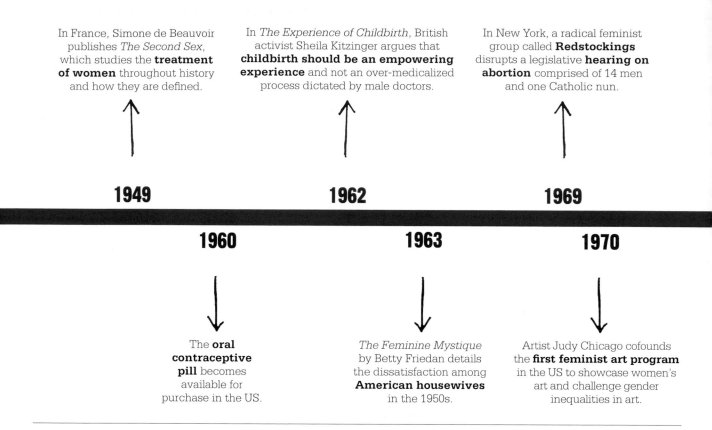

In France, Simone de Beauvoir publishes *The Second Sex*, which studies the **treatment of women** throughout history and how they are defined.

In *The Experience of Childbirth*, British activist Sheila Kitzinger argues that **childbirth should be an empowering experience** and not an over-medicalized process dictated by male doctors.

In New York, a radical feminist group called **Redstockings** disrupts a legislative **hearing on abortion** comprised of 14 men and one Catholic nun.

1949

1962

1969

1960

1963

1970

The **oral contraceptive pill** becomes available for purchase in the US.

The Feminine Mystique by Betty Friedan details the dissatisfaction among **American housewives** in the 1950s.

Artist Judy Chicago cofounds the **first feminist art program** in the US to showcase women's art and challenge gender inequalities in art.

A second, more radical wave of feminism flourished between the 1960s and the early '80s, influenced by ideas that had begun to develop after 1945. Seeing women's position as both different from and unequal to men, second-wave feminists analyzed every aspect of society, including sexuality, religion, and power, redefining them in relation to the oppression of women. Feminists developed ideas about how culture and society could be changed to liberate women. As new ideas formed, feminist political activism and campaigns intensified.

A key concept within second-wave feminism was the idea that women are not born but created—the product of social conditioning. First expressed by Simone de Beauvoir in 1949, this distinction between biological sex and gender as a social construct had a huge impact on second-wave feminist thinking. Arguing that a woman's biology should not determine her life, feminist writers such as Betty Friedan and Germaine Greer described and challenged the image of idealized femininity imposed on women by upbringing, education, and psychology, urging them to challenge the stereotype.

Liberating personal politics

Second-wave feminism, often known as the Women's Liberation Movement (Women's Lib or WLM), developed in the context of the political activism of the civil rights and anti–Vietnam War movements of the period. Its proponents saw feminism as a cause for liberation rather than simply a struggle for equal rights. For them, women's personal experiences were political and reflected the power structures that kept women oppressed.

Radical feminists of this period, such as American writer and activist Kate Millett, defined patriarchy—the universal social and political system of male power over women—as the main source of women's oppression. Some feminists focused on the nuclear family as a key mechanism in preserving the hold of patriarchy, while others attacked the patriarchy and misogyny of the Christian Church, calling for a feminized form of religion.

Sex and violence

Second-wave feminists explored issues of sexuality more deeply than any feminists before. The American feminist Anne Koedt

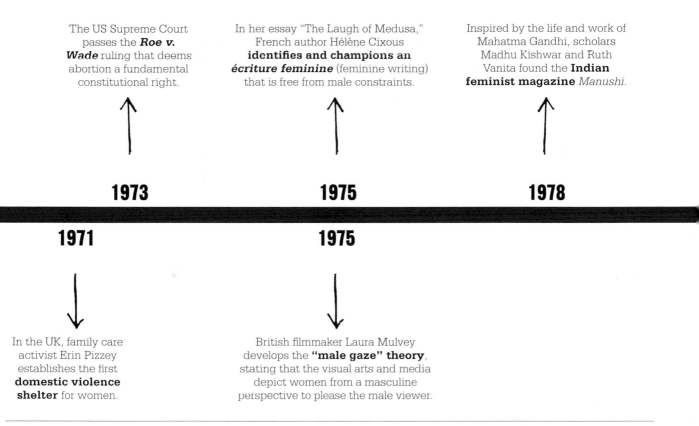

The US Supreme Court passes the **Roe v. Wade** ruling that deems abortion a fundamental constitutional right.

In her essay "The Laugh of Medusa," French author Hélène Cixous **identifies and champions an écriture feminine** (feminine writing) that is free from male constraints.

Inspired by the life and work of Mahatma Gandhi, scholars Madhu Kishwar and Ruth Vanita found the **Indian feminist magazine** *Manushi*.

1973   **1975**   **1978**

1971   **1975**

In the UK, family care activist Erin Pizzey establishes the first **domestic violence shelter** for women.

British filmmaker Laura Mulvey develops the **"male gaze" theory**, stating that the visual arts and media depict women from a masculine perspective to please the male viewer.

argued in her essay "The Myth of the Vaginal Orgasm" that it was men who had shaped attitudes toward and opinions about female sexuality because men defined women's sexual activity only in terms of their own desires. Her work, and the publication in 1976 of *The Hite Report*, a study of female sexuality, shattered received notions about women's sexuality by presenting a realistic picture of women's sexual behavior.

Reproductive rights and the ability of women to control their own fertility continued as feminist issues. The new contraceptive pill provided one answer, enabling women to enjoy sex without the fear of pregnancy. Acquiring it, though, was difficult, and feminists campaigned intensively for access to free, safe contraception and a

woman's right to legal abortion. Linked to these demands was the emergence of a women's health movement in the US and elsewhere, which called for women to gain control of their own health care.

Second-wave feminists also raised the political profile of rape and domestic violence, which men used, they argued, to control and intimidate women. From the late 1970s the American feminist Andrea Dworkin spearheaded an attack on pornography, arguing that it not only oppressed women but also incited violence toward them.

Battles old and new

Equal rights feminists continued the work of their first-wave sisters, focusing in particular on achieving equal pay for women. In Britain and Iceland, equal pay legislation,

in 1970 and 1976 respectively, followed working-class women's strike action. Closely linked to this was a global Wages for Housework Campaign, which began in Italy in 1972 and drew attention to women's unpaid labor as mothers and homemakers. Feminists argued that women's work for the home and family should be paid.

By the late 1970s, feminists were applying their ideas to many areas of society, arguing that all issues, even overeating, were feminist issues. Historians such as British-born Sheila Rowbotham highlighted the exclusion of women from history; artists such as the American Judy Chicago worked to create specifically feminist art; while British academic Laura Mulvey and others explored misogyny within film. ■

ONE IS NOT BORN, BUT RATHER BECOMES, A WOMAN

THE ROOTS OF OPPRESSION

IN CONTEXT

PRIMARY QUOTE
Simone de Beauvoir, 1949

KEY FIGURE
Simone de Beauvoir

BEFORE
1884 Friedrich Engels'
*Origin of the Family, Private
Property and the State*
locates the source of women's
oppression in the family.

1944 French women win
the vote and France's 19th-
century laws giving men
absolute control over their
wives are amended.

AFTER
1963 In the US, Betty
Friedan's *The Feminine
Mystique* explores how
the suburban nuclear family
oppresses women.

1970 *The Female Eunuch* by
Germaine Greer is published
in the UK.

The main goals of first-wave
feminism were to achieve
legal, social, intellectual,
and political equality with men.
Second-wave feminism broadened
the struggle. Demands for equality
continued but feminists also
examined women's personal
experiences—how they were
viewed and treated in the home
and in society. They also analyzed
the roots of women's oppression
with a view to gaining liberation.

Simone de Beauvoir's groundbreaking book *The Second Sex*
probably provided the most
significant contribution to the
thinking and theoretical basis of
second-wave feminism. Published

See also: Institutions as oppressors 80 ▪ Patriarchy as social control 144–145 ▪ Uterus envy 146 ▪ Poststructuralism 182–187 ▪ Language and patriarchy 192–193

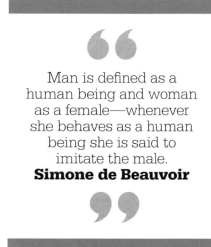

> Man is defined as a human being and woman as a female—whenever she behaves as a human being she is said to imitate the male.
> **Simone de Beauvoir**

in France in 1949, it came between the end of first-wave feminism and the emergence of the second-wave in the 1960s. An unprecedented and profound exploration of the myths, social pressures, and life experiences of women, the book reaches a radical conclusion. De Beauvoir states that womanhood or femininity is a social or cultural construct, formed over generations. In this construct, she argues, lie the causes of women's oppression.

Women as "Other"

De Beauvoir begins with a simple question: What is a woman? Noting that philosophers had generally defined women as imperfect men, she goes on to say that women are the "Other;" that is they are defined only in relation to men. She explains that woman is simply what man decrees and is defined and differentiated with reference to man, and not he with reference to her. Woman is the "incidental," the "inessential," as opposed to the "essential." He is the "Subject," the "Absolute"—she is the "Other,"

the "Object." In other words, society sets up the male as the norm, and woman as the secondary sex.

In the first volume of *The Second Sex*, de Beauvoir explores biology, psychology, and historical materialism in search of reasons for women's subordination and finds that there are none. These various disciplines reveal unarguable differences between the two sexes but provide no justification for women's second-class status. While recognizing the particular processes of a woman's biology—puberty, menstruation, pregnancy, and menopause—de Beauvoir nevertheless denies that they establish a fixed and inevitable destiny for her.

De Beauvoir then examines history, tracing social changes from nomadic hunters through »

Simone de Beauvoir

Born into a bourgeois Parisian family in 1908, Simone de Beauvoir was one of the most significant philosophers of the 20th century. She studied at the Sorbonne, where she met Jean-Paul Sartre, her lover and companion for more than 50 years. Even though the couple both had other affairs, they worked and traveled together, their partnership shaping their philosophical and practical lives.

From 1944, de Beauvoir published many works of fiction and nonfiction. She and Sartre jointly edited the political journal *Les Temps Modernes* and supported many left-wing political causes, including Algerian and Hungarian independence, the student protests of May 1968, and the anti–Vietnam War movement. She died in Paris aged 78 in 1986.

Key works

1947 *The Ethics of Ambiguity*
1949 *The Second Sex*
1954 *The Mandarins*
1958 *Memoirs of a Dutiful Daughter*
1958 *Adieux: A Farewell to Sartre*

SIMONE DE BEAUVOIR

LE DEUXIÈME SEXE

I

LES FAITS ET LES MYTHES

nrf

GALLIMARD

The first French edition of *The Second Sex*, published by Gallimard in 1949, was conceived in two parts. The first, shown here, was titled "Facts and Myths"; the second, "Lived Experience."

The causes of women's oppression

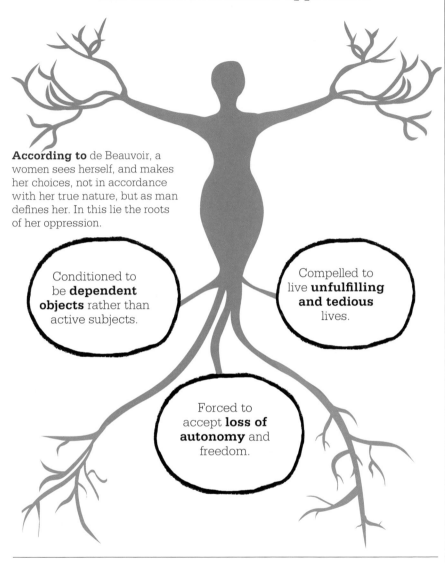

According to de Beauvoir, a women sees herself, and makes her choices, not in accordance with her true nature, but as man defines her. In this lie the roots of her oppression.

Conditioned to be **dependent objects** rather than active subjects.

Compelled to live **unfulfilling and tedious** lives.

Forced to accept **loss of autonomy** and freedom.

To emancipate woman is to refuse to confine her to the relations she bears to man, not to deny them to her.
Simone de Beauvoir

to modern times, and explores myth and literature. In all areas she finds that women have been relegated to a subordinate role, even when fighting for their rights such as the campaign for suffrage. She argues that male values always dominate, subordinating women to the point at which the whole of feminine history has been man-made. De Beauvoir regards woman as having been complicit in this process, because of her perceived need for approval and protection. She argues that, despite achieving some rights, women remain in a state of subjection.

Constructing femininity
In the second half of *The Second Sex*, de Beauvoir explores women's lived experiences, from childhood through to adulthood. She puts sexuality, marriage, motherhood, and domesticity under her intellectual and philosophical microscope. It is in this part of the book that she presents her most important thesis: that women are not born feminine but that femininity is constructed, explaining that no biological, psychological, or economic fate determines the figure that the female presents in society. Instead, she argues, it is civilization that has created this feminine creature, whom she considers intermediate between male and eunuch.

According to de Beauvoir, until the age of 12 the young girl is as strong as her brothers and shows exactly the same intellectual capacity. However, de Beauvoir spells out in great detail how the young girl is conditioned to adopt what is presented to her as femininity, saying that there is a conflict in a woman between her autonomous existence and her objective self: she is taught that to please others, and particularly men, she must make herself the object rather than the subject, and she must renounce her autonomy. For de Beauvoir, this becomes a vicious circle: the less a woman exercises her freedom to grasp the world around her, the less she dares to present herself as the subject.

From socialist to feminist

When Simone de Beauvoir wrote *The Second Sex*, she did not define herself as a feminist. She was a socialist and believed a socialist revolution would liberate women, but in the late 1960s, as feminism blossomed, she changed her mind. She told an interviewer in 1972 that the situation of women in France had not really changed over the last 20 years and that people on the left should join the women's movement while waiting for socialism to arrive.

Defining herself as a feminist, but reluctant to join traditional reformist groups, de Beauvoir joined the radical Mouvement de Libération des Femmes (MLF)—the French women's liberation movement. In 1971, when abortion was still illegal in France, de Beauvoir was one of more than 300 women who signed a pro-abortion manifesto, later known as the Manifesto of the 343, stating that she had had an abortion and demanding this right for all women.

De Beauvoir acknowledges that, due to the successes of feminism, young women are encouraged to get an education and take up sports. Nevertheless, there will not be the same pressure on them to succeed as there will be on boys. Instead, a girl aims for a different kind of accomplishment: she must remain a woman and not lose her femininity. De Beauvoir states that women reinforce their own dependency through love, narcissism, or mysticism. Conditioned to be dependent, women accept a life of tedious housework, motherhood, and sexual slavishness—roles that de Beauvoir attacked and rejected in her own life.

Liberation and legacy
De Beauvoir believed in an individual's ability to choose her own path and make her own decisions, a central tenet of existentialism, the philosophical

theory she shared with her life partner Jean-Paul Sartre. *The Second Sex* is a philosophical work, not a rallying call to action, but even so she argues that women can and should recognize and challenge the social construction of femininity. They should seek autonomy and liberate themselves through the fulfilling work, intellectual activity, sexual freedom, and social change that would include economic justice. *The Second Sex* was immensely

influential. Its long-term impact on feminism is hard to overestimate. In the shorter term, the analysis of female oppression influenced later feminists such as Shulamith Firestone, who dedicated her book *The Dialectic of Sex* (1970) to de Beauvoir. The value de Beauvoir placed on the personal experience of women was significant to feminist thought and encouraged consciousness-raising and sisterhood within early second-wave feminism. She believed that women should see themselves as a class within society. Women needed to identify their shared experiences and oppression in order to break free.

Perhaps de Beauvoir's most important contribution was to distinguish between sex and gender. De Beauvoir does not choose to use the word gender instead of sex in *The Second Sex* but she defines the difference. Her argument that biology is not destiny, and her explanation of gender as distinct from sex or biology, still resonates through feminist discourse today. ■

De Beauvoir speaks to the press in June 1970 after her release from police custody. She and Sartre (to her right) had been arrested for selling a newspaper by a banned organization that advocated overthrowing the French government.

SOMETHING IS VERY WRONG
WITH THE WAY AMERICAN WOMEN
ARE TRYING TO LIVE
THE PROBLEM WITH NO NAME

An advertisement for dishwashing liquid in 1956 portrays the stereotypical American housewife as a selfless wife and mother embodying what Friedan called the "feminine mystique."

Feminism as a movement faltered and almost disappeared during the years of the Great Depression and World War II. However, the 1960s saw the emergence of a reenergized feminist movement. The book that is often credited with inspiring this renaissance in the US is Betty Friedan's *The Feminine Mystique*, published in 1963. Exploring the unhappiness experienced by white middle-class women, the book resonated with millions of American women.

The Feminine Mystique was an instant best seller and Friedan became a leading, if sometimes controversial, spokeswoman for the revitalized feminist movement.

Survey of her peers
In 1957, Friedan, already an experienced journalist, carried out an intensive survey of her college classmates 15 years after they had all graduated. She was already feeling slightly guilty that, as a wife and mother of three small children, she was sometimes required to work away from home. This caused her to question her own situation and to speak to other women about their feelings and experiences. The women she interviewed were white, college-educated, married with children, usually living in the leafy suburbs, and to all outward appearances economically comfortable. Time and again, however, Friedan found these women were unhappy; they expressed dissatisfaction but were unable to identify its cause. The women Friedan interviewed could not articulate the problem; instead they would say they felt they did not exist, that they were inexplicably tired or had to use tranquilizers to blot out

> " The problem lay buried, unspoken for many years in the minds of American women.
> **Betty Friedan** "

See also: Female autonomy in a male-dominated world 40–41 ▪ Marriage and work 70–71 ▪ Rights for married women 72–75 ▪ The roots of oppression 114–117 ▪ Family structures 138–139

their feelings of discontent. Friedan called this sense of unhappiness "the problem that has no name."

The feminine mystique

Continuing her research into this paradox, Friedan interviewed more women, as well as psychologists, educationalists, doctors, and journalists. She discovered that these feelings of discontent were shared by women all over America.

In 1963, Friedan published her findings in the book *The Feminine Mystique*, in which she notes that while campaigning women had fought and achieved so much during first-wave feminism, women's aspirations had changed by the late 1940s. Although more women were attending college, only a small number of them embarked on a career. Women continued to see the "feminine mystique," an idealized image of femininity rooted in marriage and family, as the most desirable role open to them. She observes how they were marrying at a younger age than before, often helping their

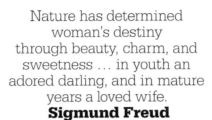

Nature has determined woman's destiny through beauty, charm, and sweetness … in youth an adored darling, and in mature years a loved wife.
Sigmund Freud

husbands to complete their college careers, and then devoting their lives to raising children and making a home for the family.

Ideal image

According to Friedan, there were huge pressures on postwar women to conform to the feminine mystique. Women's magazines, such as the *Ladies' Home Journal* and *McCall's*, which in the 1930s

had featured young, independent women, were now filled with pictures of contented American housewives in comfortable homes equipped with the latest gadgets. Articles such as "Femininity Begins at Home," "The Business of Running a Home," and "How to Snare a Male" reinforced the image of women as sexual objects and homemakers, while articles such as "Really a Man's World, Politics" implied that life outside the home was for men.

Friedan also writes about the impact of Freudian thought on creating the feminine mystique, reminding readers that Freud attributed all the problems faced by women to sexual repression. Noting how psychologists had adopted Freud's views, she says that psychoanalysis as a therapy was not in itself responsible for the feminine mystique but had informed writers, researchers, university professors, and other educators, leading to a restricting effect on women. In Friedan's words "The feminine mystique, »

Betty Friedan

Born Bettye Naomi Goldstein in Peoria, Illinois, in 1921, Friedan graduated in psychology from Smith College for women in 1942. Interested in left-wing politics, she attended Berkeley University for a year before writing for trade union publications.

Friedan married in 1947 and became a freelance writer after losing her job because she was pregnant. Committed to greater public participation for women, in 1966 she cofounded and became the first president of the National Organization for Women (NOW),

the largest equal rights feminist body in the US. In 1971, she helped set up the National Women's Political Caucus with other feminists, including Gloria Steinem and Bella Abzug.

In later life, she criticized extremism in the feminist movement. She died in 2006.

Key works

1963 *The Feminine Mystique*
1982 *The Second Stage*
1993 *The Fountain of Age*
1997 *Beyond Gender*
2000 *Life So Far*

The reasons for women's malaise

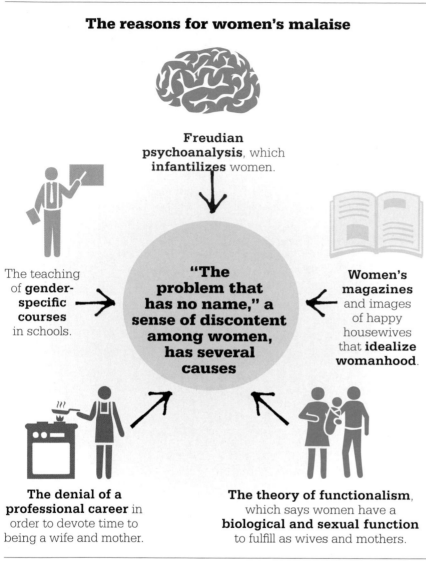

Freudian **psychoanalysis**, which **infantilizes** women.

The teaching of **gender-specific courses** in schools.

"The problem that has no name," a sense of discontent among women, has several causes

Women's magazines and images of happy housewives that **idealize womanhood**.

The denial of a professional career in order to devote time to being a wife and mother.

The theory of functionalism, which says women have a **biological and sexual function** to fulfill as wives and mothers.

> 66
> Who knows what women can be when they are finally free to become themselves?
> **Betty Friedan**
> 99

elevated by Freudian theory into a scientific religion, sounded a single, overprotective, life-restricting, future-denying note for women."

Friedan also criticizes the social theory of functionalism, which holds that each part of society contributes to the stability of the whole, a view that was popular in the social sciences at the time. Friedan argues that this theory also contributed to the feminine mystique by suggesting that women's function should be confined to their sexual and biological roles as wives and

mothers. Friedan also states that anthropologists had applied their findings of other cultures to arrive at the same conclusion. Referring to US cultural anthropologist Margaret Mead, who contributed to the feminine mystique by glorifying the reproductive ability of women, Friedan points out the contradiction inherent in Mead's views, given that she lived a professional and fulfilling life.

Friedan found that education reinforced the feminine mystique. Girls and young women at college

were prey to what she describes as "sex-directed educators," who provided what were considered to be gender-specific courses through the 1950s and '60s. There was even, she says, an attempt to put a scientific slant on this by suggesting that girls were more suited to "domestic science" than physics and chemistry.

For Friedan, the feminine mystique was an impossible ideal. For 15 years, she says, she had watched American women trying to conform to an image that made them "deny their minds." Having analyzed the causes, Friedan produces what she calls a "new life plan for women" and urges women to break free from the feminine mystique and search for meaningful work that would lead to their fulfilment. She recognizes that it might be difficult but cites women who had succeeded. For her, education and paid employment were routes out of the trap of the feminine mystique.

New support
Betty Friedan's book made an extraordinary impression on US society, introducing thousands of white middle-class women to feminism. Within a year 300,000

copies had been sold, rising to more than 3 million copies within three years of publication and 13 translations. Women in the US, the UK, and many other countries recognized descriptions of their own frustrations in the book and turned to feminism for ideas on how to overcome them.

There were criticisms, not least that Friedan had concentrated on the lives of white middle-class suburban women and had ignored working-class women, African Americans, and other ethnic

Women flood New York's Fifth Avenue in the Women's Strike for Equality March held in August 1970, an event replicated in other US cities. The march was led by the National Organization for Women, which Friedan cofounded.

groups within the US. It was also suggested that women had already begun to break through the constraints described by Friedan and were entering the professions or working outside the home. Later feminists criticized Friedan for including men in her proposals for change. Finally, some of her readers were offended by what they saw as attacks on the roles of wife and mother, a concern often voiced in second-wave feminist debates.

Friedan's legacy

Despite criticisms, Friedan's writings struck a deep chord with a great many women. The fact that she gave importance to their personal experiences resonated just as much as the ideas in the book. *The Feminine Mystique* helped to spark

the Women's Liberation Movement and the emergence of second-wave feminism; within just a few years of its publication, women were organizing and challenging sexism in the media, in schools and colleges, and elsewhere in society.

There were also practical political outcomes. A few months after the book's publication, the Equal Pay Act was introduced in the US, stipulating that women and men should receive equal pay for equal work. Three years later, in 1966, Friedan and other feminists founded the National Organization for Women (NOW), based on the proposition that "women first and foremost are humans beings, who … must have the chance to develop their fullest human potential." ■

"GOD'S PLAN" IS OFTEN A FRONT FOR MEN'S PLANS
FEMINIST THEOLOGY

IN CONTEXT

PRIMARY QUOTE
Mary Daly, 1973

KEY FIGURE
Mary Daly

BEFORE
1848 In the US, the Seneca Falls Convention calls for equal rights for women, including religious rights.

1960s Women's Studies becomes an academic discipline, and women start earning degrees in theology.

AFTER
1976 The Ecumenical Association of Third World Theologians (EATWOT) first meets in Tanzania; it admits women members in 1981.

1989 African American Barbara Harris is the first woman to become an Anglican bishop; the Church of England ordains its first women priests in 1994.

The field of feminist theology emerged in the 1960s, when feminism began to affect religious communities and the American Academy of Religion (AAR). Like feminism, it advocates equality between the sexes, but it also specifically deconstructs and reconstructs (critiques and reimagines) structures of religious thought and practice.

In this stained-glass window, Eve and Adam are ejected from the Garden of Eden after Eve introduces sin to the world by tempting Adam with fruit from the Tree of Knowledge of Good and Evil.

One of the leading lights in feminist theology was Mary Daly. Daly criticized the patriarchal structures and endorsement of the male point of view of religion, particularly within the Roman Catholic Church. She advocated an end to its male leadership, criticized the use of a male vocabulary for God (He, His), and called for the creation of spaces in which women and language are free of male domination.

Other influential women in feminist theology in the US were theologians Elizabeth Schüssler Fiorenza, Rosemary Radford Ruether, and Letty Russell, and biblical scholar Phyllis Trible. These women created new ways of reading the Bible that liberated female characters, or reinterpreted passages previously cited to subordinate women. They also studied ancient history to find women whose role in the origins of Christianity had been buried by male scholarship.

Hail the Goddess
Some feminist theologians reject the phallocentric ideologies of the main religions and embrace gynocentric traditions that praise the earth (Gaia) or the Goddess. The

Some feminists regard the term 'feminist theology' as an oxymoron.
Mary Daly

American feminist historian and theologian Carol P. Christ rejects all male symbols for God in favor of female ones. Her "thealogy" celebrates the feminine form, life cycle, and ability to give birth, and critiques Western culture's denigration of womanhood.

Beyond Christianity

Feminist theology has now moved beyond its narrow beginnings as a Christian field in North America and Europe. Jewish, Buddhist, Muslim, and Hindu feminists are also protesting against the use of their sacred texts to subordinate them, and identifying forms of oppression that religions have created or endorsed. Women of color and women in non-Western contexts have shaped their own theological domains, often stressing intersectionality—the overlapping of multiple oppressions such as race, class, and gender. Since the 1980s, feminist theologians from Africa, the Caribbean, Latin America, and Asia have been meeting at the Ecumenical Association of Third World Theologians to discuss the intersections of religion, patriarchy, and colonialism.

For many feminist theologians, their conviction that religion is liberating or redemptive underpins their commitment to both religion and feminism. For others, such as Mary Daly, the oppressive structures of patriarchal religion are what cause them to reject it. ▪

A woman priest lights a candle at her church in the UK. The Church of England first ordained women as priests in 1994; it was not until 2015 that it consecrated a woman bishop.

Mary Daly

Born in New York City in 1928 to working-class, Irish Catholic parents, Mary Daly studied philosophy and theology in graduate school, earning three doctoral degrees. In 1966, she became the first woman to teach theology at Boston College, a Catholic research university run by Jesuits, and began writing books about the patriarchy of religion and its oppression of women.

Daly had hoped to reform Catholicism but eventually she left the Church and renamed herself a radical, postchristian feminist. This led to conflict with Boston College. In 1999, a male student threatened to sue for discrimination because Daly only taught women in her Feminist Ethics lectures. After a lengthy legal battle, a settlement was reached and Daly retired. She died in 2010 at the age of 81.

Key works

1968 *The Church and the Second Sex*
1973 *Beyond God the Father*
1984 *Pure Lust: Elemental Feminist Philosophy*

OUR OWN BIOLOGY HAS NOT BEEN PROPERLY ANALYZED
SEXUAL PLEASURE

IN CONTEXT

PRIMARY QUOTE
Anne Koedt, 1968

KEY FIGURE
Anne Koedt

BEFORE
1897 Early British sexologist
Havelock Ellis examines male
sexuality in *Sexual Inversion*.

1919 Researcher Magnus
Hirschfeld opens the Institute
for Sexual Science in Berlin,
Germany. Hirschfeld states
that there are many sexual
variations in the human race.

AFTER
1987 Based on measurements
of the female sexual response,
American sexologist Beverley
Whipple asserts that women
can orgasm through their
imaginations alone.

2005 Australian urologist
Helen O'Connell asserts that
the internal structure of a
clitoris spreads over a larger
area than previously thought.

Second-wave feminists challenged the prevailing idea that women's sexuality should be dictated by men. They maintained that male domination was the driving force behind a lack of sexual pleasure in women. Sexuality, they stressed, is political.

In 1905, Austrian psychoanalyst Sigmund Freud had theorized that the clitoral orgasm was "immature;" "mature" women, he claimed, had vaginal orgasms. He considered women who did not achieve orgasm through vaginal penetration as dysfunctional or frigid.

Freud's ideas were still influential in the 1950s, but feminists were beginning to challenge them. In 1949, Simone de Beauvoir argued that sexual intercourse is driven by the male desire to objectify and penetrate the female. She considered that the woman's sexual role is largely passive, and that "resentment is the most common form of feminine frigidity."

The sexologists
Scientific study of human sexuality began to take off after World War II, as society gradually became more open about sex, at least within the context of marriage. After the success of his 1948 report on male sexuality, American biologist Alfred Kinsey published *Sexual Behavior in the Human Female* in 1953. Together, they became known as the Kinsey Reports. He

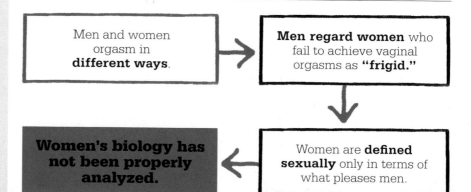

Men and women orgasm in **different ways**.

Men regard women who fail to achieve vaginal orgasms as **"frigid."**

Women are **defined sexually** only in terms of what pleases men.

Women's biology has not been properly analyzed.

See also: Sexual double standards 78–79 ▪ Achieving the right to legal abortion 156–159 ▪ Political lesbianism 180–181 ▪ Sex positivity 234–237 ▪ Raunch culture 282–283 ▪ Sexual abuse awareness 322–327

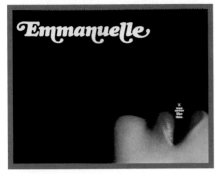

Sexually liberated women, such as Emmanuelle in this 1974 softcore porn film, were a popular subject in the media of the time. A more complex depiction of female sexuality was rare.

disagreed with Freud's view that vaginal orgasms are "superior;" the clitoris, he said, is the main site of stimulation. American researchers William Masters and Virginia Johnson also examined sexual dysfunction, response, and orgasm. Their 1966 study, *Human Sexual Response*, argued that clitoral or vaginal stimulation could both lead to orgasm.

Author Shere Hite holds a copy of *The Hite Report*. The study concluded that sexuality was culturally, not biologically, created and therefore attitudes needed to be challenged.

By the late 1960s, attitudes to sex had changed exponentially, as sex before marriage became more acceptable. In 1968, Anne Koedt wrote the influential essay "The Myth of the Vaginal Orgasm," which was published as a book in 1970. According to Koedt, vaginal stimulation alone was not enough for women to achieve orgasm, and because conventional sex positions did not stimulate the clitoris, women were left "frigid." This term, she says, placed the blame on women rather than on men.

Koedt argues that women who claimed to have vaginal orgasms were either confused by their lack of knowledge of their own anatomy, or were "faking it," and that men maintained this myth for a variety of reasons, including an overriding desire for penetration and a fear of becoming sexually expendable. Koedt's essay challenged views about heterosexual sex and about female sexuality. Some women used the work to promote lesbianism; others objected to the suggestion that they were faking orgasms.

Later feminists were influenced by Koedt's work. In 1976, American writer Shere Hite published a report on female sexuality based on a survey of 100,000 women. The responses indicated that most women did not achieve orgasm through vaginal penetration. Hite linked this failure to women's subordinate role in sex and demanded sexual pleasure for women as a right. ▪

Anne Koedt

US-based artist Anne Koedt was born in Denmark in 1941. Koedt's "The Myth of the Vaginal Orgasm" (1968) was first published in the New York Radical Women's journal of collected essays entitled *Notes from the First Year.* In 1968, she gave a well-known speech in which she called for feminist activists to learn from other revolutions. Later that year she cofounded a separatist group called The Feminists with the radical feminist and philosopher Ti-Grace Atkinson, but left the group in 1969 to form New York Radical Feminists (NYRF) with Shulamith Firestone. In 1978, Koedt became an associate of the Women's Institute for Freedom of the Press.

Key works

1968 "The Myth of the Vaginal Orgasm"
1973 *Radical Feminism*

> We are fed the myth of the liberated woman and her vaginal orgasm—an orgasm which in fact does not exist.
> **Anne Koedt**

I HAVE BEGUN TO MAKE A CONTRIBUTION

FEMINIST ART

IN CONTEXT

PRIMARY QUOTE
Judy Chicago, 1999

KEY FIGURES
**Carolee Schneemann,
Yoko Ono,
Marina Abramovich,
Judy Chicago,
Miriam Schapiro,
Barbara Kruger**

BEFORE
1930s–1960s Frida Kahlo
uses her own experiences as
her primary subject matter.

AFTER
2007 *WACK!* at the Museum
of Contemporary Art in Los
Angeles is the first major
retrospective of feminist art.

2017–2018 *Roots of "The
Dinner Party"* at the Brooklyn
Museum's Center for Feminist
Art in New York examines
Judy Chicago's landmark work.

In the 1960s, female artists
began to produce a new kind
of "feminist" art. Some of it
celebrated the female body, some
expressed anger at the inequalities
women faced, but all of it brought
female realities to the fore, rejecting
traditional attitudes about women.
There had been forerunners—
women such as the Mexican artist
Frida Kahlo—who were largely
unknown at the time, but were later
recognized for their vivid depictions
of women's experiences.

Female artists of the new era
were more forthright. They openly
challenged the canon of "great,"
mainly male, artists and their
traditional media of painting and

See also: Female autonomy in a male-dominated world 40–41 ▪ Intellectual freedom 106–107 ▪ Modern feminist publishing 142–143 ▪ Writing women into history 154–155 ▪ Guerrilla protesting 246–247

Frida Kahlo explored issues such as gender and race in a style that combined modern influences and Mexican folk art. Her first solo exhibition was in New York in 1938, her second in Paris in 1939.

sculpture. They found new ways of working and new types of spaces that circumvented the conventional art world. Embracing modern media and materials, they used performance and body art, video, photography, and installation.

Acting out art

Performance allowed artists to explore the relationship between the body as an active agent in a work of art and its more traditional role as an object to be observed. One of the first such projects was Carolee Schneemann's *Eye Body: 36 Transformative Actions* in 1963. Using her own body as "an integral material," she covered herself with paint, grease, chalk, and plastic and posed naked in the setting of her New York loft for a black-and-white film, shot by the Icelandic artist Erró. In *Interior Scroll*, Schneemann's most shocking and controversial piece, she stood naked on a table, unraveled a long scroll from her vagina, and read out the extracts from feminist texts inscribed on it.

Other artists, such as Yoko Ono and Marina Abramovich, used performance to explore themes of passivity and subjugation. In *Cut Piece* (1964), Ono sat motionless as members of the audience cut away pieces of her clothing until only her

I am trying to make art that relates to the deepest and most mythic concerns of human kind and I believe that, at this moment of history, feminism is humanism.
Judy Chicago

underwear was left. In *Rhythm 0* (1974), Abramovich presented the audience with 72 objects, ranging from a feather to a gun, and invited them to use them on her for her pleasure or to inflict pain.

Bea Nettles was among those who parodied and challenged earlier depictions of women in art. Her *Suzanna...Surprised* (1970) is a defiant new take on the biblical story of Susanna, startled by two »

Forgotten women artists

There are countless women artists whose names are no longer widely known. In the early 1900s, for example, Swedish artist Hilma af Klint produced abstract paintings predating those of Wassily Kandinsky and Piet Mondrian. In the 1920s and '30s, Hannah Höch, a leading German Dada artist, was one of the first to use photomontage, while Ukrainian-American Abstract Expressionist painter Janet Sobel, working in 1940s New York, influenced Jackson Pollock. In 1968, Nancy Graves became the first female artist to have a solo show at the Whitney Museum of American Art in New York, and in 1972, the Abstract Expressionist painter Alma Thomas's show at the Whitney was the first by an African-American woman.

Altarpiece no. 1 was one of three that af Klint created in 1915 to conclude her *Paintings of the Temple*. Its rainbow pyramid and sun reflect her spirituality.

Judy Chicago's *The Dinner Party* comprises a dining table set for major female figures in myth and history. To qualify for inclusion, each guest had to fulfil certain criteria set down by the artist.

Tried to **improve** the **lives of women**.

Made a **worthwhile contribution** to society.

Work **illuminates women's history**.

A **role model** for a more **equal future**.

lecherous elders as she bathed—a common subject in Renaissance painting. Combining photographic materials, quilting, and paint, Nettles creates a powerful, nude Suzanna gazing out defiantly from a faint backdrop of a garden.

In *Some Living American Women Artists* (1972), Mary Beth Edelson took a reproduction of Leonardo da Vinci's fresco of the Last Supper and collaged the heads of living artists, including Georgia O'Keefe, Lee Krasner, and Yoko Ono, onto the figures of Christ and his 12 disciples around the table. It is an ironic comment on the exclusion of women from the upper echelons of both society and organized religion. On a personal note, Louise Bourgeois exorcized memories of her overbearing father with her installation, *The Destruction of the Father* (1974), in which rounded forms frame a cavelike space enclosing a dining table covered with flesh-colored objects.

Martha Rosler's video *Semiotics of the Kitchen* (1975) parodies a television cooking show to attack domestic oppression. Slowly naming and demonstrating an alphabet of kitchen utensils, which at times seem to become weapons, she turns their everyday meaning into "a lexicon of rage and frustration," and ends by slashing the air with a knife to make the letter Z.

Down with hierarchies

In January 1971, art historian Linda Nochlin's essay "Why Have There Been No Great Women Artists?" argued that the absence of female artists from art history was due not to an innate inability to create great art, but to their exclusion from training, patronage, and exhibiting in the male-dominated art world. In 1976, Nochlin co-organized *Women Artists: 1550–1950* at the

Judy Chicago

Born Judith Sylvia Cohen in 1939, Chicago trained as a painter at the University of California in Los Angeles, where her tutors criticized her use of female imagery. Frustrated by the male-dominated art world, she created the first Feminist Art Program and, in 1973, opened the Feminist Studio Workshop. Her book *Through the Flower; My Struggles as a Woman Artist* was published in 1975. After her epic feminist work *The Dinner Party*, she turned to a broader range of subjects, while continuing to teach, write, and work with other artists; two later,

large-scale collaborative works—the *Holocaust Project* and *Resolutions*—employ a variety of crafts and art media. In 2018, *Time* magazine named Chicago as one of the 100 most influential people in the world.

Key works

1969–1970 *Pasadena Lifesavers*
1975–1979 *The Dinner Party*
1980–1985 *Birth Project*
1985–1993 *Holocaust Project: From Darkness into Light*
1995–2000 *Resolutions: A Stitch in Time*

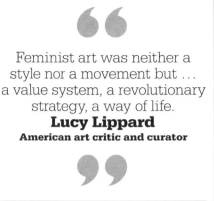

> " Feminist art was neither a style nor a movement but … a value system, a revolutionary strategy, a way of life.
> **Lucy Lippard**
> American art critic and curator "

Los Angeles County Museum of Art, the first such international exhibition in the US.

Judy Chicago founded the first college-level feminist art study course at California State University in 1970. A year later she moved it to the California Institute of the Arts with Miriam Schapiro. Out of this grew *Womanhouse* (1972), a collaborative project in which 28 artists and students turned each room of an old Hollywood house into a feminist installation.

Incorporating crafts

Miriam Schapiro became a leading member of the P&D (Pattern and Decoration) movement. Its members opposed divisions between high art and decorative art, and Schapiro collaged painting and fabrics in works she called "femmages." In 1975, Chicago embarked on *The Dinner Party*. One of feminist art's most iconic pieces, the multi-media installation incorporates ceramics, needlework, metalwork, and textiles. More than 100 artists contributed their work, highlighting crafts rather than male-dominated fine art and rejecting the notion of a single artist. All but one dinner plate is decorated with an elaborate vulva design; the

imagery was later criticized by some feminists, who thought it diminished, rather than honored, the women in the work.

Challenging stereotypes

During the 1980s, female artists produced works that directly challenged traditional notions of womanliness, especially as portrayed in mass media. They characterized such representations as artificial constructions by a male-dominated

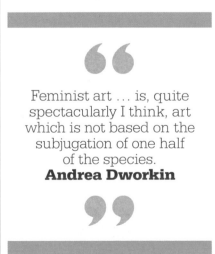

> " Feminist art … is, quite spectacularly I think, art which is not based on the subjugation of one half of the species.
> **Andrea Dworkin** "

This still from American artist Kara Walker's animated film *Song of the South* (2005) about the creation of African-America touches on the issues of gender, equality, and race commonly found in her work.

society. In *Untitled Film Stills* (1977–1980), photographer Cindy Sherman explores the idea that femininity is a series of poses that women take up in order to conform to society's expectations. Barbara Kruger's collages and conceptual art similarly show how graphic design and advertising reinforce female stereotypes. In 1985, the art-activist group Guerrilla Girls was formed to draw attention to sexism and racism in the art world.

In the 1990s, female artists focused more on individual concerns, in a variety of forms. These range from British artist Tracey Emin's autobiographical pieces to works by Iranian Shirin Neshat, such as *Women of Allah*, that investigate questions of gender, identity, and society in the Muslim world. ∎

NO MORE MISS AMERICA!
POPULARIZING WOMEN'S LIBERATION

IN CONTEXT

PRIMARY QUOTE
New York Radical Women, 1968

KEY FIGURE
Robin Morgan

BEFORE
1949 Simone de Beauvoir uses the term "liberation" in *The Second Sex*, urging women to liberate themselves from oppressive social expectations.

1966 The equal rights feminist group National Organization of Women (NOW) is founded in Washington, D.C.

AFTER
1970 British feminists protest at the Miss World beauty contest in London's Albert Hall.

1973 Arguing that civil rights activists and white feminists do not address black women's specific needs, the National Black Feminist Organization is founded in New York.

The Women's Liberation Movement burst onto the national stage in the US on September 7, 1968. On that day, about 400 feminists mounted a dramatic protest at the annual Miss America beauty pageant in Atlantic City, New Jersey. Their aim was to highlight the many ways in which women were objectified by men and to highlight the contest's racism. The protest made media headlines and "women's liberation" became a household term.

Sisterhood is powerful

The protest was the brainchild of New York Radical Women (NYRW), the city's first feminist organization, which had formed in the fall of 1967. Founding members included Shulamith Firestone (who later cofounded Redstockings), Pam Allen, Carol Hanisch, and Robin Morgan. Many members had experience of civil rights and anti–Vietnam War activism and were angered by the condescending attitudes of male activists toward them and women generally.

Initially, NYRW had just a dozen or so members. Their first public protest had been in

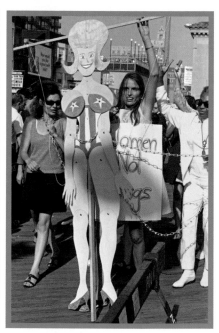

A chained marionette in mandatory high heels, scanty costume, and bouffant hair—so detested by feminists—is paraded during the 1968 Miss America protest.

Washington, D.C., in January 1968. While 5,000 women took part in an anti–Vietnam War march led by the politician and pacifist Jeannette Rankin, NYRW had organized a counter-event to highlight feminist concerns. Carrying banners with

See also: Radical feminism 137 ▪ Guerrilla protesting 246–247

slogans such as "Don't cry. Resist," they had conducted a mock burial of "traditional womanhood" and distributed leaflets emblazoned with the phrase "Sisterhood is Powerful"; this would become a famous slogan of the early years of women's liberation.

Street theater

It was the Miss America protest that captured public attention. Robin Morgan understood that it needed to be sensational. Feminists flooded into Atlantic City, paraded with placards, and crowned a sheep as Miss America while making sheep noises. They set up a "Freedom Trash Can," into which they threw an assortment of items associated with stereotypical femininity and "instruments of torture to women," including bras, girdles, high-heeled shoes, and copies of *Playboy* magazine. The intention was to set the trash can on fire; permission was refused, but news headlines gave rise to a long-lasting myth that feminists were "bra burners." The Miss America

> We are the women men warned us about.
> **Robin Morgan**

protest ended with a group of women unfurling a banner that read "Women's Liberation."

At much the same time, a second protest in Atlantic City targeted the Miss America event for its racist standards of beauty. Black women activists, who declared that the pageant upheld whiteness as the exclusive criterion, staged an alternative pageant. After riding through the city in a motorcade, contestants took the stage in the Ritz-Carlton Hotel, where 19-year-old Saundra

Williams from Philadelphia was crowned. Dressed in the conventional tiara and white gown, she wore her hair Afro style, performed an African dance, and told news reporters that black women were beautiful.

Telling the world

Both protests made headline news, with events streamed live to millions of viewers. Their impact was enormous. The Miss America protest brought the Women's Liberation Movement to the forefront of public consciousness and highlighted the commercial and social oppression and sexualization of women that the NYRW activists so abhorred. Similarly the Miss Black America event revealed the double standard of sexism and racism experienced by black women.

Women's liberation activism had taken off and other protests and demonstrations followed. By 1973, there were more than 2,000 Women's Liberation groups in the US alone, and the movement had spread worldwide. ▪

Robin Morgan

Born in Florida in 1941, Robin Morgan was a child actor. After studying at Columbia University, she worked with the Curtis Brown Literary Agency, where she published her own poetry. Politically active in the 1960s, she became a radical feminist and set up the Women's International Terrorist Conspiracy from Hell (W.I.T.C.H.) in 1968. In 1970, Morgan compiled *Sisterhood is Powerful*, an anthology of women's liberation writings.

In 1984, Morgan joined forces with Simone de Beauvoir and other feminists to found the

Sisterhood is Global Institute (SIGI), an international feminist think tank. Among other honors, in 2002, Morgan won a lifetime award from Equality Now, which promotes the human rights of women and girls worldwide.

Key works

1972 *Monsters*
1977 *Going Too Far*
1982 *The Anatomy of Freedom*
1984 *Sisterhood is Global*
2003 *Sisterhood is Forever*

OUR FEELINGS WILL LEAD US TO ACTIONS
CONSCIOUSNESS-RAISING

IN CONTEXT

PRIMARY QUOTE
Kathie Sarachild, 1968

KEY FIGURE
Kathie Sarachild

BEFORE
1949 In *The Second Sex*, Simone de Beauvoir identifies women as a class, sharing common experiences.

1963 Betty Friedan's *The Feminine Mystique* analyzes the unhappiness and isolation of white middle-class American women.

AFTER
1975 American feminist Susan Brownmiller publishes *Against Our Will*. She argues that men use rape to subordinate women.

2017 The #MeToo movement uses social media to raise awareness among women of sexual harassment in many areas of life.

One of the main ways in which the Women's Liberation Movement raised awareness was through consciousness-raising (CR). Women-only groups met in private homes and cafés to talk about aspects of their lived experiences, from childhood through to marriage and sexuality. Their aim was to show how personal difficulties were rooted in political issues that needed to be changed.

The concept of consciousness-raising emerged in 1967, when a group of women, some of whom were already left-wing or Civil Rights activists, formed New York Radical Women (NYRW). It was the first women's liberation group

Women join hands at the National Women's Conference in Houston, Texas, in 1977. The purpose of the event was to develop a plan of action to present to President Jimmy Carter.

See also: The roots of oppression 114–117 ▪ Patriarchy as social control 144–145 ▪ Rape as abuse of power 166–171 ▪ Trans-exclusionary radical feminism 172–173 ▪ Language and patriarchy 192–193

> Because we have lived so intimately with our oppressors, we have been kept from seeing our personal suffering as a political condition.
> **The Redstockings Manifesto**

in the city and among the first in the US. One evening, a member, Anne Forer, asked others in the group to provide examples of how they had been oppressed in their own lives. She said she needed to hear this in order to raise her own consciousness.

In 1968, Kathie Sarachild, another founding member of NYRW and a member of the radical feminist group Redstockings, wrote and also presented "A Program for Feminist Consciousness-Raising" at the first National Women's Liberation Conference, held near Chicago. Sarachild asserted that a mass liberation movement would develop when increasing numbers of women began to perceive the reality of their own oppression. The primary task of feminists, she believed, was to awaken a "class consciousness" among women.

CR takes off
In 1970, the phrase "the personal is political" appeared in print to encapsulate the importance of recognizing and sharing women's experience through consciousness-raising. It was used as a title for an article by NYRW member Carol Hanisch in *Notes from the Second Year*. By 1973, some 100,000 women were in CR groups across the US. Such gatherings typically consisted of no more than 12 women. Topics were decided in advance and each woman spoke in turn, sharing their experiences of oppression at work, at home, and in intimate relationships. Understanding was the object, not advice or criticism; each experience was regarded as equally valid.

Shaping the movement
Opponents trivialized CR meetings, describing them as gossip sessions or therapy, or felt they were not sufficiently political. The movement was also criticized for excluding men. However, supporters of consciousness-raising believed that the objectives of liberation should be shaped by the realities of women's lives.

The idea that the personal is political became one of the most important concepts in the Women's Liberation Movement. It maintains that the patriarchy defines and shapes family life and that sexual intercourse is political. Dismissing women's shared problems as personal, it argues, confines them to a subordinate role, and is just another way in which men oppress women. Male power is reinforced through violence (in society and in the home), marriage and childcare, and love and sex; once women's personal lives are seen as political, the basis of sexism can be found, challenged, and changed. ▪

Kathie Sarachild
The American feminist Kathie Sarachild was born Kathie Amatniek in 1943. In 1968, she dropped her father's surname and began using her mother's name, Sara, instead. She was the first to use the slogan "Sisterhood is Powerful" at a women's peace march in Washington, D.C., in 1968.

In 1969, Sarachild became an early member of the radical feminist group Redstockings; much later, in 2013, she edited the Redstockings anthology. Also in 2013, along with Carol Hanisch, Ti-Grace Atkinson, and others, she contributed to an open statement that questioned the silencing of those seeking to debate issues of gender.

Key works

1968 "A Program for Feminist Consciousness-Raising"
1973 "Consciousness-Raising: a Radical Weapon"
1979 *Feminist Revolution*

> Consciousness-raising groups are the backbone of the Women's Liberation Movement.
> **Black Maria Collective**

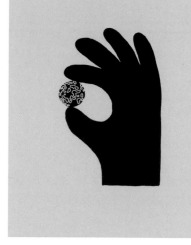

AN EQUALIZER, A LIBERATOR
THE PILL

The introduction of the oral contraceptive pill in the US in 1960 marked a scientific breakthrough and, for women, the debut of an era of unprecedented social and sexual freedom. The Pill, as it soon became known, is composed of synthetic hormones that offer far greater protection against unwanted pregnancies than earlier contraceptive methods.

The advent of the Pill was a triumph for birth-control activist Margaret Sanger, who had helped biologist Gregory Pincus secure the funds to research the drug. Within a few years, Pincus, together with reproductive scientist Min Chueh Chang, and gynecologist John Rock had developed the first Pill, Enovid. Clinical trials were carried out in the US and Puerto Rico.

A new freedom
Within two years of its approval in the US, the Pill was being taken by 1.2 million American women, although individual states could veto its use. In Britain, it began to be prescribed by the National Health

It enabled me to purposefully have a life that I designed. It allowed me to start college and a career.
Gloria Feldt
Former CEO of Planned Parenthood

Service in 1961, but was available only to married women until 1967. While social conservatives considered the Pill to be a licence for promiscuity, feminists such as Sanger knew that its advent heralded more than sexual enjoyment. It gave women control over pregnancy, enabling them to limit families and pursue careers. Although its potential health risks had still to be addressed, the Pill was liberating—and here to stay. ■

See also: Birth control 98–103 ▪ Achieving the right to legal abortion 156–159 ▪ Reproductive justice 268

WE ARE GOING ALL THE WAY
RADICAL FEMINISM

IN CONTEXT

PRIMARY QUOTE
The Redstockings manifesto, 1969

KEY ORGANIZATION
Redstockings

BEFORE
1920 With the backing of feminists such as Alexandra Kollontai, the Soviet Union legalizes abortion.

AFTER
1973 The US Supreme Court rules in favor of abortion rights up to the third trimester of pregnancy.

1989 Redstockings members hold an abortion speakout in New York to mark the 20th anniversary of their first event.

2017 US President Donald Trump signs a bill that prevents state-approved private health insurers from offering abortion coverage.

Founded by Shulamith Firestone and Ellen Willis in 1969, Redstockings (a name indicating both far-left and feminist sympathies) emerged when New York Radical Women broke up and dispersed. Similar groups included W.I.T.C.H. (Women's International Terrorist Conspiracy from Hell). The aim of this radical brand of feminism was to end women's oppression by reclaiming their sovereignty over the female body and enacting radical social change.

Redstockings' tactics consisted of "zaps," a form of direct action protest, and street theater. Largely based in New York City, they also had a chapter in Florida, while Redstockings West of San Francisco operated independently.

Abortion activism
In February 1969, a Redstockings protest disrupted a New York State hearing on abortion reform. Noting that of 15 speakers, the only female was a nun, the group appealed for the right of women to testify on the issue, citing their own experiences.

A month later, Redstockings activists staged a public abortion speakout at the Washington Square Methodist Church in New York. At this event, 12 women spoke about their own illegal abortions and the extreme pain, fear, danger, and exorbitant costs involved. Gloria Steinem, who reported on the speakout, said that it turned her from objective journalist to activist. ∎

A member of W.I.T.C.H. (Women's International Terrorist Conspiracy from Hell) rides down a San Francisco street in 1974. W.I.T.C.H. was Redstockings' more extreme twin.

See also: Marxist feminism 52–55 ▪ Anarcha-feminism 108–109 ▪ Uterus envy 146 ▪ Wages for housework 147 ▪ Achieving the right to legal abortion 156–159

FEMINISM WILL CRACK THROUGH THE BASIC STRUCTURES OF SOCIETY
FAMILY STRUCTURES

IN CONTEXT

PRIMARY QUOTE
Shulamith Firestone, 1970

KEY FIGURES
**Shulamith Firestone,
Gayle Rubin**

BEFORE
1950s After World War II,
women in North America and
Britain are encouraged to leave
their wartime careers and
return to the domestic sphere.

1963 Betty Friedan's *The
Feminine Mystique* identifies
dissatisfaction among white,
middle-class housewives
as "the problem that has
no name."

AFTER
1989 The United Nations'
Convention on the Rights of
the Child includes the right to
be free from all discrimination.

2015 American retailer Target
announces it will no longer
divide children's toys and
bedding by gender.

A woman prepares lunch while her
family relaxes in this 1950s image of
a white American family at home in
the suburbs. This patriarchal family
structure was the national "ideal."

I n the 1950s, white, middle-
class American families,
benefiting from the postwar
economic boom, moved to the
suburbs in droves. The image of
success they created led to the
idealization of the white, heterosexual
nuclear family, in which men were
responsible for earning an income
and women played a lesser role. The
subordination of women contrasted
with the independence many of
them had gained in wartime.

In her 1970 book *The Dialectic of
Sex*, radical feminist Shulamith
Firestone argues that the inequality
between men and women is the
foundation for all other forms of
oppression in society and is
closely bound up in the notion

See also: Emancipation from domesticity 34–35 ▪ The roots of oppression 114–117 ▪ The problem with no name 118–123 ▪ Patriarchy as social control 144–145

Unless revolution uproots the basic social organization, the biological family … the tapeworm of exploitation will never be annihilated.
Shulamith Firestone

Shulamith Firestone

Born in Ottawa, Canada, in 1945 as the oldest daughter of a German mother and an American father, Shulamith Firestone grew up in an Orthodox Jewish household. The family moved to St. Louis, Missouri, when she was a child.

Firestone's father exerted a patriarchal control over the household, which Shulamith railed against. She earned two bachelor's degrees before moving to New York City in 1967, where she cofounded New York Radical Women. She also formed the Chicago Women's Liberation Union with feminist Jo Freeman as an anticapitalist, multi-issue coalition, and the group Redstockings with Ellen Willis.

A revolutionary feminist, Firestone argued that women should overturn the nuclear family structure in her 1970 book, *The Dialectic of Sex.* Withdrawing from political life in the 1970s, Firestone became a painter. She struggled with schizophrenia for decades before dying in 2012, aged 67.

of the nuclear family. She argues against philosophers Karl Marx and Friedrich Engels' theory that the origin of women's oppression dates from the establishment of private property. Instead, Firestone claims, men's oppression of women goes further back, "beyond recorded history," to sexual inequality in the animal kingdom and the biological family.

Burden of child-bearing

Locating inequality in reproduction, Firestone states that women's inferior position in society can be traced to their vulnerability during pregnancy and their responsibility for children. Challenging these limitations, Firestone declares "We are no longer just animals," and proposes a range of radical changes to society. She calls for raising children in a gender-neutral fashion that would render sex differences culturally irrelevant, and she also imagines the invention of new technologies that would allow children to be born outside of women's bodies.

Firestone argues for the abolition of the heterosexual nuclear family altogether, instead replacing it with unmarried egalitarian couples and collectives of people who would raise children together. Children, she emphasizes, must also be given greater rights and freedom of expression.

Underpinning Firestone's ideas for a future egalitarian society is socialist feminism. She argues that technological advances have the

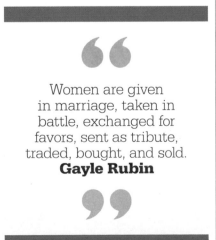

Women are given in marriage, taken in battle, exchanged for favors, sent as tribute, traded, bought, and sold.
Gayle Rubin

potential to eliminate intellectually deadening work, freeing up the workforce for jobs that people find rewarding. She suggests that women would also be freed from performing limited roles in the domestic sphere.

Critique of nuclear family

Other feminists besides Firestone have critiqued the heterosexual nuclear family structure, including Gayle Rubin in her 1975 article "The Traffic in Women: Notes on the 'Political Economy' of Sex." Rubin writes that the history of Western marriage is largely the history of men exchanging women as commodities. She also argues that women's confinement to the domestic sphere results in women performing various types of labor to sustain the male worker (cooking, raising children, doing the laundry, and cleaning the house, for example). Yet because these types of labor go unpaid, women are unable to acquire the economic capital that typically results from men's work. ▪

WOMEN HAVE VERY LITTLE IDEA HOW MUCH MEN HATE THEM

CONFRONTING MISOGYNY

IN CONTEXT

PRIMARY QUOTE
Germaine Greer, 1970

KEY FIGURES
Germaine Greer

BEFORE
1792 British reformer Mary Wollstonecraft describes in *A Vindication of the Rights of Woman* how social conditioning in a patriarchal society trivializes women.

1963 American feminist Betty Friedan defines the "feminine mystique" as an idealized femininity impossible for women to attain.

AFTER
1975 In *Against Our Will*, American feminist Susan Brownmiller argues that men use rape as a tool to keep women fearful and oppressed.

1981 Radical American feminist Andrea Dworkin asserts that pornography dehumanizes women.

The Women's Liberation Movement of the 1960s and '70s saw an outpouring of writings by feminists. One of the liveliest and most provocative was *The Female Eunuch* by Germaine Greer. Published in 1970, it was a best seller and became one of the key texts of second-wave feminism. Greer's main thesis is that women are effectively castrated socially, sexually, and culturally—hence the book's title.

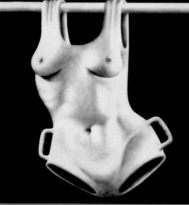

Arguing that women must learn to question basic assumptions about female "normality," Greer begins by looking at the female "Body," from cells through to curves, sex, and "the wicked womb"—the source of menstrual blood. She claims that women are regarded as sexual objects for the use of other sexual beings, specifically men, and that women's sexuality is misrepresented as passive. The qualities that are valued in women, she says, are those of the castrate: timidity, languor, and delicacy.

Moving on to the "Soul," Greer explores the stereotypes that mold women from birth through puberty and into adulthood, arguing that women are conditioned to avoid independent thought and behavior, and to encourage a view of themselves as "illogical, subjective, and generally silly." For Greer, the castration of women is carried out in terms of a masculine-feminine polarity, in which men have commandeered all the energy and

This arresting cover, designed by British artist John Holmes for the 1971 edition, has been described by writer Monica Dux as "a work of art that has in itself become iconic."

See also: Sexual pleasure 126–127 ▪ Family structures 138–139 ▪ The male gaze 164–165 ▪ Rape as abuse of power 166–171 ▪ Trans feminism 286–289 ▪ Sexism is everywhere 308–309

> Women have somehow been separated from their libido, from their faculty of desire, from their sexuality.
> **Germaine Greer**

streamlined it into an "aggressive, conquistatorial power," which reduces heterosexuality to a sadomasochistic pattern. Greer argues that love itself has been perverted and distorted by either the presentation of a romantic myth or by the pornographic creation of women as male sexual fantasies.

Greer makes a powerful assault on the nuclear family: not only is it stifling for women, she says, but tensions within the family are harmful for children's wellbeing.

She proposes that children should instead be brought up more freely and communally.

Women haters

In what was perhaps one of the most provocative statements in *The Female Eunuch*, Greer claims that love has been so perverted it has turned to hate, loathing, and disgust. She argues that deep down, men hate and resent women and are disgusted by them, particularly during sex. To prove her point, she cites examples of criminal attacks on women, domestic abuse, gang rapes, and the many and varied sexual insults used by men to describe women.

In the final section of her book, Greer suggests that women should refuse to enter into patriarchal relationships such as marriage— and that if they do and are unhappy, they should leave. They should refuse to be unpaid workers and should question all stereotypic assumptions about women. Above all, she argues that women should reclaim their sexuality, energy,

and power. By freeing themselves from the processes of a misogynist society, Greer claims, women can work toward their own sexual and social liberation.

Greer wanted *The Female Eunuch* to be subversive, and it stands alone as a radical feminist text that does not slot into any particular feminist perspective. With its explicit sexual language, its provocative call to liberation influenced countless women. ▪

> Womanpower means the self-determination of women … all the baggage of paternalistic society will have to be thrown overboard.
> **Germaine Greer**

Germaine Greer

Born in Melbourne, Australia, in 1939, Germaine Greer attended a Catholic school before winning a scholarship in 1964 to study English literature at Cambridge University in the UK. From 1968 until 1972, she was an assistant lecturer at the University of Warwick, and contributed to the underground magazine *Oz*.

With the success of *The Female Eunuch*, Greer became a major public figure, appearing on talk shows and writing articles. She founded the journal *Tulsa Studies in Women's Literature* in the US, started a publishing company, and

returned to Warwick University as professor of English. In 2018, she angered many feminists by criticizing aspects of the #MeToo movement and by suggesting that rape sentences should be lowered in some cases.

Key works

1970 *The Female Eunuch*
1979 *The Obstacle Race*
1984 *Sex and Destiny: The Politics of Human Fertility*
1991 *The Change: Women, Aging and the Menopause*
1999 *The Whole Woman*

MS. AUTHORS TRANSLATED A MOVEMENT INTO A MAGAZINE
MODERN FEMINIST PUBLISHING

IN CONTEXT

PRIMARY QUOTE
Letty Cottin Pogrebin, 1999

KEY FIGURES
**Gloria Steinem,
Florence Howe,
Carmen Callil**

BEFORE
1849 America's first feminist magazine begins publishing monthly editions.

1910 *Seito* (Bluestocking), a monthly literary magazine for women, is launched in Japan.

1917 *The Woman Citizen* launches in the US; it focuses on women's political education.

AFTER
1996 *Bitch* magazine is launched in Portland to provide a thoughtful feminist response to popular culture.

2011 Emily Books is founded in New York by Emily Gould and Ruth Curry; it sends subscribers selected e-books (mostly by women) each month.

Women's periodicals and journals flourished in the 19th century, especially in the US, where securing the right to vote was a major goal for women. With suffrage largely achieved by the late 1920s on both sides of the Atlantic (though not in France until 1944), the number of feminist publications began to dwindle.

A few writers such as Virginia Woolf and Simone de Beauvoir remained potent voices. De Beauvoir's 1949 book *The Second Sex*, which deplored the historical subordination of women, has been credited with inspiring second-wave feminism.

Feminist publishing emerged in the 1970s to highlight issues that troubled contemporary women. Suffocating domesticity, as depicted by Betty Friedan's best-selling *The Feminine Mystique* (1963), was an early spur to action, as was the journalist and activist Gloria Steinem's account of the demeaning exploitation she experienced as a Playboy Bunny, also published that year. Publishing by and for women was part of the "revolution" that Steinem talked about in her speeches, arguing that women should not merely seek reform: the world—and especially politics—needed fundamental change.

Taking up the challenge
Off our Backs was the combative title of one of the new American feminist periodicals, edited by a collective of women and first

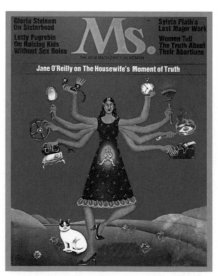

***Ms.* magazine** was launched in spring 1972. The cover of its first issue depicts the Indian goddess Durga with eight arms, here representing the many roles a woman fulfills, including ironer, driver, cook, and correspondent.

See also: Intellectual freedom 106–107 ▪ The roots of oppression 114–117 ▪ Consciousness-raising 134–135 ▪ Writing women into history 154–155 ▪ Bringing feminism online 294–297

Gloria Steinem

Born in 1934, Gloria Steinem became perhaps the best-known of second-wave American feminists. After graduating from Smith College in the US in 1956, she spent two years in India on a scholarship, where she absorbed Ghandian principles that guided her activism. She soon became one of the Women's Liberation Movement's most prolific writers and most articulate advocates. In 1963, her first-person exposé of the vulnerability of the young women who worked as Playboy Bunnies fueled the feminist cause, helped improve conditions at the clubs, and is still used in journalism classes today. She cofounded *Ms.* magazine in 1972 and has remained a lifelong campaigner for women's rights. In 2013, she received the Presidential Medal of Freedom, the highest US civilian honor.

Key works

1983 *Outrageous Acts and Everyday Rebellions*
1992 *Revolution from Within*
1994 *Moving Beyond Words*
2015 *My Life on the Road*

published in 1970. In Britain, *Spare Rib*, launched in 1971, voiced the ideas and concerns of the Women's Liberation Movement, examining topics such as body image, race, class, and women's sexuality. A year later, *Broadsheet* became New Zealand's first feminist magazine, focusing on both national and international women's issues. In 1972, Steinem and Dorothy Pitman Hughes founded *Ms.* magazine; its initial test issue sold 300,000 copies nationwide in eight days. It was the first American magazine to feature prominent women speaking out on controversial subjects, including criminalized abortion, domestic violence, pornography, sexual harassment, and date rape.

Feminist publishing houses

In Britain and the US, feminist book publishing also sprang to life in the early 1970s. Together with her husband Paul Lauter, the American author and publisher Florence Howe launched The Feminist Press in 1970 to reprint feminist classics, as well as textbooks for the new field of women's studies. In 1973, British publisher Carmen Callil founded Virago Press; its name means "a warlike woman," and its apple logo refers to the forbidden fruit of knowledge tasted by Eve in the Bible. In 1978, Virago began its Modern Classics series, which revived the work of hundreds of female writers. By the mid-1980s, there were at least seven feminist publishers in the UK, as well as

> ❝
> Steinem's seminal essay ["A Bunny's Tale"] marked one of the first times a woman publicly challenged society's stance on female beauty standards.
> *Vogue*
> September, 2017
> ❞

mainstream publishers that had their own feminist lists. In the US, Aunt Lute Books began publishing multicultural feminist works in 1982.

New female authors

Further powering the women-in-print movement was a wave of new authors, such as Alice Walker, Margaret Atwood, Alice Munro, and Toni Morrison, and a female audience hungry for their stories and views. Feminist bookshops appeared—at least 100 in Britain and North America by 1980—making the works of these authors and the discussion of women's issues accessible to a wider public.

Eventually, however, the rise of huge bookstore chains took its toll on the independents. In the 1980s, a number of feminist presses and magazines also folded, although of the 64 women's publishing companies launched in the US between 1970 and 1991, 21 were still trading in 1999. Recent accounts suggest that feminist publishing is finding fresh impetus in the 21st century. ▪

PATRIARCHY, REFORMED OR UNREFORMED, IS PATRIARCHY STILL
PATRIARCHY AS SOCIAL CONTROL

IN CONTEXT

PRIMARY QUOTE
Kate Millett, 1970

KEY FIGURE
Kate Millett

BEFORE
1895 American suffragist Elizabeth Cady Stanton challenges the religious orthodoxy of male supremacy in *The Woman's Bible*.

1949 Simone de Beauvoir describes the historical, social, and psychological roots of women's oppression in *The Second Sex*.

AFTER
1981 In the US, radical feminist Andrea Dworkin argues in *Pornography: Men Possessing Women* that pornography is linked to violence against women.

1986 American feminist historian Gerda Lerne publishes *The Creation of Patriarchy*.

Patriarchy, the social and political system of male power over women, was a key target for radical feminists in the 1960s and '70s. Their theories on the subject were laid out in *Sexual Politics* by the American writer and activist Kate Millett. Published in 1970, the book defines and analyzes patriarchy and examines the multiple ways in which it oppresses women. The book's title reflects Millett's argument that sex, like other areas of life that are usually considered personal, has a political dimension

To radical feminists such as Kate Millett, the family was inherently patriarchal, with girls learning to be passive and boys taking on more assertive roles soon after birth.

See also: Family structures 138–139 ■ Rape as abuse of power 166–171 ■ Language and patriarchy 192–193

> Sex is a status category with political implications.
> **Kate Millett**

that is frequently neglected. If politics refers to power-based relationships, where one group of people controls another, then sexual relations are, by their very nature, political. For Millett, sexual politics refers to male control over women, and underpins a patriarchal society where all areas of power—including government, political office, religion, military, industry, science, finance, and academia—are entirely within male hands.

Patriarchy begins at home

Like other radical feminists, Millett sees no biological reason for male dominance. Instead, she argues, the gender identities of men and women are formed early in life through parental and cultural notions of gender. The family is "patriarchy's chief institution" because it mirrors and reinforces patriarchal structures in society, and behavior within the family is established and controlled by men.

Education, too, Millett believes, reinforces patriarchy, creating an imbalance by directing young women toward humanities and social sciences, while channeling young men into science, technology, engineering, the professions, and business. Control in these fields is political, serving the interests of patriarchy in industry, government, and the military.

Force and habit

Millett argues that socialization, or the process of acquiring learned behaviors, within patriarchy is so efficient that force is rarely needed. However, she points to one exception where the power of patriarchy does rely on sexual force: rape, in which aggression, hatred, contempt, and the desire to violate combine in a particularly misogynistic form of patriarchy.

For Millett, patriarchy is so embedded in the psychology of men and women that the character structure it creates in both sexes becomes "even more a habit of mind and a way of life than a political system." The shifts in women's legal, social, and sexual status achieved by feminists since the 1830s, Millett argues, did nothing to change patriarchy. Even winning the vote for women did not damage patriarchy because the political system was still defined by men. ■

> A sexual revolution begins with the emancipation of women, who are the chief victims of patriarchy.
> **Kate Millett**

Kate Millett

American feminist Kate Millett was born in St. Paul, Minnesota, in 1934. She studied at the University of Minnesota; St. Hilda's College, Oxford, UK; and at New York City's Columbia University. She became a committee member of the National Organization for Women (NOW) when it was formed in 1966, although her feminism proved to be more radical. The publication of *Sexual Politics* in 1970 was followed by other feminist works, including *Three Lives* (1971), a documentary film.

Also a sculptor, Millett married a fellow sculptor in 1965. Plagued by mental illness from the early 1970s, she then added mental health to her politics and activism. After divorce, she came out as a lesbian and married a photographer, Sophie Keir. The pair remained together until Millett's death in 2017.

Key works

1970 *Sexual Politics*
1974 *Flying*
1990 *The Loony-Bin Trip*
1994 *The Politics of Cruelty*
2001 *Mother Millett*

UTERUS ENVY PLAGUES THE MALE UNCONSCIOUS
UTERUS ENVY

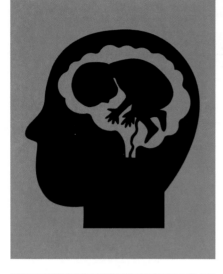

IN CONTEXT

PRIMARY QUOTE
Antoinette Fouque, 2004

KEY ORGANIZATION
Psychanalyse et politique

BEFORE
1905 Sigmund Freud advances the concept of "penis envy" in *Three Contributions to the Theory of Sexuality*.

1970–1971 Jacques Lacan develops the theory "Woman does not exist" into the concept "there is no such thing as Woman."

AFTER
1979 Antoinette Fouque registers the Mouvement de Libération des femmes as a commercial trademark of "Psych et po," which prevents other feminists from using it.

1989 Influenced by Fouque, the Women's Alliance for Democracy (AFD) and the Misogyny Observatory are founded in France.

Formed in France in 1968, the Mouvement de Libération des femmes (MLF) was an umbrella feminist organization that prided itself on its diversity and disregard for "masculine" concepts of hierarchy. It came to prominence in 1970, when members laid a wreath for the Wife of the Unknown Soldier near the Tomb of the Unknown Soldier, at the Arc de Triomphe in Paris.

One group within the MLF was the Psychanalyse et politique ("Psych et po") led by psychoanalyst Antoinette Fouque. While most French feminists linked women's biological difference with their oppression, Psych et po asserted that this difference, which had been suppressed by the "phallic order" of patriarchy, was the source of women's potential liberation.

Fouque believed misogyny was driven by men's envy of women's ability to give birth. Influenced by the ideas of the psychoanalyst Jacques Lacan, Fouque said that it was only through psychoanalytic exploration of the unconscious that

women could "return to the Mother;" reject the Father; and produce a new, authentic, feminine consciousness, a sexual and symbolic power that was not constructed by men. She strongly criticized the rest of French feminism as "phallic feminism," and as much the enemy as patriarchy.

In 1972, Fouque established the publishing house Editions des femmes, founded to distribute women's writings that were "repressed, censored, and rejected" by bourgeois publishers. ∎

> The feminism of non-difference—sexual, economic, political—is the master trump card of gynocide.
> **Antoinette Fouque**

See also: The roots of oppression 114–117 ∎ The male gaze 164–165 ∎ Poststructuralism 182–187 ∎ Gender is performative 258–261

WE ARE ALWAYS THEIR INDISPENSABLE WORKFORCE
WAGES FOR HOUSEWORK

IN CONTEXT

PRIMARY QUOTE
Selma James, 1975

KEY ORGANIZATION
Wages for Housework

BEFORE
1848 In *The Communist Manifesto*, philosophers Karl Marx and Friedrich Engels argue that women in bourgeois society are exploited as "mere instruments of production."

1969 Leftist students in Italy agitate for social reform, culminating in "Hot Autumn," a period of strikes.

AFTER
1975 Margaret Prescod and Wilmette Brown found Black Women for Wages for Housework in New York.

1981 Ruth Taylor Todasco sets up the No Bad Women, Just Bad Laws Coalition in Tulsa, Oklahoma, focusing on the decriminalization of sex work.

T he idea that the state should pay women for the domestic work they perform for their families was first raised in Italy in 1972. The concept captured the imagination of the media (pro and anti) and quickly transmuted into the international campaign, Wages for Housework.

The movement's leaders—Selma James, Mariarosa Dalla Costa, Silvia Federici, and Brigitte Galtier—were members of the Italian intellectual movement Operaismo (Workerism). Drawing upon Marxist theories, Operaismo advocated that work was the seat of one's power base

in society and that a fair wage was essential for any work to be recognized as socially valuable. Wages for Housework argued that domestic work, childcare, and even sex formed women's power base and that women should demand both payment for their services and better working conditions.

The activists argued that the work women did at home—which included maintaining the health of the family and producing future workers—underpinned industry and profit. They viewed welfare and child benefit payments as wages that women were owed. They also criticized feminists who saw women's work outside the home as more valuable and liberating.

Since 1975, the campaign has expanded to include groups such as Wages Due Lesbians, which have similar financial and social goals. ∎

A 1950s housewife runs the household laundry through a wringer. Unpaid and often unseen, such work was, feminists argued, the basis of women's powerlessness.

See also: Unionization 46–51 ▪ Marxist feminism 52–55 ▪ Gross domestic product 217 ▪ Pink-collar feminism 228–229

HEALTH MUST BE DEFINED BY US

WOMAN-CENTERED HEALTH CARE

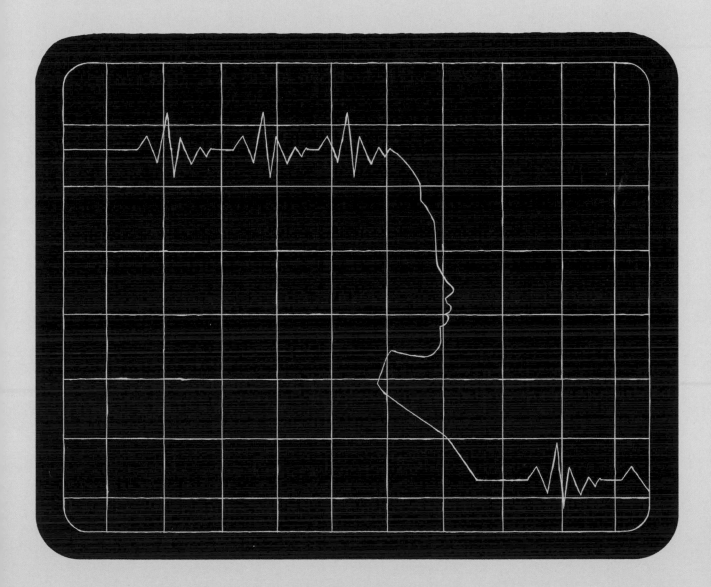

IN CONTEXT

PRIMARY QUOTE
**The Doctor's
Group, 1970**

KEY ORGANIZATION
**Boston Women's Health
Book Collective**

BEFORE
1916 American activist
Margaret Sanger opens the
first birth control clinic in
Brooklyn, New York.

Early 1960s The FDA (Food
and Drug Administration)
approves use of the Pill. It is
soon widely available, but only
for married couples.

AFTER
1975 The Federation of
Feminist Women's Health
Centers is established, with
branches in major US cities.

1975 The National Women's
Health Network—the "action
arm" of the American women's
health movement—carries out
its first demonstration.

> When women give birth
> they are controlled by a
> male-dominated,
> autocratic, hierarchical
> medical system.
> **Sheila Kitzinger**

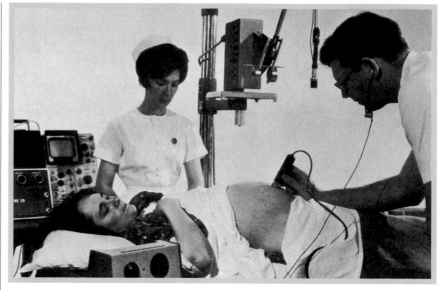

A pregnant woman has an ultrasound
at Winnipeg General Hospital, Canada.
Many women benefited from high-tech
prenatal care in the 1970s, but some
felt "over-medicalized."

Until the 1970s, women's
sexual and reproductive
health was rarely discussed
or even understood by women
themselves. Doctors would typically
give medical diagnoses to the
husbands of the women they
examined and women's own
experiences were discounted.
Access to contraception was
restricted and childbirth was often
a medicated, surgical procedure.

Second-wave feminism and
the contraceptive pill changed
women's relationship to pregnancy
and sex. Out of this context arose
the women's health movement: a
revolution that challenged medical
and male control over women. Its
aim was to enable women to have
knowledge of, and power over,
their own bodies.

Body knowledge
In 1969, at a sexual health
workshop at a conference of the
Women's Liberation Movement in
Boston, 12 women ranging in age
from 23 to 39 discussed their
struggle to find good medical care.
This led them to form the Doctor's
Group and to publish a 193-page

booklet entitled "Women and
Their Bodies: a Course." The
booklet sought to educate women
about their bodies, dispel feelings
of shame, stigma, or self-blame,
and improve their relationships
with medical professionals. The
text was distributed by hand and
contained candid discussions of
female anatomy, menstruation,
sexuality and relationships, sexual
health, nutrition, pregnancy, birth,
and contraception.

In 1971, the booklet's title was
changed to *Our Bodies, Ourselves*
(*OBOS*) and the Doctor's Group
became the Boston Women's Health
Book Collective. In 1973, the first
commercial, expanded edition of
OBOS went on sale. Its frank advice
on lesbianism, masturbation, and
abortion shocked the public.

The book was updated many
times over the years. Early editions
focused on the idea of patients
as the passive victims of the

See also: Better medical treatment for women 76–77 ▪ Birth control 98–103 ▪ Achieving the right to legal abortion 156–159 ▪ Reproductive justice 268 ▪ Campaigning against FGC 280–281

medical establishment. Much writing from the women's health movement stressed the inherent imbalance of power in doctor-patient relationships and argued for women's right to have more knowledge to redress this.

Accessibility was a key aspect of the women's health movement. According to *OBOS*, doctors used medical jargon to maintain their power. Crucially, the text of *OBOS* was filled with personal experiences and anecdotes, which became just as important to the women's health movement as scientific and medical data. Echoing Germaine Greer's famous rallying cry in *The Female Eunuch* (1970) for feminists to taste their menstrual blood, the authors told readers: "You are your body and you are not obscene."

Early versions of *OBOS* were more politically focused, emphasizing the connection between women's health and their socioeconomic background. Knowledge of women's bodies, the writers argued, demands knowledge of the social and political climate in which women move. Women

It was exciting to learn facts about our bodies, but it was even more exciting to talk about how we felt about our bodies.
Our Bodies, Ourselves

Nearly every physical experience we have as a woman is so alienating that we have been filled with extreme feelings of disgust and loathing for our own bodies.
Our Bodies, Ourselves

did not just need to learn about their own bodies; they had to use that knowledge to question the medical establishment and push for better access to health care for all strata of society.

Birth control
Nowhere was the political relevance of the women's health movement more evident than when it came to reproductive choices. The *OBOS* chapter on birth control opens with the declaration that women should have the right to make their own decisions about having children, including whether and when they will have children, and if so how many. This declaration continued the close connection between birth control and women's rights that existed throughout the 20th century.

As well as advising women to make contact with their local branch of Planned Parenthood, a nonprofit organization for sexual and reproductive health care, the book also details the safety and »

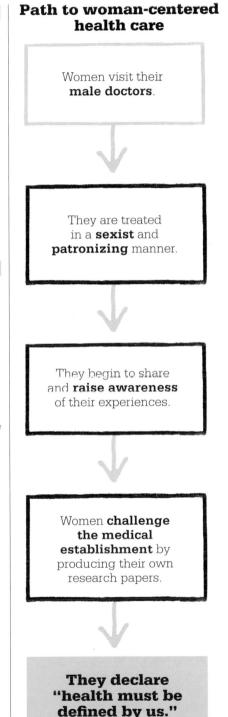

Path to woman-centered health care

Women visit their **male doctors**.

↓

They are treated in a **sexist** and **patronizing** manner.

↓

They begin to share and **raise awareness** of their experiences.

↓

Women **challenge the medical establishment** by producing their own research papers.

↓

They declare "health must be defined by us."

Sheila Kitzinger

Born in Somerset, UK, in 1929, the daughter of a midwife and campaigner for birth control, Sheila Kitzinger brought about a major change in attitudes to childbirth. After studying social anthropology at Oxford, she married and gave birth to the first of five daughters at home—an experience she found overwhelmingly positive. An advocate of woman-centered childbirth and home births for low-risk pregnancies, in 1958 Kitzinger helped found the Natural Childbirth Trust (as it became known from 1961). She wrote many books on pregnancy and parenting and lectured all over the world. She believed childbirth should be seen as a natural, even joyful event.

In 1982, Kitzinger was made an MBE (Member of the British Empire) in honor of her services to childbirth. She died in 2015.

Key works

1962 *The Experience of Childbirth*
1979 *The Good Birth Guide*
2005 *The Politics of Birth*
2015 *A Passion for Birth*

efficacy of birth control methods such as the Pill, IUDs, diaphragms, and spermicides. It also includes warnings about the withdrawal method and the potential side-effects of the Pill.

Much feminist writing about birth control emphasizes its psychological impact on women: they are the ones who get pregnant if it fails, and they resent having to take sole responsibility. Until men take an unwanted pregnancy as seriously as women do, *OBOS* argues, they will continue to consider contraception a female problem. "What will it take," the text asks, "for us to have pleasurable, fulfilling, guilt-free sexual relations? Far more than just good birth control methods. But that, at least, is a start."

Having children

It was widely accepted in mid-20th-century America and elsewhere that pregnancy and motherhood were key to women's fulfilment. In *The Second Sex* (1949), Simone de Beauvoir says that in pregnancy and motherhood women lose their sense of self and become "passive instruments." She writes that motherhood leaves a woman

> 66
> We have been ignorant of how our bodies function and this enables males, particularly professionals … to intimidate us in doctors' offices and clinics of every kind.
> **Our Bodies, Ourselves**
> 99

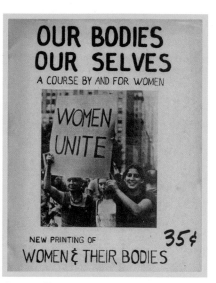

Our Bodies, Ourselves has gone through many different versions since 1970, and had been published in 31 languages by 2017. This cover is from the 1971 version of the book.

"riveted to her body" like an animal, vulnerable to domination by men and nature.

A few years later, author and academic Sheila Kitzinger began to promote a contrasting approach toward pregnancy and childbirth, encouraging women to see the delivery process as a positive event. Her highly influential 1962 book *The Experience of Childbirth* was a manifesto for the idea of a woman-centered birth, encouraging mothers to have autonomy over pregnancy and childbirth and resist the medicalization of labor and the dominance of male doctors.

The *OBOS* chapters on pregnancy and childbearing fall between de Beauvoir's view and Kitzinger's, declaring that women and children fare better when conception is chosen freely. With detailed descriptions of fertilization, physical symptoms, pregnancy, labor, and post-labor, *OBOS* encourages women to become

Cher Sivey prepares to give birth to baby Wilde in Stroud, UK, in 2011. During labor in a birthing pool, she affirmed that her body and her baby did not need outside help in this process.

active participants in conception. Like Kitzinger, they challenge the traditional doctor–pregnant woman relationship, and like de Beauvoir, emphasize that pregnancy involved a struggle to come to terms with an identity change. It is this struggle, the authors believe, that could lead to conditions such as post-natal depression, because women have no language to express how they feel, or may feel guilt about their feelings. In the same vein as Kitzinger, *OBOS* argues that it is necessary to come to terms with the pregnancy and childbirth process. Emphasizing anecdote over medical evaluation, they challenge women's guilt over their "unmotherly" feelings.

Read by millions worldwide, *OBOS* continues to be updated and republished, and reflects changing attitudes. While the work has become less political as reforms have been introduced, its overall impact cannot be overstated. ∎

We as women are redefining competence: a doctor who behaves in a male chauvinist way is not competent, even if he has medical skills.
Our Bodies, Ourselves

Labor pains

Feminists are divided on managing the pain of labor. Some believe that Sheila Kitzinger's preference for home birth and her insistence on a non-medicalized approach, advocated by the natural childbirth movement, denies a woman's right to pain relief. They argue that there is nothing noble about labor pains and that to endure them stoically is to reinforce the biblical view that they are women's punishment for Eve eating from the Tree of Knowledge of Good and Evil in the garden of Eden. They see second-wave feminism's critique of medicalization as reversing first-wave feminism's desire for women to break free of the tyranny of their biology.

Others fiercely defend an opposing view, saying that pain serves a purpose during childbirth. They describe women who elect to deliver their child by Caesarean section—the most extreme form of medicalization—as being "too posh to push."

THERE IS NO BEGINNING TO DEFIANCE IN WOMEN
WRITING WOMEN INTO HISTORY

IN CONTEXT

PRIMARY QUOTE
Sheila Rowbotham, 1972

KEY FIGURE
Sheila Rowbotham

BEFORE
1890 The first Daughters of the American Revolution chapter is organized after men refuse to allow women to join the patriotic society, Sons of the American Revolution.

1915 British historian Barbara Hutchins publishes *Women in Modern Industry*, one of the first books promoting a feminist view of history.

AFTER
1977 The National Women's Studies Association, the first academic association of historians of women's history, is founded in the US.

1990 The first PhD program in women's studies is established at Emory University, Georgia.

Historians have ignored or trivialized women's roles in almost all fields of human endeavor, including those motivated by egalitarian principles, such as working-class struggles and revolutionary movements. British historian Sheila Rowbotham sought to challenge this injustice in *Hidden from History: 300 Years of Women's Oppression and the Fight Against It*. Published in 1973, the book set out to record the integral part women have played in history.

Amateur historians
The first sustained attempt to uncover the silenced history of women was not by professional historians, however, but by members of American women's organizations founded in the late 19th century—such as Colonial Dames of America, Daughters of the American Revolution, and United Daughters of the Confederacy—which sought to record the part played by women in the two great schisms in US history: the American Revolution (1775–1783) and the Civil War (1861–1866). Not only did these organizations serve as powerful examples of women's ability to alter the previously male-dominated narrative of US history but they also challenged the 19th-century view on "separate spheres" based on the biological differences between the sexes.

Academic discipline
With the rise of second-wave feminism in the 1960s, Sheila Rowbotham encouraged others to consider women's history as an academic discipline in its own right. In 1969, the first women's studies course was taught at Cornell University, in the US. Several professional associations were created, as well as a handful of academic journals, such as

> 66
>
> Values linger on after the social structure which conceived them.
> **Sheila Rowbotham**
>
> 99

See also: Enlightenment feminism 28–33 ▪ Working-class feminism 36–37 ▪ Marxist feminism 52–55 ▪ The roots of oppression 114–117

> 66
>
> Women's history is the primary tool for women's emancipation.
> **Gerda Lerner**
>
> 99

The Journal of Women's History and *Women's History Review*, both founded in 1989.

The growth of women's studies in the 1970s and '80s coincided with the rise of social history, which aims to recover the lives of historically inarticulate groups of individuals, silenced in historical narratives. In seeking to write history from the bottom up, the goal of social historians resonated with those researching women's history and provided a methodology not only for recovering female voices but also for showing how women's role in history had been socially constructed, with a view to maintaining patriarchal control and the status quo. History was shown to be yet another root of female oppression.

Among the pioneers during this period were American academics Carroll Smith-Rosenberg, Natalie Zemon-Davis, Mary Beth Norton, Linda Kerber, and Gerda Lerner. The field of women and gender studies continues to grow, and attests to the enduring campaign to advocate and commemorate the role women have played throughout history. ▪

Cornell University offered the first women's studies course in the US. Now called Feminist, Gender, and Sexuality Studies, the course has broadened to include queer theory and gender.

Sheila Rowbotham

A founder of the Women's Liberation Movement in Britain, socialist feminist theorist and writer Sheila Rowbotham was born in Leeds, UK, in 1943. After studying at St. Hilda's College, Oxford, she obtained her first post in gender politics at the University of Amsterdam in the Netherlands.

As a fellow of the Royal Society of Arts and a professor of gender and labor history at the University of Manchester, Rowbotham has gained international recognition as a historian of feminism and radical social movements. Strongly influenced by Marxist thought, she argues that the oppression of women must be examined through both economic and cultural categories of analysis.

Key works

1973 *Hidden from History: 300 Years of Women's Oppression and the Fight Against It*
1997 *A Century of Women: The History of Women in Britain and the United States*
2010 *Dreamers of a New Day: Women Who Invented the Twentieth Century*

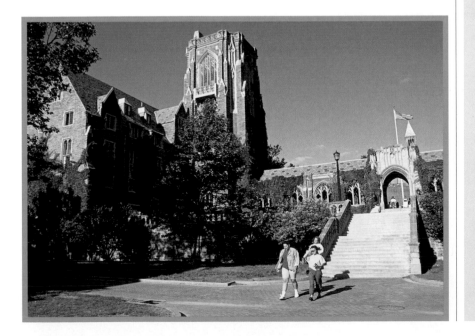

THE LIBERTY OF WOMAN IS AT STAKE

ACHIEVING THE RIGHT TO LEGAL ABORTION

IN CONTEXT

PRIMARY QUOTE
Justices O'Connor, Kennedy, and Souter, 1992

KEY ORGANIZATIONS
Our Bodies, Ourselves; Planned Parenthood

BEFORE
1967 The UK legalizes abortion in Great Britain for pregnancies under 28 weeks (reduced to 24 weeks in 1990).

1971 Simone de Beauvoir publishes the Manifesto of the 343—a list of French women who admitted to having illegal abortions.

AFTER
1976 In the US, Congress's Hyde Amendment bans federal funding of abortion for most women on Medicaid.

2018 In Ireland, the Eighth Amendment restricting abortion is repealed.

T he fight for access to safe and legal abortion in the 1960s and '70s was a key part of the Women's Liberation Movement, which saw it as a human rights issue rather than a moral question. Legal restrictions meant that women were dying or being seriously injured as a result of illegal abortions. Feminists focused on women's right to control their own bodies and their reproductive choices, and argued that only they had the right to decide whether a pregnancy should be terminated.

In the 19th and early 20th centuries, feminists had held mixed views. While some disagreed with abortion on moral grounds, many

See also: Sexual double standards 80–81 ▪ Birth control 102–107 ▪ Woman-centered healthcare 142–147 ▪ Sex positivity 230–233

Abortion was punishable by drowning in the Habsburg empire of Charles V, as prescribed in 1532 in *Constitutio Criminalis Carolina*, the first book of German criminal law.

The case for legalizing abortion

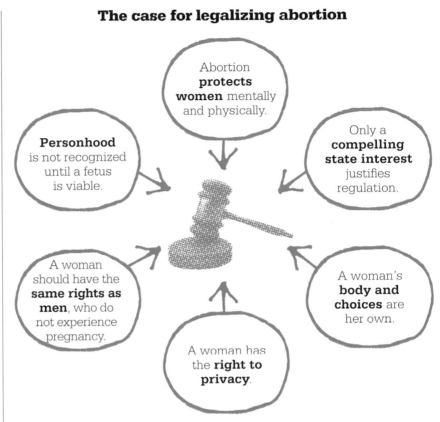

Abortion **protects women** mentally and physically.

Personhood is not recognized until a fetus is viable.

Only a **compelling state interest** justifies regulation.

A woman should have the **same rights as men**, who do not experience pregnancy.

A woman has the **right to privacy**.

A woman's **body and choices** are her own.

thought it was a necessary evil. *The Revolution*, a feminist newspaper in New York City, ran an anonymous article in 1869 that argued against anti-abortion laws because they would punish women, not men, whom the writers blamed for unwanted pregnancies. Margaret Sanger, founder of the first birth control league in 1916, was morally against abortion. Her primary aim in providing contraception was to prevent the back-street abortions that endangered women's lives.

A feminist issue

Abortion became a central issue in the feminist movement of the late 1960s, with the British Women's Liberation Movement making "abortion on demand" one of its key goals. The 1967 Abortion Act legalized abortion for women up to 28 weeks pregnant in England,

Scotland, and Wales, but two doctors had to agree that the pregnancy would harm the woman's physical or mental health. In the US, while Betty Friedan, author of *The Feminine*

To become a mother without wanting to, is to live like a slave or a domestic animal.
Germaine Greer

Mystique, is often credited with linking women's liberation and abortion rights, Rachel Fruchter's "A Matter of Choice: Women Demand Abortion Rights" emphasized that laws restricting access to abortion disproportionately affect women who are non-white and poor.

In 1971, the influential women's health book *Our Bodies, Ourselves* posited that anti-abortion laws were driven by the notion that sex for pleasure is negative, pregnancy is a punishment for pleasure, and fear of pregnancy reinforces conventional sexual morality. While most feminists acknowledged the trauma of abortion, a lack of control over their own bodies was considered to be a greater harm to women. »

The Jane Collective

Before abortion laws changed at federal level in the US, a number of groups helped women access safe—albeit still illegal—abortions in an effort to combat costly and dangerous procedures. The Jane Collective was launched in Chicago, Illinois, in 1965 by Heather Booth, then a 19-year-old student. Booth had become aware of the problems faced by women seeking an abortion when a friend became pregnant.

The members of the collective trained themselves to operate safe abortions. The organization never advertised; women discovered it by word of mouth and then called and asked for Jane. The group charged $100 for an abortion, which most women could not afford, so they also provided interest-free loans. By 1973, when abortion was legalized throughout the US, the collective had performed around 11,000 procedures. No deaths were reported.

Abortion is our right ... as women to control our own bodies. The existence of any abortion laws (however 'liberal') denies this right to women.
Our Bodies, Ourselves

Canadians protest in support of pro-choice activist Dr. Henry Morgentaler in 1975. The doctor was jailed several times for providing unauthorized abortions.

Changing laws

English abortion law originally applied in the US, too, and allowed women to abort a fetus—using drugs or instruments—before it began to move (usually around 15 weeks). After abortion was made illegal in Britain in 1802, anti-abortion legislation was also enacted in the US, from 1821.

The demographic of women seeking terminations in the UK and US also changed: before the 19th century, most were unmarried, but by the 1880s more than half were married and many already had children. The medical profession and government blamed this on the rise of women's rights movements. The UK's 1861 Offences Against the Person Act criminalized abortion even for medical reasons, and in the US, the 1873 Comstock Law prohibited—among other things—the publication of information on abortion. By 1900, every US state considered abortion a felony in almost all circumstances.

The Abortion Law Reform Association formed in 1936 won British women the right to have an abortion if their mental health was at risk. However, this only included women who could afford to see a psychiatrist. The number of illegal abortions—and the deaths that resulted—continued to rise.

By the 1960s, women were campaigning in large numbers to repeal abortion laws. In the US in 1964, a woman named Gerri Santoro died in a Connecticut motel from a self-induced abortion; the graphic photograph of her dead body later became a catalyst in the campaign for legal abortion.

The influence of veteran campaigner Margaret Sanger on the Connecticut Birth Control League led to the 1965 *Griswold v. Connecticut* case, when Estelle T. Griswold of the Planned Parenthood League of Connecticut successfully challenged the Comstock Law banning the sale or purchase of contraceptive drugs or devices.

> The right of privacy ... is broad enough to encompass a woman's decision whether or not to terminate her pregnancy.
> *Roe v. Wade*

Two years later, in 1967, Colorado became the first US state to legalize abortion in cases of rape, incest, or risk to the mother's health; 13 other states followed. Hawaii became the first state to legalize abortion at the woman's request in 1970, and Washington became the first state to legalize abortion through a referendum. By 1973, abortion had been partly legalized in 20 states.

Roe v. Wade

The legal case that led to abortion being legalized at federal level was *Roe v. Wade* in 1973. It concerned Norma McCorvey, who had become pregnant with a third child in June 1969. As abortion was legal in Texas in the case of rape, she went to Dallas seeking an abortion, falsely asserting that she had been raped. Denied because she had no police report, she then tried to seek an illegal abortion, but found the clinics had been closed by the police. In 1970, two lawyers, Linda Coffee and Sarah Weddington, filed suit on her behalf, under the alias Jane Roe, against Dallas County district attorney Henry Wade. That year (too late for McCorvey, who had already given birth), a three-judge panel declared Texas law to be unconstitutional as it violated the Ninth Amendment right to privacy.

The case reached the Supreme Court, which in January 1973 ruled in favor of Roe with a seven-to-two majority, declaring Texas laws against abortion unconstitutional. The court held that, under US statutes, "the unborn have never been recognized ... as a person in the whole sense" and abortion fell within the parameters of the right to privacy. After *Roe v. Wade*, states could not ban abortion for pregnancies under 12 weeks. However, in 1992,

The *Roe v. Wade* case inspired a movie made for television in 1989. Actress Holly Hunter (right) played Norma McCorvey, or "Jane Roe."

another landmark case, *Planned Parenthood v. Casey*, restored the right of states to regulate abortions in the first trimester. Americans today remain almost equally divided between "pro-life" and "pro-choice," and dissatisfaction with abortion laws is widespread. Meanwhile, there are more than 60 countries in the rest of the world where abortion is illegal. ∎

Simone Veil

Simone Veil is known for advancing women's rights in France, particularly for her work on legalizing abortion. Born Simone Jacob in Nice in 1927, she was just 17 when she was sent to Auschwitz by the Nazis. She survived the Holocaust and went on to study law and political science. After practicing law, she worked as a magistrate, improving the treatment of female prisoners.

In 1974, Veil was appointed Minister of Health—the first female minister in the French government. At this time, women in France were demanding legal access to abortion. After the publication in 1971 of the Manifesto of the 343—women who had undergone illegal abortions—331 doctors signed a similar manifesto declaring they supported a woman's right to choose. Subsequently, Veil drafted and pushed through the Veil Law in 1975, which legalized abortion during the first trimester—despite violent attacks by the far-right.

In 1979, Veil became the first female president of the European Parliament. She died in 2017, aged 89.

YOU'VE GOT TO PROTEST, YOU'VE GOT TO STRIKE

WOMEN'S UNION ORGANIZING

IN CONTEXT

PRIMARY QUOTE
Gwen Davis, 2013

KEY FIGURES
Esther Peterson, Rose Boland, Eileen Pullen, Vera Sime, Gwen Davis, Sheila Douglass

BEFORE
1900 The International Ladies Garment Workers Union is established in New York City.

1912 Action by women working in the textile industry in Massachusetts leads to minimum wage law in the US.

AFTER
1993 In the US, the Family and Medical Leave Act provides employees with job-protected leave to care for a child or other family member.

2012 Icelandic unions help to draw up the Equal Pay Standard to encourage employers to pay women the same as men.

The employment of women in defense industries during World War II moved feminist labor concerns to the forefront of public debate. At first, unions in the combatant countries were more interested in protecting the jobs of returning servicemen than in addressing women's rights. However, with economic growth and increased demand for women workers in the 1950s, some unions began to challenge pay inequalities that were based on sex alone.

In the US, after repeated attempts to bring in equal pay legislation, continuous political and feminist agitation at last resulted in the issuing in 1963 of the Equal Pay Act, championed by the labor and union activist Esther Peterson and encouraged by President John F.

Striking Dagenham machinists take their protest to Whitehall, London, on June 28, 1968. It took another 16 years—and another strike—for their work to be recognized as "skilled."

See also: Unionization 46–51 ▪ Marxist feminism 52–55 ▪ Marriage and work 70–71 ▪ Pink-collar feminism 228–229 ▪ The pay gap 318–319

Kennedy. In Europe, however, it took the collaborative strike action of women to put into power the rule of equal pay for equal work.

Making a stand

In the UK, it was a strike in 1968 by sewing machinists at the Ford Motor Company's Dagenham plant in London that hastened legislation. The strike was sparked by Ford's decision to downgrade women's work (making car seat covers) as Category "B" (semi-skilled) labor, instead of Category "C" (skilled), and to pay women in Category "B" 15 percent less than men in the same position. On June 7, 1968, female sewing machinists walked out, led by Rose Boland, Eileen Pullen, Vera Sime, Gwen Davis, and Sheila Douglass. Their three-week strike halted all car production.

To persuade the machinists to return to work, Barbara Castle, the Secretary of State for Employment and Productivity, negotiated a pay rise to 92 percent of the men's rate and instigated a government review of the issue of "equal pay." A year later, inspired by the Ford strike, women trade unionists formed the National Joint Action Campaign Committee for Women's Equal Rights, which organized an equal-pay demonstration in London. In 1970, in line with EU legislation, the UK's Equal Pay Act prohibited unequal treatment between men and women at work.

Island solidarity

Every year on October 24 in Iceland, working women celebrate "Women's Day Off." It marks the day in 1975 when 25,000 women, almost 90 percent of the workforce, took part in a national strike. They gathered in Reykjavik to protest unequal economic conditions for women, requesting equal pay in the workplace and compensations for their housework and childcare at home. Iceland's leading feminist group, the Redstockings, organized the protest and decided that a strike would be the most powerful and effective action. As a result of the "Day Off," many industries and services that relied on female workers were forced to shut down, including schools, banking, telephone services, newspapers, and theaters. The strike lasted until midnight, and achieved its goal of demonstrating to the whole country the equal value of women workers throughout society.

A year after the strike, Iceland passed the Gender Equality Act, which guaranteed equal rights for women and men. In 2018, Iceland became the first country in the world to pass legislation aimed at forcing employers to pay women and men the same amount for doing the same job. ▪

There was a tremendous power ... and a great feeling of solidarity and strength among all those women standing on the square in the sunshine.
Vigdís Finnbogadóttir
Former president of Iceland

Spanish Women's Strike, 2018

While 170 countries planned public protests on March 8, 2018 (International Women's Day), Spain was the only one where a general strike gained union backing. More than 5 million workers, mainly women, joined a "feminist strike" organized by the 8M Commission, a collective of feminist groups inspired by Iceland's "Women's Day Off" in 1975. Under the slogan "If we stop, the world stops," hundreds of thousands of women took part in 24-hour demonstrations and other actions in around 200 Spanish towns and cities, bringing a halt to work, study, and housework. The protestors' demands ranged from battling unequal pay based on gender to opposing violence against women. The demonstrators also highlighted inequalities endured by women within the home and the rising level of violent crime against women. A poll conducted by the *El Pais* newspaper suggested that 82 percent of the Spanish population were in favor of the strike. While many unions backed 24 hours of action, Spain's two largest unions, the UGT and CCOO, limited their support to two-hour strikes.

SCREAM QUIETLY
PROTECTION FROM DOMESTIC VIOLENCE

Until the 1970s, the plight of women facing violence from male partners was rarely discussed in public, although feminists had been fighting against domestic violence since at least the 1800s. In the UK, the 1937 Matrimonial Causes Act had included cruelty as grounds for divorce, but the process of proving this was difficult and expensive.

It was not until women began to share their personal experiences at consciousness-raising groups in the late 1960s and early '70s that women began to realize that the abuse they faced was not an individual problem but a collective one demanding political redress.

Refuges for women

Erin Pizzey, an early member of the UK's Women's Liberation Movement, set up the first women's

Women and children crowd into the UK's first women's shelter in Chiswick, West London, in 1974. Following a public awareness campaign, the numbers seeking sanctuary rocketed.

See also: Rights for married women 72–75 ■ Consciousness-raising 134–135 ■ Rape as abuse of power 166–171 ■ Fighting campus sexual assault 320

> We have to foster the attitude that violence in the home is shameful and unmanly.
> **Anne Summers**

shelter in Chiswick, London, in 1971. It was an important step in exposing the realities of what it meant to be a "battered wife," as survivors of domestic violence were then called. The shelter gave victims material and emotional support, and the publicity that it generated exposed a problem that had previously been viewed as a matter between husband and wife.

Pizzey's 1974 book *Scream Quietly or the Neighbours Will Hear*, focusing on women's personal stories, further highlighted the issue. Pizzey's strategy of opening new shelters by squatting in abandoned buildings angered local authorities, but her work was also widely praised, including by members of parliament and Lord Hailsham, head of the judiciary, who said she was providing a unique service.

Further initiatives
In Australia, feminist writer Anne Summers, who had formed a Women's Liberation Movement (WLM) group in Adelaide in 1969, also established women's shelters. After moving to Sydney in 1970, she and other feminists occupied two abandoned buildings owned

by the Church of England and opened the Elsie Refuge there in 1974. They received government funding a year later.

In Canada, the National Action Committee (NAC), formed from a coalition of 23 feminist groups in 1972, pressed for explicit protection for women in law. The federal changes they demanded were finally included in the 1985 Charter of Rights and Freedoms.

The White Ribbon Campaign, founded by Canadian men in 1991 to cultivate healthy masculinity free from misogyny, is now active in more than 60 countries. In 1993, the United Nations published *Strategies for Confronting Domestic Violence* in a bid to press countries around the world to rethink their approach to violence against women. New or updated laws in the US, Australia, and the UK have been passed to protect women from abuse. Domestic violence continues, but is a problem far fewer nations can now ignore. ■

> At least one in three women is beaten, coerced into sex or otherwise abused by an intimate partner in the course of her lifetime [globally].
> **United Nations Department of Public Information 2008 report**

Erin Pizzey

Born in Qingdao, China, in 1939, Erin Pizzey was the daughter of Western diplomats and lived in many countries as a child, including South Africa, Lebanon, Canada, Iran, and the UK. She grew up in an emotionally and physically abusive household, in which both parents were bullies. She later upset radical feminists with her claim that women were just as likely as men to perpetuate violence.

Pizzey's controversial opinions provoked protests and death threats from militant feminists. She relocated to Santa Fe, New Mexico; the Cayman Islands; and Italy to write, before returning to London in the 1990s. Chiswick Women's Aid (now called Refuge), which Pizzey established in 1971, is the UK's largest domestic violence organization.

Key works

1974 *Scream Quietly or the Neighbours Will Hear*
1998 *The Emotional Terrorist and the Violence-Prone*
2005 *Infernal Child: World Without Love*

THE MALE GAZE PROJECTS ITS PHANTASY ON TO THE FEMALE

THE MALE GAZE

In the movies, the **viewpoint of the camera** is **male** and **active**, while the **female on the screen** is **passive**, being looked at.

↓

The determining male gaze projects its phantasy on to the female figure, which is styled accordingly.

↓

The **woman** thus becomes an **erotic object of desire:** both for the male characters within the film and for the audience.

↓

The **man** ultimately **holds** the **power**.

S ince feminist film theorist Laura Mulvey coined the term "the male gaze" in 1975, it has become a part of the everyday feminist lexicon. Widely used to refer to the sexism and the sexual objectification of women in popular culture, Mulvey's original argument about the male gaze was one that drew on psychoanalysis to examine representations of women in classic Hollywood cinema.

Objects of desire
In her essay "Visual Pleasure and Narrative Cinema," Mulvey argues that in Hollywood film, the (male) filmmaker uses the camera to reflect male desire for women and assumes a (heterosexual) male viewer. Mulvey analyzes how the camera's presentation of shots— segmenting women's bodies into separate parts rather than as a whole, zooming in on those parts, and slowly panning up the body in a sexualized manner—results in depicting women on screen as objects of male desire. While men are presented on screen as active protagonists driving the narrative, women are seen as passive props for male subjects and as passive fetishes of men's sexual fantasies.

See also: The roots of oppression 114–117 ▪ The problem with no name 118–123 ▪ Antipornography feminism 196–199 ▪ Sex positivity 234–237 ▪ The beauty myth 264–267 ▪ Sexual abuse awareness 322–327

Using psychoanalyst Sigmund Freud's theory of scopophilia, or the pleasure gained through looking, Mulvey theorizes that women's "to-be-looked-at-ness" in film is a form of male voyeurism. This creates a problem: if the audience is meant to identify with the male subject of the film, how are female viewers supposed to relate to the screen?

The oppositional gaze

In 1992, black feminist theorist bell hooks published the book *Black Looks: Race and Representation*, in which she challenges Mulvey's thesis by critically examining the pervasive whiteness in Hollywood cinema and questioning how black women are supposed to relate to cinema. Finding themselves limited to racist "mammy" or "jezebel" stereotypes on screen, hooks argues, black women have two key strategies for accessing the scopophilia Mulvey writes about. They either have to suppress their blackness and attempt to

This French poster for *The Postman Always Rings Twice* (1946) flaunts the film's male gaze. Cora Smith, the female protagonist, is first seen through a series of close-ups, forcing the viewer to look at her in a voyeuristic way.

identify with the white women on screen to find some degree of representation, or they have to create viewing pleasure in watching films with a critical eye. Deconstructing the racism and sexism in film, suggests hooks, can be a way of contesting not only the male gaze but black women's erasure in film, in the process gaining a type of scopophilic joy.

Theorizing ways for black women to find pleasure in film, hooks coined the term "the oppositional gaze"—a critical gaze that both assesses the dominant gaze and returns its own gaze. It is a gaze that actively reclaims power. For hooks, a black feminist oppositional gaze can be found in black feminist independent film, a medium that creates powerful representations of black women

rather than simply reacting in criticism to black women's exclusion from the screen.

Queer gaze

Scholars have also argued for reading film through a queer gaze. Patricia White's *UnInvited: Classical Hollywood Cinema and Lesbian Representability* (1999) asks what it means for the male gaze if queer female audiences are also consuming films meant to titillate heterosexual men. ▪

Woman lives her body as seen by another, by an anonymous patriarchal Other.
Sandra Lee Bartky
Professor of gender studies

Laura Mulvey

Born in Oxford in 1941, Laura Mulvey studied at St. Hilda's College, Oxford University. She became known as a feminist film theorist in the 1970s with her groundbreaking article "Visual Pleasure and Narrative Cinema," pioneering the field of feminist film theory. Between 1974 and 1982, Mulvey co-wrote and co-directed six films with her husband Peter Wollen—most of these contained feminist themes, especially *Penthesilea: Queen of the Amazons* (1974)

and *Riddles of the Sphinx* (1977). In 1991, she also co-directed *Disgraced Monuments*. Mulvey was elected as a Fellow of the British Academy, in 2000, and is professor of film theory at Birkbeck, University of London.

Key works

1975 "Visual Pleasure and Narrative Cinema"
1989 *Visual and Other Pleasures*
1996 *Fetishism and Curiosity*

RAPE IS
A CONSCIOUS PROCESS OF
INTIMIDATION
RAPE AS ABUSE OF POWER

IN CONTEXT

PRIMARY QUOTE
Susan Brownmiller, 1975

KEY FIGURES
**Susan Brownmiller,
Antonia Castañeda**

BEFORE
1866 In the US, Frances
Thompson, Lucy Smith, and
other black women testify
before Congress about the
gang-rape of black women by
white police officers during the
Memphis riots.

1970 Chicago Women Against
Rape issues a statement of
purpose, linking rape with
unequal power in society.

AFTER
1993 After decades of
struggle, marital rape is made
illegal in all 50 US states.

2017 The #MeToo feminist
movement to hold perpetrators
of sexual violence accountable
spreads internationally.

When Susan Brownmiller wrote *Against Our Will: Men, Women, and Rape* in 1975, rape was a hidden issue, widely considered to be rare because it was seldom reported. When rape was discussed, it was in hushed tones, and the blame was often put on the female victims, the logic being that men were driven by biology to "need" sex. According to the prevailing wisdom of the time, it was women's responsibility to control, or at least limit, male lust.

Rape is political

In the 1970s, feminists began to challenge society's response to sexual violence against women, introducing the concept of rape being motivated by power. Brownmiller's book served as a catalyst. Based on four years of research, the book postulates that since prehistory, rape has been the primary mechanism through which men asserted their dominance over women. She claims that far from being a crime of passion driven by sexual desire, rape is a tool consciously and calculatedly deployed by men to assert power over women's bodies. This is the

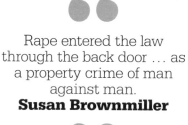

> Rape entered the law through the back door … as a property crime of man against man.
> **Susan Brownmiller**

case in domestic rape, stranger rape, and during wide-scale acts of terror, such as enslavement, warfare, and genocide. As such, rape has to be considered in political terms.

Men are given permission to rape, writes Brownmiller, partly through the widespread belief that women's bodies are men's to possess, and partly through systemic discrimination, which forces women into subordinate positions. The age-old concept of the female body as male property, she finds, still haunts modern-day perceptions of rape.

Susan Brownmiller

Journalist and feminist Susan Brownmiller was born in Brooklyn, New York, in 1935. Growing up in a working-class Jewish household, Brownmiller attributed her motivation to confront violence against women to her early education on the holocaust and the historical treatment of Jews.

In 1964, Brownmiller became involved with the Civil Rights Movement, and in 1968 she became interested in feminism after attending consciousness-raising groups hosted by New York Radical Women. While her 1975 book *Against Our Will: Men,* *Women, and Rape* was met with controversy, Brownmiller's thesis—that rape had always been the fundamental way men exerted power over women—had a profound influence on the feminist movement's approach to sexual violence.

Key works

1975 *Against Our Will: Men, Women, and Rape*
1984 *Femininity*
1989 *Waverly Place*
1990 *In Our Time: Memoir of a Revolution*

See also: Protection from domestic violence 162–163 ▪ Indian feminism 176–177 ▪ Survivor, not victim 238 ▪ Women in war zones 278–279 ▪ Sexism is everywhere 308–309 ▪ Men hurt women 316–317 ▪ Fighting campus sexual assault 320 ▪ Sexual abuse awareness 322–327

Brownmiller was also one of the first journalists to draw attention to the sexual abuse of children, arguing that the rape of adult women and sexual violence committed against children are often perpetrated by seemingly well-adjusted and upstanding men who are known to those they victimize, and are often within the same family. Such crimes, she says, are not confined to a small number of "perverts," as society often likes to maintain.

Rape as mass violence

Subsequent feminist scholarship has looked at the use of rape against women as a method of both humiliating terrorized groups and establishing dominance over the population. In her 1993 essay "Sexual Violence in the Politics and Policies of Conquest," Mexican American feminist Antonia Castañeda examines how mass rape was used to subdue populations in the 18th and 19th centuries. Raping indigenous women and children across what is now California, she says, was a way for Spanish soldiers to assert their claim to both the land and the bodies of the people they conquered. Although some Catholic priests were opposed to this mass sexual violence, military conquest in the name of Spain's Catholic monarchy enabled the spread of the mission system across California.

The Native American studies scholar and feminist Andrea Smith took this argument further. In her 2005 book *Conquest: Sexual Violence and American Indian Genocide* she asserts that the mass rape of indigenous women in North America represented an extension

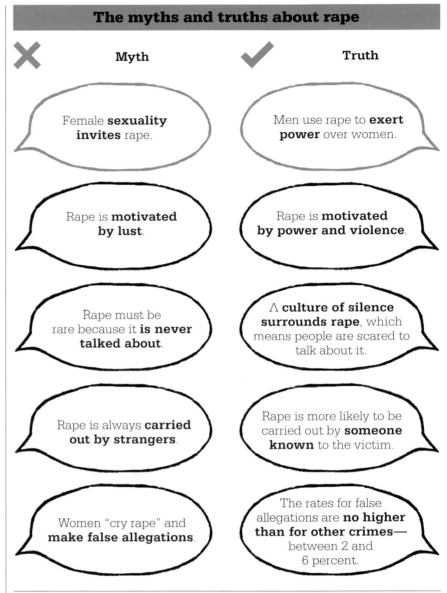

The myths and truths about rape

✕ Myth	✓ Truth
Female **sexuality invites** rape.	Men use rape to **exert power** over women.
Rape is **motivated by lust**.	Rape is **motivated by power and violence**.
Rape must be rare because it **is never talked about**.	A **culture of silence surrounds rape**, which means people are scared to talk about it.
Rape is always **carried out by strangers**.	Rape is more likely to be carried out by **someone known** to the victim.
Women "cry rape" and **make false allegations**.	The rates for false allegations are **no higher than for other crimes**— between 2 and 6 percent.

of white colonists' belief that the land on which the indigenous people lived was inherently rapable and susceptible to invasion.

Rape under slavery

In the essay "The 'Sexual Economy' of American Slavery" (2009) and other works, African American feminist academic Adrienne Davis argues that white enslavers in the US routinely used rape to terrorize black women and remind black men that they had no power to protect them. In addition, she says, when the US banned the importation of enslaved people from abroad after 1808, southern »

> Rape became not only a male prerogative, but man's basic weapon of force against woman, the principal agent of his will and her fear.
> **Susan Brownmiller**

states adapted by expanding America's domestic slave trade. Black women supported the white southern economy by producing future generations of enslaved people, often conceived through rape. Sexual violence against black women, argues Davis, was central to the historic development of America's economy.

Feminist activism
The creation of rape crisis centers was a key part of second-wave feminist activism. The women who set them up—some of whom had

The largest center of its kind in New England, the Boston Area Rape Crisis Center was set up in 1973. It provides free services to survivors of sexual violence, no matter when it occurred.

experienced sexual violence themselves—wanted to provide refuge and support for victims.

The fact that the centers were created by and for women was important. Victims who reported rape often distrusted the police who took down details of the crime. Mainly male, police officers were notoriously unsympathetic and known for shaming victims and disbelieving their stories. In addition to wanting to give raped women a safe place to turn for resources and support, rape center activists wanted to change the laws surrounding rape to ensure rapists were always held accountable.

In 1972, radical feminists in Washington, D.C., published the pamphlet "How to set up a rape crisis center." Groups soon formed throughout the country. In 1973, San Francisco Women Against Rape (SFWAR) set up a rape crisis help line for 20 hours per week, which by the early 1980s had

become a 24-hour hotline, while also providing support groups and individual counseling.

International initiatives
The same kind of initiatives sprang up in other countries through the 1970s and early '80s. In the UK, the London Rape Crisis Centre (LRCC) opened in 1976, offering a 24-hour rape crisis hotline as well as one-on-one help and medical referrals. Its aim was to support victims without making judgements, to provide resources on reporting sexual violence to the police, and to offer help in navigating the legal system for those who chose to take their case to court. The center also provided psychological healing.

In Australia, the organization Women Against Rape opened the first rape crisis center in Sydney in 1974. Canada's Women Against Violence Against Women/Rape Crisis Centre (WAVAW/RCC) was formed in Vancouver in 1982.

During the 1970s, feminists also started to use the term "rape culture" to describe how rape is

Rape in marriage

In the 17th century, English judge Sir Matthew Hale ruled that marital rape cannot exist under the law. He decreed that by entering into marriage a woman gave her consent to sex with her husband for life. This view was common in other English-speaking countries, although during the 19th century, American suffragists Elizabeth Cady Stanton, Lucy Stone, and Victoria Woodhull argued that women should determine when they had

sex with their husbands, as did British feminist Harriet Taylor Mill.

Rape in marriage did not become illegal in the UK until 1991. In the US, it became illegal in all 50 states in 1993, but marital rape was treated the same way as non-marital rape in only 17 states. That year, the United Nations High Commissioner for Human Rights also established that rape in marriage was a violation of international human rights.

> Another thing about equality is that it cannot coexist with rape.
> **Andrea Dworkin**

rendered normal and routine in misogynistic societies. The 1975 US documentary *Rape Culture* argued against the prevailing belief that rape was an individual act committed by a deranged person and emphasized the connection between rape, sexism, and violence against women. The film was influential in changing society's views about rape and in growing the movement to combat sexual violence against women. In 1978, the film was mentioned in the US Congressional Record, the first known time that the concept of rape culture was referenced in US politics at a national level.

Since the 1970s, there have been numerous rape prevention and anti-survivor shaming initiatives in many countries, with an emphasis on public education about consent; the modernization of rape laws; and best practice in hospitals, courts, and the media. Terminology around rape has also changed, with people who have experienced sexual violence identified as "survivors" rather than "victims."

Many groups founded in the 1970s and '80s continue to operate today. SFWAR became an official nonprofit organization in 1990 and continues to thrive. Australia's original rape crisis group eventually became 15 government-funded centers known as the Centres Against Sexual Assault (CASA).

In the US, the Rape, Abuse and Incest National Network (RAINN) was founded in 1994 and runs the National Sexual Assault Hotline.

The 1994 Violence Against Women Act established government sources of funding for efforts to combat rape culture. In some countries, funding for these groups is an enduring challenge. For instance, there were 68 rape crisis centers operating in UK cities by 1984. However, by 2010 that number had fallen to 39, and only an estimated one in five centers had the full funding they required.

Violence persists

Despite some positive steps, sexual violence remains a hidden, or barely acknowledged problem in many countries. After many decades of campaigning, it was only in 2013 that the Irish government admitted to the state's active role in sending "fallen women," including women who had become pregnant through rape, to the notorious Magdalene laundries—essentially labor camps run by the Sisters of Mercy, an order of Catholic nuns, who treated the young women punitively and sold their babies to wealthy families. The practice continued in Ireland from the 18th century until as late as 1996.

In Japan, the 2018 documentary *Japan's Secret Shame* told the story of one woman's fight to bring her alleged rapist, a well-known journalist, to trial in a country where talk of rape and other sexual violence is taboo. Rape culture may be increasingly recognized but it persists across the world, in both poor and wealthy countries, in the West and the global South, without discriminating. ∎

Women in Mumbai light candles during a vigil to mark the gang rape and murder of Jyoti Singh Pandey, a 23-year-old physiotherapist, on a bus in South Delhi in December 2012.

WOMYN-BORN-WOMYN IS A LIVED EXPERIENCE
TRANS-EXCLUSIONARY RADICAL FEMINISM

IN CONTEXT

PRIMARY QUOTE
Lisa Vogel, 2013

KEY FIGURES
Janice Raymond, Sheila Jeffreys, Germaine Greer, Lisa Vogel

BEFORE
1973 In California, West Coast Lesbian Conference co-organizer Beth Elliott walks out after being attacked by lesbian separatist group The Gutter Dykes for being trans.

1977 Gloria Steinem suggests that transsexualism is a distraction from more relevant feminist issues.

AFTER
2008 Australian writer and blogger Viv Smythe—a cisgender woman—coins the term trans-exclusionary radical feminism to distinguish it from the trans-inclusive radical feminist community to which she belongs.

Since the 1970s, there has been a vocal sub-group of feminists who believe that because they were assigned "female" at birth and have always identified as female (cisgender), their lives and experience of oppression are entirely different from those of trans women. These women are now referred to as Trans-Exclusionary Radical Feminists, or TERFs, though this is not a term they generally use themselves.

In the 1970s, during the height of second-wave feminism, some radical feminists such as Mary Daly, Janice Raymond, and Sheila Jeffreys considered trans women as

"interlopers." They had strong and hostile views as to who counted as a woman, developing their own arguments against the validity of trans people's identities. Some—though not all—of these women were also proponents of "political lesbianism," the idea that all feminists can and should give up men and live a separatist life.

Janice Raymond published *The Transsexual Empire: The Making of the She-Male* in 1979—the first overtly trans-exclusionary radical feminist text. In it, she accuses trans women of being mentally ill men who want to invade women's spaces due to their sense of entitlement. She also specifically singles out fellow lesbian feminist Sandy Stone, the sound engineer for women's music label Olivia Records, as being a trans imposter in the women's music scene.

Sheila Jeffreys expanded on these views in the 1990s and later stated that trans people uphold

Activists demonstrate for trans rights in Chicago in 2017. They are protesting against the removal of policies that had allowed trans students to use toilet facilities appropriate to their gender identities.

See also: Confronting misogyny 140–141 ▪ Political lesbianism 180–181 ▪ Privilege 239 ▪ Intersectionality 240–245 ▪ Gender is performative 258–261 ▪ Trans feminism 286–289

Germaine Greer addresses the audience at the NSW Teachers' Conference Centre in Sydney, Australia, in 2008. Currently a very vocal TERF, Greer has been "no platformed" at many universities.

the exclusion and bullying of marginalized groups deserves to be called feminism at all.

Critics such as Julia Serano argue that TERFs violate their own feminist principles, which have long sought to understand women as complex subjects rather than mere bodies. Intersectional critics point out that race and class also greatly impact an individual's experience of privilege before, during, and after medical transition.

TERFs are routinely challenged for refusing to respect the identities of trans people and contributing to damaging perceptions that trans women are "men in dresses" preying on women with their "male energy." Opponents of TERF ideology say such dehumanizing rhetoric contributes to the high murder rate of trans women. ▪

harmful stereotypes about the gender binary. She claimed that feminine trans women buy into damaging patriarchal directives about how a woman should look and behave. Jeffreys also argued that the medical establishment harms "women's" bodies in granting trans men access to surgery. The medical transition of trans men who had previously identified as masculine lesbians has, she said, led to a crisis in the lesbian community.

All transsexuals rape women's bodies by reducing the real female form to an artifact, appropriating this body for themselves.
Janice Raymond

Germaine Greer is now one of the most highly publicized TERFs. She claims that trans women have no authentic reason to transition; in her view, someone born with male genitalia is only, and can only ever be, a man.

Trans-inclusive feminism
Criticism of TERF views is both trenchant and wide-ranging. Trans-inclusive feminists question whether a feminism that endorses

Michigan Womyn's Music Festival

The battle over prohibiting trans women from women's spaces erupted at the Michigan Womyn's Music Festival, also known as MichFest, held in Hart, Michigan, beginning in 1976. Like many other feminist organizations at the time, it used "womyn"to avoid the last syllable in "women."

The festival enforced a controversial "womyn-born-womyn" (identified as female at birth) policy that resulted in organizers confronting and

expelling trans attendee Nancy Burkholder in 1991. In the many years of protest that followed, Camp Trans was established in the early 1990s as an alternative event, while an initiative called Trans Women Belong Here attempted to change the festival from within.

When founder Lisa Vogel repeatedly refused to change the policy, attendance declined and acts canceled their performances. MichFest finally closed down in 2015.

FAT IS A WAY OF SAYING "NO" TO POWERLESSNESS
FAT POSITIVITY

IN CONTEXT

PRIMARY QUOTE
Susie Orbach, 1978

KEY FIGURES
**Susie Orbach,
Marilyn Wann**

BEFORE
1969 The National Association to Advance Fat Acceptance is founded in the US.

1972 A group called Fat Underground forms at the Radical Psychiatry Center in Berkeley, California.

1973 American activists Dr. Sara Fishman and Judy Freespirit publish the *Fat Liberation Manifesto*.

AFTER
2003 The Association for Size Diversity advocates the Health at Every Size model for public health care policy in the US.

2012 The first issue of *Fat Studies: An Interdisciplinary Journal of Body Weight and Society* is published in the US.

F at positivity is the concept that fat people have the right to love and accept their bodies as they are. It rejects the view of fat bodies as inherently unhealthy and criticizes the way in which Western views of the body often equate health with moral virtue. British psychoanalyst Susie Orbach, along with other proponents of fat positivity, argue that fat women are socially policed to conform to sexist, Eurocentric, heterosexist, and cissexist (discrimination against transgender people) standards of beauty that punish fat bodies. They assert that this hierarchy of bodily value must be overthrown. Orbach's 1978 book, *Fat Is A Feminist Issue*, was an early intellectual contribution to fat-positive feminist movements.

Unruly bodies
Western attitudes about the body were framed by Christian teaching that bodies are sinful and that women's bodies in particular are susceptible to temptation. Enlightenment-era concepts of the body also had a major influence, especially the idea of mind-body dualism, which asserts that the rational mind must govern the libidinous body. Scholars in the academic field of Fat Studies criticize these core ideas, arguing that both have played a role in society judging some bodies as inferior and those of marginalized communities—especially women, people of color, poor people, LGBT people, and those with disabilities—as particularly unruly and requiring social control.

Challenging ideology
Feminists first identified anti-fat stigma as a form of discrimination worth combatting in the 1960s. Banding together with those in

> The only thing anyone can diagnose … by looking at a fat person is their own level of stereotype and prejudice toward fat people.
> **Marilyn Wann**

See also: The problem with no name 118–123 ▪ The male gaze 164–165 ▪ Sex positivity 234–237 ▪ The beauty myth 264–267 ▪ The Riot Grrrl movement 272–273

Women belly dance together at the National Association to Advance Fat Acceptance convention in Boston, promoting the fat positivity movement through their positive body image.

the burgeoning fat-acceptance movements, feminists objected to the systemic oppression of fat people at a time when ultra-thin fashion models such as Twiggy were heralded as icons for women.

More organizations challenging fat phobia emerged in the 1980s, and in the 1990s the Fat Liberation and Riot Grrrl movements led to fat feminist zines (small-circulation magazines). Activist Marilyn Wann's *FAT!SO?*, published as a zine in 1994, was developed as a book in 1998. Around the same time, organizations such as the Council on Size and Weight Discrimination, set up in 1991, reported that women of size both earned less than thin women and were given fewer pay raises by their employers, while doctors often assumed that medical problems were due to excess weight without performing diagnostic tests.

Fat positivity has increased in the internet age, with heightened awareness of fat-shaming, the proliferation of "fatshion" and plus sized models, and huge followings on social media. Poet and activist Sonya Renee Taylor's intersectional feminist movement and her 2018 book *The Body Is Not An Apology* seek to "dismantle the systems of body-based oppression."

Out of fat positivity has sprung the body positivity movement, emphasizing the worthiness and beauty of all bodies. However, some advocates of fat positivity criticize the body positivity movement, arguing that those most marginalized, especially "superfat" people and women of color, are underrepresented in the body positivity movement. ∎

Susie Orbach

Born into a Jewish family in London in 1946, Susie Orbach is a psychoanalyst, feminist writer, and social critic. In 1978, she published *Fat Is A Feminist Issue*, which looks at women's troubled relationships with their bodies, the emotional reasons women eat, and, crucially, the ways in which thinness is held up as an ideal.

Orbach has gone on to publish work in similar areas including *Fat Is A Feminist Issue II, Hunger Strike, On Eating,* and *Bodies.* She also writes about the dynamics of relationships, particularly within heterosexual couples. Orbach worked with Unilever to co-originate the Dove Campaign for Real Beauty in 2004 (using women of all ages and sizes in place of professional models) and is on the steering committee of the UK-based Campaign for Body Confidence. Orbach is married to the writer Jeanette Winterson.

Key works

1978 *Fat Is A Feminist Issue*
1983 *What Do Women Want?*
(with Luise Eichenbaum)
2005 *The Impossibility of Sex*

WOMEN'S LIBERATION, EVERYONE'S LIBERATION

INDIAN FEMINISM

Before independence in 1947, feminism in India was pioneered by upper-caste Indian men who drew the subject of women's status into anticolonial campaigns, and before that by the British, who wished to outlaw certain cultural practices. After 1947, a "Third Phase" of feminism—led by women, for women—was freed of the anticolonial agenda to focus on women's issues alone. Yet by 1970, when Indira Gandhi was India's first female prime minister, there were few other women in politics and most women in the rest of society had little or no say over their daily lives. It was left to feminist groups to tackle issues such as the bias of social and legal systems in favor of men, unequal property rights, and low pay.

A mural in the Indian state of Andhra Pradesh, where there is a high incidence of crimes against women, proclaims "Women's empowerment is the basis of women's development."

New initiatives

In 1972, the gang rape of an orphan tribal girl, Mathura, by policemen who were later acquitted, sparked a campaign against police violence against women. The campaign eventually succeeded in amending the law in 1983, so that a victim's claim that she did not consent to sexual intercourse must be accepted unless proven otherwise. Further laws included making rape while in custody a punishable offence.

Since Indian feminism had to consider gender inequality within the power structures of caste, tribe, language, region, and class, women in academia were reluctant to accept the Western concept of feminism and argued for a more Indian-specific approach. In 1978, academics Madhu Kishwar and

See also: The global suffrage movement 94–97 ▪ Anticolonialism 218–219 ▪ Postcolonial feminism 220–223 ▪ Indigenous feminism 224–227 ▪ Bringing feminism online 294–297

Madhu Kishwar

Born in 1951, Madhu Purnima Kishwar studied at Miranda House and Jawaharlal Nehru University in Delhi. An academic, writer, and human rights and women's rights activist, she cofounded *Manushi*, a pioneering magazine about women and society. She is Senior Fellow at the Centre for the Study of Developing Societies (CSDS) in Delhi, and Director of the Indic Studies Project based at CSDS. Kishwar is president of *Manushi Sangathan*, a forum for organizing citizens' groups for action on specific issues, to promote social justice and strengthen human rights, especially for women.

Key works

1984 *In Search of Answers: Indian Women's Voices*
1986 *Gandhi and Women*
1990 *Why I Do Not Call Myself a Feminist*
2008 *Zealous Reformers, Deadly Laws: Battling Stereotypes*

Ruth Vanita founded *Manushi* magazine, which airs critical issues of patriarchy in society, law, and the economy, and the violence faced by women "from all quarters." Now in digital form, the magazine was originally inspired by the life and work of Mahatma Gandhi, and seeks a peaceful resolution to social conflict, helping women deal with the challenges of their time.

Feminism in India today

While women in India theoretically have rights that make them equal to men under the law, in reality these rights are still frequently ignored. Mainstream Indian feminism continues to fight for women on issues such as child marriage, sex-selective abortions, dowry crimes, rape, and violence against marginal women. Online forums target body image, menstruation taboos, sex

education, motherhood, and queer love, and social media is now leading what academic and author Alka Kurian calls "Fourth Wave" feminism, which combines women's freedom with a broader call for social justice for minorities.

Protests have gained support via the media, and groups such as the Gulabi Gang (Pink Gang) confront women's issues locally. Campaigns also exist against issues like "eve-teasing," the sexual harassment of a woman in a public place.

Hindu fundamentalists advocate the ideal of the traditional Indian woman. Hindu women who battle against orthodox notions of Hindu marriage and family are accused of being westernized, and violence against such women is widespread. ▪

The pink sari-clad Gulabi Gang, formed in 2002, publicly shames perpetrators of violence and injustice toward women and children, and puts pressure on the police to act.

OUR VOICES HAVE BEEN NEGLECTED
FEMINIST THEATER

Feminist theater emerged during the 1970s, inspired by the activism of the Women's Liberation Movement. Rather than the "room of one's own" that Virginia Woolf had demanded, women now wanted their own stage—a platform for feminist ideas and experiences. Theater collectives sprang up across the world, ranging from the Women's Theatre Group (now The Sphinx) and Monstrous Regiment in the UK to Spiderwoman and At the Foot of the Mountain in the US, Melbourne Women's Theatre Group in Australia, Dotekabo-ichiza in Japan, Sistren in Jamaica, and Canada's Nightwood Theatre.

What I feel is quite strongly a feminist position and that inevitably comes into what I write.
Caryl Churchill

These burgeoning groups shared a common aim of challenging female stereotypes and the objectification of women's bodies. While all endorsed the general principle of women's equality, they differed in how this should be addressed and achieved. Nightwood's priority, for example, has been to stage plays by and about Canadian women, while Spiderwoman's indigenous women's troupe reflects the politics of Native American women's experience.

Creating a feminist theater

Different political dynamics and styles of feminism influenced the direction each group took. In a radical feminist approach, At the Foot of the Mountain explored female experiences and sought to create from them an art form distinct from a "theater of patriarchy," where male themes and characters rule. The socialist-feminist Monstrous Regiment was committed to new writing and collectively organized to give women the chance to work in all aspects of theater.

British playwright Caryl Churchill, who went on to win international acclaim, was among those commissioned by Monstrous Women. Like other European

Body language

Eve Ensler's one-woman show *The Vagina Monologues* surfaced quietly at the Off Off Broadway HERE Arts Center in 1996, but soon caused a stir. The original monologues were based on Ensler's interviews with 200 women and their accounts of sex, relationships, and associated violence. Her dramatic delivery of stories that were alternately hilarious and disturbing could not be ignored; translated into 48 languages, the monologues are now known across the world.

While the show sparked conservative outrage, and some feminists criticized it for being too narrow and bodycentric, many applauded the political issues it raised. Since 1998, Ensler has used the monologues as part of her global V-Day movement to protest against violence toward women and tackle issues such as assault, incest, female genital mutilation, and human trafficking.

playwrights of the time—such as French Tunisian-born Simone Benmussa, Germany's Gerlind Reinshagen, and Italy's Franca Rame—Churchill was influenced by socialist feminism. Her plays were theatrically inventive, as were those of experimental feminist dramatists, such as Cuban American María Irene Fornés or African American Adrienne Kennedy.

Top Girls (1982), perhaps Churchill's best-known play, opens with a dinner scene that brings together historical and fictional women to celebrate the promotion of the lead character Marlene. As the plot unfolds, Marlene's past is revealed, and the audience learns that her success has been achieved at great cost to other women.

A new generation

Top Girls' cautionary message about material success and individual empowerment proved prophetic for both feminism and its theater movement in the ensuing years. The free-market capitalism and neoliberalism, embraced by

Dinner-party drama sets the scene for Caryl Churchill's *Top Girls*. This 1991 revival at the Royal Court Theatre, London, included some of the cast from the original 1982 production.

Margaret Thatcher's government in the UK and Ronald Reagan's administration in the US, were at odds with the collective ethos that had characterized feminist theater.

In the 1990s, new feminist issues galvanized a younger generation of activists. American dramatist Eve Ensler used the success of her solo show *The Vagina Monologues* (1996) to create the V-Day movement highlighting violence against women.

Inequalities and injustices continue to inform 21st-century feminist drama. Trenchant voices include award-winning women of color, such as Suzan-Lori Parks and Lynn Nottage in the US, debbie tucker green in the UK, and the Australian cabaret troupe of First Nations women, Hot Brown Honey. All in their turn have demanded a feminist stage of their own. ■

"Women's Talk," Lina Khoury's 2006 Arab version of *The Vagina Monologues*, is advertised in Beirut.

ALL FEMINISTS CAN AND SHOULD BE LESBIANS
POLITICAL LESBIANISM

IN CONTEXT

PRIMARY QUOTE
Leeds Revolutionary Feminist Group, 1981

KEY ORGANIZATION
Leeds Revolutionary Feminist Group

BEFORE
1955 The Daughters of Bilitis group—the first lesbian political and social group in the US—is founded.

1969 In Washington, D.C., the Furies Collective is established as a feminist lesbian separatist group.

AFTER
1996 American sociologist Vera Whisman publishes *Queer by Choice*.

2008 In *Sexual Fluidity: Understanding Women's Love and Desire*, American psychologist Lisa Diamond argues that women's sexuality can shift over time.

From the early 1960s, many feminists began to identify heterosexuality as a primary means by which men control women. Radical lesbian feminists questioned heterosexual marriage as the default destiny for girls and women and urged them to practice lesbianism as a political identity.

Political lesbians argued that women could only be truly free of men's violence and control if they excluded men from their romantic and sexual lives completely. Leaving heterosexuality behind voluntarily, they maintained, was a way for women to deepen their commitment to the Women's Liberation Movement.

Lesbian feminism, however, was not always accepted within wider feminist movements. In the US, for example, esteemed heterosexual feminist Betty Friedan—one-time president of the US-based National Organization for Women (NOW)—tried to distance herself from the case for lesbianism. Critics of Friedan condemned her alleged 1969 remarks that lesbians constituted a "lavender menace" that threatened the respectability of feminism.

Resisting patriarchy

In response to Friedan, a loosely organized band of radical lesbian feminists reclaimed her insult and formed a group called the Lavender Menace. In 1970, they produced a manifesto, "The Woman Identified Woman," which asked women to stop aligning themselves with men's sexist expectations and divert their energies from men through political lesbianism.

A lesbian couple march at New York's Gay Pride Parade in 1989. The first parade took place in 1970, one year after the Stonewall Riots in Greenwich Village, where violence erupted between LGBT people and the police.

See also: Compulsory heterosexuality 194–195 ▪ Sex positivity 234–237 ▪ Intersectionality 240–245 ▪ Feminism and queer theory 262–263 ▪ Bisexuality 269

> " Lesbianism is a necessary political choice, part of the tactics of our struggle, not a passport to paradise. "
> **Leeds Revolutionary Feminist Group**

The concept of political lesbianism was given its fullest expression by the UK-based Leeds Revolutionary Feminist Group (LRFG) in the pamphlet "Political Lesbianism: The Case Against Heterosexuality," produced in 1979. In this pamphlet the LRFG analyzed heterosexual sex, and penetration in particular, as an act of violation by men and a constant reminder of women's status as the "invaded center."

Political lesbians were not necessarily expected to have sexual relationships with women. The LRFG defined a lesbian as a woman who did not have sex with men. While many political lesbians had women partners, some were sexually abstinent or asexual.

Many heterosexual feminists were angry at the LRFG's bold assertion that continuing to have sex with men was colluding with

Reclaim the Night marches took place across the UK until the 1990s. They were revived in 2004, the march pictured is from Bristol in 2015, with campaigners against sexual violence demanding an end to rape.

the "enemy." Other lesbians were outraged that lesbianism could be defined as simply not having sex with men. Those who believed their sexuality was inborn rejected the assertion that lesbianism could be any woman's choice.

The sex wars

Feminists continued to debate what constituted an appropriately "feminist" expression of sexuality through the 1980s. In the US, radical lesbian feminist Andrea Dworkin rejected penetration, criticized porn and sex work as violence against women, and emphasized egalitarianism over sexual roles. Other lesbians, such as Gayle Rubin, also in the US, explored BDSM (Bondage, Domination, Sadism, Masochism), and referred to themselves as "pro-sex" feminists. ▪

Leeds Revolutionary Feminist Group

Political lesbianism had its roots in the US, but it was the Leeds Revolutionary Feminist Group (LRFG), from the north of England, that had perhaps the movement's greatest impact. The group was formed in 1977, and first came to prominence in November that year when it organized the Reclaim the Night marches throughout the UK. The marches were in response to police advice to women not to go out at night, in reaction to the "Yorkshire Ripper" serial murders

then taking place. Reclaim the Night (Take Back the Night in the US), was a call to action for the right of women to occupy public space without the threat of physical or sexual violence.

The LRFG remained active through the 1980s. In 1981, it republished its 1979 pamphlet "Political Lesbianism: The Case Against Heterosexuality" as a book called *Love Your Enemy? The debate between heterosexual feminism and political lesbianism*.

WOMAN MUST PUT HERSELF INTO THE TEXT

POSTSTRUCTURALISM

PRIMARY QUOTE
Hélène Cixous, 1975

KEY FIGURES
Hélène Cixous, Luce Irigaray, Julia Kristeva

BEFORE
1960s In France, a new intellectual movement opposed to Structuralism develops.

1968 The French economy is disrupted by student protests and general strikes against capitalism, traditional values, and American imperialism.

AFTER
1970 Mouvement de libération des femmes (MLF), the French women's liberation movement, forms, declaring 1970 "year zero" for their struggle.

1990 Poststructuralist feminist thought finds an American audience with Judith Butler's *Gender Trouble: Feminism and the Subversion of Identity.*

Language reflects traditional **male power structures**. → This leads to **patriarchal dominance** of literature and intellectual culture.

↓

Woman must put herself into the text by her own movement. ← Women are **urged to create** a new *écriture féminine* **(feminine writing)** that will lead to social change.

Poststructuralism is a philosophical movement that emerged in France during the 1960s. It developed as a critique of Structuralism, a French philosophy of the 1950s and '60s, which argued that cultural products, such as literary texts, have underlying logical principles or "structures." Structuralists used the idea of "binary opposition," identifying opposites such as rational/emotional and male/female in texts, to uncover universal organizing principles.

In contrast, poststructuralists argued against the idea of binary opposition, using the philosophical tool of deconstruction. For poststructuralists, texts cannot be relied on as a source of self-evident "truth," because they are shaped by history and culture—both of which, as systems of human knowledge, are subject to bias. They questioned not only what we know but how we think we know it, and how our position in the world affects our idea of what is objective truth.

Many French feminists, including Hélène Cixous, Luce Irigaray, Julia Kristeva, and others, embraced poststructuralism as a way of critiquing dominant assumptions about knowledge

---

Hélène Cixous

Hélène Cixous was born in Oran, French Algeria, in 1937, to a physician father and a mother who had escaped Nazi Germany. She later said that her identity as a member of a Jewish French family in Algeria was marked by alienation.

Moving to France, Cixous studied and lectured in English literature, and was involved in the French student revolution of 1968. She became a powerful voice in French feminism during the 1970s, and published her most influential work, "The Laugh of the Medusa," on *écriture féminine* (feminine

writing). In 1974, she established the first doctoral program in women's studies in Europe, at the experimental University of Paris 8, which she cofounded in direct response to the student protests of 1968. She is a novelist, poet, and playwright, and holds honorary degrees from universities around the world.

Key works

1975 "Le rire de la Méduse" (The Laugh of the Medusa)
1983 *Le Livre de Promethea* (The Book of Promethea)

See also: Political lesbianism 180–181 ▪ Language and patriarchy 192–193 ▪ Gender is performative 258–261

Cixous teaches students at the first center for feminist studies in Europe, at the University of Paris 8. Cixous is an intellectual and radical thinker who developed a new feminist language.

and power. In particular, they drew attention to the ways that philosophical texts have been written from the perspective of men while being presented as objective and all-encompassing fact.

Ecriture feminine
French philosopher Hélène Cixous emerged as an early French poststructuralist feminist in the 1970s. In 1975, she published her career-defining essay "The Laugh of the Medusa."

In this work, Cixous calls on women to challenge the dominant modes of writing that place values typically associated with men over those associated with women. She coins the term *écriture féminine*, or feminine writing, as a challenge to "phallogocentrism," or the ways that men's writing and speech emphasize the importance of (male) reason

over (female) emotion. In her call to women, Cixous asks them to intervene and rewrite the rules of writing, linguistics, and knowledge-making. This is important, argues Cixous, because writing is a key tool for social change.

For Cixous, women's bodies play an important role in *écriture féminine*. She proposes that women experience their bodies—through masturbation, for example—in waves of energy and emotion. This complex way of inhabiting their bodies, she argues, must find expression through writing.

Discussing how women have been disparaged by men for their writing, Cixous compares the ways women have written in secret with the ways women have masturbated in secret. Both, she argues, represent ways that women have been cut off from their source of power because of men's fear and hatred of women.

Cixous reflected American theories of political lesbianism when she stressed the importance of women's connections with other women. She argued that everyone should pursue their

underlying bisexual potential, in the process creating a "multiplication" of desire.

Sexual difference
Luce Irigaray was born in Belgium and, like Hélène Cixous, became an important contributor to French feminism during the 1970s. She developed several theories, including drawing on Marxism to develop her "theory of transaction," arguing that women were reduced to commodities under capitalism, »

> ❝ Woman's *seizing* the opportunity to speak … [allows for] her *shattering* into history … for her own right, in every symbolic system, in every political process.
> **Hélène Cixous** ❞

> ❝ Women must write her self [and must] bring women to writing, from which they have been driven away as violently as from their bodies.
> **Hélène Cixous** ❞

The relationship between sex and language

Beyond logic

Expression is **circular** and centers on **experience**.

It searches for **new language** and **perspective**.

It cannot yet describe **female pleasure**.

Logical

Expression is a **narrative** that leads to a **goal**.

It uses **language** that is **phallocentric**, entrenching a male point of view.

It can effectively describe **male pleasure**.

with polygamous men trading and collecting them much as men trade and collect financial assets.

In her work, Irigaray argues for the importance of women's writing as a way to challenge male-dominated communication and literary output. Through a revolution in women's writing, Irigaray hopes there will be a new language for women that was yet to be fully conceptualized or articulated.

Irigaray is perhaps best known for sexual difference feminism. She believes that the history of Western thought is one in which men have occupied a position at the top of a sexual hierarchy, with women below them as men's inferiors. Men's values and experiences have come to stand for the experiences of all humans, to the extent that women's experiences and philosophical contributions are erased and sublimated. Irigaray suggests that society must move

away from the idea of a sexual hierarchy of men as the subject and women as the "other" and acknowledge sexual difference—that is, recognize women's differences from men and their right to forge female subjectivity by occupying the position of "I."

> 66
>
> The … exclusive—and highly anxious—attention paid to erection … proves to what extent the imaginary that governs it is foreign to the feminine.
> **Luce Irigaray**
>
> 99

Irigaray also notes that women (whom she imagines here in a cisgender context, identifying with the gender assigned to them at birth) have a special relationship to bodily fluids—specifically menstrual blood, breast milk, and amniotic fluid—and connects these physical fluids to women's capacity for conceptual fluidity in writing. In her book *This Sex Which Is Not One* (1977), she writes extensively about women's sexuality as fluid and multiple, with numerous erogenous zones compared with men.

In highlighting the multiplicity of women's sexual organs and potential sites of pleasure, Irigaray seeks both to challenge the primacy of the phallus in male-controlled understandings of sexuality and to explore avenues for sensuality between women. This latter theme is central to Irigaray's piece "When Our Lips Speak Together" (1980).

> " … as in true theater, without makeup or masks, refuse and corpses show me what I permanently thrust aside in order to live.
> **Julia Kristeva**

An advocate for women to take part in "mimesis" or imitation, Irigaray drew on psychoanalysis to suggest that women turn male-created stereotypes about their femininity on their head and take on strange and unusual versions of femininity.

Kristeva and the abject
Born in Bulgaria, Julia Kristeva moved to France in the mid-1960s, and is known for her writing on psychoanalysis, linguistics, and literary criticism. In her 1982 book *Powers of Horror: An Essay on Abjection*, she explores the idea of "abjection"—the process by which a person's sense of the boundaries between the self and the not-self, or the subject and the object, become blurred. In particular, abjection occurs when a person is forced to grapple with that which threatens to destroy the self, namely mortality. Eventually each of us will be reduced to the status of an object, as a corpse.

The figure of the mother, in particular, writes Kristeva, is the target of social abjection. Through the process of reproduction and birth, the mother's body challenges the boundary between subject and object: she belongs to herself, but another being is growing inside her and emerging from her body. She transgresses the boundaries between civilization and the wild through her unruly body, which leaks all manner of fluids through the processes of pregnancy, birth, and breastfeeding.

A mixed response
French feminist work has been criticized as promoting biological essentialism, or the idea that men and women are fundamentally culturally different due to biology.

Julia Kristeva's theory of abjection and the maternal body has influenced feminist scholars of the body. However, she has been criticized for her emphasis on biological difference.

Many feminists object to Irigaray's theory of sexual difference, and to Cixous and Irigaray's emphasis on *écriture féminine*, as reinforcing existing gendered stereotypes. Others criticize poststructuralist feminist writing for being overly theoretical, elitist, and inaccessible. ∎

Men trade women as commodities in Victor-Julien Giraud's *The Slave Market* (1867), which shows a new slave acquired for a classical harem.

The Theory of Transaction

Influenced by Marxist theory, Irigaray argued in her book, *This Sex Which Is Not One,* that in a patriarchal society, women are reduced to the status of commodities, objects exchanged between men based on their perceived market value. Men look upon women as essential for the group's survival through reproduction, but also as things that must be controlled.

Irigaray argued that just as men seek to accumulate maximum wealth under capitalism through exploitation, they also seek to "accumulate" as many women as possible. Her theory claimed that within this transactional context, women are separated into three categories: mother, virgin, and whore. Mothers are exchanged according to their "use value," or reproductive value, while virgins are assessed based on their "exchange value," as a commodity passed between men. Prostitutes, who possess both use and exchange value, are demonized by men.

THE POL OF DIFFE

1980s

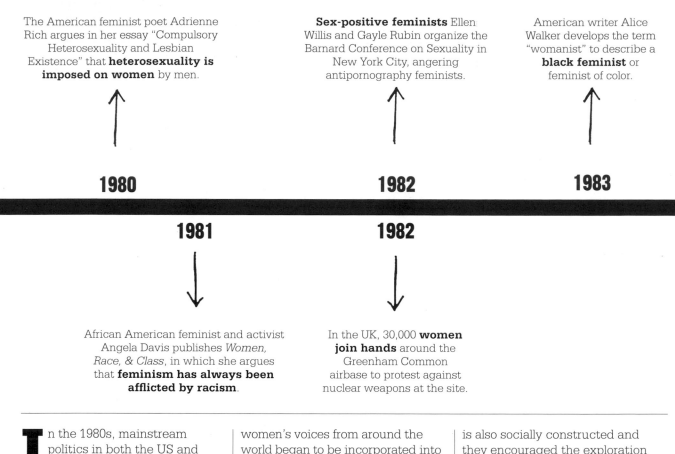

The American feminist poet Adrienne Rich argues in her essay "Compulsory Heterosexuality and Lesbian Existence" that **heterosexuality is imposed on women** by men.

Sex-positive feminists Ellen Willis and Gayle Rubin organize the Barnard Conference on Sexuality in New York City, angering antipornography feminists.

American writer Alice Walker develops the term "womanist" to describe a **black feminist** or feminist of color.

1980

1982

1983

1981

1982

African American feminist and activist Angela Davis publishes *Women, Race, & Class*, in which she argues that **feminism has always been afflicted by racism**.

In the UK, 30,000 **women join hands** around the Greenham Common airbase to protest against nuclear weapons at the site.

I n the 1980s, mainstream politics in both the US and the UK shifted to the right, as the governments of US president Ronald Reagan and British prime minister Margaret Thatcher embraced free-market capitalism, an ideology less conducive to radical activism than the thinking that was prevalent in the 1960s and '70s. Some feminists challenged this, including thousands of women who protested against the installation of nuclear weapons at Greenham Common, a military airbase in the UK. However, others started to re-examine feminism itself, especially in the context of sexuality, race, and gender. Women of color analyzed how white-dominated feminism had ignored the realities of racial difference. At the same time,

women's voices from around the world began to be incorporated into the body of feminist ideas.

At the beginning of the 1980s, American feminist Adrienne Rich challenged what she defined as "compulsory heterosexuality," which, she asserted, was a powerful tool used by patriarchy and capitalism to control women. She urged all feminists to reject men and heterosexual sexuality as a political statement.

By the end of the decade, another key feminist idea, queer theory, was emerging. Continuing into the 1990s and beyond, queer theory questioned the ideology that viewed heterosexuality as the norm and superior to same-sex sexuality. Building on feminist theories about gender, queer theorists suggested that sexuality

is also socially constructed and they encouraged the exploration of sexual identity.

Race and imperialism
For feminists of color, the subject of race, especially racism within feminism, had become a major concern. In her book *Women, Race, & Class*, the activist and academic Angela Davis highlighted the racism and classism within the women's suffrage movement of the late 19th and early 20th centuries, and suggested that early feminism reflected the interests of white middle-class women. Her work stimulated a discussion within feminism about the needs and concerns of women of color and how their history and culture should be represented and voiced, with feminists such as bell

Guerrilla Girls, an anonymous group of feminist artists, forms in New York City to fight **sexism and racism in the art world**.

Sisters in Islam (SIS) is formed in Malaysia, committed to promoting the **rights of Muslim women** based on the principles of equality and freedom.

1985

1988

1984

1986

1989

Feminist Susie Bright cofounds *On Our Backs*, the first **lesbian erotica magazine** in the US.

"Under Western Eyes: Feminist Scholarship and Colonial Discourses," an essay by Indian-born writer Chandra Talpade Mohanty, **challenges Western feminist views** on women in the developing world.

US civil rights advocate Kimberlé Crenshaw coins the term **"intersectionality"** to describe how different types of discrimination are interconnected and interact.

hooks putting forward strategies to make feminism accessible to women of all classes and ethnicities.

Some black feminists, such as the writers Alice Walker and Maya Angelou, suggested that black women should use the word "womanism" as an alternative to "feminism," which to them reflected the culture of privileged white women. Other feminists, such as the cultural scholar Gloria Anzaldúa, who grew up on the Texas-Mexico border, addressed the situation of women in anticolonial movements, arguing that they were ignored by mainstream feminism.

From these perspectives emerged a specifically anticolonial strand of feminism, which analyzed indigenous women's experiences in liberation movements and drew attention to cultural patriarchal practices forced on women, such as female genital cutting (FGC) and polygamy. Chandra Talpade Mohanty, an Indian academic, took this further by advocating a "postcolonial" feminism that found Western feminists' image of "third-world women" as poorly educated victims stereotypical and over simplistic.

Joined-up oppression
At the end of the 1980s, African American feminist Kimberlé Crenshaw introduced the idea of "intersectionality," or intersectional thinking. This analytical tool identified the ways in which class, race, and gender interact and create multiple oppressions, particularly for the most marginalized women in society, such as indigenous women and women of color. Developed from the exploration of black women's experiences of domestic violence, intersectionality provided a new theoretical dimension to feminist thought.

Feminist perspectives were applied to an increasing number of issues. The American activist Barbara Ehrenreich highlighted the low pay and the lack of job opportunities (the "pink-collar ghetto") for women, while the Guerilla Girls, an all-woman collective, burst onto the New York art scene, using dramatic tactics to protest the under-representation of women artists in the art world. Feminist ideas also continued to spread worldwide, with Muslim women opposing forced marriage and women in China campaigning for women's studies programs. ■

THE LINGUISTIC MEANS OF PATRIARCHY
LANGUAGE AND PATRIARCHY

IN CONTEXT

PRIMARY QUOTE
Dale Spender, 1980

KEY FIGURE
Dale Spender

BEFORE
1949 Simone de Beauvoir in *The Second Sex* claims that society is underpinned by a view of men as the norm, and women as the "other."

1970 In *Sexual Politics*, American feminist Kate Millett argues that male writing is misogynist and reinforces patriarchal views of women.

AFTER
2003 Articles in *The Handbook of Language and Gender*, edited by New Zealand sociolinguists Janet Holmes and Miriam Meyerhoff, explore how women and men manage their gender identities through language.

anguage is fundamental to all societies. It allows people to communicate and to receive and share ideas or values. As such, many feminists have seen language as a critical area for study and analysis, particularly to explore the ways in which language helps to perpetuate patriarchy and discrimination against women.

In 1980, Australian feminist Dale Spender published *Man Made Language*, which became a key text in the study of language from a feminist perspective. As its title suggests, the book claims that men, in their dominant role, have created a language that reinforces women's subordination to them.

> 66
> Language and the conditions for its use structure a patriarchal order.
> **Dale Spender**
> 99

For Spender, language and the rules of language are under male control and reflect male values. As a result, women are either invisible or defined as the "other." They find it difficult to change or challenge this situation, since they have to use the language they inherited. Language, therefore, perpetuates male supremacy and entrenches patriarchy.

Mankind speaking
Spender sees language as a reflection of the way society is structured to favor males, and calls this linguistic bias sexism. For Spender, sexism in language appears in many forms: an obvious example is the use of the pronoun "he" to refer to both men and women, which assumes male supremacy and subjugates women.

Spender explores the roots of what she calls "he/man language" and its use of "he" as a generic pronoun and "mankind" to describe the entire human race. She points to the 17th and 18th centuries, when male grammarians laid down rules that explicitly stated males should take pride of place in language and that the male gender was "more comprehensive" than the female. This not only implies that men are

See also: Institutions as oppressors 80 ▪ Patriarchy as social control 144–145 ▪ Poststructuralism 182–187 ▪ Gender is performative 258–261

> The monopoly over language is one of the means by which males have ensured their own primacy, and ... ensured the invisibility ... of females.
> **Dale Spender**

Dale Spender

Feminist, teacher, writer, and literary critic, Dale Spender was born in 1943 in Newcastle, New South Wales, Australia. She studied at Sydney University and taught English at James Cook University before leaving Australia for London, where her PhD research at the University of London formed the basis of *Man Made Language*.

A prolific writer, Spender has authored more than 290 books, including a literary spoof, *The Diary of Elizabeth Pepys* (1991).

She has also edited literary anthologies and—a habitual wearer of purple in honor of the suffragettes—writes a blog called Shrieking Violet.

Key works

1980 *Man Made Language*
1982 *Women of Ideas and What Men Have Done to Them*
1983 *There's Always Been a Women's Movement This Century*
1995 *Nattering on the Net: Women, Power, and Cyberspace*

more powerful than women, but also effectively states that men are the "norm." Women cannot then identify or find themselves in these terms.

Terms such as "chairman," "fireman," or "policeman" similarly assume male dominance in those roles. For Spender, all "he/man" language serves to "construct and reinforce the divisions between the dominant [male] and muted [female] groups." It makes women invisible linguistically and promotes male imagery at the expense of female in everyday life. In effect, women are absorbed into male experience.

Spender also provides examples of language that in her view encourages positive views of men and a negative image of women.

The word "bachelor" applied to a man, for instance, suggests independence and virility, while the word "spinster" reflects a negative and derogatory view of women.

Sexism and silence

A consequence of male-controlled language, Spender argues, is that women lack their own language, and so are largely silenced. Forced to use language defined by men, women are muted, their skills are unrecognized or devalued, and their social and cultural roles disappear. Spender cites the lack of prominent women in many academic fields and those women whose experiences and roles in historical events have been overlooked. Thanks to her work in raising these issues, today's feminists and educators seek to challenge sexist language, behavior, and omissions. ■

A woman takes the minutes while the men make decisions at a meeting in the 1950s. As in many areas of society, business has built a language based on men as the central figures.

HETEROSEXUALITY HAS BEEN FORCIBLY IMPOSED ON WOMEN

COMPULSORY HETEROSEXUALITY

IN CONTEXT

PRIMARY QUOTE
Adrienne Rich, 1980

KEY FIGURE
Adrienne Rich

BEFORE
1949 Simone de Beauvoir advances the theory that lesbianism can be a protest against the patriarchal system.

1970 The Radicalesbians, an activist group in the US, issues its manifesto linking lesbians' and women's liberation.

AFTER
1988 British researcher Helena Whitbread publishes extracts from the diaries of a 19th-century gentlewoman called Anne Lister. They include descriptions of lesbian sex.

1991 In the US, queer theorist Michael Warner coins the term "heteronormativity" to describe the assumption that all people are heterosexual until identified otherwise.

Scholar and poet Adrienne Rich was one of the first feminists to state that heterosexuality is not simply a natural state of being or default sexuality but something that society mandates. She argued that heterosexuality has been enforced throughout history because it is the means by which patriarchy controls women. In her 1980 essay "Compulsory Heterosexuality and Lesbian Existence," Rich uses the term compulsory heterosexuality as a way to understand how it functions as, in her words, a "political institution."

Male control

Rich identifies compulsory heterosexuality as a capitalist mechanism to enforce women's economic subservience to men within the confines of marriage and motherhood. She writes that it has been behind many of the world's abuses of women, such as witch burnings; the denial of women's economic viability outside the realm of heterosexual marriage; and male control of law, religion, and science. She outlines the multiple ways in which men have controlled women's bodies and prevented them from obtaining an education and a career.

Rich also analyzes the erasure of lesbian existence from historical texts written by men. She argues that in denying modern women

Matrimony is idealized in this stained-glass window from a church in London, UK. Adrienne Rich saw marriage as a key component of men's patriarchal control over women.

See also: Trans-exclusionary radical feminism 172–173 ▪ Political lesbianism 180–181 ▪ Antipornography feminism 196–199 ▪ Preventing forced marriage 232–233 ▪ Sex positivity 234–237

… the social relations of the sexes are disordered and extremely problematic, if not disabling, for women.
Adrienne Rich

the knowledge that women have in the past found alternatives to heterosexuality, men continue to try to control women's choices.

Patriarchal exploitation and abuse of women, argues Rich, have resulted in women internalizing the idea that they are sexual objects and accepting men's violations of their boundaries in order to survive. This complicity, she says, teaches women to compete with other women to gain men's attention, and also to

In the film *Carol*, based on a 1950s' novel by Patricia Highsmith, a married mother (Cate Blanchett) and a young woman (Rooney Mara) defy heterosexual assumptions and have a lesbian affair.

invest their energies in men—a way of relating that she calls "male-identification."

The lesbian continuum

In order to counter compulsory heterosexuality and male-identification, Rich recommends the radical feminist concept of the "woman-identified-woman"—someone who spends her emotional, romantic, and erotic energy on women, and withdraws this energy from men. This idea inspired radical lesbian separatism during the 1970s, with women forming women-only spaces and matriarchal communities on "womyn's land," often in rural areas or by the beach.

Rich expands the idea of who counted as lesbian in her concept of the "lesbian continuum." Drawing on the idea that girls' first love is their mother, Rich argues that all women,

"CATE BLANCHETT AND ROONEY MARA ARE SUPERB." THE WALL STREET JOURNAL.

EXQUISITELY DIRECTED BY TODD HAYNES
The New York Times

A THOUGHTFUL, BEAUTIFULLY BUILT FILM THAT TRANSCENDS EXPECTATIONS."
VANITY FAIR

CAROL

however they identify sexually, exist on a continuum of love for other women. This prompted feminists to debate whether the term "lesbian" has any coherence if not rooted in sexuality. Many rejected Rich's concept of a continuum, but the way she conceptualized compulsory heterosexuality as a patriarchal political institution was a revolution in feminist theory. ■

Adrienne Rich

Award-winning poet, writer, and activist Adrienne Rich was born in Baltimore, Maryland, in 1929. She studied poetry and writing at Radcliffe College, ultimately publishing more than 20 volumes of poetry and books on feminism, lesbian sexuality, race, and Jewish identity.

During the 1960s, Rich was radicalized by her experiences as a wife and mother, and by political unrest in American society. She became involved in the New Left and protested against the Vietnam War and for women's rights and black civil rights. After separating

from her husband Alfred Haskell Conrad, a professor of economics, in 1970, she met Jamaican-American author Michelle Cliff in 1976. They remained partners until Rich died in 2012.

Key works

1976 *Of Woman Born: Motherhood as Experience and Institution*
1979 *On Lies, Secrets and Silences: Selected Prose*
1980 "Compulsory Heterosexuality and Lesbian Existence"

PORNOGRAPHY IS THE ESSENTIAL SEXUALITY OF MALE POWER

ANTIPORNOGRAPHY FEMINISM

IN CONTEXT

PRIMARY QUOTE
Andrea Dworkin, 1981

KEY FIGURES
**Andrea Dworkin,
Catherine MacKinnon**

BEFORE
1953 Hugh Hefner launches
Playboy magazine, featuring
nude photos of Marilyn Monroe
without her consent.

1968 America's voluntary film
rating system introduces the
X rating, which comes to be
associated with pornography.

AFTER
1986 The US Attorney
General's Commission on
Pornography (the Meese Report)
determines that pornography
has a harmful effect on society.

1997 The US Supreme Court
limits restrictions against
internet pornography as an
issue of free speech.

For a short period in the
1980s, radical feminists and
right-wing conservatives in
the US worked together to make
pornography illegal. Although their
aims were the same, their motives
were different. The conservatives
believed that pornography was
morally depraved and a threat
to marriage and society; the
antipornography feminists argued
that depicting women as sex
objects rather than human beings
encouraged violence against them.

The leading antipornography
feminist was the philosopher
Andrea Dworkin. Having survived
sexual assault and domestic
violence, she believed that such

See also: Sexual pleasure 126–127 ▪ Confronting misogyny 140–141 ▪ The male gaze 164–165 ▪ Sexism is everywhere 308–309

Andrea Dworkin

Born in New Jersey in 1946, Andrea Dworkin endured sexual violence as a child and in prison after her arrest at an anti–Vietnam War protest as a college student. In 1971, she fled an abusive marriage, and in 1974, *Woman Hating*, her first feminist book, was published. That year she met John Stoltenberg, a gay gender-critical feminist, whom she later married in 1998.

A critic of pornography, Dworkin formulated an antipornography bill with lawyer Catharine MacKinnon in the 1980s, which passed in Minneapolis and Indianapolis before being vetoed. In 1985, she led a large antipornography protest in New Orleans, and the following year testified before the Attorney General's Commission on Pornography. Dworkin died in 2005.

Key works

1981 *Pornography: Men Possessing Women*
1983 *Right-Wing Women: The Politics of Domesticated Females*
1987 *Intercourse*
1988 *Letters from a War Zone: Writings 1976–1987*

The Show World Center Strip Club, seen here in 1984, is one of the last remaining sex clubs on Eighth Avenue, New York City. In the 1980s, it was a key player in a booming sex industry.

This relaxation of social mores provoked a strong reaction. In 1973, the US Supreme Court tried two cases relating to pornography and obscenity laws. In *Miller v. California*, the Court ruled that deeming pornography "free speech" cheapened the level of speech protected by the First Amendment. In *Paris Adult Theater I v. Slaton*, the Court determined that censorship and the limitation of commercial pornography was in society's best interest. Both judgements were based on the conservative view that pornography threatened "good traditional values" and morality. The fact that pornography might cause harm to women, either directly or indirectly, was not taken into account at the trials.

In 1976, the producers of the porn film *Snuff* claimed that the film featured the real-life murder and dismemberment of its female lead. Even though the film's producers later admitted that »

Pornography is the theory, rape is the practice.
Robin Morgan

violence was sexualized and normalized in pornography. In Dworkin's view, pornography did not celebrate human sexuality but encouraged men to view women as less than human, a conviction she set out in her widely read book *Pornography: Men Possessing Women*, published in 1981.

New liberties

In the late 1960s and early '70s, before video and the internet made pornography freely and readily available at home, anyone interested in watching a pornographic film could rent a "stag film" reel or visit an adult cinema. For a brief period, it seemed that pornography had entered the mainstream. Popular porn films such as *Hot Circuit* (1971), *School Girl* (1971), and the highly successful *Deep Throat* (1972), starring Linda Lovelace, seemed to edge toward cultural legitimacy. For homosexual men, cinemas that aired gay adult films, such as *Boys in the Sand* (1971) and *The Back Row* (1972), were a liberating space.

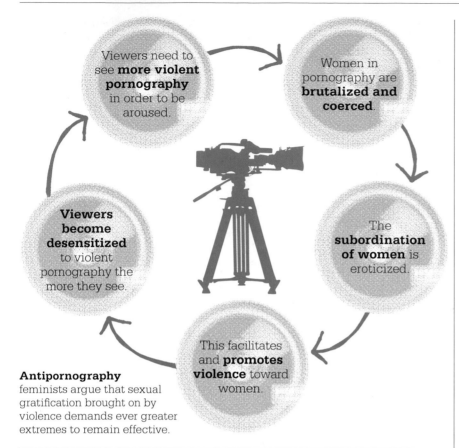

Viewers need to see **more violent pornography** in order to be aroused.

Women in pornography are **brutalized and coerced**.

The **subordination of women** is eroticized.

This facilitates and **promotes violence** toward women.

Viewers become desensitized to violent pornography the more they see.

Antipornography feminists argue that sexual gratification brought on by violence demands ever greater extremes to remain effective.

There can be no 'equality' in porn, no female equivalent, no turning of the tables in the name of bawdy fun.
Susan Brownmiller

this was an advertising gimmick, the stunt inspired a feminist backlash. The use of a woman's purported death to promote the film demonstrated the feminist view that pornography eroticized violence against women.

In the mid- to late 1970s, three feminist activist groups formed in the US in direct opposition to pornography and violence against women: Women Against Violence in Pornography and Media (WAVPM), Women Against Pornography (WAP), and Women Against Violence Against Women (WAVAW). Feminist groups protested outside cinemas from San Francisco, San Jose, Los Angeles, and San Diego to Denver, Buffalo, Philadelphia, and New York, handing out pamphlets discouraging people from viewing *Snuff*.

In 1980, Linda Lovelace (whose real name was Linda Boreman, later Linda Marchiano), the star of *Deep Throat*, published *Ordeal*, an autobiography that directly challenged the fun, free-love, free-speech image of pornography in the 1970s. She revealed that her abusive husband, Chuck Traynor, had beat her, raped her, and forced her to perform sexual acts on film, including bestiality. While the conceit of the film *Deep Throat* was that the female character's clitoris was in her throat, and therefore performing oral sex on men was fun and empowering, in real life Boreman was the victim of brutal violence and coercion. Boreman famously stated that to watch *Deep Throat* was to watch herself being repeatedly raped.

In response to these revelations, Catharine MacKinnon, a Yale-educated lawyer, teamed up with Andrea Dworkin, to try to bring a civil case against Traynor, but there were no laws in place that enabled sex workers and pornographic film stars to sue their employers. The pair campaigned for change and three years later the Minneapolis City Council commissioned MacKinnon and Dworkin to draft an ordinance (local law) that would outlaw pornography as a violation of the rights of women. When Dworkin and MacKinnon achieved some success, they began to collaborate with right-wing antipornography pressure groups. In Indianapolis, for example, MacKinnon worked with council member Beulah Coughenour, an antifeminist Republican woman, to get pornography banned.

Different dangers
Radical feminists found the coalition of the antipornography movement and right-wing conservatives troubling. In an essay entitled "Sexual Politics, the New Right, and the Sexual Fringe" in 1981, feminist Gayle Rubin points out

The Barnard Conference on Sexuality, held in New York in 1982, revealed bitter divisions between sex positive feminists and antipornography feminists, who picketed the event.

the only feminist stance on pornography was censorship, the organizers of the conference invited a number of sex-positive speakers to share their perspective. WAP members picketed the conference and also distributed leaflets explaining their reasons for protesting, arguing that the conference was promoting sadomasochism and pedophilia. Meanwhile, speakers at the conference included Alice Echols, a lesbian academic and advocate for lesbian sadomasochism, whose speech entitled "The Taming of the Id" advocated sexual freedom.

Despite the legal battles and public protests of the early 1980s, antipornography feminism did little to end the proliferation of pornography. Its ready availability during the internet age has raised new questions about the long-term impact of easy-access pornography on children, women, men, and wider society. ∎

how censorship of sexuality almost always has a repressive impact on marginalized sexualities. While Dworkin and MacKinnon insisted that all pornography was violent to women, Rubin counters that sexuality could be liberating. Categorizing sex into "good" and "bad" kinds, she argues, can cause harm to sexual minorities. Rubin's view of sexuality is that all sex, including pornography, should be legal, provided it is consensual.

In 1984, a group of lesbians began to publish an erotica magazine called *On Our Backs*, a response to the antiporn feminist journal, *Off Our Backs*.

Confrontation

The fight between antipornography feminists and the pro-sex or sex-positive line of feminist thought culminated at the 1982 Barnard Conference on Sexuality. Wanting to counteract the assumption that

Pornography is a direct denial of the power of the erotic, for it represents the suppression of true feeling. Pornography emphasizes sensation without feeling.
Audre Lorde

Consent and the feminist sex wars

In the so-called "feminist sex wars" ignited at the Barnard Conference in New York City in 1982, feminists who saw pornography and much of heterosexual sex as violent against women took part in debates with feminists who found sex liberating.

To an antipornography feminist, sadomasochistic sex involving violent role-play and sexualized submissiveness is inherently oppressive. Sex-positive feminists do not oppose sadomasochism as long as it takes place among consenting adults. As antipornography feminists began to see nearly all heterosexual sex as violent and coercive, sex-positive feminists defended healthy, communicative sexual relationships.

The sex wars have continued into the 21st century, as third-wave feminists defend women's right to be sexually active while sex-critical feminists question why women need to be seen as sexy in order to feel empowered.

WOMEN ARE GUARDIANS OF THE FUTURE
ECOFEMINISM

IN CONTEXT

PRIMARY QUOTE
Vandana Shiva, 2005

KEY FIGURE
Vandana Shiva

BEFORE
1962 Rachel Carson's book
Silent Spring highlights the
devastating impact pesticides
have on the environment.

1973 In India, women in the
Chipko Movement use non-
violent direct action to prevent
deforestation caused by
government-backed logging.

AFTER
2004 Wangari Maathai
becomes the first African
woman to receive the Nobel
Peace Prize for her contribution
to sustainable development.

2016 The West Coast
Ecofeminist Conference in
California explores the
degradation of women, animal
rights, and the environment in
a violent, patriarchal world.

rench feminist Françoise
d'Eaubonne coined the
term "ecofeminism" in 1974
for a new branch of feminism that
focused on ecology, the study of the
interactions between organisms
and their environment. It holds that
the domination and degradation of
nature and the exploitation and
oppression of women have
significant connections.

Several environmental disasters
in the US—most notably the 1979
near meltdown at the Three Mile
Island nuclear power plant in
Pennsylvania—brought 600 women
together in 1980 for "Women and
Life on Earth," the first ecofeminist
conference. Held in Massachusetts
during the spring equinox, the
conference explored the links
between feminism, militarization,
healing, and ecology. Ecofeminism

Hundreds of women farmers from
10 southern African countries, whose
crop production had suffered as a result
of erratic weather extremes, protest
outside the 2011 UN climate change
conference in Durban.

See also: Indian feminism 176–177 ▪ Women against nuclear weapons 206–207

Rachel Carson, pioneering American biologist, takes notes beside a river near her home. Her book *Silent Spring* (1962) ignited the environmental movement and led to a ban on destructive pesticides such as DDT.

was defined as a "women-identified movement" that sees Earth's devastation and the threat of nuclear annihilation as feminist concerns because they are underpinned by the same "masculinist mentality" that oppresses women. Ecofeminism holds that women have a special role to play in protecting the environment and campaigning against damage to the planet.

Cultural ecofeminism

As ecofeminism developed, it began to splinter into different approaches, one of which is sometimes described as cultural ecofeminism. This strand is rooted in spirituality, goddess worship, and nature-based religions. Its adherents, including American writer and activist Starhawk (Miriam Simos), argue that women have an intrinsic kinship with the natural environment, and, as instinctive carers, should be at the forefront of its protection. Other feminists criticize this approach for reinforcing gender stereotypes, claiming women's moral superiority, and taking little account of class, race, or the economic exploitation of resources.

A radical standpoint

Ecofeminists such as Vandana Shiva take a more politically radical position. Science and technology are not gender neutral, says Shiva. Global corporate initiatives such as the technology-driven Green Revolution, which by the late 1960s had vastly increased agricultural production worldwide, reflect a dominant ideology of economic growth created, in her own words, by "Western technological man." In this drive for growth, women and nature are viewed as objects to be owned and controlled, and both are exploited.

The struggle, says Shiva, is to save life on the planet from a dominant, patriarchal, and capitalist worldview. Unless women take the lead, she believes, there can be no sustainable future. ∎

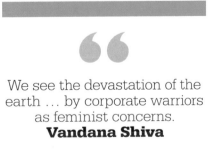

> We see the devastation of the earth … by corporate warriors as feminist concerns.
> **Vandana Shiva**

Vandana Shiva

Born in 1952, Vandana Shiva studied physics in India, then the philosophy of science in Canada. She has written extensively about agriculture and food production, and has actively campaigned for biodiversity and against genetic engineering, working with grassroots groups in Africa, Asia, Latin America, and Europe. In 1982, she founded the independent Research Foundation for Science, Technology, and Ecology in India.

Other projects founded by Shiva include Navdanya (Nine Seeds)—an Indian initiative to promote diversity, organic farming, and the use of indigenous seeds—and Bija Vidyapeeth, a college for sustainable living. In 2010, *Forbes* magazine dubbed her one of the seven most powerful women in the world.

Key works

1988 *Staying Alive: Women, Ecology and Survival in India*
1993 *Ecofeminism* (co-written with Maria Mies)
2013 *Making Peace with the Earth*

"WOMAN" WAS THE TEST, BUT NOT EVERY WOMAN SEEMED TO QUALIFY

RACISM AND CLASS PREJUDICE WITHIN FEMINISM

IN CONTEXT

PRIMARY QUOTE
Angela Davis, 1981

KEY FIGURE
Angela Davis

BEFORE
1965 The Voting Rights Act in the US prohibits racial discrimination in voting.

1973 The National Black Feminist Organization is founded to press for action on issues that affect black women in the US.

AFTER
1983 Black American author and feminist Alice Walker coins the term "Womanism" in her book *In Search of Our Mothers' Gardens*.

1990 Black American sociologist Patricia Hill Collins explores the "loose" black woman stereotype in her book *Black Feminist Thought*.

Much of the feminist scholarship during the first and second waves of the Women's Liberation Movement in the US and UK was written by white, middle-to-upper-class women. As such, it tended to reflect their experiences and biases even while claiming to apply to all women. The same was true of feminist movements, many of which were led by, and attracted the support of, white, class-privileged women.

While women of color had always been part of feminist movements for change, the unique concerns of women of color and poor and working-class women

See also: Racial and gender equality 64–69 ▪ Black feminism and womanism 208–215 ▪ Intersectionality 240–245

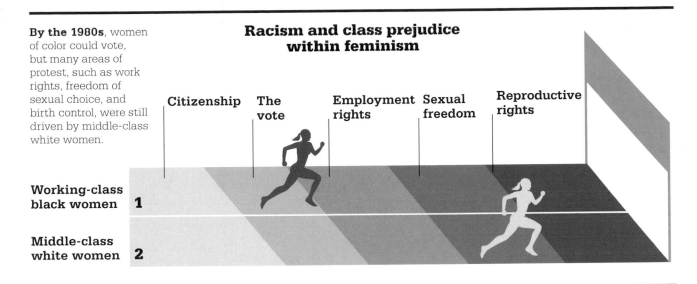

Racism and class prejudice within feminism

By the 1980s, women of color could vote, but many areas of protest, such as work rights, freedom of sexual choice, and birth control, were still driven by middle-class white women.

Citizenship | The vote | Employment rights | Sexual freedom | Reproductive rights

Working-class black women **1**

Middle-class white women **2**

had often been ignored within mainstream feminism. From the 1970s and into the 1980s, feminists of color, poor and working-class feminists, and feminists at the intersections of those two groups began to draw attention to the racism and prejudice undermining the "sisterhood" of feminism.

Rights for whites

In 1981, the black activist, academic, and writer Angela Davis published *Women, Race, & Class*. This study of the history of the Women's Liberation Movement in the US, from the days of slavery onward, reveals how feminism has always been hampered by race and class prejudices. Its publication was to be a watershed moment for feminism.

In the book, Davis examines how the institution of slavery set black women on a course for

subhuman treatment that reflected very different assumptions about womanhood, race, and class than those projected onto white women. Davis also explores how white feminists reinforce antiblack racism and class prejudice in their own struggle for equality.

Writing about the first women's rights convention, held in Seneca Falls, New York, in 1848, Davis points out how the 19th-century suffragists highlighted the institution of marriage and the exclusion of women from professional employment as the two major forms of oppression impacting women. Davis argues that these concerns were specific to white and economically privileged women and failed to address the plight of poor and »

A housekeeper sweeps a fireplace in a wood-paneled den in Virginia. In the postwar period, a white woman's status was reflected by her "help," who was often African American.

The mothers of slaves

White feminists in the US in the 19th century often called for women's equality based on their unique role as mothers, but that plea was not extended to black women during the era of slavery. Angela Davis explained that black women then were not seen as mothers at all, but more like animals, responsible for "breeding" to increase the slave workforce. White enslavers' focus on their reproductive function was heightened after the US Congress banned the international importation of enslaved people from Africa in 1807. From then on—with some exceptions, such as slave ships brought secretly to American ports—enslavers had to rely solely on "breeding" and slave auctions within the US to grow their enslaved population.

As a result, sexual abuse was rife—both white enslavers' rape of enslaved black women and the forcing of black men and women to reproduce, until the US abolished slavery in 1865.

white enslavers' widespread sexual violence under slavery, slavery-endorsing society created the victim-blaming stereotype of the sexually "loose" black woman, which still endured. While they physically and sexually abused black women, male enslavers refused to view black women in the same light as white women. White women were considered physically weak and delicate, whereas black women were expected to work in the fields alongside the men. With black women forced to perform the same tasks as men, the image of black women as "unfeminine" and "unladylike" was reinforced in white society.

Meanwhile, as the Industrial Revolution took hold, argues Davis, white women's work inside the home became increasingly devalued and rendered irrelevant as machines took over their labor. As a result, strict gender roles

working-class white women and enslaved black women, as well as the racism endured by free black women in the states of the North.

White suffragists also called for the ban of black women from membership of the National Woman Suffrage Association, in order, Davis argues, to retain the membership of Southern white women opposed to integration. Additionally, there were many white suffragists incensed after the passage in 1870 of the 15th Amendment, which allowed black men to vote. For Davis, suffragists exposed their underlying racism when they objected to the idea of black men voting before white women could, and neglected to focus on the potential importance of this milestone in obtaining the vote for black women.

The legacy of slavery

Davis holds up slavery as the cause of many of the prejudices that persisted into modern life for women of color. She writes that in order to deflect from the reality of

A banner reading "Women fight back" is unfurled at an outdoor protest in 1980. At this time, both black and white feminists pushed for the passing of the Equal Rights Amendment, which promised equal legal rights for women.

[The Seneca Falls] Declaration … ignored the predicament of white working-class women, as it ignored the condition of Black women in the South and North.
Angela Davis

> Every inequality ... inflicted on American white women is aggravated a thousandfold among Negro women, who are triply exploited—as Negroes, as workers, and as women.
> **Elizabeth Gurley Flynn**
> US labor leader

governing white "men's work" outside the home and white "women's work" inside the home became cemented.

Reproductive rights

After the 1865 abolition of slavery, when breeding more slaves was no longer profitable for white enslavers, white supremacists reasserted their desire for a white nation "untainted" by people of color. The eugenics movement of the late 19th and early 20th centuries aimed to "purify" the human race by selecting who should and should not breed. This left women of color, and those from poor backgrounds, vulnerable to involuntary sterilization.

While women of color were encouraged to curb reproduction, white women, writes Davis, were expected to have as many children as possible. Early feminist family planning advocates such as Margaret Sanger—who coined the term "birth control"—were heralded as champions for women's reproductive rights. However, Sanger also believed in "weeding out the unfit ... preventing the birth of defectives."

For Davis, these historical double standards in how women's bodies have been policed based on race and class had led many feminists of color to regard white-dominated feminist activism on reproduction issues with suspicion. Having had forms of birth control forced upon them in the past, women of color could not necessarily view the issue of reproductive rights in the same liberating light.

Embracing difference

Davis's insights began a new conversation about whose voices should be heard in feminist movements; which issues should be seen as "women's issues;" and the need for diversity in leadership, thought, and tactics. She made it clear that the experiences of white, class-privileged feminists were not those of poor or black feminists.

The growth of a more diverse feminism in the 1980s led to a flourishing of feminist thought. The idea of "woman" was no longer limited to the white middle-class woman. It went beyond that to consider the ways that all women are embodied, not simply as a gender but also as part of a race, class, or sexual group. ∎

> As long as women are using class or race power to dominate other women, feminist sisterhood cannot be fully realized.
> **bell hooks**

Angela Davis

As an activist, scholar, and professor, Angela Davis rose to prominence in the 1960s for her work in the black civil rights movement, especially in the Black Panther Party and the black communist group Che-Lumumba Club. Davis's activism was driven by her background. She was born in Birmingham, Alabama, in 1944, grew up in an area exposed to anti-black bombings during the 1950s, and attended a segregated elementary school.

Davis was fired from her teaching post at University of California, Los Angeles (UCLA) in 1970 for her links to communism, but won her job back. That same year, she was implicated in the supply of guns to a black prisoner who died trying to escape. She was released from prison in 1972, and continues to lecture on women's rights, race, and criminal justice.

Key works

1974 *Angela Davis: An Autobiography*
1983 *Women, Race, & Class*
1989 *Women, Culture, & Politics*

THE MILITARY IS THE MOST OBVIOUS PRODUCT OF PATRIARCHY
WOMEN AGAINST NUCLEAR WEAPONS

On August 27, 1981, a small group of 36 women in the UK, calling themselves "Women for Life on Earth," set off from Cardiff, Wales, to walk 120 miles (190 km) to Greenham Common in Berkshire. Their purpose was to draw attention to the fact that American nuclear-powered cruise missiles were due to be located at the Greenham Common air base.

On September 4, the group arrived at Greenham, where four women chained themselves to the perimeter fence and a letter was delivered to the base commander explaining the reasons for the protest—that the women were against cruise missiles being located in Britain and believed the nuclear arms race represented the greatest threat ever faced by humanity.

The women set up camp outside the main gate. Over the following weeks and months, they were

Women hold hands in a "peace chain", as part of the 1982 "embrace the base" protest at Greenham. Some women came for short visits; others stayed for years in "benders" made out of tree branches and plastic.

See also: Women uniting for peace 92–93 ▪ Ecofeminism 200–201 ▪ Guerrilla protesting 242–243 ▪ Women in war zones 276–277

The protest's long-term impact

The legacy of the Greenham Women's Peace Camp, especially its impact on the proliferation of nuclear weapons, is almost impossible to quantify. However, the women-only space created at Greenham was very powerful, not least for clearly showing that women could work collectively, even in difficult conditions. The Camp attracted thousands of women to the site, developed a powerful camaraderie, and enabled women to discuss not just their role as campaigners for a nuclear-free world but also their roles and situations as women. The Camp proved that they could challenge the nuclear state. Their creative actions, or "protest as spectacle," and commitment to non-violent direct action helped to shape antiwar and environmental campaigns that followed.

Cruise missiles left Greenham in 1991, but some women stayed until 2000, as a general protest against nuclear weapons. In 2002, the Camp was designated a Commemorative and Historic Site.

This sculpture at Greenham Peace Garden represents a camp fire. It is engraved with the words "You can't kill the spirit"—lyrics from Greenham's unofficial anthem.

joined by many others, and a decision was made early on to make the camp women-only. The first major demonstration took place in December 1982, when some 30,000 women arrived to "embrace the base" by forming a human chain around its perimeter.

Action steps up

The protest escalated when the cruise missiles arrived. Women cut the perimeter wire, entered the base, picketed it, and monitored and publicized the deployment of missiles on training exercises. Many women were charged with criminal damage, arrested, and fined or imprisoned. Violence toward the women from police and bailiffs who tried to evict them also increased.

Within its first year, the Greenham Women's Peace Camp made news headlines around the world. Images of Greenham women proliferated. They were shown dancing on silos; decorating the wire with toys or weaving webs of silk and wool into it; blockading the base and congregating at the various "gates" or small camps that made up the larger camp. This joyful chaos served as a vivid contrast with the power of the state and its commitment to nuclear deterrence.

By 1983, the Greenham Women's Peace Camp was not only a powerful focus for peace campaigners but also the most visible strand of British feminism. Reflecting key elements of the Women's Liberation Movement, the camp was non-hierarchical

Take the toys away from the boys!
The Fallout Marching Band

and its decisions were based on consensus, with a strong focus on debate and personal experience.

Challenge to the patriarchy

For many British feminists, Greenham was the most visible expression of women challenging not just nuclear weapons but also male military power. Nuclear weapons symbolized all forms of male violence toward women.

Some women at Greenham argued that only women, as nurturers and caretakers, could truly resist militarism. Reflecting this maternalist perspective, they hung photographs of their children on the wire surrounding the base. Other feminists were unhappy with this traditional attitude, arguing that it propped up the determinist view of women as mothers first and foremost, and also pointed out that mothers had long been used in war to remind their sons of their duty to fight. Some also felt that placing too much focus on a single issue risked deflecting attention from all the other issues affecting women. ▪

WOMANIST
IS TO FEMINIST AS
PURPLE
IS TO LAVENDER
BLACK FEMINISM AND WOMANISM

IN CONTEXT

PRIMARY QUOTE
Alice Walker, 1983

KEY FIGURE
Alice Walker, Maya Angelou, bell hooks

BEFORE
1854 The National Association of Colored Women's Clubs forms in Washington, D.C., to promote job training and equal pay. Its motto is "Lifting As We Climb."

1969 Maya Angelou's *I Know Why the Caged Bird Sings* outlines her experiences of racism and sexual abuse.

AFTER
2018 African American writer Brittney C. Cooper publishes *Eloquent Rage: A Black Feminist Discovers Her Superpower*, a memoir about how Cooper found her voice as a black woman and earned the respect that transcends race and gender.

For these grandmothers and mothers of ours were … artists; driven to … madness by springs of creativity in them for which there was no release.
Alice Walker

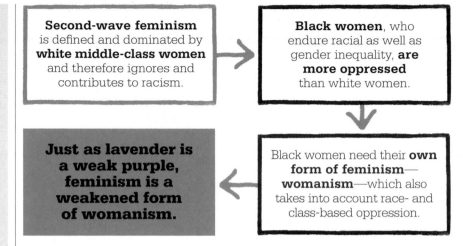

Second-wave feminism is defined and dominated by **white middle-class women** and therefore ignores and contributes to racism.

Black women, who endure racial as well as gender inequality, **are more oppressed** than white women.

Black women need their **own form of feminism— womanism**—which also takes into account race- and class-based oppression.

Just as lavender is a weak purple, feminism is a weakened form of womanism.

T he exact meaning of African American author Alice Walker's phrase "Womanist is to feminist as purple is to lavender" has been the subject of debate over many years. Her term "womanism" appears in her 1983 book *In Search of Our Mothers' Gardens: Womanist Prose*, a collection of poetry, essays, interviews, and reviews that form an exploration of what it is like to be an African American woman. In particular, the book examines the relationship between African American women and literature, art, and history.

Defining terms

Walker begins the book with a definition of "womanism," which is derived from the slang term "womanish;" for example, black mothers might say their daughters are "acting womanish," meaning they are trying to be like an adult. Walker describes it as the opposite of "girlish"—that is, "frivolous, irresponsible, not serious." A womanist is therefore someone who should be taken seriously.

Walker expands on this by saying that when black women are accused of "acting womanish" it is

because their behavior is being seen as "outrageous, audacious, courageous, or wilful". When black women want to "know more" or understand something in greater depth, they risk being criticized for behaving inappropriately.

This description could apply to women who go against the grain or do not embrace societal norms—exactly the sort of behavior feminists were accused of exhibiting in the early 1980s. In fact, Walker directly describes womanists as black feminists, establishing a strong link between womanism and feminism, though she saw womanism as the primary and stronger state (the color purple) of which feminism (the paler color lavender) forms just a part.

Womanists for all

In the second part of her definition of "womanist," Walker broadens the description to include all women "that love other women." She says that love may or may not be a sexual love, and emphasizes a bond between women that celebrates their emotional life and their strength. She goes on to claim that womanism is for heterosexual women who have a male partner as

See also: Racism and class prejudice within feminism 202–205 ▪ Postcolonial feminism 220–223 ▪ Privilege 239 ▪ Intersectionality 240–245

well as for lesbian women and women who love men as friends. This statement was controversial, because attached to it was the notion that a womanist might not want to separate herself from men. This challenged some radical and lesbian feminists, who insisted that the collective fight against the patriarchy had to exclude men.

Outlining her universalist philosophy for womanists, Walker describes it as a garden in which all flowers are present, a metaphor for the fact that there are many races in the world and many kinds of womanist, in terms of their sexuality, class, and so on. This analogy also appears in the book's title essay "In Search of our Mothers' Gardens," in which she uses the idea of a well-tended, colorful garden to describe black women's creativity. Her own mother always kept a flourishing garden full of flowers, which Walker saw as an outlet for her mother to express her creativity.

A womanist, Walker goes on to assert, is committed to the survival of all humans in a world where men and women can live together while still maintaining their cultural distinctiveness. She describes womanists as having the potential to become activists, able to lead oppressed people to safety—in the way that slaves were able to escape from their captors—and fight for the survival of all races.

To achieve this, womanism takes into account the whole lives of black women, their sexuality, family, class, and poverty, and their history, culture, mythology, folklore, oral traditions, and spirituality. »

Alice Walker

Born in 1944 in Eatonton, Georgia, Alice Malsenior Walker was the eighth child of African American sharecroppers. When she was accidentally blinded in one eye, her mother gave her a typewriter, allowing her to write instead of doing chores. She received a scholarship to attend Spelman College in Georgia. After graduating in 1965, she moved to Mississippi and became involved in the Civil Rights Movement.

Walker is best known for her novels, short stories, and poems, with their insight into African American culture, particularly female lives. Her most famous work is the novel *The Color Purple*. The book won a Pulitzer Prize and was adapted into a film by Steven Spielberg in 1985. A musical adaptation produced by Oprah Winfrey premiered in 2004.

Key works

1981 *You Can't Keep a Good Woman Down*
1982 *Meridian*
1982 *The Color Purple*
1983 *In Search of Our Mothers' Gardens: Womanist Prose*

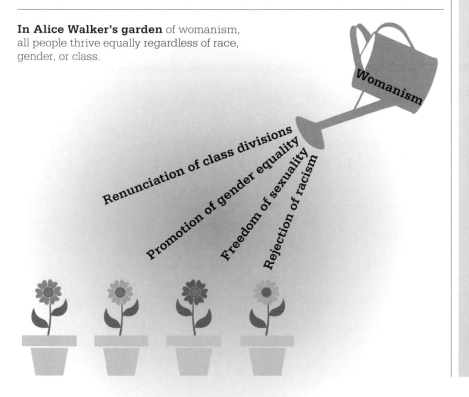

In Alice Walker's garden of womanism, all people thrive equally regardless of race, gender, or class.

Renunciation of class divisions

Promotion of gender equality

Freedom of sexuality

Rejection of racism

Womanism

The third part of Walker's definition lists areas of life that the womanist should embrace and celebrate. Walker points to how the love of spirituality, dance, and music can lead to a loving of the self, opening up womanism to the inclusion of self-care—a subject that African American feminist bell hooks later wrote about in her book *Sisters of the Yam* (1993).

Finally, comparing purple with lavender, womanism is compared with feminism. Walker views feminism as an aspect of womanism but not the whole story. In summary, she affirms the experiences of African American women while also promoting a vision for the whole world based on those experiences.

Zora Neale Hurston

Walker was particularly interested in black women writers who had been overlooked or forgotten. Zora Neale Hurston (1891–1960) was a writer, journalist, and anthropologist whom Walker discovered while reviewing a course on black literature. Walker noticed that Hurston's work was mentioned only briefly compared to that of the black male writers. While searching for Hurston's work, she discovered *Mules and Men* (1935), a collection of African American folklore.

Black folklore helped inspire Walker's concept of womanism and the discovery of Hurston's work was integral to its development. When Walker gave *Mules and Men* to her family to read, they discovered that the stories were folk tales told to them by their grandparents when they were children. As adults, they had moved away from this legacy, mostly through embarrassment or shame at their old traditions, dialect, and accounts of experiences under slavery. Under slavery, black people had been ridiculed and stereotyped, and their descendants had aspired to be more like Europeans.

In Walker's 1979 essay "Zora Neale Hurston," she concludes that the writer was ahead of her time, not only in the way in which she lived her life, but in her positive attitude to

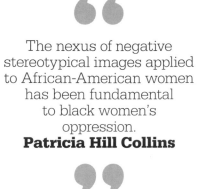

> The nexus of negative stereotypical images applied to African-American women has been fundamental to black women's oppression.
> **Patricia Hill Collins**

her black heritage. Being a pioneer came with its drawbacks—Walker found that while many loved Hurston's work, there were strong opinions about her lifestyle, which was unconventional for the 1930s. Unmarried, she enjoyed several relationships, was flamboyant, and wore dramatic African head wraps before they became fashionable. Hurston was also accused by some African American critics of taking money from "white folks" in the form of a grant for research. Interested in Africa and in countries such as Jamaica, Haiti, and Honduras, Hurston studied the speech of black people from the American Deep South.

Walker's "rediscovery" of Hurston made a big impression on her life and work, mainly because she found in Hurston a black woman who was wholly "herself." Walker called her essay on Hurston "a cautionary tale" because she had suffered for her outspokenness, yet showed that

Zora Neale Hurston wrote books, plays, collections of folklore, magazine articles, and a study of voodoo. She died in obscurity in 1960, but Alice Walker's writings led to a revival of interest.

black people had a responsibility to celebrate their black intellectuals and not let them be overlooked.

The caged bird sings

Womanism aspires to encompass black women's whole lives and celebrate the ways in which they negotiate multiple oppressions in their individual lives. In 1969, African American author Maya Angelou had published her first autobiography, *I Know Why the Caged Bird Sings*, in which she writes about her rape at the hands of her mother's boyfriend and her experiences of prejudice as a child and as a young woman.

The book's depiction of racism and sexual violence confirmed that black feminists were right to be concerned about this intersection of gender and racial oppression. They faced a particular set of

issues, which was why womanism was needed instead of feminism. The black people of Angelou's community were an essential backdrop for her autobiography. She describes how both men and women were affected by racism,

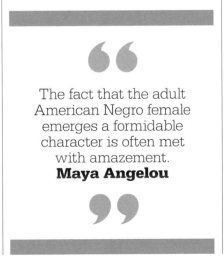

> The fact that the adult American Negro female emerges a formidable character is often met with amazement.
> **Maya Angelou**

The 1976 Broadway show *For Colored Girls Who Have Considered Suicide/When the Rainbow is Enuf* by Ntozake Shange, highlighted the particular experiences of black women.

how religion and the church were central to every aspect of her community, and the consequences of poverty. Growing out of the belief that the fight against racism and sexism could not be carried out separately, black feminism sought to address inequalities in both these areas for black women.

Black feminists had some historical black female figures to look to as role models, such as Ida B. Wells, a founding member of the National Association for the Advancement of Colored People, who had fought a campaign against lynching in the US during the 1890s. However, this organization » was seen as old-fashioned in the 1960s and '70s, when black American women began to search for an ideology that reflected their experience. For most of them, feminism failed to describe how they related to the world.

A new chapter

In 1973, as a result of wanting to address racism and sexism, black feminists formed the National Black Feminist Organization (NBFO) in New York City. Issuing a Statement of Purpose, they expressed their dissatisfaction with black women's near invisibility in second-wave feminism and in the Civil Rights and Black Liberation movements, as well as their resolve to address the needs of "the larger but almost cast-aside half of the black race in Amerikkka, the black woman."

The following year, a splinter group formed the more radical Combahee River Collective (CRC) in Boston. In 1977, Demita Frazier, Beverly Smith, and Barbara Smith, former members of the NBFO, authored the Combahee River Collective Statement, which affirmed that black women suffered from both racism and sexism. This

was the first time that there had been an express acknowledgement that black women were the victims of multiple oppressions: sexual oppression in the black community and racism within wider society and within the feminist movement. The collective did not state that the Women's Liberation Movement was wrong for concentrating on sexual oppression, simply that black women had other issues besides sexism that needed to be addressed.

The authors focused on identity politics and racial-sexual oppressions. They also dealt with what they saw as damaging ideologies that compounded their situation, such as capitalism, imperialism, and patriarchy. Like Walker, they rejected lesbian separatism. The Collective sponsored seven black feminist retreats between 1977 and 1980. Attracting thousands of women, these consciousness-raising events built support for women who had previously worked in isolation.

New voices

By the time Walker wrote *The Color Purple* in 1982, a novel that highlighted not only domestic

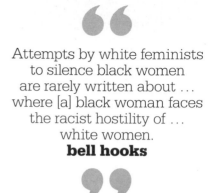

> Attempts by white feminists to silence black women are rarely written about ... where [a] black woman faces the racist hostility of ... white women.
> **bell hooks**

violence and love between women but also the cultural vibrancy of the American Deep South, both the NBFO and the CRC had dissolved and black women were crying out for a different way to bring their whole existence into focus.

It was at this time that bell hooks, who was beginning to carve a place for herself within academia, experienced some of the racism from feminists that the CRC and NBFO had discussed at their conferences and in publications. In her own book, *Feminist Theory:*

---

bell hooks

Born Gloria Jean Watkins in Hopkinsville, Kentucky, and growing up in a racially segregated community in the American South, bell hooks adopted her pseudonym from her maternal great-grandmother as a way to honor female legacies. She chose to spell it without capital letters to focus attention on her message rather than herself. She earned her BA from Stanford University, her MA from the University of Wisconsin, and her PhD from the University of California, Santa Cruz. An acclaimed intellectual, feminist

theorist, artist, and writer, hooks has written more than 30 books. Her work examines the varied perceptions of black women, and spans several genres, including cultural criticism, autobiography, and poetry.

Key works

1981 *Ain't I a Woman: Black Women and Feminism*
1984 *Feminist Theory: From Margin to Center*
1993 *Sisters of the Yam: Black Women and Self-Recovery*

The Color Purple was released as a film in 1985. The tale of abuse and prejudice suffered by a black woman in the American South won the Pulitzer Prize and was nominated for 11 Oscars.

From Margin to Center, which she published in 1984, she argues that the curricula for women's studies and feminist theory marginalized black authors. She also asserts that feminism cannot make women equal to men because in Western society, not all men are equal and not all women share a common social status either.

Using this work as a platform to offer a more inclusive feminist theory, hooks encourages the sisterhood but also advocates—as did Audre Lorde, another American activist and writer of color—for women to acknowledge their differences while still accepting one another. However, when hooks challenged feminists to consider their relationship to race, class, and sex, some black feminists doubted that white women would ever be able to fully debate racism, given the legacy of colonialism and slavery.

As well as including white women, hooks also argued for the importance of male involvement in the equality movement, stating that, in order for change to occur, men must play their part.

Womanism today

Although many of the early black women's groups disbanded in the early 1980s, black feminism and womanism grew out of this formative period in the lives of African American women. Womanism is still debated but is used as a historical term. By demanding their own space within feminism, academics and activists such as bell hooks and Alice Walker created space for more intellectual debate and alternative theories to develop within feminism.

In 1993, for example, African American academic Clenora Hudson-Weems totally rejected not just feminism but black feminism, calling the term Eurocentric. Instead she advocated for "Africana womanism," an approach that aspired to encompass black women's African heritage. Prejudice against black people is still rife in 21st-century society, and black women have been at the forefront of efforts to confront this. Formed in the US in 2013, Black Lives Matter is a movement that aims to intervene whenever violence by the state or vigilantes affects black people. It was set up by three black women—Alicia Garza, Patrisse Cullors, and Opal Tometti—following the acquittal of the killer of Trayvon Martin, an unarmed black youth, in Florida in 2012.

The women used social media to spread the word and connect with like-minded people across the US. They wanted to form a grassroots movement to highlight the contributions made to society by black people, to affirm their humanity, and to resist oppression. Black Lives Matter has since become a new civil rights movement with a global network of activists. ■

Supporters of Black Lives Matter at a Pride march in Toronto, Canada, in 2017. They demanded that police in uniform did not join the march, in protest of police violence against black people.

THE MASTER'S TOOLS WILL NEVER DISMANTLE THE MASTER'S HOUSE
ANGER AS AN ACTIVIST TOOL

Although the Women's Liberation Movement in the 1960s and '70s was said to represent all women, Audre Lorde felt that some women—notably poor women and black women—were excluded. Drawing parallels with the relationship between slave and master to describe women's struggle for freedom, she asserted that women should embrace the differences between each other and use them as a strength to fight their enemies. She pronounced that change would not come from fear and prejudice—the instruments, or tools, of the oppressor—but from changing the rules and working together.

Anger as energy

In her poem "For each of you" (1973), Lorde advises women to use anger in a constructive way to fight authority. If used correctly, she says, anger can be a powerful source of energy to fight inequality. Anger should not be directed at other women, but instead at those who restrict women's lives. In Lorde's 1981 address to the National Women's Studies Association, she used anger to accuse the movement of refusing to debate the issue of racism, as it insisted that racism could only be unraveled by black women and not by the movement as a whole. Lorde argued that this meant that white women never noticed their own prejudice. ∎

Audre Lorde was an African American writer, feminist, and civil rights activist. She used her poetry to express her anger at political and social injustice.

See also: Racial and gender equality 64–69 ∎ Black feminism and womanism 208–215 ∎ Privilege 239 ∎ Intersectionality 240–245

HALF THE POPULATION WORKS FOR NEXT TO NOTHING
GROSS DOMESTIC PRODUCT

IN CONTEXT

PRIMARY QUOTE
Marilyn Waring, 1988

KEY FIGURE
Marilyn Waring

BEFORE
1969 In her book *Housework*, American feminist Betsy Warrior argues that women's domestic labor is the basis for all economic transactions.

1970 Danish economist Ester Boserup examines the effects of economic growth on women in the developing world in her book *Woman's Role in Economic Development*.

AFTER
1994 The journal *Feminist Economics* is founded in the US. Its mission is to find new approaches for improving the lives of women and men.

2014 The anthology *Counting on Marilyn Waring* gathers a range of feminist economic theories into one volume.

I n the last decades of the 20th century, Marilyn Waring—a university lecturer, farmer, and activist for international women's rights from New Zealand—became an important voice in economic and political ideologies. She pioneered the feminist critique of mainstream economics for disregarding the essential part women's unpaid work plays in all countries' economies.

Gross domestic product

Waring's groundbreaking work *If Women Counted* (1988) examines how economic orthodoxies exclude most of women's work, making half of the world's population invisible. She convincingly argues for the need to rethink basic economic concepts, in particular Gross Domestic Product (GDP), so the whole community's wellbeing is taken into consideration, including the productivity of women's unpaid work. Waring was the first to emphasize the importance of women's time at micro and macro community levels. She turned women's time into a tool to challenge patriarchal traditions in both economics and government. Previously invisible domestic work performed by women was finally linked to its economic value.

Waring's *If Women Counted* persuaded the United Nations to recalculate GDP and inspired new accounting methods in numerous countries. Her book is also considered the founding source of feminist economics, helping gain increased visibility for women. ◼

> The most important question is not what is the value of the work [women] are doing, but do they have time to do it?
> **Marilyn Waring**

See also: Marxist feminism 52–55 ▪ Socialization of childcare 81 ▪ Wages for housework 147

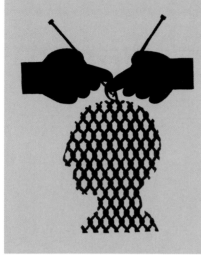

WHITE SOCIETY STOLE OUR PERSONHOOD

ANTICOLONIALISM

IN CONTEXT

PRIMARY QUOTE
Gloria Anzaldúa, 1987

KEY FIGURES
**Awa Thiam,
Gloria Anzaldúa**

BEFORE
1930s French-speaking African and Caribbean writers based in Paris begin the Négritude literary movement in protest against French colonial rule and assimilation.

1950s Martinican philosopher Frantz Fanon publishes works that analyze women's colonial and neocolonial oppression, as well as sexist domination.

AFTER
1990 South African writer Bessie Head publishes her autobiography, in which she describes growing up under South Africa's apartheid system and being subject to both racism and patriarchal black nationalism.

Colonial policy-makers often believed that the status of women in a society indicated the extent to which it was "civilized." They partly justified intervention, oppression, and occupation by claiming they were "protecting" women of color from the "savage" customs of their men. This made it difficult for women of color to assert their racial and gender rights and led to gender divisions within independence movements. Even though women contributed to nationalist causes, their male counterparts remained suspicious of their motives, often

> Challenging the status of women amounts to challenging the structures of an entire society when this society is patriarchal in nature.
> **Awa Thiam**

accusing them of embracing a European agenda. Some feminists were torn between fighting for their country's independence or advancing women's rights.

Double domination

Among the feminists who have written about women's experiences under colonialism is Senegalese writer Awa Thiam. Her book *Speak Out, Black Sisters: Feminism and Oppression in Black Africa* (1977) examines how traditional and colonial oppression shaped the lives of women in West and Central Africa. Breaking many taboos by openly discussing institutionalized patriarchy, polygamy, female genital mutilation, sexual initiation, and skin whitening, she highlights women's double oppression by colonial and traditional patriarchal systems.

To use one example, Thiam describes how the introduction of cash crops grown for export in the Belgian Congo under colonial administration from 1908 to 1960 led to the increased exploitation of women, because horticulture was considered women's work under the traditional gender division of labor. Yet it was the men who received payment for such

See also: Postcolonial feminism 220–223 ▪ Indigenous feminism 224–227 ▪ Privilege 239 ▪ Intersectionality 240–245 ▪ Campaigning against FGC 280–281

work, because only men were considered "adult and valid" under the colonial system.

Another key work on the topic, *Fighting Two Colonialisms* (1979), by South African-born journalist Stephanie Urdang, looks at women's participation in Guinea Bissau's fight for independence from Portugal in 1974 and 1976. It highlights women's crucial role as mobilizers

A Chicana woman takes part in La Marcha de la Reconquista, a 1,000 mile (1,600 km) march from Calexico, on the US-Mexico border, to Sacramento in 1971 to protest against discrimination.

in the guerrilla war, persuading their husbands and sons to join the cause, but also describes how many women took up arms. Yet the end of colonialism did not bring the gender equality promised by independence leader Amílcar Cabral. Instead, the patriarchy reasserted itself and women were forced back into traditional roles.

New questions

The racist and sexist structure that anticolonialism exposed opened up debate and stimulated ideas that challenged oppression. In the US, Chicana feminism grew

out of the Chicano movement, which emerged in the 1960s to protest against the discriminatory treatment of people of Mexican descent in the border areas seized by the US in the Mexican-American War of 1846–1848. Chicana feminists found that the feminism espoused by white women in the US did not address the racial and class discrimination they faced in addition to sexism. The Chicana feminist Gloria Anzaldúa, who emphasized the intertwining of different identities and oppressions, described this disregard of their issues as a kind of neocolonialism. ▪

Gloria Anzaldúa

Born in Texas in 1942, as a young woman Gloria Anzaldúa took part in Chicano activism, such as securing farm workers' rights. As a researcher in inclusionary movements, she focused on the hierarchy within colonialism and on how issues of gender, race, class, and health interlink. Anzaldúa's most famous work *Borderlands/La Frontera: The New Mestiza* (1987), analyzed colonialism and male control in the borderlands between the US and Mexico. Anzaldúa died in 2004.

Key works

1981 *This Bridge Called My Back: Writings by Radical Women of Color*
1987 *Borderlands/La Frontera: The New Mestiza*
2002 *This Bridge We Call Home: Radical Visions for Transformation*

A COMMUNITY OF SISTERS IN STRUGGLE
POSTCOLONIAL FEMINISM

IN CONTEXT

PRIMARY QUOTE
Chandra Talpade Mohanty, 1984

KEY FIGURES
Chandra Talpade Mohanty, Gayatri Chakravorty Spivak

BEFORE
1961 Frantz Fanon, a Martinican psychiatrist who had served in the French colony of Algeria, publishes *The Wretched of the Earth*, which deals with colonialism's dehumanizing effects.

AFTER
1990s Transnational feminism emerges. It focuses on migration, globalization, and modern communications.

1993 Toni Morrison is the first African American to win the Nobel Prize for Literature. Her writing brings black experiences into mainstream American literature.

Postcolonial feminism is a sub-discipline of postcolonialism, a field of inquiry concerned with the effects of Western colonialism on current economic and political institutions and with the persistence of neocolonial or imperial practices in the modern world. It re-examines the history of people subjugated under forms of imperialism and analyzes the power relationship of colonizer-colonized in cultural, social, and political spheres.

Postcolonial feminism is a response to the failure of both postcolonialism and Western feminism to acknowledge the concerns of women in the

See also: Early Arab feminism 104–105 ▪ Indian feminism 176–177 ▪ Anticolonialism 218–219 ▪
Indigenous feminism 224–227 ▪ Feminism in post-Mao China 230–231

Sisterhood cannot
be assumed on the
basis of gender.
**Chandra Talpade
Mohanty**

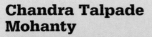

postcolonial world. Before the 1980s,
most postcolonial theory was written
by men. Significant texts included
Discourse on Colonialism (1950)
by Martinican Aimé Césaire; *The
Wretched of the Earth* (1961) by
Frantz Fanon, also from Martinique;
and *Orientalism* (1978) by the
Palestinian-American academic
and critic Edward Saïd. The term
"postcolonialism" itself was and is
considered contentious. The word
implies that there is a homogeneity
across former colonized nations,

that they are permanently linked
to their colonial past, or that there
is no lingering colonial influence.
The reality, however, is often very
different. Former colonial nations
are often torn apart by patriarchal
power struggles and subject to
international interventions that
are another form of occupation.

Real women
In the 1980s, postcolonial feminists
began to critique the theories put
forward by feminists in developed
countries, who saw white, middle-
class women of the West—in the
northern hemisphere—as the norm.
They accused Western feminism
of homogenizing women's struggles
in the West and then applying them
to Third World women in the
southern hemisphere's developing
nations. These assumptions were
seen as patronizing, and were said
to reduce real women with real
issues to a universal monolith.

In India, Chandra Talpade
Mohanty argued that women living
in non-Western countries were
assumed to be poor, ignorant, ››

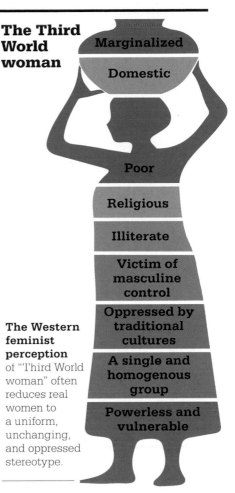

**The Third
World
woman**

Marginalized

Domestic

Poor

Religious

Illiterate

Victim of
masculine
control

Oppressed by
traditional
cultures

A single and
homogenous
group

Powerless and
vulnerable

**The Western
feminist
perception**
of "Third World
woman" often
reduces real
women to
a uniform,
unchanging,
and oppressed
stereotype.

**Chandra Talpade
Mohanty**

Born in Mumbai, India, in 1955,
Chandra Talpade Mohanty is one
of the most important scholars in
postcolonial and transnational
feminist theory. Mohanty studied
English at the University of
Delhi and later earned a PhD
in Education at the University
of Illinois. Her 1986 essay
"Under Western Eyes: Feminist
Scholarship and Colonial
Discourses" gained widespread
recognition. Her main fields
of interest are the politics of
difference and solidarity,
decolonizing knowledge, and
feminist transborder solidarity.

She is now Distinguished
Professor of Women's and
Gender Studies, and Dean's
Professor of the Humanities at
Syracuse University, New York,
and her current works examine
the politics of neoliberalism.

Key works

2003 *Feminism Without Borders:
Decolonizing Theory, Practicing
Solidarity*
2013 *Transnational Feminist
Crossings: On Neoliberalism and
Radical Critique*

Gayatri Chakravorty Spivak

Born in Kolkata in 1942, and one of the most authoritative voices in postcolonial theory, Gayatri Chakravorty Spivak is best known for her pioneering essay "Can the Subaltern Speak?," published in 1983.

Spivak began a long association with the US in 1961, when she left India to join the graduate program at Cornell University. She is currently Professor in the Humanities at Columbia University. However, she remains close to India, where she has been funding primary schools in West Bengal since 1986. When she won the Kyoto Prize in Arts and Philosophy in 2012, she donated the cash award to her foundation supporting primary education in India. Spivak also translates works in Indian languages, such as those of Mahasweta Devi, into English.

Key works

1983 "Can the Subaltern Speak?"
1999 *A Critique of Postcolonial Reason: Toward a History of the Vanishing Present*

Two women veiled in burqas walk along a street in Herat, Afghanistan. Women's oppression by the Islamic fundamentalist Taliban was one of the reasons given for the invasion of the country by the US and its allies in 2001.

uneducated, sexually constrained, tradition-bound, and victimized, irrespective of whether they were powerful or marginal, prosperous or not. Western women, on the other hand, were assumed to be modern, sexually liberated, well-educated, and capable of making their own decisions.

Home-grown struggle

In rejecting Western stereotypes of themselves, Mohanty and others gave voice to indigenous feminist movements. They argued that to be truly authentic, feminism in developing countries cannot be "imported." It must emerge from each society's own ideologies and culture to reflect the complex layers of oppression that exist there. They also argued that it was the duty of Western feminists to recognize forms of difference as part of their movement.

While some Western feminists fear that postcolonial arguments risk breaking up the feminist movement into smaller groups and advocate a "global sisterhood," many feminists of color in the West acknowledge and echo postcolonial arguments. In her book *Sister Outsider* (1984), African American Audre Lorde argues that denying differences reinforces old forms of oppression. White women, she asserts, disregard their privilege of whiteness and define woman in terms of their own experience, so that women of color "become 'other,' the outsider whose experience and tradition is too 'alien' to comprehend."

Black feminists such as bell hooks took the argument further, saying that Western feminism not only neglects the subject of race but also fuels racism.

"Triple colonization"

Western feminism's oppression of Third World women is referred to as "triple colonization." According to postcolonial feminists, such women

> To ignore the subaltern today … is to continue the imperialist project.
> **Gayatri Chakravorty Spivak**

are "colonized" first by colonial power, secondly by patriarchy, and thirdly by Western feminists. Race has thus become a central point in postcolonial feminist discourse.

In her essay "Can the Subaltern Speak?" (1983), postcolonial critic Gayatri Chakravorty Spivak reflects on the Eurocentric "Self" and the anonymous, non-European "Other." She asks if the "subaltern"—the term given to populations that are outside the patriarchal power structure of the colony and its motherland—can even speak for themselves. Her answer is that they cannot, because they are not understood or supported. Spivak writes: "Everything that has limited or no access to the cultural imperialism is subaltern."

On the curriculum

Historically, Western feminist theory has dominated university curriculums and been made to stand for all feminism. Although a reassessment of European feminist texts in light of postcolonial thought has seen changes to women's studies programs—Goldsmith's, University of London, in the UK, for example, has made a concerted effort to decolonize the curriculum—postcolonial feminism is still

regarded as being outside the main canon. This conforms with what Spivak calls "neocolonialist, multiculturalist, culturally relativist knowledge production," which neglects the diversity of other peoples' differences to produce a simpler and more politically correct brand of cultural studies.

There is a great deal of important postcolonial women's fiction in English, such as the work by Indian novelist Anita Desai, Nigerian author Flora Nwapa, and Jamaican novelist and poet Olive Senior. However, the continued lack of female writers on university syllabi, and the fact that postcolonial women writers are less well known than their male counterparts, reflects not only the greater struggle that women writers experience, but also the realities of multiple colonization, through which women continue to be marginalized on grounds of race, class, and gender. For example, in 1986, it was Wole Soyinka, a male Nigerian playwright, who became the first African to win the Nobel Prize for

Literature, and postcolonial literature written by men, such as *Things Fall Apart* (1959), by the Nigerian author Chinua Achebe, and *Midnight's Children* (1981) by the British Indian writer Salman Rushdie, that received widespread recognition and awards.

Nonetheless, postcolonial feminism has succeeded in making the boundaries of mainstream feminism more porous. Since the 1980s, Indian academics have also questioned the term "feminism," arguing for an Indian-specific alternative. Postcolonial feminists continue to campaign for a more inclusive and useful mainstream feminism, based on shared values among women worldwide, which works toward a truer understanding of their goals and particular struggles. ∎

South Sudanese women unite for peace in 2017. Their mouths are taped over to symbolize their silencing by both the government and rebel forces in a postcolonial country torn apart by civil war.

LET US BE THE ANCESTORS OUR DESCENDANTS WILL THANK

INDIGENOUS FEMINISM

IN CONTEXT

PRIMARY QUOTE
Winona LaDuke, 2015

KEY FIGURES
**Winona LaDuke,
Mary Two-Axe Earley,
Paula Gunn Allen**

BEFORE
1893 Queen Lili'uokalani is
forced off her throne during
the takeover of the Kingdom
of Hawaii by the US. The
colonizers impose Christianity
on Hawaii and force women to
adopt "Christian names" and
patrilineal surnames.

AFTER
1994 In Chiapa, southern
Mexico, the Zapatista Army of
National Liberation unveils the
Women's Revolutionary Law,
including a woman's right to
work, fair pay, education, and
choice of partner.

2015 Canada's prime minister
Justin Trudeau announces the
creation of a National Inquiry
into Missing and Murdered
Indigenous Women and Girls.

Indigenous feminism focuses
on the experiences and
concerns of women whose
racial background is that of one
of the native peoples in countries
that were settled by European
colonists. It is active in the US,
Canada, Australia, and New
Zealand, but also in places such
as Chiapas in Mexico, where the
Zapatistas revolutionary movement
protests against the oppression of
indigenous people by the state.
Activists and scholars protest and
write about the impact on the lives
of indigenous women of colonization,

See also: Anticolonialism 218–219 ▪ Postcolonial feminism 220–223 ▪ Intersectionality 240–245

Indigenous women suffer **inequalities** for reasons relating to both **gender and ethnicity**.

⬇

They sustain a **dual oppression**.

⬇

To combat this, they **increase their role in the ethnic struggle**, bringing women's issues to the fore.

⬇

Through this strategy, female autonomy and ethnic autonomy are linked.

A scene from *Rabbit-Proof Fence,* a 2002 Australian film about three mixed-race girls who try to return to their Aboriginal mother after being forcibly separated from her by the state.

white supremacy, genocide, sexual violence, anti-indigenous nationalism, and the European patriarchy introduced into colonized lands.

Outside pressures
Indigenous feminists point out that colonization has had a profound impact on native family structures and the ability of women to give birth to and raise their children in an environment appropriate to their racial origin. Andrea Smith (1966–), a Native American studies scholar and feminist, has documented

the wide-ranging oppression of indigenous women and their families under colonialism, including sexual and domestic violence, white appropriation of native cultures, the devaluation of indigenous women's lives, and the grim legacy of state-sanctioned Indian boarding schools in the US and Canada in the 19th and 20th centuries. Run by Christian missionaries, these schools stripped indigenous children of their cultures and native languages to forcibly "reeducate" them into "civilized" European culture.

In the same way, mixed-race children born to Aboriginal women in Australia, often as a result of rape, were forcibly removed from their mothers and placed in residential schools, a policy that prevailed from 1910 until 1970. Now known as the Lost, or Stolen,

Generation in Australia, such children were taught to reject their indigenous heritage and forced to adopt white culture. They were given new names, forbidden from speaking their own languages, and in the often harsh conditions of the institutions where they were placed, child abuse was rife.

Indigenous activism
In the US, the American Indian Movement (AIM) emerged in 1968 as one of a growing number of civil rights groups. AIM sought economic independence for Native American communities after what it saw as centuries of land theft, ecological destruction, and impoverishment by the US government. Many Native American women participated in AIM and championed its goals, but were nonetheless frustrated by the organization's lack of focus on issues that particularly affected women, such as health care and reproductive rights.

In 1974, the Native American women's group Women of All Red Nations (WARN) was formed to »

Mary Two-Axe Earley

Indigenous activist Mary Two-Axe Earley was born on the Kahnawake reserve near Montreal, Canada, in 1911. She is remembered for her lifelong work in challenging laws that discriminated against the rights of indigenous women, specifically parts of the 1876 Indian Act that denied some indigenous women the rights to own property and to live on the reserve of their birth.

Earley migrated to the US at age 18 in search of work, and by the 1960s she was active in women's rights organizations, including Indian Rights for Indian Women (IRIW). Forced to battle the inherent male prejudice of both the Canadian government and the National Indian Brotherhood, Earley finally secured an amendment to the Indian Act in 1985. In her own words, she was now "… legally entitled to live on the reserve, to own property, die, and be buried with my own people." In 1996, her final year, Earley was honored with a National Aboriginal Achievement Award.

I am a woman. And I am part of … the Indian nation. But people either relate to you as an Indian or as a woman.
Winona LaDuke

address these issues. It embarked on a series of indigenous rights campaigns, such as highlighting issues relating to Native American women's health, restoring and securing of treaty rights violated by the US federal government, and combating the commercialization of Indian culture.

Forced sterilization

Activist Winona LaDuke, whose father was a Native American actor, was one of the founders in 1985 of the US-based Indigenous Women's Network (IWN), focusing on Native American women and their families and communities. She also worked with WARN to publicize the US government's forced sterilization program, which was a central concern of indigenous feminists. Scholars had estimated that from 1970 to 1976, 25–50 percent of

Winona LaDuke speaks outside the Capitol in Washington, D.C., in 1997, to protest the use of Yucca Mountain, Nevada, a sacred Native American site, as a store for radioactive waste.

Native American women in the US were sterilized by the Indian Health Service. Women and girls were often either forced into sterilization, lied to about the procedure as being reversible, or sterilized without their consent or knowledge.

As a result of these actions, the birth rate of indigenous women declined between 1970 and 1980, interfering not only in women's autonomy but also in the right of indigenous families to have children and continue their tribal lineages in the face of historical extermination. This was in line with America's long history of sterilizing marginalized

> I am intensely conscious of popular notions of Indian women as beasts of burden, squaws, traitors, or, at best, vanished denizens of a long-lost wilderness.
> **Paula Gunn Allen**

populations of women, such as low-income women of color and women with disabilities.

Missing and murdered

Another crucial area of indigenous feminist activism in North America has been the issue of missing and murdered indigenous women (MMIW). In Canada, the MMIW controversy has been classified as a national crisis. For decades, activists have been protesting the lack of resources allocated to the issue. Highway 16, a remote road in British Columbia bordering 23 communities of indigenous peoples and known for hitchhiking, has been the scene of the abduction and murder of indigenous girls and women since the late 1960s. Most of the murders have gone unsolved. In 2016, the Canadian government agreed to introduce a public bus route along the highway that would provide safe transport for low-income indigenous women.

Beyond white feminism

A key component of indigenous feminism is to articulate a vision for indigenous women's lives and activism against a background of white-dominated feminism. Native American writer and activist Paula Gunn Allen, who grew up close to the Laguna Pueblo reservation in New Mexico, laid the foundations for this development of indigenous feminism in the 1980s.

In her 1986 book *The Sacred Hoop: Recovering the Feminine in American Indian Traditions*, Allen argues that indigenous women have rich matriarchal tribal traditions, with social, political, and spiritual leadership roles that existed in their communities long before European colonization. Allen seeks to recover and revive that legacy, emphasizing Native American women's tradition of power and highlighting the ways in which contemporary ideas about gender have been strongly influenced by the fixed patriarchal views of gender that were imported into North America by European colonizers. This knowledge, claims Allen, has much to teach the, mainly white-led, feminist movement, as the historical social oppression of women has not been a universal, inevitable, cross-cultural reality. ■

> I think the Black sense of male and female is much more sophisticated than the Western idea.
> **James Baldwin**

James Baldwin, the American author, believed that whiteness lay at the heart of racism, including the treatment of indigenous women.

Whiteness studies

In 1903, African American historian and activist W.E.B. Du Bois wrote of the "color line" as the defining problem that would dominate the 20th century. By the 1980s, the academic field of critical whiteness studies had emerged as a subset of critical race studies, particularly in the US, the UK, and Australia. It seeks to examine whiteness as a racial category as it has evolved and shifted over time and across geographic boundaries. Scholars challenge whiteness as the unstated racial norm that communities of color are compared against. They argue that "white" is in reality the assimilation of various ethnically European cultures. Many of these cultures, such as the Irish, Italians, and Greeks, were treated as "other" before "becoming" white and being folded into the dominant white "culture." Those deemed to be white then benefit from white racial dominance. In other words, whiteness is part of a process of expanding racism.

WOMEN REMAIN LOCKED INTO DEAD-END JOBS
PINK-COLLAR FEMINISM

IN CONTEXT

PRIMARY QUOTE
Karin Stallard, Barbara Ehrenreich, Holly Sklar, 1983

KEY FIGURES
Karin Stallard, Barbara Ehrenreich, Holly Sklar

BEFORE
1935 The US Social Security Act—the first attempt at a government safety net—includes maternal and child welfare and public health benefits for the most deprived.

1982 The US Congress fails to ratify the Equal Rights Amendment (ERA) to the US Constitution, barring discrimination based on sex.

AFTER
1996 President Bill Clinton signs the Personal Responsibility and Work Opportunity Reconciliation Act, reducing government aid to poor families, especially to single mothers.

The term "pink-collar" was first used in the US in the early 1970s to mean "female" non-professional office jobs. It soon came to mean work performed primarily by women, such as waitressing, nursing, and house-cleaning. Such jobs tend to pay lower than both male-dominated white-collar jobs (office and managerial work) and blue-collar jobs (manual labor).

Pink-collar feminists challenge the economic exploitation of such employees. Writers Karin Stallard, Barbara Ehrenreich, and Holly Sklar, among others, have highlighted the impact on women of poverty, wage inequality, job discrimination, and unequal division of labor in the home. In their book *Poverty in the American Dream: Women & Children First* (1983), they show how all these factors limit women's ability to lead autonomous, joyful, and healthy lives. They describe the "pink-collar ghetto" in which women often found themselves—underpaid, overworked, and with little room for advancement or career change. Male leaders, they say, seldom promote women past a certain rank, even in white-collar work, contributing to women's career stagnation and inability to break through the "glass ceiling"—a term coined by American management consultant Marilyn Loden in 1978 for this invisible barrier to success.

Women and poverty
American researcher Diana Pearce spoke of the "feminization of poverty," to describe the high number of women in poverty

A boss dictates to his secretary in an early 20th-century cartoon. Demand for typists fueled a boom in employment for women, but such work, especially in "typing pools," was often tedious and much like a factory production line.

See also: Marriage and work 70–71 ▪ Family structures 138–139 ▪ Leaning in 312–313 ▪ The pay gap 318–319

> ❝ For more and more women poverty begins with divorce.
> **Karin Stallard, Barbara Ehrenreich, Holly Sklar** ❞

around the world as a result of structural oppression—the way in which institutions and society limit women's economic resources and opportunities. Charting the increase in the number of American households headed by women between 1950 and the 1970s, Pearce observes how paid work, and sometimes divorce, can lead to women's independence from men but can also bring financial insecurity, especially if women also have to pay for childcare while they work. The situation is even worse for women in same-sex relationships who are both in poorly paid pink-collar jobs.

The impact of racism
Women of color are often doubly affected by the feminization of poverty and structural racism, as Stallard, Ehrenreich, and Sklar also point out. They denounce the influential theory of "black matriarchy" that US Senator and sociologist Daniel Patrick Moynihan had advanced in his 1965 report on African-American families known as the Moynihan Report. Moynihan had infamously argued that black women's matriarchal control of the family was responsible for the

erosion of the black nuclear family and the inability of black men to act as authority figures within their families. Psychologist William Ryan—who had refuted lies about poverty in his 1971 work, *Blaming the Victim*—joined the chorus of criticism against Moynihan's arguments. Ryan argues that blame is just a convenient substitute for analyzing the inequality in society that creates marginalized groups.

Few advances
Structural racism has intensified the feminization of poverty for American black women since the 1980s. The incarceration of many black men during President Reagan's "war on drugs" (1982–1989), and a crackdown on crime in poorer neighborhoods, vastly increased the number of families headed by single black women, creating racist stereotypes of black women as "welfare queens."

In 2011, the US government's *Women in America* report largely confirmed the lack of progress for all women in the US. While excelling in education, women—especially women of color—still earned less than men and were more likely to live below the poverty line. ▪

> ❝ When someone works for less pay than she can live on, then she has made a great sacrifice for you.
> **Barbara Ehrenreich** ❞

Barbara Ehrenreich

Born in Butte, Montana, in 1941 to a working-class union family, Barbara Ehrenreich is a lifelong political activist who has written extensively on women's health, class, and poverty, and is involved with the Democratic Socialists of America. She has won multiple awards for her investigative journalism during her career. Her best-known book is *Nickel and Dimed* (2001), which chronicles three months of working in minimum-wage "female" jobs across America.

Ehrenreich has said that when she gave birth to her daughter in a New York public clinic in 1970, the clinic, which primarily served communities of color, induced her labor simply because the doctor on call wanted to go home. The experience enraged her and became the source of her passionate feminism.

Key works

1983 *Women in the Global Factory*
2003 *Global Women: Nannies, Maids, and Sex Workers in the New Economy*
2008 *This Land Is Their Land: Reports From a Divided Nation*

WOMEN'S ISSUES HAVE BEEN ABANDONED
FEMINISM IN POST-MAO CHINA

IN CONTEXT

PRIMARY QUOTE
Li Xiaojiang, 1988

KEY FIGURE
Li Xiaojiang

BEFORE
1919 The nationalist May Fourth Movement for social and political reform raises the Chinese public's awareness of gender discrimination.

1950 The New Marriage Law legalizes equality between men and women for the first time in China.

AFTER
2013 A 23-year-old graduate becomes the first Chinese woman to win a gender discrimination lawsuit after being turned down by an employer for a job as a tutor.

2015 Five young Chinese feminists (the "Feminist Five") are arrested for "disorderly conduct" on the eve of International Women's Day.

After the death of Chairman Mao Zedong in 1976, Deng Xiaoping eventually emerged as the preeminent power and policy-maker in China. His decision to introduce a so-called "socialist market economy" and to open up the country to global capitalism changed all aspects of life in China, including the position of women in society.

Changing role
Under Mao's state-controlled economy and policy of collective farms and factories, women had experienced relative equality with men in education and work. After Mao, the treatment of women—despite laws that protected them

> 66
> Women can hold up half the sky.
> **Mao Zedong**
> 99

from discrimination in employment, education, and housing—was influenced by the demands of a capitalist market and the subjective decisions of employers, bringing increased discrimination against women in hiring and promotion.

In 1979, Deng also introduced a "one-child" policy to limit the size of the family and control population growth, which held back living standards. A cultural preference for boy children led to the abortion of female fetuses and abandonment of baby girls, and some critics in the West branded the policy an attack on human and reproductive rights.

Deng's socialist modernization prioritized economic development at the expense of women's status. Following the collapse of Mao's collectives, the household became an important economic unit. The "iron" women-workers of the Maoist era were replaced with "socialist housewives." Women were denied access to new technologies and banned from studying subjects such as engineering.

A new awareness
Despite the new restrictions on women, the Women's Liberation Movement in China began to

See also: Marxist feminism 52–55 ▪ Feminism in Japan 82–83

独生优生

晚婚晚育

广渠门内大街
GUANGQUMENNEI DAJIE

establish a new identity. In 1983, the Beijing Municipal Women's Federation formed a company to recruit and train female domestic workers from rural areas and place them in urban households. Even though this strengthened the stereotype of domestic work being "women's work," it was still considered to be an advance in women's interests in that women became independent earners.

An important development for women in post-Mao China was the establishment of women's studies programs and academic research on women. Up to this point, Chinese women had lacked a cultural space for articulating a collective consciousness around gender. Historically, feminist movements in China had been led by men, such as Yu Zhengxie (1775–1840). Yu criticized practices such as foot binding and widow chastity, but also saw women as passive objects that needed to be liberated by men.

China's "one-child" policy, initiated in 1979, was widely advertised as an attempt to improve living standards. The controversial policy began to be phased out in 2015.

The pioneer of women's studies in 1980s China was Li Xiaojiang, who, in 1983, published the essay "Progress of Mankind and Women's Liberation." Two years later, the first non-official women's professional organization—the Association of Women's Studies—was founded, and the first academic conference on the subject took place in Zhengzhou, capital of Henan province.

From that point, women's studies in China grew significantly. In 1985, the Center for Women's Studies in China opened at Zhengzhou University, heralding a number of similar research centers across China. For the first time in Chinese history, women were engaging in discussion about their status, without state surveillance and on an equal footing with men. ▪

Li Xiaojiang

One of the leading feminist thinkers in China, Li Xiaojiang is often credited with bringing women's studies into the arena of academic debate in post-Mao China. Born in 1951, the daughter of an academic father who was president of Zhengzhou University, she studied at Henan University, where, in 1985, she set up the first Chinese research center for women's studies. In the same year, Li Xiaojiang established the first women's gender awareness course and the first national independent women's conference. She continues to teach, write, and lecture.

Key works

1983 "Progress of Mankind and Women's Liberation"
1988 *The Exploration of Eve*
1989 *Gap Between Sexes*
1989 *Study on Women's Aesthetic Awareness*
1999 *Interpretation of Women*

> The precondition of a Marxist theory of feminism in post-Mao China is to abstract entire women.
> **Li Xiaojiang**

FORCED MARRIAGE IS A VIOLATION OF HUMAN RIGHTS
PREVENTING FORCED MARRIAGE

IN CONTEXT

PRIMARY QUOTE
United Nations, 2009

KEY FIGURE
Zainah Anwar

BEFORE
Before 622 CE Forced marriage of widowed step-mothers to their husband's eldest son is common practice in the Arabian Peninsula.

622–632 During the Prophet Muhammad's years in Medina, a young girl complains to his wife Aisha that she is being forced to marry; he intervenes to stop the marriage.

8th–10th century Law books compiled by both the Sunni and Shia schools of Islam demand the consent of both parties to a marriage.

AFTER
2012 Amina Filala commits suicide in Morocco after being forced to marry her rapist. In 2014, the law that permits this is repealed.

The practice of forcing a woman, sometimes a very young girl, to marry a man against her wishes is most often associated with the Muslim faith. Forced marriage is not condoned by Islam, but it is culturally enforced, especially in the Middle East and South Asia—usually in order to preserve property or wealth within a family (the couple are often cousins), prevent unsuitable relationships, fulfil a promise, or settle a debt. Muslim, Sikh, Hindu, and Christian women can all be victims, including those living in the West, who may find themselves married off while being taken to their family's home country on vacation.

Forced marriages are different from arranged marriages, where the parties are free to accept or reject the intended marriage partner. A woman who rejects forced marriage, or who chooses to marry someone regarded as unsuitable, can become the victim of an "honor" crime, in which she is murdered for bringing shame on the family.

Forced marriage is also linked to human trafficking. The global organization Girls Not Brides, which

A woman seeks justice from a sharia court in a marriage dispute in northern Nigeria. Though deemed "unIslamic," forced marriage in parts of the region is said to be as high as 75 percent.

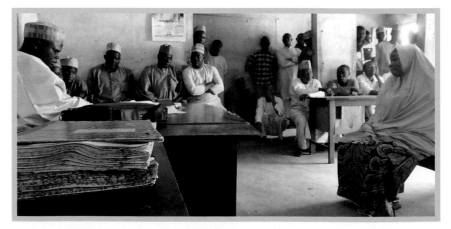

See also: Rape as abuse of power 166–171 ▪ Indian feminism 176–177 ▪ Survivor, not victim 238 ▪ Modern Islamic feminism 284–285

A child bride protests in Yemen, where rates of child marriage are high. Charities are trying to put a stop to this, and young women who were once child brides themselves join the protests.

focuses on the forced marriage of children, reports on girls being sold for marriage in countries as diverse as Costa Rica, Nicaragua, Dominican Republic, Vietnam, Indonesia, and China, among others.

Stamping it out

In the 1980s, the United Nations, national governments, NGOs (non-governmental organizations), and pressure groups joined forces to combat forced marriage. Education was seen as key to prevention, as the practice is highest among the least educated members of society. However, government efforts can be patchy and equivocal. For example, some countries—including Algeria, Bahrain, Kuwait, and Libya—effectively legitimize forced marriage by exonerating rapists provided they marry their victims (who have no choice in the matter). Women's rights groups have sprung up to tackle the problem of forced marriage head on. In

Malaysia in 1988, the feminist Zainah Anwar founded Sisters in Islam, an organization of female lawyers and activists who seek to reform family law in the Muslim world, including laws permitting forced marriage, stating that the practice contravenes sharia (Islamic law). Several Muslim countries declared forced marriages to be unlawful in the 2000s; in 2005, Saudi Arabia's top religious clerics banned the practice.

In the UK, Jasvinder Sanghera, a British Sikh woman who ran away from home after learning that she was to enter a forced marriage at the age of 14, set up the charity Karma Nirvana in 1992 to support victims of forced marriage and honor crimes. Even though the UK, like other European countries and the US, has laws in place to prosecute those who facilitate forced marriage, shame and secrecy mean that many cases never come to light. The practical and emotional support offered by groups set up and run by women from the communities that are most at risk are vital to the eradication of this violation of human rights. ▪

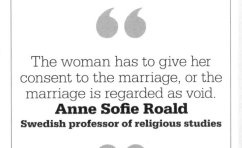

The woman has to give her consent to the marriage, or the marriage is regarded as void.
Anne Sofie Roald
Swedish professor of religious studies

Zainah Anwar

Feminist and activist Zainah Anwar was born in Johor, Malaysia, in 1954. After training as a journalist, she studied law in the US, and worked for various think-tanks. In 1988, together with American Muslim feminist Amina Wadud and five other women, Anwar cofounded Sisters in Islam in Malaysia to promote the rights of women, challenge discrimination, and outlaw practices such as forced marriage. The women were motivated by a burning question: "If God is just, if Islam is just, why do laws and policies made in the name of Islam create injustice?"

The work of Sisters in Islam draws on progressive interpretations of the Quran, as well as international human rights protocols to further its work. Anwar served as the organization's leader for more than 20 years, and remains on its board of directors.

Key works

1987 *Islamic Revivalism in Malaysia*
2001 *Islam and Family Planning*
2011 *Legacy of Honor*

BEHIND EVERY EROTIC CONDEMNATION THERE'S A BURNING HYPOCRITE

SEX POSITIVITY

IN CONTEXT

PRIMARY QUOTE
Susie Bright, 1990

KEY FIGURES
Susie Bright, Carol Queen, Gayle Rubin, Ellen Willis

BEFORE
1965 *Penthouse*, an erotic men's magazine, launches in the US.

1969 Artist Andy Warhol's *Blue Movie* is the first adult film depicting sex to be released in the US.

AFTER
1992 Feminist writer Rebecca Walker coins the term "third-wave feminism" after Clarence Thomas is appointed to the US Supreme Court; he had been accused of sexual harassment, but denied the claims.

2011 The first "SlutWalk" protest takes place in Toronto in response to comments made about campus rape.

The sex positivity feminist movement that began in the early 1980s was partly a backlash against the clampdown on pornography that other feminists supported. It was underpinned, however, by the wider sex-positive movement, which promoted physical pleasure, experimentation, and safe-sex education. Pro-sex feminists, as they were also known, emphasized sexual freedom for women, supported LGBTQ groups, and opposed any legal or social restrictions on consensual adult sex. They believed that accepting lesbianism, bisexuality, and gender fluidity was necessary for women's liberation. Unlike many radical

See also: Birth control 98–103 ▪ Sexual pleasure 126–127 ▪ The Pill 136 ▪ Antipornography feminism 196–199 ▪ Supporting sex workers 298

> When a young woman discovers her power, both sexual and intellectual, she unleashes her own voice, her righteousness.
> **Susie Bright**

feminists, they did not denounce male sexuality, but warned that patriarchal governments would continue to discriminate against women's sexuality via legislation.

Pleasure v. censorship

Earlier in the 20th century, sex reformers and educators in the US, such as Margaret Sanger and Betty Dodson, had championed birth control, sex education, and masturbation, challenging deeply held moral convictions. Scientific works such as the Kinsey reports (1948 and 1953) and Hite report (1976) also led to a shift in thinking about female sexuality, while advances in contraception and the 1960s culture of "free love" revolutionized sexual behavior.

In 1975, American entrepreneur, writer, and sex educator Joani Blank founded Down There Press and

published *The Playbook for Women About Sex*. Two years later, she opened Good Vibrations, only the second feminist sex toy business in the US, which became a key hub of sex-positive feminism and feminist literature. Susie Bright, one of the first women to be called a "sex-positive feminist" was an early employee; the American author and sociologist Carol Queen is its staff sexologist today.

Teenage promiscuity

Some people perceived the new sexual freedom as a threat. Public unease grew as businesses exploited the relaxed social mores and loosened restrictions around pornography by making it publicly available. Widely publicized porn films such as *Deep Throat* (1972) and *Snuff* (1975) provoked fears that the sexual revolution would encourage teenage promiscuity and violence against women.

The antipornography feminist movement of the 1980s was born of such concerns. Radical writers, »

Mick Jagger, Michèle Breton, and Anita Pallenberg star in a sex scene from Donald Cammell and Nicolas Roeg's 1970 cult film *Performance*, which Warner made in London in 1968 and then toned down prior to release.

Susie Bright

Writer, editor, and sex expert Susie Bright was born in Virginia in 1958. By the late 1970s, she was active in left-wing causes such as pacifism, and became a member of the International Socialists. She worked as a laborer in California and Detroit and wrote for the underground newspaper *The Red Tide*.

A champion of sex-positive feminism, Bright founded the Erotic Video Club and later wrote reviews of pornographic films for Penthouse Forum. She became the first woman in the X-Rated Critics Organization. While editing the sex-positive magazine *On Our Backs*, she styled herself as sex advice columnist Susie Sexpert. Bright also founded the first women's erotica series, *Herotica*, and publishes *The Best American Erotica* series.

Key works

1997 *Susie Bright's Sexual State of the Union*
2003 *Mommy's Little Girl: On Sex, Motherhood, Porn, and Cherry Pie*
2011 *Big Sex, Little Death: A Memoir*

Gayle Rubin's theory of sexuality

Rubin outlined a sex hierarchy divided between practices considered normal (left)—which she called the "charmed circle"—and those thought to be outside the norm (right), such as sadomasochism.

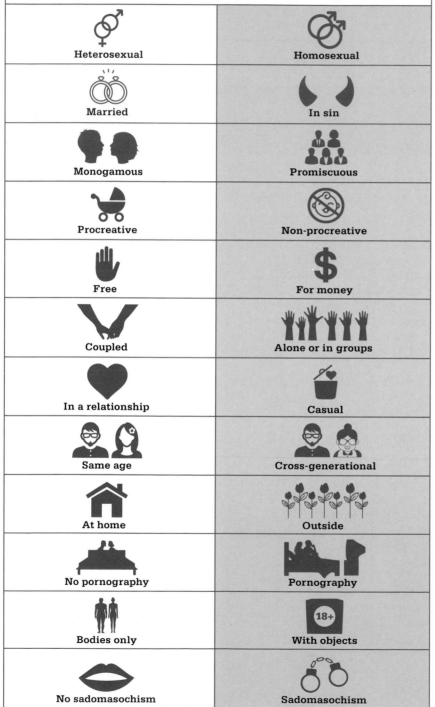

Heterosexual	Homosexual
Married	In sin
Monogamous	Promiscuous
Procreative	Non-procreative
Free	For money
Coupled	Alone or in groups
In a relationship	Casual
Same age	Cross-generational
At home	Outside
No pornography	Pornography
Bodies only	With objects
No sadomasochism	Sadomasochism

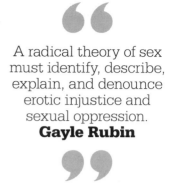

A radical theory of sex must identify, describe, explain, and denounce erotic injustice and sexual oppression.
Gayle Rubin

such as Catharine MacKinnon, Dorchen Leidholdt, Andrea Dworkin, and Robin Morgan, saw pornography as an assault on civil rights and a tool of women's oppression. New groups, such as Women Against Violence Against Women (WAVAW) and, later on, Women Against Pornography (WAP) pressed for antipornography legislation across the US and Canada.

The Feminist Sex Wars

Sex-positive supporters were angered by the stance taken by antipornography campaigners against prostitution and BDSM (various practices such as bondage, domination, and sadomasochism); the campaigners viewed both as inherently misogynistic and violent. Samois, a lesbian-feminism BDSM group in the US, founded by writer Pat Califia and anthropologist Gayle Rubin, maintained that consensual BDSM acts were fully compatible with feminism, but that passing moral judgment on women's desires was clearly antifeminist. Samois's criticism was echoed by feminist advocates of decriminalized prostitution, who demanded recognition of sex workers' rights.

As the sex-positive feminist movement grew, its supporters challenged the ever more strident antipornography campaign. In 1979, American journalist Ellen Willis published an essay "Feminism, Moralism and Pornography," which outlines her concerns that laws against pornography could infringe on the right to free speech, threaten sexual freedom, and endanger women and sexual minorities.

In 1982, Willis and Rubin were among the organizers of the highly controversial Barnard Conference on Sexuality, whose stated aim was to move beyond violence and pornography to focus on sexuality as an issue apart from reproduction. The event sparked a furious response from antipornography groups but gained considerable publicity for sex-positive feminism.

The Feminist Sex Wars, as they became known, raged on in various forms. In 1984, in response to the proposed Dworkin-MacKinnon Ordinance, which declared that pornography was a violation of women's civil rights, Willis set up the Feminist Anti-Censorship Taskforce. The same year, Susie Bright cofounded the first women's

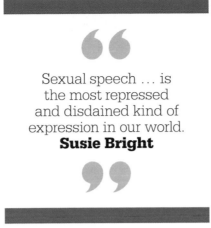

> Sexual speech ... is the most repressed and disdained kind of expression in our world.
> **Susie Bright**

erotica magazine, *On Our Backs*; its title was a parody of the radical feminist magazine *Off Our Backs* which published articles by antipornography feminists. *On Our Backs*, the only sex magazine produced by women at the time, came to encapsulate sex-positive feminism and the lesbian culture of the 1980s.

Criticisms and consent

One of the most influential essays of the early 1980s was Rubin's "Thinking Sex," which became a cornerstone of pro-sex feminism. Examining historical attitudes to

sexuality, it also highlights the conflicting sexual mores of the time. On one side, "sex-negative" thinkers viewed sex as potentially dangerous and corrupting, unless practiced conventionally. Rubin, in support of sex-positivism, calls for "erotic creativity," an end to sexual persecution, and the freedom for individuals to express their sexuality as desired.

Sex-positive feminists did not agree on all issues, such as whether all forms of consensual sex are positive, as some sexual practices might be considered degrading to one partner. In 1996, American playwright Eve Ensler's controversial play *The Vagina Monologues* also divided opinions. Sex-positive pioneer Betty Dodson denounced its focus on the vagina and sexual violence against women rather than the clitoris and sexual pleasure; others praised its openness and its embracing of sexuality.

Questions surrounding consent, pornography, and sexuality are still debated, but sex-positivism has undoubtedly gained ground. In the 21st century, most Western women enjoy a sexual freedom unknown only a few generations ago. ∎

Carol Queen

Born in 1958, sex-positive author and educator Carol Queen studied at the University of Oregon. She was inspired to become a sex educator by the diversity she encountered in San Francisco. She started writing about sexuality and became involved with Down There Press, which has published some of her books.

In 1990, Queen began working at Good Vibrations where she is still staff sexologist. In 1998, her video *Bend Over Boyfriend* (about female to male anal sex) became a best-selling series for the retailer. She also helped to develop its

first video production unit, Sexpositive Productions, which began making innovative porn movies featuring bisexual characters. Queen, herself bisexual, still runs the Center for Sex & Culture in San Francisco, which she founded in 1994 with her partner, Robert Morgan Lawrence; it is a gathering place for communities across the gender spectrum.

Key work

2015 *The Sex and Pleasure Book*

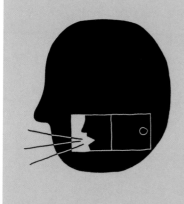

EVERYONE HAS THE RIGHT TO TELL THE TRUTH ABOUT HER OWN LIFE
SURVIVOR, NOT VICTIM

IN CONTEXT

PRIMARY QUOTE
**Ellen Bass and
Laura Davis, 1988**

KEY FIGURES
Ellen Bass, Laura Davis

BEFORE
1857 French pathologist
Auguste Ambroise Tardieu
writes the first known book on
child sexual abuse.

1982 Three women found
Survivors of Incest Anonymous
in Baltimore, Maryland.

1984 US Congress passes
the Child Abuse Victims'
Rights Act.

AFTER
2014 Every member of the
United Nations agrees to
ratify the newest incarnation
of the UN Convention on the
Rights of the Child (originally
ratified in 1990) except for the
US and South Sudan.

Before the 1980s, open discussion of incest and the sexual abuse of children was publicly stigmatized. Both were considered rare, as was rape in general. Second-wave feminists challenged these cultural precepts and called for sexual violence against women and girls to be taken seriously. They argued that women who had been abused as children should be encouraged to talk about their experiences in order to not only expose the crime but allow their psychological wounds to heal.

Inspired by feminist campaigns against sexual violence, in 1988 American feminists Ellen Bass and Laura Davis published a self-help book for female survivors of child sexual abuse called *The Courage to Heal*. Bass and Davis include survivors' accounts to validate women's experiences and reassure them that they are not alone. Using the language of "survivors," the authors focus on resilience rather than vulnerability.

Some feminists are critical of the term "survivor." They argue that the word "victim" reiterates the magnitude of systemic violence against women and bolsters efforts to secure government funding for remedying human rights violations. ∎

Survivors attend a hearing in 2018 to decide changes to be made by US sports bodies following the conviction of former US Gymnastics team doctor Larry Nassar for sexual assault.

See also: Protection from domestic violence 162–163 ▪ Rape as abuse of power 166–171 ▪ Men hurt women 316–317 ▪ Fighting campus sexual assault 320

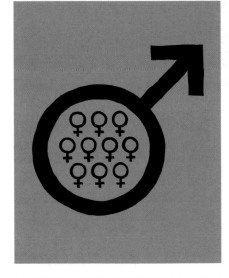

UNEARNED PRIVILEGE IS PERMISSION TO DOMINATE
PRIVILEGE

IN CONTEXT

PRIMARY QUOTE
Peggy McIntosh, 1988

KEY FIGURE
Peggy McIntosh

BEFORE
1970s Second-wave feminists start producing academic material on the phenomenon of male privilege.

AFTER
2004 *White Like Me: Reflections on Race From a Privileged Son* by antiracist author, activist, and public speaker Tim Wise is published in the US.

2017 American writer and amateur genealogist Jennifer Mendelsohn begins publishing the ancestral immigration stories of modern anti-immigrant politicians and media figures on Twitter as a commentary on privilege and American hypocrisy.

P rivilege refers to the unearned advantages a person accumulates over the course of their lifetime, such as being born a citizen of a country that persecutes illegal immigrants, or being born into a wealthy family. Systems of oppression privilege people with power at the expense of those without it.

Privilege theory
In 1988, American feminist and antiracist scholar Peggy McIntosh wrote an article, "White Privilege: Unpacking the Invisible Knapsack," on how she became aware of her own white privilege. She uses the metaphor of the knapsack to discuss the ways in which whiteness gives a white person helpful "tools" for life that people of color cannot access.

McIntosh gives 46 examples of white privilege. They range from her children being taught only about white people's achievements in school to the fact that adhesive bandages are made to match white skin. All are the result of the systemic valuation of white people

When you're accustomed to privilege, equality feels like oppression. (It's not.)
Franklin Leonard
American film producer and founder of *The Black List*

over people of color. She argues that white-dominated society promotes denial about the realities of white privilege in order to maintain the myth of meritocracy.

A major challenge for feminism continues to be the courage to take accountability for privilege. Today, feminist activists identify many different forms of privilege: able-bodied privilege, Christian privilege, cisgender privilege, citizenship privilege, and more. ∎

See also: Indian feminism 176–177 ▪ Black feminism and womanism 208–215 ▪ Anticolonialism 218–129 ▪ Indigenous feminism 224–227 ▪ Intersectionality 240–245

ALL SYSTEMS OF OPPRESSION ARE INTERLOCKING
INTERSECTIONALITY

IN CONTEXT

PRIMARY QUOTE
Combahee River Collective, 1977

KEY FIGURE
Kimberlé Crenshaw

BEFORE
1851 In the US, former slave Sojourner Truth delivers her speech "Ain't I a Woman?" at the Women's Convention in Akron, Ohio.

1981 American Civil Rights leader Angela Davis publishes *Women, Race, & Class*, which looks at how the feminist movement has always been blighted by the racism and classism of its leaders.

AFTER
2000 Black author bell hooks publishes *Feminism Is for Everybody: Passionate Politics*.

2017 Experts from the United Nations report that racism and human rights abuses in the US are on the rise.

In many countries during the 1970s, white, middle-class women dominated feminist groups. These women experienced oppression mainly in the context of gender, whereas poor and working-class white women experienced oppression because of gender and class, and women of color because of gender, race, and possibly class. Women who suffered oppression on a number of fronts—such as poor, indigenous, lesbian women—were often made to feel as if their quest for a feminist movement relevant to their own lives was "divisive."

Men first

Other social justice movements of the time tended to be dominated by those with the most power. Left-wing groups, for example, were often led by white men, some of whom treated women as potential sexual partners and secretarial back-up. Black women found that black liberation groups also tended to be dominated by men, and lesbians complained that the Gay Liberation Front focused on the experiences of gay men. These and other organizations failed to tackle cohesively the simultaneous and

> The struggle against patriarchy and racism must be intertwined.
> **Kimberlé Crenshaw**

intersecting problems of racism, sexism, homophobia, class oppression, and other prejudices.

Groups such as the Combahee River Collective, a black lesbian feminist socialist organization in Boston, Massachusetts, were formed to address the needs of women facing multiple forms of oppression. Its Combahee River Collective Statement, issued in 1977, is one of the first published accounts of the way multiple oppressions intersect. Proposing a bottom-up approach to social justice, the collective's members argued that prioritizing the needs of the most marginalized would lift

Kimberlé Crenshaw

Born in Canton, Ohio, in 1959, Kimberlé Williams Crenshaw is Distinguished Professor of Law at UCLA, where she has taught since 1986. She studied government and Africana studies at Cornell University, earned a law degree at Harvard in 1984, followed by an LLM (Master of Law degree) from the University of Wisconsin in 1985.

Crenshaw coined the term "intersectionality," a concept that is widely seen as a foundation of third- and fourth-wave feminism. It was also reportedly influential in drafting the equality clause of the post-apartheid South African Constitution. In 1996, Crenshaw founded The African American Policy Forum. She also served as the first director for the Center for Intersectionality and Social Policy Studies, established in 2011 at Columbia University.

Key works

1989 "Demarginalizing the Intersection of Race and Sex"
1991 "Mapping the Margins"
1993 *Words that Wound*
1995 *Critical Race Theory*
2013 *The Race Track*

See also: Racism and class prejudice within feminism 202–205 ▪ Black feminism and womanism 208–215 ▪ Disability feminism 276–277 ▪ Trans feminism 286–289 ▪ Universal feminism 302–307 ▪ The feminist killjoy 314–315

Black women in the US, such as the protesters at this Civil Rights demonstration in 1965, faced—and still face—levels of police brutality that are not experienced by white women.

society as a whole. Black American feminist writers and activists such as Angela Davis, bell hooks, and Audre Lorde also wrote about the need for race-, class-, and sexuality-based analysis within feminism, and their books shaped the terrain that would later become known as intersectionality.

Multiple jeopardy

The Combahee River Collective's analysis was similar to the concept of "multiple jeopardy" used by black feminist scholars such as Patricia Hill Collins and Deborah K. King. The term denotes the ways in which sexism is "multiplied" when combined with racism, and then further multiplied by class and other oppressions.

King and others identify the multiple jeopardy of being a black woman under slavery. Enslaved black women were expected to

perform the same back-breaking labor in the fields as black men, but were also subjected to rape that was used both as a form of torture and control and as a means of producing children to expand the enslaved labor force. King believes that by understanding multiple jeopardy, black women will be able to work toward their own liberation as free, autonomous subjects.

Naming intersectionality

The term "intersectionality" was first used in 1989, by American law professor and critical race theorist Kimberlé Crenshaw in her essay "Demarginalizing the Intersection of Race and Sex." In a later essay, "Mapping the Margins" (1991), she divides intersectionality into three main types: structural, political, and representational. Structural intersectionality refers to the ways in which the

oppression experienced by women of color is fundamentally different from that experienced by white women. Political intersectionality addresses the specific impact that laws and public policies have on women of color, even when they are designed for feminist or antiracist reasons. Representational intersectionality describes how women of color are misrepresented in popular culture and how this affects them in everyday life.

Crenshaw also stresses that when we consider the multiplicity of oppression, we should not take an additive approach—racism plus sexism plus classism—but rather we should understand how class oppression is racialized, how racism is gendered, and so on. For example, the 1980s stereotype of the "welfare queen" was mainly associated with black single mothers. Black women experience the stigma of poverty in ways not shared by poor white »

> If we aren't intersectional, some of us ... are going to fall through the cracks.
> **Kimberlé Crenshaw**

women. Citing women's shelters in communities of color in Los Angeles as an example, Crenshaw shows the ways in which the intersections of power, privilege, and oppression operate. These shelters, she says, seek to protect women from domestic violence, yet many of them cannot be reached by public transport, and information is often given only in English, which some women cannot understand. While claiming to be spaces for women to seek help, in reality these shelters fail many of the women they intended to serve.

In addition, Crenshaw argues, every woman's experience with domestic violence varies greatly, depending on race, class, and other factors. Migrant women, for example, risk deportation if they try to escape their abusive situation, because notifying the police about their partner's violence could result in the immigration authorities investigating the family's undocumented status.

Crenshaw also points out that the policies of many NGOs created to help women are shaped by their reliance on funding. Their felt obligation to understand an issue such as domestic violence from the perspective of their funders—who are more likely to be white and class-privileged—can mean that specific requirements of their users, such as the need for interpreters and translation services, may not be prioritized.

Whose lives matter?

Movements for social change in many countries continue to exclude people based on race, gender, class, sexuality, gender identity, religion, ability, and more, either by accident or design. In the US, for example, Black Lives Matter, a liberation movement supporting black people in the face of police violence, was founded by radical black organizers Alicia Garza, Patrisse Cullors, and Opal Tometi in 2013. Two of these three women also identify as queer. Despite the founders' commitment to intersectional activism, LGBTQ activists and other black women are still concerned at the lack of visibility and public support given to female victims of anti-black brutality, especially those who are queer and transgender.

In response to these concerns, the #SayHerName movement was started by female Black Lives Matter supporters. This was given particular impetus by the suspicious death in 2015 of Sandra Bland—an African American woman who died in jail after an alleged traffic violation.

Intersectionality today

When Donald Trump was elected US president in 2016, exit polls showed that 52 percent of white female voters had voted for him, while 96 percent of black women had voted for Hillary Clinton. These statistics renewed the debate about

The entertainer Josephine Baker left the US to become a superstar in 1920s Europe. Although she returned in 1936, the intersecting racism and sexism she experienced there as a black woman drove her back to France.

white women's lack of concern for racial justice. Pointing to Trump's record of anti-black and anti-Latino remarks and his silence on incidents of racial violence, critics questioned the collective tendency of white women to enable systemic racism.

The 2017 Women's March, which took place in Washington, D.C., and around the world during Donald Trump's inauguration weekend, was also subject to intersectional feminist analyses. These ranged from questions about whose bodies the iconic pink pussy hat worn by many at the marches was supposed to represent, to challenges to white

A woman confronts police in Charlotte, North Carolina, after the fatal shooting of African American Keith Lamont Scott in 2016. The Black Lives Matter movement, founded by African American women, led the protests.

women to show up for Black Lives Matter or immigrants' rights rallies in the same vast numbers as turned out for the Women's March.

Debates such as these suggest that intersectionality's insights remain as relevant as ever, but it is not without its critics. For example, Jennifer Nash, a professor of African-American Studies and Gender and Sexuality Studies, argues that its definition and methodology are insufficiently rigorous. While Nash also cites the dangers of generalizing black women as a group, she emphasizes that distinguishing concrete identity groups such as "women" or "black people" is useful for building political coalitions.

Intersectionality is now widely regarded as an essential part of inclusive and innovative feminist writing in the 21st century, and continues to drive activism in the long march toward justice. ∎

There is no such thing as a single-issue struggle because we do not live single-issue lives.
Audre Lorde

The kyriarchy

The term "kyriarchy" was coined by feminist theologian Elisabeth Schüssler Fiorenza in 1992. Taken from the Greek roots *kyrios*, "lord, master," and *archo*, "to lead, govern," it means "rule by a sovereign."

Kyriarchy looks beyond the single issue of gender to the many ways power is held and experienced in society, resulting in both privilege and oppression, and encompassing racism, sexism, Islamophobia, classism, transphobia, and so on. Every individual has multiple simultaneous roles, some privileged, some not: a person could be, for example, Indian, upper-class, and lesbian. Everyone experiences the world according to their individual realities.

Kyriarchy holds that all forms of oppression are linked, and that this oppression is institutionalized and self-sustained: those who already have power tend to remain in power; those without tend to assume the oppressor's views toward others in their group and remain disenfranchised.

Identity politics ... frequently conflates or ignores intra group differences.
Kimberlé Crenshaw

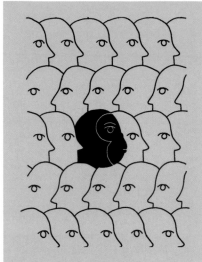

WE COULD BE ANYONE AND WE ARE EVERYWHERE
GUERRILLA PROTESTING

IN CONTEXT

PRIMARY QUOTE
Guerrilla Girls website

KEY ORGANIZATION
Guerrilla Girls

BEFORE
1979 American artist Judy Chicago exhibits her massive feminist art installation *The Dinner Party*, a tribute to the history of Western women.

AFTER
2009 The Guerrilla Girls' archives are acquired by the J. Paul Getty Museum in Los Angeles, California.

2016 The Guerrilla Girls appear on America's *The Late Show* with Stephen Colbert to discuss their activism.

2017 On International Women's Day, a group of 100 female artists in the UK protest outside the National Gallery, London, where only 20 of the 2,000 works are by women.

Founded in New York City in 1985, the Guerrilla Girls are an anonymous collective of female artists who protest against the absence of female artists and artists of color in the world's top art galleries. The group formed in response to the 1984 International Survey of Painting and Sculpture at the Museum of Modern Art (MoMA), a "definitive" exhibition of art from around the world. Only 13 of the 169 works featured in the exhibition were by female artists.

Like guerrilla fighters, Guerrilla Girls employ surprise tactics. Their hallmark is "culture jamming"—putting up posters, and even billboards, often in the middle of the night. Members of the group protect their identity by wearing gorilla masks (said to have come about after a misspelling of guerrilla) and taking the names of deceased female artists such as Frida Kahlo, Käthe Kollwitz, and Hannah Höch. Their stunts were designed to combat the 1970s stereotype of feminists as humorless, and to attract new generations of feminists. The Guerrilla Girls routinely contrast humorous images and "weenie counts" with statistics about inequality in the art world. Their

most famous poster, created in 1989, is a parody of Jean Auguste Dominique Ingres' 1814 painting *Grande Odalisque*, in which his nude is given a gorilla head. Statistics about sexism and racism in the art world and the slogan "Do women have to be naked to get into the Met Museum?" surround the figure. The same issues inspired their 1998 book, *The Guerrilla Girls' Bedside Companion to the History of Western Art*.

Political activism
In addition to targeting the art world, the Guerrilla Girls routinely speak out on political issues,

> When racism and sexism are no longer fashionable, what will your art collection be worth?
> **Guerrilla Girls**

See also: Feminist art 128–131 ▪ Radical feminism 137 ▪ Writing women into history 154–155 ▪
The Riot Grrrl movement 272–273

Guerrilla Girls pose for the camera in 1990. Over the years, the group has included around 60 women artists, including some founding members who are still active today.

especially those affecting women. The group created posters for the 1992 abortion rights march on Washington, D.C., and protested against the widely televised acts of police brutality against black taxi driver Rodney King during the Los Angeles riots of 1992. In recent years, the Guerrilla Girls have used their art to publicly criticize Hollywood's white-male-dominated Academy Awards, anti-gay politicians, and the election of Donald Trump as US president.

White bias

There has been criticism that the Guerrilla Girls, despite accusing the art world of being a mostly white space, are themselves an overwhelmingly white group. Some female artists of color who have been past members have reported feeling alienated in the group. In 2008, a former Guerrilla Girl who used the pseudonym "Alma Thomas," after the African

American artist, said that she felt uncomfortable wearing a gorilla mask, because it was harder for her to speak with authority as a black woman while her identity was obscured, and because of the anti-black history associated with the figure of the gorilla.

The Guerrilla Girls also tread a fine line between being critics of the capitalist commodification of art and being part of it themselves. Galleries across the world have held exhibitions of their protest materials: exhibitions spanning their careers have taken place at the Fundación Bilbao Arte in Bilbao, Spain; the Hellenic American Union Galleries in Athens, Greece; Tate Modern in London, UK; and the Pompidou Centre in Paris, France. ▪

Culture jamming

A form of "subvertising," culture jamming aims to undermine advertising by turning it on its head. By subverting well-known logos, slogans, and images, culture jammers question the original intent of the advertisement while also attracting the attention of those who might not otherwise listen.

While the term "culture jamming" was coined in 1984 by American musician Don Joyce, who recognized how advertising shaped people's inner lives, scholars have dated the practice to at least 1950s Europe, where it was used to attack consumerism. Today, the Canadian pro-environment journal *Adbusters* runs "subvertisements" that are a classic example of culture jamming, as is the work of the anonymous British artist Banksy, who stencils politically charged images on the sides of buildings in the dead of night.

> Everyone hates to see women complain. But I think we have found a way to do it so that no one complains.
> **Guerrilla Girls**

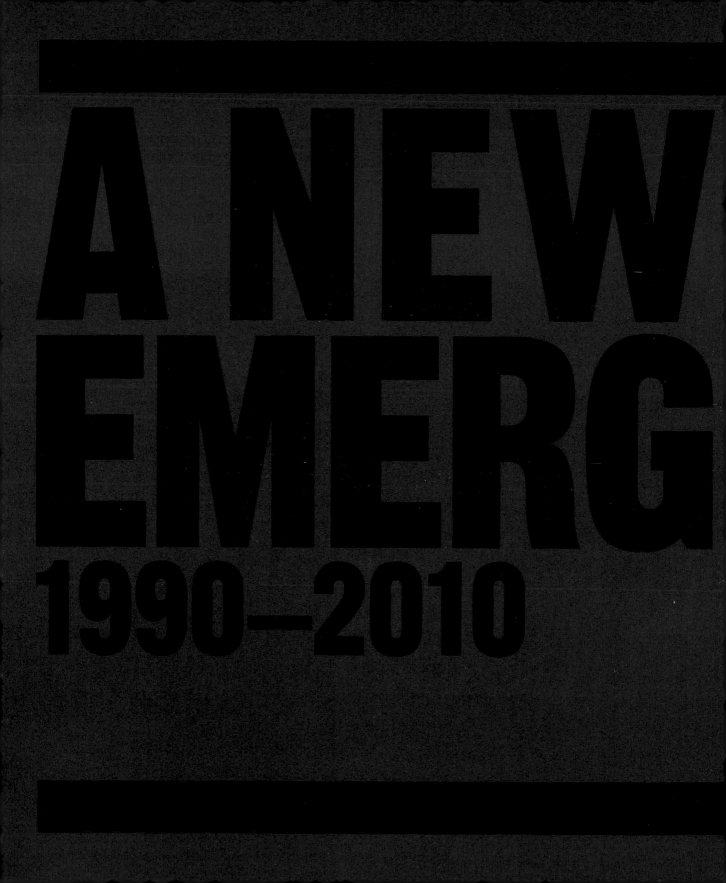

A NEW
EMERG
1990—2010

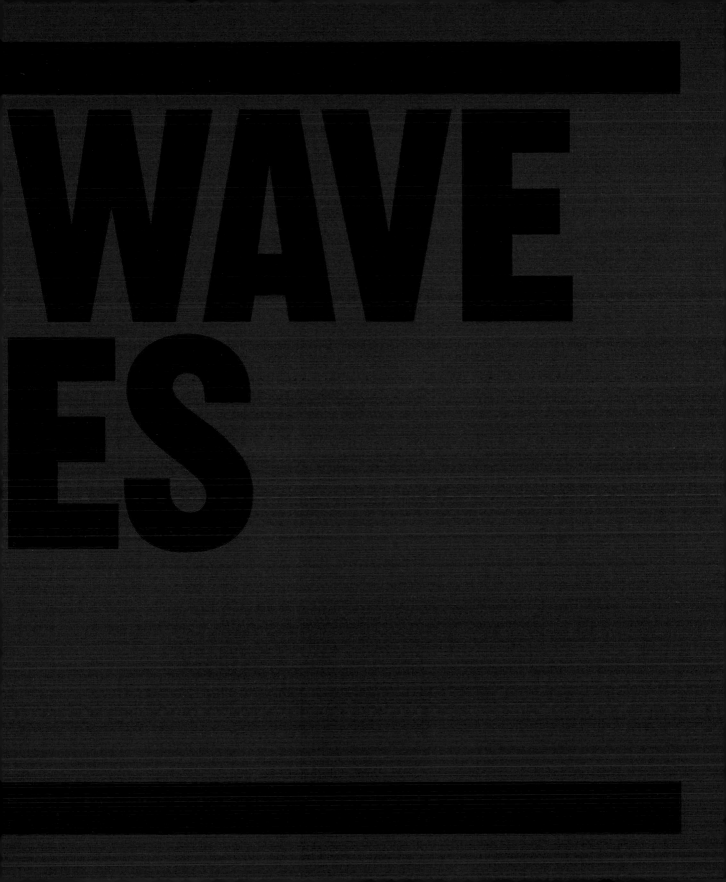

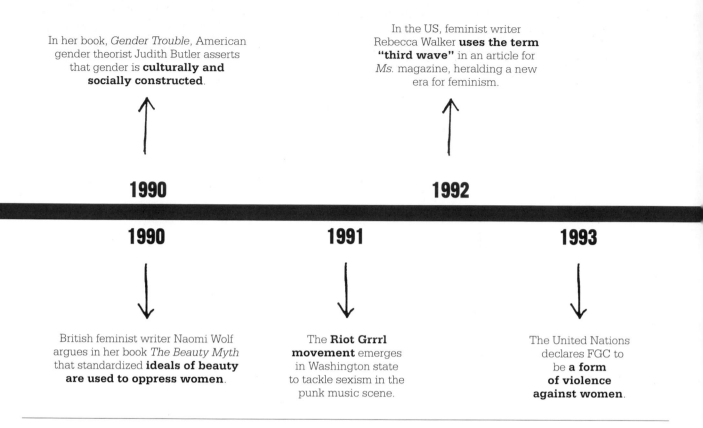

In her book, *Gender Trouble*, American gender theorist Judith Butler asserts that gender is **culturally and socially constructed**.

In the US, feminist writer Rebecca Walker **uses the term "third wave"** in an article for *Ms.* magazine, heralding a new era for feminism.

1990

1992

1990

1991

1993

British feminist writer Naomi Wolf argues in her book *The Beauty Myth* that standardized **ideals of beauty are used to oppress women**.

The **Riot Grrrl movement** emerges in Washington state to tackle sexism in the punk music scene.

The United Nations declares FGC to be **a form of violence against women**.

At the end of the 1980s, some feminists, such as Susan Faludi in the US, began to notice a powerful backlash against feminism. Antifeminists argued that women had gained equal opportunities in education and employment and were starting to emasculate men. There was much media talk of a postfeminist era, in which women no longer needed to strive for equality.

Many American feminists disagreed with this view, among them Rebecca Walker, Jennifer Baumgardner, and Amy Richards. They did not believe equality for women had been achieved, or that it was feminism's only goal. They recognized the achievements of second-wave feminism, and wished to build upon them, but argued that feminism also needed to adapt to changing circumstances, in particular the rise of the right-wing philosophy of neoliberalism. A key catalyst in the development of this new phase of feminism was the appointment of Judge Clarence Thomas to the US Supreme Court despite the fact that the attorney Anita Hill had accused him of sexual harassment—claims that he denied. In response to what she saw as blatant misogyny, the feminist writer Rebecca Walker declared her support for a new kind of feminism in "Becoming the third wave," an article she wrote for *Ms.* magazine.

A punk wave

For many young feminists born in the late 1960s and '70s, the Riot Grrrl movement of the early 1990s marked the start of the third wave. Combining feminist consciousness and punk music, "riot grrrls" stressed personal empowerment. They projected a powerful image, dressed as they pleased, reclaimed words such as "slut" and "bitch," and explored issues such as rape, domestic abuse, sexuality, and patriarchy through music and zines (handmade magazines). They celebrated female culture and friendships.

How women presented themselves was a matter of fierce debate among feminists during this period, especially between second-wave feminists and members of the new third wave. American feminist Ariel Levy coined the phrase "raunch culture" to describe the overtly sexual behavior adopted by some young women as a protest against what they saw as the prudishness of

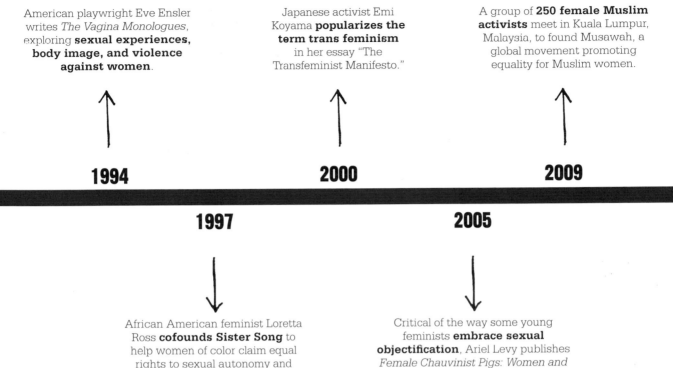

American playwright Eve Ensler writes *The Vagina Monologues*, exploring **sexual experiences, body image, and violence against women**.

Japanese activist Emi Koyama **popularizes the term trans feminism** in her essay "The Transfeminist Manifesto."

A group of **250 female Muslim activists** meet in Kuala Lumpur, Malaysia, to found Musawah, a global movement promoting equality for Muslim women.

1994

2000

2009

1997

2005

African American feminist Loretta Ross **cofounds Sister Song** to help women of color claim equal rights to sexual autonomy and reproductive justice.

Critical of the way some young feminists **embrace sexual objectification**, Ariel Levy publishes *Female Chauvinist Pigs: Women and the Rise of Raunch Culture*.

second-wave feminism exemplified by antipornography campaigners such as Andrea Dworkin. Levy believed that this played directly into the hands of misogynist culture and reinforced women's subordination. Other feminists disagreed with such views and called for a more sex-positive approach, arguing that women had a right to sexual freedom and pleasure. From this came a movement in support of feminist-created pornography.

Building on well-established feminist ideas about idealized femininity, American writer Naomi Wolf put forward her theory of the "beauty myth." She argued that women were being seriously harmed by images of idealized beauty peddled by marketing and modeling agencies. In her view,

women were being forced to direct their energies toward an impossible ideal by commercial forces imposed by men.

Issues and campaigns

Third-wave feminism was also characterized by new and sometimes conflicting theories about sex, gender, and identity. In 1990, American feminist philosopher Judith Butler published *Gender Trouble*, in which she put forward the theory that gender is continually acted out according to cultural expectations, creating the illusion of stable gender identities. She saw gender as fluid, not binary. At the same time, the issue of bisexuality claimed attention, as bisexuals complained of being treated with hostility by both heterosexual and lesbian women.

While many Western feminists debated issues of gender, others continued to campaign against actions that oppressed women, drawing attention to issues that had been sidelined or covered up, such as the inferior provision of health care to poor women, especially women of color and indigenous women, in the US. Elsewhere in the world, the Ghanaian-British activist Efua Dorkenoo campaigned against female genital cutting (FGC), which was widely carried out on young women in Africa, and Iraqi-born Zainab Salbi exposed the existence of "rape camps," established by the Serbian regime in Bosnia and Herzegovina during the Bosnian war. Salbi went on to found Women International to support rape survivors in war zones. ∎

I AM THE THIRD WAVE

POSTFEMINISM AND THE THIRD WAVE

IN CONTEXT

PRIMARY QUOTE
Rebecca Walker, 1992

KEY FIGURES
**Rebecca Walker,
Jennifer Baumgardner**

BEFORE
1960s–early 1980s Second-wave feminism examines the roots of female oppression and focuses on women's rights over their own bodies.

1983 Alice Walker uses the term "womanist" for black feminists who challenge combined sexism and racism.

AFTER
2012 A new fourth wave of feminism emerges, facilitated by the use of social media to raise consciousness.

2015 In a national survey, fewer than a quarter of LGBTQ, Latina, Asian, Pacific Islander, and Muslim women say it is a good time to be a US citizen.

I n 1992, 22-year-old American feminist and writer Rebecca Walker wrote "Becoming the Third Wave," an article for *Ms.* magazine in which she declared having joined a new, third wave of feminism that recognized and challenged the racism, classism, and sexism still prevalent in society. The article highlighted women's powerlessness to stop the sexual harassment—both verbal and physical—around them and also dismissed the widespread belief that, in a postfeminist era, most young women were enjoying equality with men and feminism was no longer needed. "The fight is far from over," Walker declared.

Like many women born in the 1960s and later, Walker, whose mother was the novelist and poet Alice Walker, could see that, in a misogynistic, right-wing age, feminism needed to be reinvented. As Jennifer Baumgardner and Amy Richards note in their 2000 book *Manifesta: Young Women, Feminism, and the Future*, women have to remold feminism to make it relevant to their generation's needs and sensibilities. From the early 1990s until around 2012, third-

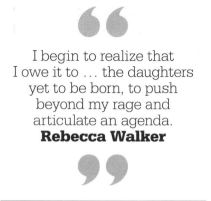

> I begin to realize that I owe it to … the daughters yet to be born, to push beyond my rage and articulate an agenda.
> **Rebecca Walker**

wave feminists let it be known that they were unconvinced that women had "arrived" and were fulfilling their dreams.

New conservatism

In the 1980s and early 1990s, the UK and US experienced an extended backlash against the social progress made during the civil rights movements of the 1960s and '70s. Margaret Thatcher's UK premiership of 1979–1990 brought the right-wing conservatism, free-market capitalism, and British nationalism that would later be

---

Jennifer Baumgardner

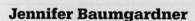

Born in North Dakota in 1970, Jennifer Baumgardner became a feminist activist as a college student in Wisconsin. Moving to New York City in the early 1990s, she worked as an intern for *Ms.* magazine before becoming its youngest editor in 1997.

Baumgardner rose to feminist prominence with the publication of her book *Manifesta* (2000), celebrating the emergence of third-wave feminism. She has also written about bisexuality as well as reproductive justice, abortion, and rape. In 2002, with Amy Richards, she founded Soapbox

Inc. to provide a platform for feminist activism. Her films "I Had an Abortion" (2004) and "It Was Rape" (2008) urged women to share their own experiences. From 2013 to 2017, Baumgardner was executive director of The Feminist Press.

Key works

2000 *Manifesta: Young Women, Feminism, and the Future*
2007 *Look Both Ways: Bisexual Politics*
2011 *F 'em!: Goo Goo, Gaga, and Some Thoughts on Balls*

See also: The birth of the suffrage movement 56–63 ▪ Racial and gender equality 64–69 ▪ The roots of oppression 114–117 ▪ Consciousness-raising 134–135 ▪ Privilege 239 ▪ Intersectionality 240–245 ▪ The Riot Grrrl movement 272–273

The birth of third-wave feminism

Feminist concerns evolved as successive generations won new freedoms but confronted and addressed different social problems.

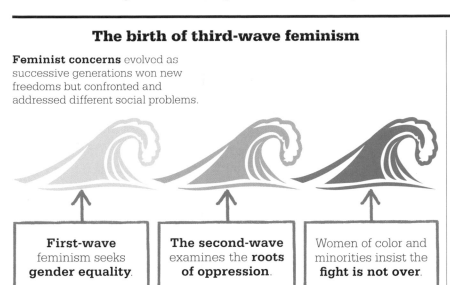

First-wave feminism seeks **gender equality**.

The second-wave examines the **roots of oppression**.

Women of color and minorities insist the **fight is not over**.

dubbed "Thatcherism." While Thatcher had voted to legalize homosexuality in 1967, in 1988 her government enacted Section 28, banning local authorities from "promoting" homosexuality, and state schools from suggesting that same-sex relationships were acceptable "as a pretended family relationship." Despite an outcry from many quarters, Section 28 was not repealed until 2003.

From 1980, US President Ronald Reagan's conservative brand of free-market economics led to a widening income gap in the US. Reagan openly opposed equality for gay and lesbian people, and gay rights groups charged him and his administration with contributing to thousands of deaths by failing to respond proactively to HIV/AIDS as a public health emergency. Reagan did not mention the word "AIDS" in public until September 1985, in response to questions from a reporter. Determined to end the silence, the radical grassroots gay rights group ACT UP, standing for "AIDS Coalition To Unleash Power," was founded in 1987.

Baptist minister Jerry Falwell's Moral Majority organization, founded in 1979, was a key player in the rise of the Christian Right during the Reagan era. Throughout the 1980s, this movement mobilized evangelical Christians into a "family values" coalition that opposed feminism, reproductive choice, and LGBT rights. In 1982, the Equal Rights Amendment (ERA), first introduced to Congress in 1923, failed to meet its deadline

for ratification by the requisite majority of 38 states. In 1989 and again in 1992, women marched demanding abortion rights.

In 1991, Judge Clarence Thomas was confirmed by Congress to the US Supreme Court despite his alleged sexual harassment of Anita Hill, which was the starting point of Walker's "Third Wave" article in *Ms.* in 1992. In 1995, at the Rally for Women's Lives, feminists protested en masse about violence against women. After the 1995 Million Man March in Washington, D.C., for black civil rights, in 1997 black women organized a Million Woman March in Philadelphia. Gay rights activists also protested at the Capitol many times during the 1990s, and the 2000 Millennium March called for LGBTQ equal rights.

Race, class, and sexuality

Conservative policy shifts had given many young women—especially those who were not white and middle class—plenty to protest about. Activists such as Walker highlighted their daily experiences of misogyny, racism, classism, and homophobia, which they believed were clearly a by-product of the political climate of the time.

While second-wave feminist gains were recognized, third-wave feminists wanted to dig deeper and analyze what American civil rights advocate Kimberlé Crenshaw first called "intersectionality" in a 1989 paper discussing the intersection of race, gender, and class from a »

Queen Latifah, a pioneer hip-hop feminist, raps about issues affecting black women. Her song "Ladies First" (1989) urges black women to be proud of their bodies and gender.

black feminist perspective. The term is used to describe the way that power systems interlock to oppress the most marginalized in society, including LGBT people, people of color, the lower classes, and people with disabilities. If Robin Morgan's declaration that "Sisterhood is Powerful" was the mantra of second-wave feminism, third-wave feminists were asking which groups of women were actually included in this sisterhood. It was a question that feminists of color had highlighted throughout the 1970s and '80s.

Crenshaw's paper was far from the only influence on third-wave feminists. Important scholarly work by postcolonial feminists, such as Chandra Talpade Mohanty, was also emerging. American feminist Peggy McIntosh had published an influential article on white privilege in 1988, Judith Butler was looking at the social construction of sex and gender, and there was a wealth

of new writing on gay and lesbian issues. The women's studies programs that feminists had fought to introduce in colleges and universities during the 1970s were making inroads into higher education by the 1990s.

Outside the academic world, the Riot Grrrl feminist punk movement of the early 1990s exploded onto the scene in the US as a response to male-dominated punk music and a misogynistic culture at large. Riot Grrrl activists reclaimed labels used to degrade women, such as "bitch" and "slut." They created a powerful girl culture that publicly denounced violence and sexual abuse against women and girls. In songs such as Bikini Kill's "Rebel Girl," they celebrated the strength of female relationships.

The belief that women had a right to express their sexuality and to enjoy sex was also a cornerstone of third-wave feminism. While second-wave feminists such as

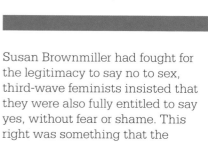

> Being liberated doesn't mean copying what came before but finding one's own way—a way that is genuine to one's own generation.
> **Jennifer Baumgardner and Amy Richards**

Susan Brownmiller had fought for the legitimacy to say no to sex, third-wave feminists insisted that they were also fully entitled to say yes, without fear or shame. This right was something that the feminist sex positivity movement called for throughout the 1980s. However, it was at odds with the beliefs of antipornography feminists, who had built coalitions with right-wing political groups in their bid to demonize not only pornography but also sexual practices such as BDSM (bondage, domination, and sadomasochism).

The sexuality dilemma

Back in the early 1980s, *The New York Times* had run "Voices of the Post-Feminist Generation," an article about young women who agreed with feminist goals but cringed at being associated with "women's libbers" of the older generation, whom they found to be negative, angry, and antagonistic

The characters Charlotte, Carrie, Miranda, and Samantha in the TV show *Sex and the City* (1998–2004) embodied sexual freedom yet their happiness often depended on men.

Young women in a 2017 London march demonstrate their support for Care International, whose missions include both fighting poverty and "empowering women and girls."

toward men. A divide now opened up between feminists of the second and third wave. Some second-wave feminists argued that women of the third-wave generation were insufficiently critical of their culture. They criticized the reclamation of "bitch" or "slut" and the habit of women referring to themselves as "girls." Using such language, practicing casual sex, conforming to hypersexualized feminine images, or consuming porn were, they thought, markers of a postfeminist generation that had lost its feminist way.

From the 1990s, critical feminists maintained that young women's desire for sexual liberation risked reinforcing their subordination. In her book *Female Chauvinist Pigs: Women and the Rise of Raunch Culture* (2005), American feminist Ariel Levy examines the rise of highly sexualized female behavior. She views this not as any kind of advance, but as the expression of an unresolved 1980s feminist conflict between the women who supported sex-positivism and those who opposed pornography. Women wanted to be sexually free, but that sexual freedom made them vulnerable to male exploitation.

Perpetuated in the media

Some feminists targeted the media for purporting to celebrate women's sexual freedom, while cynically sexualizing female characters for profit. One example cited by British cultural theorist Angela McRobbie was the American TV series *Sex and the City*. While claiming to portray sexually liberated, successful working women in New York City, the series' plotlines and characters often perpetuated anti-feminist messages. The central character Carrie Bradshaw, for instance, was obsessed with finding a man to complete her life. A further issue of concern has been increasing levels of sexual violence against women depicted in the news, on television, and at the cinema.

Postfeminist concerns are still hotly debated—and now by new, younger feminists. The emergence of social media has brought an explosion of activism, marking the movement's fourth wave. ∎

GENDER IS A SET OF REPEATED ACTS

GENDER IS PERFORMATIVE

IN CONTEXT

PRIMARY QUOTE
Judith Butler, 1990

KEY FIGURE
Judith Butler

BEFORE
1949 Simone de Beauvoir says that "one is not born a woman" and suggests that gender is established through a social process of "becoming" woman.

1976 Monique Wittig proposes that binary gender is the foundation of a compulsory heterosexuality.

AFTER
1990s Psychologist Nancy Chodorow explains how gender roles are entrenched by replication over generations.

I n part thanks to the work of Simone de Beauvoir, feminists of the second wave began to distinguish between "sex" and "gender" when discussing the differences between men and women. Sex refers to biological differences, whereas gender refers to social differences—what are often called gender roles. In 1986, the philosopher Judith Butler wrote a paper entitled "Sex and Gender in Simone de Beauvoir's *Second Sex*," acknowledging that de Beauvoir had provided an important new understanding of gender. However, Butler went on to form her own theories on the subject and critique the distinction between the terms.

In 1990, Butler published her ground-breaking work *Gender Trouble*. Butler's work is notoriously

See also: The roots of oppression 114–117 ▪ Poststructuralism 182–187 ▪ Feminism and queer theory 262–263

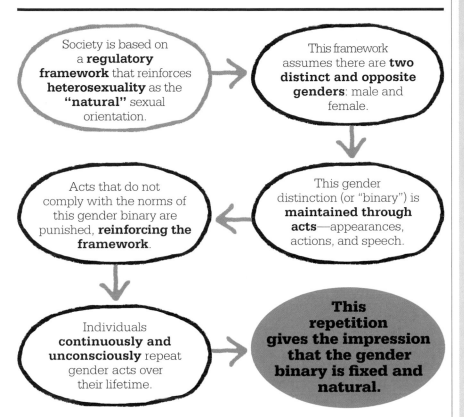

Society is based on a **regulatory framework** that reinforces **heterosexuality** as the **"natural"** sexual orientation.

This framework assumes there are **two distinct and opposite genders**: male and female.

This gender distinction (or "binary") is **maintained through acts**—appearances, actions, and speech.

Acts that do not comply with the norms of this gender binary are punished, **reinforcing the framework**.

Individuals **continuously and unconsciously** repeat gender acts over their lifetime.

This repetition gives the impression that the gender binary is fixed and natural.

Judith Butler

Born in Cleveland, Ohio, in 1956, Judith Butler became interested in philosophy in Jewish ethics classes at the age of 14. Butler studied at Bennington College and Yale University, earning her PhD in Philosophy in 1984. She first proposed her theory of performativity in an essay entitled "Performative Acts and Gender Constitution" (1988), and went on to become a leading proponent of gender theory. Her later work moves beyond conceptions of gender to discuss a philosophical theory of violence. Butler also writes about the concept of "precarity"—when the conditions in which one lives become unbearable. Butler has been outspoken about feminism, LGBTQ+ issues, and the Israeli-Palestinian conflict. Her partner, Wendy Brown, is a political theorist.

Key works

1990 *Gender Trouble*
1993 *Bodies That Matter: On the Discursive Limits of "Sex"*
2004 *Undoing Gender*
2015 *Notes Toward a Performative Theory of Assembly*

complex. It draws on the theories of the poststructuralist philosopher Michel Foucault and the ideas of poststructuralist feminists such as Julia Kristeva. Foucault and other poststructuralists believe that social reality is constructed through the language that is used to describe it. Butler therefore tends to focus on linguistic structures, discourse, and acts.

When Butler talks about "acts," she is talking about how social reality is created through language and gestures. Speech is an act, but so is nonverbal communication— such as a person's body language, appearance, and behavior. Both, Butler believes, are key to the creation of gender identity. Within a social context, Butler suggests

that there are rules and restrictions on how free a person is to "act" differently to societal expectations.

Gender as performative

To Butler, gender is created and maintained through the constant repetition of acts. These acts, when observed together, give the appearance of a coherent and natural gender identity. Butler calls this repetition of acts within a given context "performativity." When Butler says that gender is performative, she means that gender is a thing that people do, and not a thing that they innately are. According to Butler, a person is not born with a gender identity that leads them to behave in a particular way—instead, they »

> Gender is always a doing, though not a doing by a subject who might be said to preexist the deed.
> **Judith Butler**

are perceived to have a gender identity because of how they walk, talk, and present themselves. Because these acts are constantly repeated, they give the appearance of a fixed gender identity.

The gender binary

Readers have often misconstrued the ideas in *Gender Trouble*. Butler herself has responded, "The bad reading goes something like this: I can get up in the morning, look in my closet, and decide which gender I want to be today." Yet gender, as a system of expectations, is more heavily entrenched than that. A person cannot simply decide to do it "differently" overnight. Butler does not see the performance of gender as a free choice. She likens performativity to a trap in which people repeat acts that reinforce restrictive and oppressive gender norms. These norms are socially constructed, and position "man" and "woman" as polar opposites with no middle ground—something known as gender dimorphism, or the "gender binary."

Butler argues that a perception of gender as black and white, or binary, also applies to sex, and often leads to intersex people undergoing surgeries at a young

age, in order to make their bodies align more closely with medical designations of "male" and "female." In a sense, she says, sex is just as socially constructed as gender is, because the language used to describe genitalia—as being either male or female—is the same as that describing gender. Therefore, our understanding of sex is already bound up in notions of what it means for something to be masculine or feminine.

Queer theory

Butler's work has been significant not only to feminism, but to queer theory. In *Gender Trouble*, Butler criticizes many of the feminists who came before her for their assumptions that heterosexuality is the natural state of being. Butler argues that this is not the case; in fact, she says, the gender binary exists largely in order to support the imposition of heterosexuality on society. Belief in an oppositional and complementary gender binary is necessary for people to believe that heterosexuality (oppositional desire) is a fact of nature. Butler writes that sex, gender, and

> It is important to resist the violence that is imposed by ideal gender norms, especially against those who are gender different, who are nonconforming in their gender presentation.
> **Judith Butler**

The Gothic drag troupe Black Lips poses in New York City, in March 1993. Formed by the singer Anohni, the group performed gender-bending theater in the early 1990s.

sexuality are constructed to go hand in hand—meaning that a person classified as "male" at birth is expected to identify as masculine and to experience heterosexual attraction toward women. She argues that this "coherent identification"—when sexuality, sex, and gender align—has been repeated so many times that it has become a cultural norm. In other words, it comes about through actions in society. Any deviance from this, she says, will be punished. Homosexuals, for example, and those whose gender performance does not match their sex, can be shamed and subjected to violence in order to punish their deviance from societal norms.

Such punishments are functions of what is known as hegemonic heterosexuality—"hegemonic" meaning the most dominant force in a sociopolitical context that

> Every taxi driver I have ever spoken to has a theory of gender. … Everyone has a set of presuppositions: what gender is, what it's not.
> **Judith Butler**

is considered normal, natural, and ideal. Queer theorists after Butler have called this idea "heteronormativity"—a worldview in which heterosexuality has become such a dominant idea that people begin to view every interaction or relationship as fitting into a perceived male/female dynamic. Heteronormativity relies on the belief that men and women are two opposite and complementary genders; or what Butler calls the gender binary.

Impact on feminism

Butler's ideas have a specific application when it comes to feminist theory. Butler has argued that feminists have formed new constructions of what it means to be a woman. By this, she means that feminists assume that gender is real, and that women as a group share some sort of common nature, or cultural reality. Here, Butler quotes Julia Kristeva's contention

that "women" do not really exist and argues that there is no single point of view, common essence, or life experience shared by all women that means they should be grouped into a single category. Butler believes that the commonalities among women that are cited by feminists as unifying them too often associate experiences of the female gender with female bodies.

In turn, however, Butler has been criticized by those who find her work to be inaccessible, and to focus too much on complex philosophy and not enough on practical solutions to the realities of injustice and inequality. Still, Butler

has been an active campaigner for women's and LGBTQ+ rights, and her ideas have now become an integral part of even popular (nonacademic) feminist thinking.

While belief in the gender binary is still common, *Gender Trouble* introduced generations of feminists to the idea that gender is not set in stone—and that there are restrictive societal norms at play that women can work to undermine. While Butler's critiques in *Gender Trouble* do not prescribe ways to break the trap of performativity, she hoped that her work would open up new possibilities for thinking about and "doing" gender. ∎

Protesters burn an effigy of Butler during a symposium in São Paulo, Brazil, in 2017. The group, Ativistas Independente, here mingling with other conservative protesters, criticized her as an implanter of gender ideology.

FEMINISM AND QUEER THEORY ARE BRANCHES OF THE SAME TREE
FEMINISM AND QUEER THEORY

IN CONTEXT

PRIMARY QUOTE
Elizabeth Weed, 1997

KEY FIGURE
Eve Kosofsky Sedgwick

BEFORE
1894 Irish playwright Oscar Wilde is called queer by his lover's father. It is the first recorded use of the term as a homophobic insult.

1990 Italian feminist Teresa de Lauretis coins the term "queer theory."

AFTER
1997 Elizabeth Weed and Naomi Schor publish *Feminism Meets Queer Theory*, reflecting on the shared politics of the two fields.

2009 In the US, Harvard University establishes a professorship in LGBT studies.

2011 Queer theorists in the US publish a collection of essays entitled *After Sex?*, examining the place of sex in queer theory.

E merging from feminist theory, poststructuralism, and lesbian and gay studies, queer theory developed to question the ideology that positions heterosexuality as superior while stigmatizing same-sex desire.

In 1976, French critical theorist Michel Foucault wrote *The History of Sexuality Volume I*, which was the intellectual starting point for queer studies. In it, Foucault argues that sexuality, rather than being a biological fact, is actually constructed by society. He challenges the popular assumption

> 66
> The study of sexuality is not coextensive with the study of gender; correspondingly, antihomophobic enquiry is not coextensive with feminist enquiry.
> **Eve Kosofsky Sedgwick**
> 99

that the Victorian era was simply a time of sexual repression. Instead, its sexual prohibitions indicated a fascination with sex. Through this naming, regulating, and punishing of perversions, Foucault writes, a science of sexuality was born, to control and regulate sexuality on behalf of the state.

Foucault's ideas fit well with those of some feminist theorists in the US, notably Gayle Rubin, who looked at what society considered acceptable and unacceptable sex, and Adrienne Rich, who wrote about compulsory heterosexuality. Queer theorist Eve Kosofsky Sedgwick built on all these ideas in her book *Epistemology of the Closet* (1990), challenging the binary division of heterosexual and homosexual, and emphasizing the importance of recognizing gender differences between lesbians and gay men.

The question of identity
Feminism—as a movement and a set of philosophical and political principles—relies on the category "woman" in order to make its claims. However, feminist women of color from the 1980s onward began to ask "Which women?,"

See also: Poststructuralism 182–187 ▪ Compulsory heterosexuality 194–195 ▪ Sex positivity 234–237 ▪ Gender is performative 258–261 ▪ Bisexuality 269 ▪ Trans feminism 286–289

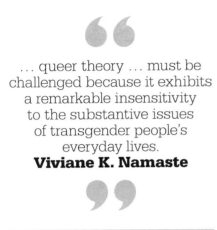

> ... queer theory ... must be challenged because it exhibits a remarkable insensitivity to the substantive issues of transgender people's everyday lives.
> **Viviane K. Namaste**

Eve Kosofsky Sedgwick

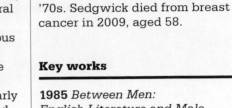

Born to a Jewish family in Dayton, Ohio, in 1950, Eve Kosofsky Sedgwick was a literary scholar whose work was central to the development of queer theory. She taught in prestigious American universities, using literary criticism to challenge norms related to gender and sexuality. This was particularly controversial in the 1980s and '90s, when the US was embroiled in the HIV/AIDS crisis within the larger context of the "culture wars," a time of conservative Christian backlash against the progressive social movements of the 1960s and '70s. Sedgwick died from breast cancer in 2009, aged 58.

Key works

1985 *Between Men: English Literature and Male Homosocial Desire*
1990 *The Epistemology of the Closet*
1999 *A Dialogue on Love*

as did lesbian groups, who were particularly concerned with uncovering a gay and lesbian history. Such questioning was based on expanding the idea of who counted in a particular identity.

Queer theory, on the other hand, developed less as a way to stake a claim on behalf of marginalized identities and more as a way to critique identity politics. Queer theorists have sought to destabilize these fixed identity categories, because they often become limiting.

Many scholars have critiqued queer theory. Canadian feminist scholar Viviane K. Namaste argues in her book *Invisible Lives* (2000) that queer theorists hypothesize about transgender people as mere examples, without putting the realities of trans lives, such as their vulnerability to violence, at the center of their theories. Meanwhile, trans-exclusionary radical feminist Sheila Jeffreys argues in *Unpacking Queer Politics* (2003) that queer theory perpetuates the interests of gay men at the expense of lesbians.

Feminists of color such as Gloria Anzaldúa have written at length about the importance of honoring identities that are at risk of being erased by colonialism, white supremacy, class oppression, misogyny, and homophobia. Queer of color theorists embrace these insights, challenging queer theory for being built on whiteness, and seeking to center queer studies on how these issues intersect. Many feminists are equally wary of abandoning identity politics when large numbers of people still face oppression, inequality, and harm due to their gender or sexuality. ▪

The singer Conchita destabilizes traditional gender categories—a central element of queer theory. "Conchita" is the drag persona of Austrian performer Thomas Neuwirth.

THE BEAUTY MYTH IS PRESCRIBING BEHAVIOR, NOT APPEARANCE

THE BEAUTY MYTH

IN CONTEXT

PRIMARY QUOTE
Naomi Wolf, 1990

KEY FIGURE
Naomi Wolf

BEFORE
1925 American writer and satirist Dorothy Parker famously observes, "Men seldom make passes at girls who wear glasses."

1975 British feminist and film theorist Laura Mulvey writes about how films are shot with the "male gaze," objectifying women by default.

AFTER
1999 In the US, girl group TLC release the song "Unpretty" as a social commentary on the beauty-related pressures that girls and women face.

2004 Dove's Campaign for Real Beauty uses non-models to advertise its skin care range.

F eminists have been critiquing patriarchal standards of female beauty since at least the 1968 protest by radical feminists at the Miss America pageant in Atlantic City, New Jersey. The idealized beauty norms represented by pageants, feminists say, are used as a method of controlling women's behavior. Their opponents frequently dismiss such feminists as "ugly," an insult also leveled at women fighting for female suffrage in the 19th century.

In the eyes of men
In 1990, American feminist and journalist Naomi Wolf published *The Beauty Myth*, in which she

See also: Sexual pleasure 126–127 ▪ Popularizing women's liberation 132–133 ▪ Patriarchy as social control 144–145 ▪ The male gaze 164–165 ▪ Fat positivity 174–175 ▪ Antipornography feminism 196–199

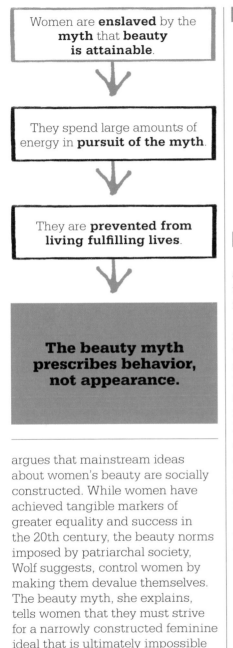

Women are **enslaved** by the **myth** that **beauty is attainable**.

↓

They spend large amounts of energy in **pursuit of the myth**.

↓

They are **prevented from living fulfilling lives**.

↓

The beauty myth prescribes behavior, not appearance.

> If we are to free ourselves from [the beauty myth] … it is not ballots … that women will need first; it is a new way to see.
> **Naomi Wolf**

argues Wolf, the more distracted they become from agitating for feminist social change.

Wolf analyzes multiple arenas in which the beauty myth oppresses women, through work, culture, religion, sex, hunger, and violence. In the chapter on the workplace, she gives the example of female news anchors, who are expected to look feminine, wear makeup, and appear youthful. Such standards are not, she points out, applied to men, whose ageing is considered distinguished and imparting an impression of gravity and wisdom.

Mainstream magazines for women, writes Wolf, devalue those who fall outside the male-imposed parameters of beauty. By shifting their focus, she argues, from domesticity in the 1950s to beauty by the 1990s, as women left the domestic sphere for the workplace, these magazines gave women new reasons to self-consciously monitor themselves. The new focus on losing weight, sexually pleasing men, and dressing to project an image of upwardly mobile white femininity

promotes the beauty myth—and helps drive the profits of those advertising in the magazines.

A new religion

From a cultural perspective, writes Wolf, the earlier obsession with women's sexual purity, dictated by religion, has shifted. Pursuing the beauty myth has become a new moral imperative. This insight by Wolf has since been echoed by fat studies scholars, who denounce the way a thin body is now equated with moral superiority in many contemporary Western cultures.

The moral imperative for women to be beautiful results in what Wolf terms "Rites of Beauty." Women are expected to adhere to an array »

A model sashays down the catwalk. Ultra-slim and white, she embodies the ideal of beauty promoted by the Western fashion industry, which excludes the majority of the world's women.

argues that mainstream ideas about women's beauty are socially constructed. While women have achieved tangible markers of greater equality and success in the 20th century, the beauty norms imposed by patriarchal society, Wolf suggests, control women by making them devalue themselves. The beauty myth, she explains, tells women that they must strive for a narrowly constructed feminine ideal that is ultimately impossible to achieve.

The more time women spend focusing on and berating themselves over their physical looks, fearing they will not be loved or valued unless they are beautiful and thin,

Conforming to the beauty myth

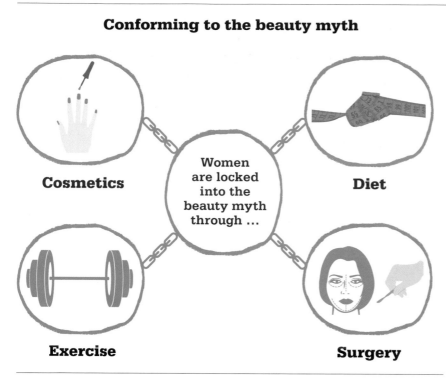

Cosmetics

Women are locked into the beauty myth through ...

Diet

Exercise

Surgery

Girls, Wolf suggests, are taught not how to desire others but how to be desired. This, she says, also teaches men to view women as two-dimensional caricatures rather than as complex human beings, thereby fostering gendered inequality and alienation between the sexes. Under such conditions, sexual pleasure between women and men is diminished.

In her chapter on hunger, Wolf links the beauty myth to anorexia and bulimia, which lead to depression, anxiety, guilt, and fear. Women with eating disorders, she says, learn to self-police and obey the dictates of constant hunger, denying themselves physical and emotional nourishment.

Wolf also describes how the beauty myth leads to violent interventions, such as cosmetic surgery, which are then normalized by society. Rather than "solving" women's unhappiness and self-hatred, society helps create the neuroses that lead to them.

Commodities and profits
The beauty myth also has an economic impact both on women as individuals and on capitalist society.

of beauty rituals and to feel as if they have "sinned" if they depart from them. American feminist scholar Susan Bordo's 1993 book *Unbearable Weight* mirrors some of these theories in her analysis of the cultural and gendered basis of the 1990s anorexia nervosa epidemic. Dessert commercials targeting women in the US, for example, often used religious references such as "Devil's food cake" and "sinfully good."

Wolf goes on to discuss the sexual objectification of women by men. As a consequence, she says, women continually labor to be seen as sexually desirable by them.

Naomi Wolf

Author, journalist, and adviser to former US President Bill Clinton and Vice President Al Gore, Naomi Wolf was born in San Francisco, California, in 1962. She attended Yale University before studying as a Rhodes Scholar at Oxford University in the UK.

In 1990, Wolf's *The Beauty Myth* became an international best seller and influenced feminist interventions in mainstream beauty culture. *The New York Times* called the book "one of the 70 most influential books of the 20th century." Wolf also writes for newspapers such as *The*

Washington Post and *The Wall Street Journal* and has worked as a visiting lecturer at Stony Brook University, New York, and as a fellow at the Barnard Center for Research on Women, New York City.

Key works

1990 *The Beauty Myth*
1998 *Promiscuities: A Secret History of Female Desire*
2007 *The End of America: Letter of Warning to a Young Patriot*

Historically, argues Wolf, women's access to economic security through marriage depended on how well they fulfilled the male-imposed ideal, making women a commodity. This is compounded by the huge range of products and services they buy, from dieting to undergoing vaginoplasty after comparing themselves with porn stars—all of which generate billions of dollars a year for corporations.

New future

Wolf's aim in writing about the beauty myth is to uncover its depths and then dismantle it. She argues for a feminist future in which women's worth is not dependent on a male definition of beauty, but one defined by women themselves. She writes that she does not wish to forbid women from indulging in their sexuality, or wearing lipstick, but wants them to stop viewing themselves negatively. Women should have choices and be recognized as multi-dimensional people, respected by society as both serious and sexual, and to have rich and fulfilling lives. As long as women feel beautiful, it does not matter what they look like.

Since Wolf wrote *The Beauty Myth* in 1990, other feminist scholars have expanded on her findings, and women in general have sought to dismantle the beauty myth. Feminists of color have continued to call out the racism of white-dominated beauty

We can dissolve the myth and survive it with sex, love, attraction, and style not only intact, but flourishing more vibrantly than before.
Naomi Wolf

Women in the Philippines protest against skin-whitening products containing mercury. Such products are common in Asia, where Eurocentric ideals of beauty are widely promoted.

norms and institutions, and the "heroin chic" look promoted by the fashion industry in the 1990s, then typified by British model Kate Moss, has been challenged. The plus-size modeling industry is growing each year, and the terms "fat positivity" and "body positivity" are popular topics of feminist discussion. Even some skin care and cosmetics companies have heeded Wolf's plea, with Dove's Campaign for Real Beauty leading the way in 2004—although sceptics point out that Unilever, the company behind Dove, also make Fair & Lovely, a skin-whitening product popular in Asia.

While women still struggle with self-worth in patriarchal, racist societies, Wolf's exploration of the harms posed by the beauty myth helped instigate a turning point for late 20th-century feminism. ∎

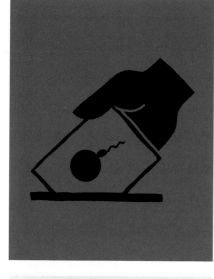

ALL POLITICS ARE REPRODUCTIVE POLITICS
REPRODUCTIVE JUSTICE

IN CONTEXT

PRIMARY QUOTE
Laura Briggs, 2017

KEY FIGURE
Loretta Ross

BEFORE
1965 A survey of Puerto Rican residents finds that a third of mothers aged 20 to 49 have been sterilized under US eugenics laws.

1994 Loretta Ross and other black women coin the term "reproductive justice" after the UN's International Conference on Population and Development in Cairo, Egypt.

AFTER
2013 In the US, the Center for Investigative Reporting reveals that, in California prisons, at least 148 women were illegally sterilized from 2006 to 2010.

2017 American feminist Laura Briggs analyzes the effect of public policy in *How All Politics Became Reproductive Politics*.

The term "reproductive justice" is used to address the widely differing rights over childbearing that women of different races and classes can exercise. It rose to prominence in the 1990s, as black feminists in the US, such as Loretta Ross, began to highlight the plight of poorer women, especially women of color, who had few of the health care choices enjoyed by their more affluent counterparts.

Ross has maintained that, for such women, the terms "pro-life" or "pro-choice" do not reflect their limited options. Historically in the US, poor women of color have received inadequate sex education, unsafe abortions, and inferior provision of contraception, prenatal care, maternity leave, and childcare.

Fighting inequalities

Ross cofounded SisterSong in 1997 to fight for better family health care for underprivileged American women. In *Radical Reproductive Justice* (2017), she and other members outline how systemic oppression affects women's childbearing choices. In what Ross has termed "reprocide," ethnic groups have been suppressed through reproductive control. The forced sterilization of Mexican immigrant women in Los Angeles in the late 1960s and early '70s, explored in the 2015 film *No Más Bebés*, is one example. Such practices may be rarer today, but huge inequalities still exist. ∎

Pro-choice spoken word artist Natalya O'Flaherty performs at a rally in Dublin in April 2018, prior to the referendum on legalizing abortion in Ireland in May.

See also: Birth control 98–103 ▪ The Pill 136 ▪ Achieving the right to legal abortion 156–159 ▪ Racism and class prejudice within feminism 202–205

SOCIETY THRIVES ON DICHOTOMY
BISEXUALITY

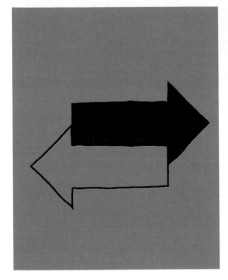

In second-wave feminism, lesbians played a central role, but bi women—women who can love and be attracted to both men and women—were isolated, invisible, and treated with hostility. Mainstream society still strongly condemned any woman who had sex with another woman, while many lesbians thought bi women should give up men altogether.

Challenging invisibility

From the early 1980s, attitudes began to change as mixed-gender, bisexual, social, and support groups in which women were prominent sprang up in Canada, the US, and the UK. American bisexual activist Robyn Ochs, among others, also set up women-only groups.

In the early 1990s, a surge in books on bisexuality went some way to support those not in groups. They were mainly collections of essays by people who identified as bisexual, and covered a range of issues. *Bi Any Other Name* (1991), edited by Loraine Hutchins and Lani Ka'ahumanu, was the first and most

I remember sitting there grinning … There were 20 bisexual women in the world. I was not the only one. What a powerful feeling.
Robyn Ochs

influential. In the UK, Sue George's *Women and Bisexuality* (1993) looks at bi women's experiences, such as feminist guilt and motherhood. These writers argue that bi women had always been a key part of the lesbian and feminist movements.

Slowly, over the next 25 years, bisexuality and the bi community became increasingly recognized, encompassing the more complex views of gender that exist today. ∎

See also: Political lesbianism 180–181 ∎ Compulsory heterosexuality 194–195 ∎ Sex positivity 234–237 ∎ Feminism and queer theory 262–263

THE ANTIFEMINIST BACKLASH HAS BEEN SET OFF
ANTIFEMINIST BACKLASH

IN CONTEXT

PRIMARY QUOTE
Susan Faludi, 1991

KEY FIGURE
Susan Faludi

BEFORE
1972 In the US, the Equal Rights Amendment (ERA), first proposed in 1923, is passed by Congress, but is not yet ratified by state legislatures.

1981 Ronald Reagan is sworn in as 40th President of the US, marking a swing to the right in American politics.

AFTER
2017 The #MeToo movement, a social media campaign against sexual assault, becomes the rallying cry for a new feminist resurgence.

2018 Illinois becomes the 37th state to ratify the Equal Rights Amendment, one short of the 38 states necessary for an amendment of the US constitution.

In 1986, American journalist and feminist Susan Faludi investigated a Harvard-Yale study in *Newsweek* magazine that claimed college-educated single women over 30 had only a 20 percent chance of getting married, a statistic that fell to 1.3 percent for women over 40. These statistics, which Faludi exposed as wrong, led her to investigate other misleading media stories about the impact of feminism on society. She identified an antifeminist backlash that blamed feminism for society's ills.

In 1991, Faludi published *Backlash: The Undeclared War Against American Women*, in which

Donald Trump's attacks on his opponent Hillary Clinton during the presidential debates in the run-up to the 2016 election helped spark a pro-feminist backlash in the US.

See also: Institutions as oppressors 80 ▪ Global suffrage movement 94–97 ▪ Achieving the right to legal abortion 156–159 ▪ Bringing feminism online 294–297 ▪ Sexual abuse awareness 322–327

Susan Faludi

Born in Queens, New York, in 1959, Susan Faludi graduated from Harvard in 1981. She became a journalist, writing on feminism through the 1980s and reporting for *The New York Times* and the *Wall Street Journal*. In 1991, one of her reports won the Pulitzer Prize for explanatory journalism.

Faludi has held several prestigious academic posts, including as a Tallman Scholar and Research Associate in Gender, Sexuality and Women's Studies at Bowdoin College, Maine. Faludi's father, a Holocaust survivor, came out as a transgender woman in 2004, aged 76. This transition inspired Faludi's 2016 memoir *In the Darkroom* on transsexualism and gender fluidity, which won the Kirkus Prize for non-fiction.

Key works

1991 *Backlash: The Undeclared War Against American Women*
1999 *Stiffed: The Betrayal of the American Man*
2007 *The Terror Dream: Fear and Fantasy in Post-9/11 America*
2016 *In the Darkroom*

she identifies the "New Right," with its pro-family agenda, as leading the backlash, which she attributes to fear of feminism's success. The backlash manifested itself politically in opposition to ratification of the 1972 Equal Rights Amendment, which was designed to ensure equal rights for US citizens regardless of sex, and in attacks on women's right to legal abortion. Faludi also criticizes the widening gender pay gap and the hypocrisy of "backlash emissaries" who block bills to improve childcare while blaming working women for being bad mothers, or male senators who encourage women to return to traditional roles even though their own wives work.

Fueled by the press

Faludi emphasizes the role of the media in encouraging the backlash against feminism. She argues that the press has built an image of working women as dissatisfied and propagate myths of "man shortages" and "barren wombs." The backlash then seizes on this supposed misery and blames feminism, helped by the media's portrayal of feminists as bra-burning militants.

Faludi examines fashion and popular culture for manifestations of the antifeminist backlash, noting how a trend for business suits in the 1970s gave way to impractical or restrictive feminine fashion with body-hugging silhouettes and frills, and how Hollywood portrays single career women as unpleasant, or even malevolent, as in the film *Fatal Attraction* (1987). She also notes an increase in the use of cosmetics and cosmetic surgery as women feel pressurized to look younger, and criticizes pop psychology and self-help books for being antifeminist.

Fresh impetus

Backlash won the National Book Critics Circle Award for nonfiction in 1992 and became a best seller, reigniting feminist debate. Faludi was nevertheless criticized for contradictions, biased data, and her focus on white, middle-class, heterosexual society. In an updated edition in 2006, she reflects on women's economic and political gains since the 1990s. She claims there is no longer a backlash "because … some things are worse," and laments that women are disenchanted with a distorted feminism they believe no longer applies to them. Even so, Faludi believes this disillusionment is a start: "Being disappointed is not the same as being defeated … We aren't yet down for the count." ▪

This counterassault … stands the truth boldly on its head and proclaims that the very steps that have elevated women's position have actually led to their downfall.
Susan Faludi

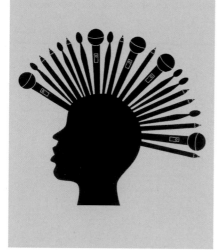

GIRLS CAN CHANGE THE WORLD FOR REAL
THE RIOT GRRRL MOVEMENT

IN CONTEXT

PRIMARY QUOTE
Riot Grrrl manifesto, 1991

KEY FIGURES
Jen Smith, Allison Wolfe, Molly Neuman, Kathleen Hanna, Tobi Vail

BEFORE
Late 1970s There is a surge in commercially successful female punk rock musicians, such as Patti Smith and Neo Boys in the US, and Siouxsie Sioux and Chrissie Hynde in the UK.

1988 *Sassy*, a magazine aimed at teenage girls who like alternative and indie rock music, is launched in the US.

AFTER
2010 Sarah Marcus publishes the first official history of the Riot Grrrls movement, *Girls to the Front: The True Story of the Riot Grrrl Revolution.*

Emerging in the Pacific Northwest in the 1990s, the punk feminist movement Riot Grrrl urged female musicians to express themselves with the same freedom as men. The movement was mainly linked to the bands Bratmobile and Bikini Kill, which developed out of the broader punk scene of Washington state. A flourishing subculture included art, fashion, and political activism against sexual abuse, homophobia, and racism.

Adopting a do-it-yourself culture, the movement sought to create non-hierarchical ways of making music that prioritized information over profits and used punk-rock fanzines (handmade fan magazines) to disseminate political ideas. Its manifesto stated: "Us girls crave records and books and fanzines that speak to US that WE feel included in and can understand in our own ways." Riot Grrrl is often cited as the starting gun of third-wave feminism, with its focus on individual identity.

The road to action
Back in 1988, *Puncture* magazine had published an article entitled "Women, sex and rock and roll," words that would head Riot Grrrl's first manifesto. The punk scene was dominated by male rock music—"beergutboyrock" was how the Riot Grrrl manifesto later described it—and women wanted to represent themselves via their own feminist zines and art.

Singer Kathleen Hanna from Bikini Kill performs at the Hollywood Palladium, Los Angeles, in 1994. Hanna once punched a man harassing a woman at one of the band's concerts.

See also: Radical feminism 137 ▪ Modern feminist publishing 142–143 ▪ Guerrilla protesting 246–247 ▪ Bringing feminism online 294–297

BECAUSE we are angry at a society that tells us Girl = Dumb, Girl = Bad, Girl = Weak.
Riot Grrrl manifesto

Several political developments in the US helped to fuel the sense of outrage that led to the formation of Riot Grrrl in 1991: the Christian Coalition's Right to Life campaign threatened access to abortions; a Salvadoran man was shot dead by a police officer in Washington, D.C., in May, triggering the Mount Pleasant race riots; and in October Clarence Thomas was confirmed as a Supreme Court Justice by the United States Senate, despite being accused of sexual assault by his assistant, Anita Hill, which he denied.

Jen Smith, zine editor and musician in Bratmobile, wrote to fellow band member Allison Wolfe to propose a "girl riot" that summer. Wolfe and Molly Neuman (also in Bratmobile) created a zine called *Riot Grrrl*, an homage to influential fanzine *Jigsaw*'s repeated phrase: "Revolutionary Grrrl Style Now." Wolfe, Neuman, and Smith joined up with Kathleen Hanna of Bikini Kill and her drummer and *Jigsaw* founder Tobi Vail, holding weekly women-only meetings.

In July 1991, a Riot Grrrl manifesto was published in *Bikini Kill Zine 2,* giving 16 reasons for

the Riot Grrrl spirit. The following month, the International Pop Underground Convention in Olympia, Washington, boasted an all-female lineup on the first night, featuring Bratmobile, Heavens to Betsy, 7 Year Bitch, Lois Maffeo, and Bikini Kill, among others. Bringing together key musicians and zine editors, the event galvanized the Riot Grrrl movement.

Development and legacy
The sound and ethos of Riot Grrrl spread through the US and then the UK. Eventually, the label applied to a wide variety of female-fronted acts. Male artists were also influenced by the movement, in particular Calvin Johnson, Dave Grohl, and Kurt Cobain.

In 1992, Riot Grrrl was criticized in *Newsweek* as being too middle-class and white. By 1994, the spirit and political radicalism had been watered down by "girl power," soon exemplified by bands such as the UK's Spice Girls. However, most of the founders of the Riot Grrrl movement remained politically and musically active, influencing other female bands and setting up "rock camps" to encourage girls and women to make music. ▪

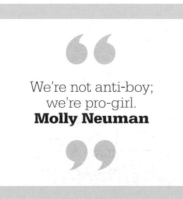

We're not anti-boy; we're pro-girl.
Molly Neuman

Kathleen Hanna

American punk singer and feminist activist Kathleen Hanna was born in Portland, Oregon, in 1968. She became interested in feminism while studying photography at Evergreen State College and working as a counselor at a domestic violence and rape shelter. She went on to perform spoken word poetry on feminist themes. The punk poet and feminist Kathy Acker suggested she start a band.

In 1990 Hanna formed the band Bikini Kill with bassist Kathi Wilcox, drummer Tobi Vail, and guitarist Billy Karren (the only male). The band liked to create a female-centric environment for their shows, with women invited forward and men sent to the back.

Bikini Kill broke up in 1998, after which Hanna formed Le Tigre, which she describes as "punk feminist electronic." Hanna currently performs with The Julie Ruin, a five-piece band.

Key works

1991 *Revolution Girl Style Now!*
1993 *Pussy Whipped*
1996 *Reject All American*

FIGURES OF WOMEN CONSTRUCTED BY MEN
REWRITING ANCIENT PHILOSOPHY

IN CONTEXT

PRIMARY QUOTE
Adriana Cavarero, 1995

KEY FIGURE
Adriana Cavarero

BEFORE
1958 In *The Human Condition*, political philosopher Hannah Arendt discusses her theory of "natality," where every person is born with the capacity for new beginnings; though silent on issues of gender and women's rights, her work inspires feminist philosophers.

1971 Alison Jaggar teaches the first course in feminist philosophy, at Miami University in Oxford, Ohio.

AFTER
1997 American philosopher Eileen O'Neill decries women's exclusion from the history of philosophy in her article "Disappearing Ink: Early Modern Women Philosophers and Their Fate in History."

Philosophy has long been an academic field dominated by the perspectives of men. This becomes a problem, argues feminist philosophers, if male philosophers presume that their theories apply to all people and that the male stands in for all. Feminist philosophers ask how those theories fare when applied to women, and look at the ways in which they are inadequate to describe how women experience the world.

New wisdom for old

In her 1995 book *In Spite of Plato*, the Italian feminist philosopher Adriana Cavarero analyzes Plato, the ancient Greek philosopher (c. 428–348 BCE), to consider how feminists might reinterpret ancient philosophy. Examining four female figures in Plato's work—including Penelope, wife of Odysseus in Greek legend—Cavarero critiques how each character is locked into a patriarchal, inferior, domestic role, in masculine, linear, death-driven narratives, and argues for a feminist analysis that centers on birth rather

In Greek legend, Penelope rebuffed her suitors by constantly weaving. Plato claims this was metaphor for the eternal nature of the soul, while feminists see her act as one of defiance.

than death. She urges feminist philosophers not to reject Plato's work as phallocentric or patriarchal but to apply their own insights as women and reclaim ancient philosophy for a feminist outlook.

Challenging the received wisdom of ancient philosophy for excluding or sidelining female views, Cavarero shows that feminist philosophers can and should take ancient philosophy and make it their own. ∎

See also: Feminist theology 124–125 ▪ Consciousness-raising 134–135 ▪ Writing women into history 154–155 ▪ Poststructuralism 182–187

THEOLOGICAL LANGUAGE REMAINS SEXIST AND EXCLUSIVE
LIBERATION THEOLOGY

IN CONTEXT

PRIMARY QUOTE
Elina Vuola, 2002

KEY FIGURE
Gladys Parentelli

BEFORE
19th century The decolonization of Latin America, formerly ruled by the Catholic powers of Portugal and Spain, begins to loosen ties with the Catholic Church in Europe.

1962–1965 The Second Vatican Council, convened under Pope John XXIII in Rome, modernizes Catholicism.

1968 Peruvian priest Gustavo Gutierrez develops liberation theology; he writes *A Theology of Liberation* in 1971.

AFTER
2013 An Argentinian cardinal becomes Pope Francis II, and, as head of the Catholic Church, addresses issues of poverty and inequality.

In Latin America in the 1960s, liberation theology emerged as a movement looking to the Roman Catholic Church for social change and to free the racially, economically, politically, and socially oppressed. While traditional theologies call for the renewal of the heart or mind, liberation theology demands physical and material action.

The basic assertion of liberation theologists is that God and the Bible prioritize the oppressed poor over the rich. Finnish academic Elina Vuola stresses the need to develop liberation theology's understanding of gender in the 21st century. The poorest in Latin America are often indigenous women, who do not have access to basic provisions because they are a political and social minority. Feminist liberation theologians believe that to free poor women from unjust structures, a new world order must replace current systems.

Latin American women are among the most powerful advocates of liberation theology.

Uruguay-born Gladys Parentelli has fought for women's reproductive rights and rebuked the Vatican for telling women what to do with their bodies. She also criticizes the patriarchy for its domination of women and nature. For her, women are "the guardians of life," who create new life and protect the planet. This intertwining of women and the earth to create a global community, free from sexual and ecological domination by men, has become known as ecofeminism. ■

> I am convinced that women are inherent guardians of life and of the earth's resources.
> **Gladys Parentelli**

See also: Institutions as oppressors 80 ▪ Feminist theology 124–125 ▪ Ecofeminism 200–201 ▪ Postcolonialism 220–223 ▪ Indigenous feminism 224–227

DISABILITY, LIKE FEMALENESS, IS NOT INFERIORITY

DISABILITY FEMINISM

Disability feminism has its roots in "the personal is political" concepts that shaped second-wave feminism in the 1970s. It first emerged in the 1980s because disabled women had difficulty getting their views heard, either in the women's movement or the disabled people's movement.

Building on the thinking of the disabled people's movement, disability feminism maintains that disability, like gender, is created by society. This view,

> Disability is something imposed on top of our impairments by the way we are unnecessarily isolated and excluded from full participation in society.
> **UPIAS**
> **(Union of the Physically Impaired Against Segregation)**

known as the social model of disability, is the antithesis of the medical model of disability as impairment. Supporters of the social model of disability believe that the removal of barriers created by society—such as inaccessible environments and discrimination in employment—will allow disabled people to achieve equality.

Language matters

In her groundbreaking texts on feminist disability, in the late 20th and early 21st centuries, American scholar and disability feminist Rosemarie Garland-Thomson looks at society's construct of disability and urges the avoidance of impairment terms to describe it. She argues for the use of phrases such as "people who identify as disabled" or "people who identify as non-disabled," to avoid labeling someone as just a body with an impairment. She points out how the word "disabled" labels one person as deficient (disabled) and the other as superior (non-disabled), thus oppressing the disabled person.

Garland-Thomson also stresses the importance of acknowledging differences within disability—such

See also: Consciousness-raising 134–135 ▪ Achieving the right to legal abortion 156–159 ▪ Intersectionality 240–245 ▪ Reproductive justice 268

Disabled women express their views at the Women's March in London, UK, in January 2017. The march was one in a chain of protests about the inauguration of US President Donald Trump.

as the various types of disability, from spinal injuries to dyslexia— and social or cultural categories that may run parallel to disability, like gender, race, ethnicity, class, and sexuality. All of these, she says, intersect in society.

Personal and political

British academic Jenny Morris explores how disabled people experience prejudice and how stereotypes of disability are defined by the non-disabled world—ideas she first set out in her book *Pride Against Prejudice* (1991). Morris discusses what it is like to be disadvantaged for being both a woman and disabled, and also to be studied under the category of "double disadvantage," saying that such studies objectify disabled women. They do so by not taking account of personal experience, she says, and by attempting to assess which is "worse"—whether sexism or disability has the most serious effect on a woman's life chances.

Morris also challenges feminists' exclusion of the medical model of disability. By excluding the specific impairments of "disabled" bodies, society cannot develop a credible politics in debates on prenatal testing, abortion, and euthanasia. The focus on external barriers to disabled people's lives, Morris says, ignores the experience of the body and important issues such as disabled women's reproductive rights and the life of the unborn, physically impaired fetus. ▪

Disability and the abortion debate

A woman's right to control her own body, including the right to choose abortion, was a key tenet of second-wave feminism. However, disability rights groups argue that to permit women to have an abortion on the grounds of impairment is to support disability eugenics and endorse the claim that disabled lives are not worth living.

Disability-equality writing on abortion does not focus on pro-life arguments about the sanctity of life on ethical grounds, but on the issue of pre-natal screening and the advice given to women in early pregnancy who are encouraged to abort fetuses that are impaired. In most countries where abortion is legal, this means that "impaired" fetuses can be aborted at a later stage in a pregnancy than is the case for "normal" fetuses. This, campaigners say, reinforces negative stereotypes about disability and is incompatible with the notion of equal rights.

WOMEN SURVIVORS HOLD FAMILIES AND COUNTRIES TOGETHER
WOMEN IN WARZONES

IN CONTEXT

PRIMARY QUOTE
Zainab Salbi, 2006

KEY FIGURE
Zainab Salbi

BEFORE
1944 Soviet soldiers rape many thousands of women in Germany during its invasion of the country.

1992 The Republic of Bosnia and Herzegovina proclaims independence from Yugoslavia; the Bosnian War breaks out, a war in which women are systematically raped.

AFTER
2008 The United Nations officially declares rape a weapon of war.

2014 Islamic State gains international attention through its use of sexual violence as a tool of terrorism, and to enslave the Yazidi minority in Iraq.

In most conflicts throughout history, male leaders have declared war, male soldiers have fought wars, and women have generally been civilians, safe from the front line—although not from many of the consequences. The American feminist and writer Susan Brownmiller, in her 1975 book *Against Our Will: Men, Women and Rape*, claims that war provides men with the psychological backdrop to give vent to their contempt for women.

Yazidi women and children sort wool at a refugee camp near the Syrian border. A religious and ethnic minority in Northern Iraq, the Yazidis were targeted by Isis from 2014.

The impact of war on women and girls is all-encompassing. They lose members of their family, their homes, their education, and their work. The most harmful consequence, however, is sexual violence. In the Bosnian conflict of 1992–1995, rape and sexual violence

See also: Women uniting for peace 92–93 ▪ Rape as abuse of power 166–171 ▪ Global education for girls 310–311 ▪ Men hurt women 316–317

Women's lives and their bodies have been the unacknowledged casualties of war for too long.
Amnesty International

were widespread, committed by all ethnic groups against men and women, but predominantly by the Serbian army and paramilitaries against women, mostly Bosnian Muslims. The number of female rape victims during the conflict is estimated at between 12,000 (UN) and 50,000 (the Bosnian Interior Ministry). "Rape camps" and detention houses, where mainly Bosniaks (Muslim Bosnians) and Croat women and children were enslaved, tortured, and repeatedly raped, were established all over the region by Serbian forces.

Almost all studies of the conflict argue that rape was not incidental to the Bosnian conflict, but an integral part of the military campaign, used as both a strategic tool of ethnic cleansing to impregnate women with ethnically Serbian babies, and a genocidal tactic to force victims to leave an area for good.

Solidarity after war
Human rights activist Zainab Salbi was 23 and living in the US when she learned about the rape camps. The reports led her to found Women

for Women International (WfWI), a humanitarian organization that publicizes sexual violence in conflict and supports women survivors. She was influenced by her experience of violence as a child during the Iran-Iraq War: her father had been Saddam Hussein's personal pilot.

Since its founding in 1993, WfWI has provided $120 million to almost half a million women in eight conflict zones. In 2006, Salbi published *The Other Side of War*, a collection of letters and first-person narratives by women survivors from former Yugoslavia and five other conflict zones where WfWI has worked (Afghanistan, Colombia, Democratic Republic of the Congo, Rwanda, and Sudan). A second book, *If You Knew Me, You Would Care*, aimed to subvert the notion of victim, interviewing women in conflict zones about survival, peace, and their hopes for the future. Both books argue that aid to women in war zones must go beyond material support and promote women's role in the peace process to effect real change. ▪

It appears easier to talk about protecting women than it is to fully include women at all decision-making levels in peace talks and post-conflict planning.
Zainab Salbi

Rape as a weapon of war
Rape has always existed in warfare, with predominantly male perpetrators and female victims. The circumstances that facilitate it include the breakdown of law during conflict and hypermasculine military culture, in which gang rape is a "bonding" exercise. The consequences of such rape include degradation, intimidation, psychological trauma, the spread of disease, and pregnancy. In many cultures, victims of rape are also ostracized, leading to the destruction of communities.

Historically, from ancient conflicts to the enforced mass prostitution of World War II, women were raped as "spoils of war." In several more recent wars, rape has been a tool of genocide or ethnic cleansing. Millions were raped during the Rwandan genocide (1994) and the two civil wars in the Congo (1990s), while conflicts in former Yugoslavia led to the first conviction of rape as a war crime. In the 21st century, accusations of rape have even been leveled at UN peacekeepers.

Bosnian Muslims watch the televised conviction in November 2017 of Serbian commander Ratko Mladić for crimes committed in the Bosnian war (1992–1995).

A GENDER POWER CONTROL ISSUE

CAMPAIGNING AGAINST FEMALE GENITAL CUTTING

IN CONTEXT

PRIMARY QUOTE
Efua Dorkenoo, 2013

KEY FIGURES
**Fran Hosken,
Efua Dorkenoo**

BEFORE
1929 Missionaries in Kenya describe FGC as "sexual mutilation," at a time when it was more usually termed "female circumcision," implying that it was similar to male circumcision.

AFTER
2014 The United Nations General Assembly passes Resolution 69/150 to end FGC by 2030.

2017 *BMJ Global Health* reports that, over 30 years, the prevalence of FGC has mostly declined, but has increased by 2 percent to 8 percent in Chad, Mali, and Sierra Leone.

Female genital cutting (FGC)—the partial or full removal of external female genital organs and the suturing of the vulva—has caused concern for decades. American anthropologist Rose Oldfield Hayes described the "excruciatingly painful" nature of the practice in a 1975 paper, and in 1977 Egyptian physician and activist Nawal El Saadawi published *Hidden Faces of Eve*, in which she describes her own experience of undergoing FGC.

Fran Hosken, an Austrian-American writer and feminist, took up the cause in 1979 with "The Hosken Report: Genital and Sexual Mutilation of Females," and soon after that, Ghanaian-born Efua Dorkenoo's determined campaign to end the practice helped to galvanize

In northeast Uganda, members of the Sebei tribe demonstrate the mud-smearing that accompanies an FGC ceremony. FGC is outlawed here, but is still practiced by several tribes.

See also: Anticolonialism 218–219 ▪ Postcolonial feminism 220–223 ▪
Preventing forced marriage 232–233

support from NGOs, the United
Nations, and the World Health
Organization. The graphic term
"mutilation" was then widely used
(hence FGM), but the more neutral
"cutting" is now often preferred.

A tradition that persists

As many as 200 million women in
30 countries—mainly in Africa, but
also in Indonesia and the Middle
East—have undergone FGC. It is
a tradition dating back at least
2,500 years, predating Christianity
and Islam. It is not specific to any
one religion or ethnic group, but is
associated with purity and
chastity, curbing sexual urges
and ensuring that women are
virgins until marriage and faithful
thereafter. In at least 15 countries,
most girls are cut before they are
five years old, while others undergo
the procedure at puberty.

Fear of unmarriageability, of
rejection, and even of exile from the
community compels girls to submit
to FGC. Many live in countries that
are poor, leaving them with little
choice but to comply or die of
poverty. Respected women village
elders often perform the procedure
and earn a living from doing so.
When families relocate to other
parts of the world, FGC often
persists. Where it is now illegal,
as in the UK, the US, and British
Commonwealth countries, some
parents continue the tradition by
returning home or finding someone
to perform the procedure illegally.

Some women brought up in
Westernized countries still choose
to undergo the procedure as adults;
they argue that criticisms of cutting
are ethnocentric. In 1997, the
Association of African Women for
Research and Development opposed
Western feminist intervention in the
issue, and impassioned calls for
FGC to be eradicated still provoke
charges of cultural imperialism.

The two counter arguments
in favor of ending FGC are the
damage it causes—from recurrent
infections, potential infertility, and
childbirth complications to fatal
bleeding—and often an absence of
choice, making it a human rights
violation. Since the 1990s, victims
have started to speak out about
undergoing FGC, with campaigns
such as Change.org in India and
Safe Hands for Girls in Gambia
publishing stories of survivors, and
Somali model Waris Dirie recording
how she underwent FGC in her 1998
autobiography, *Desert Flower*.

The way forward

At the United Nations' Vienna
World Conference on Human Rights
in 1993, FGC was declared a form
of violence against women. By
2013, 24 of the 27 African countries
where FGC is prevalent had laws
against it. Progress has been slow,
but many now point to community
initiatives, such as those run by the
NGO Tostan in West Africa, as
the effective way forward. ▪

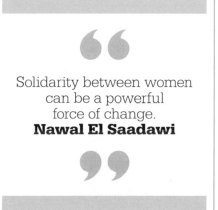

> Solidarity between women
> can be a powerful
> force of change.
> **Nawal El Saadawi**

Efua Dorkenoo

Born in Ghana in 1949, Efua
Dorkenoo trained as a nurse in
the UK in the 1970s. Seeing a
woman who had undergone
FGC suffer agonizing pain as
she gave birth, Dorkenoo was
angered by the lack of medical
criticism of the practice. While
working for the Minority
Rights Group, she began her
campaign against FGC, and
published the first-ever report
on FGC in Britain, setting up
FORWARD (Foundation for
Women's Health, Research
and Development) in 1983 to
help eliminate the practice. As
a result, FGC was banned in
the UK in 1985. For her work
with FORWARD, Dorkenoo
was awarded an OBE in 1994.
She then worked at the World
Health Organization and, later,
with Equality Now, realizing
hopes for an African-led
movement against FGC
shortly before her death from
cancer in London in 2014.

Key works

1992 *Tradition! Tradition:
A Symbolic Story on Female
Genital Mutilation*
1994 *Cutting the Rose: Female
Genital Mutilation*

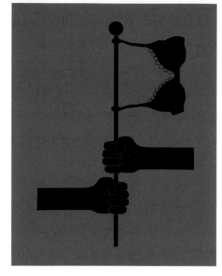

RAUNCH CULTURE IS NOT PROGRESSIVE
RAUNCH CULTURE

The 1960s, in many Western countries, was a decade of sexual revolution, which released men and women from stifling gender norms and enabled women to explore their sexuality without shame. Feminists often responded with scepticism to these claims, and by the 1980s were locked into an intra-community battle known as the "sex wars" about how best to practice feminist sexuality. Debates over sex work, porn,

penetration, kinky sex, and more divided women as to whether, or to what extent, these practices could be considered sexually exploitative of women. No clear final consensus was reached, and by the new millennium the debate was complicated further by the development of raunch culture.

The rise of raunch

The American feminist journalist Ariel Levy contributed to the discussions on raunch culture with her 2005 book, *Female Chauvinist Pigs: Women and the Rise of Raunch Culture*. Raunch culture, explains Levy, refers to the different ways in which young women participate in the sexual objectification of other women as well as themselves. It was driven by the increasing hypersexualization of the media from the 2000s onward, including the rise of men's magazines such as *Maxim* and *Stuff* in the US and *Loaded* in the UK, as well as the popularity

Playboy started publishing men's magazines in 1953, later using its iconic rabbit logo to sell merchandise for women, further promoting the sexual objectification of women.

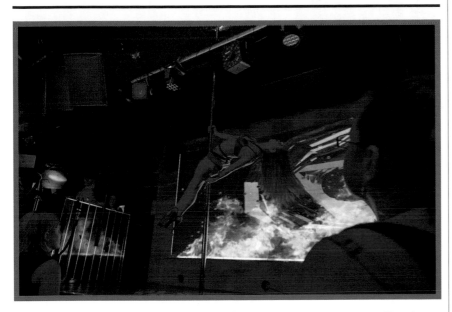

of the US video franchise *Girls
Gone Wild*, which filmed young
women on vacation flashing their
naked breasts and genitals for
viewers to ogle.

Young women, according to
Levy, are increasingly focusing on
acting "raunchy," not based on
their own desires but in an attempt
to attract men. They are expected to
uphold raunch culture in order to be
thought sexy and liberated; if they
do not, they are considered to be
uptight and retrograde.

As a result of raunch culture,
Levy argues, female sexuality has
become caricatured and, in line
with the ideology of raunch culture,
to reject the caricature is to reject
sexuality in general. Levy concludes
that raunch culture is ultimately a
symptom of a postfeminist moment
in which younger women who have
benefited from the seriousness and
militancy of older feminists can now
afford to reject feminist critiques of
the sexual objectification of women.
In its place, these young women
pursue a misguided and damaging

East London Strippers Collective
promotes strippers and lap dancers
in the UK, empowering performers to
improve working conditions within
the sex industry.

attempt at sexual "freedom" that
ultimately furthers the interests of
misogynist culture.

Feminist critiques

Some third- and fourth-wave
feminists have critiqued Levy's
concept of raunch culture. Feminists
have called into question Levy's
focus on sex workers and porn stars
rather than on the inequality found
within sex work and porn industries
at large. Queer feminist sexual
practices have served as a critique
of Levy's focus on raunch culture
and the way the "male gaze" shapes
women's sexuality. Queer femme
burlesque (performed by feminine
lesbians and other queer women),
porn, and sex parties, for example,
challenge the assumption that
women's "raunch" is performed only
to satisfy men's sexual desires. ▪

Club Burlesque Brutal

In 2010, burlesque performer
Katrina Daschner created
the Club Burlesque Brutal,
a queer femme (feminine
LGBTQ persons) burlesque
troupe based in Vienna,
Austria. Daschner wanted to
challenge the assumption that
burlesque is aimed to serve
heterosexual male desire, as
well as the assumption that
femininity is synonymous with
passive sexual objectification.

Most of the performers in
Club Burlesque Brutal are
queer femmes, and the troupe
aims to portray a diverse
range of femininities in their
performances. Daschner plays
a character named Professor
La Rose. The performances
enact overt lesbian and queer
desire on the stage in a
reclamation of both female
sexual power and an assertion
of queer eroticism.

Released in 2017, *Femme
Brutal* is a documentary film
about the troupe. It explores
the performers' lives, as well
as questions of sexual power,
bodies, femme identity, and
redirecting the male gaze.

> ❝
> Young women today
> are embracing raunchy
> aspects of our culture
> that would likely have
> caused their feminist
> foremothers to vomit.
> **Ariel Levy**
> ❞

EQUALITY AND JUSTICE ARE NECESSARY AND POSSIBLE
MODERN ISLAMIC FEMINISM

IN CONTEXT

PRIMARY QUOTE
Musawah

KEY FIGURES
Zainah Anwar, Marina Mahathir, Lila Abu-Lughod

BEFORE
2001 The US invades Afghanistan, pledging to liberate Afghan women from oppression and the veil.

2007 In Istanbul, Turkey, 12 Muslim women from 11 countries meet to plan for the promotion of women's rights and equality within Islam.

AFTER
2011 Musawah challenges Muslim countries that do not ratify the UN Convention on the Elimination of All Forms of Discrimination Against Women (CEDAW).

2017 Duru Yavan, a Turkish secular feminist, promotes working with Muslim feminism to tackle patriarchy.

Women-only carriages on trains were introduced to Malaysia in 2010. Such initiatives divide feminist opinion: some welcome the provision of a safe space; others see them as restrictive.

Within contemporary Muslim societies, there has been growing resentment about the imposition of Western ideas, in particular the Western feminist view that Muslim women are victimized by Islam. Consequently, in 2009, after two years of discussions, 250 Muslim activists from various countries formed Musawah, an organization led by women to promote justice and equality within Islam. The group believes that men and women are essentially equal and that the Quran is inherently favorable to women but has been interpreted in misogynistic ways by the patriarchy in the centuries since its revelation to the Prophet Muhammad in 610 CE. The name Musawah means "equal" in Arabic and this is a global movement that promotes equality and fairness in the family and in wider society. The organization is based in Malaysia but has a secretariat that rotates from country to country.

The niqab debate in France

Successive French governments have taken a determined secular stance against Muslim women wearing the veil. In 2011, France banned women from wearing the face veil (*niqab*) in public places, because it prevents the identification of the wearer. In 2016, several French resorts banned the "burkini"—head-to-foot swimwear.

These bans have been criticized and resisted. An anonymous French graffiti artist, Princess Hijab, constantly challenges the ban by painting veils over public images of models and rappers. However, liberal feminist Elisabeth Badinter questions the right of Muslim women to choose the veil, seeing it as a symbol of enslavement.

Rokhaya Diallo, a French author and filmmaker argues in favor of the choice to veil. In a 2018 interview with the Qatar-based news organization Al-Jazeera, she described opposition to veiling as ethnocentric, patronizing, and postcolonial.

The right to wear the veil has become a live issue in France where niqab-wearing women have taken to the streets to protest.

Musawah's threefold aim is to develop and share knowledge on equality and justice within the family, to help build similar organizations, and to support human rights groups that share its goals. Its work is modeled on another Muslim movement that promotes justice for Muslim women—Sisters in Islam (SIS), also based in Malaysia, and founded by Muslim feminist Zainah Anwar and six other women in 1988.

One of the key members of SIS is Marina Mahathir, the daughter of the Malaysian prime minister, who has used the support of Muslim scholars to promote awareness of HIV and the right of a wife to refuse sexual relations with a husband who may infect her.

A matter of choice

American anthropologist Lila Abu-Lughod in her book *Do Muslim Women Really Need Saving?* (2013) challenges the view, often held in the West, that gender inequality is the fault of religion. She argues that poverty and authoritarianism are key reasons for women's lack of freedom in Muslim societies. She also claims that Western feminism often dismisses Islam as being inherently antiwoman. This view, she states, was co-opted by politicians such as US President George W. Bush, and even his wife Laura, when the US and its allies attempted to gain support for their "war on terror" following the attack on the World Trade Center in New York in 2001. The invasion of Afghanistan in the wake of 9/11 was couched in the language of "liberation", in particular freeing Afghan women from being forced to wear the hijab (the veil or other head coverings worn by many Muslim women). However, this rhetoric ignores the view of Musawah and other Islamic activist groups that many Muslim women wear the hijab out of choice and see Islam as enshrining their basic human rights.

> The Muslim world needs a paradigm shift on how we regard and treat women.
> **Zainah Anwar**

A Western project?

Musawah has faced criticism from within the Muslim community. Some point to the organization's lack of representation from the Shia as opposed to the Sunni community, despite its claims to celebrate diversity and plurality. Others, particularly traditionalists, assert that Musawah's promotion of "progressive" interpretations of the Quran within an international, human rights framework is apologetic and symptomatic of secular Western pressure on Muslim countries. Such critics see Musawah as a Western project at heart, not an Islamic one. ▪

A NEW TYPE OF FEMINISM

TRANS FEMINISM

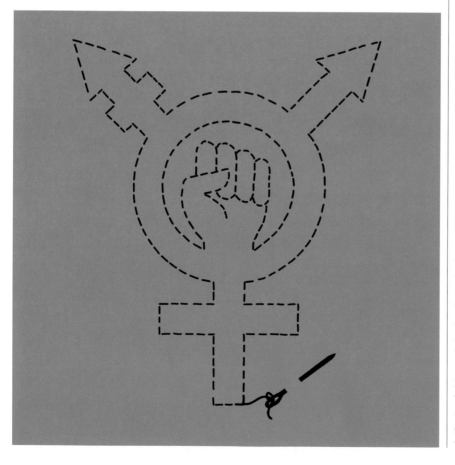

IN CONTEXT

PRIMARY QUOTE
Julia Serano, 2007

KEY FIGURES
Emi Koyama, Julia Serano

BEFORE
1959 Transgender women, along with other queer people, riot at Cooper's Do-nuts café in Los Angeles in an incident sparked by police harassment.

1966 The Compton's cafeteria riot, in San Francisco, marks the beginning of trans activism in San Francisco.

AFTER
2008 The killer of teenager Angie Zapato is the first in the US to be convicted of hate crime for violence against a trans victim.

2014 American actress and activist Laverne Cox is the first known trans woman to appear on the cover of *Time* magazine.

Transgender feminists fight for the right not only to have their genders, names, and pronouns treated with respect, but to be safe within societies that are openly hostile and violent toward them. Beyond these aims, trans feminists seek to enrich and deepen feminism with the insights they bring as transgender women, and also to bring feminist insights about gender, sexuality, and power to other trans people.

A cornerstone of trans feminism is using the insights of feminist theory and trans theory to further challenge assumptions about the gender binary, about what it means to be a "man" or "woman." They

See also: Trans-exclusionary radical feminism 172–173 ■ Intersectionality 240–245 ■ Gender is performative 258–261 ■ Feminism and queer theory 262–263

Rather than division, Julia Serano advocates a coalition between feminists and trans activists that will combat both transphobia and misogyny.

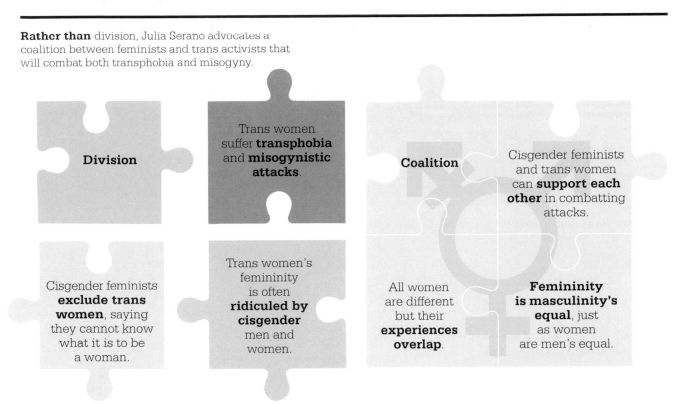

Division

Cisgender feminists **exclude trans women**, saying they cannot know what it is to be a woman.

Trans women suffer **transphobia and misogynistic attacks**.

Trans women's femininity is often **ridiculed by cisgender** men and women.

Coalition

Cisgender feminists and trans women can **support each other** in combatting attacks.

All women are different but their **experiences overlap**.

Femininity is masculinity's equal, just as women are men's equal.

fight against larger structures of power, such as the medical and prison systems, which are said to deny the experiences of trans people and withhold life-affirming resources from them.

As far back as the 1970s, there had been discrimination against trans feminist women by cisgender feminists. An early case was that of Sandy Stone, sound engineer for the women's record label Olivia Records from 1974–1978. When radical lesbian feminist Janice Raymond learned that Stone was transgender, she tried in 1976 to "expose" Stone's trans status. The Olivia Records collective, however, was already aware of this and supported Stone. Undaunted, Raymond continued her attack, publishing a manifesto against Stone in 1979 entitled *The*

Transsexual Empire: The Making of the She-Male. In the book, Raymond attacks Stone for "invading" women's spaces with her "male energy."

"The Empire Strikes Back," Stone's 1991 essay in response to Raymond's anti-trans attacks, inaugurated what became known as trans feminism: scholarship, and activism by and for trans feminists, that seeks to deepen the liberatory possibilities for a future in which people of all genders may be their most authentic and respected selves.

Developing trans feminism
Kate Bornstein was an early key figure in creating trans feminist theory. In her groundbreaking text *Gender Outlaw* (1994), Bornstein used her own experiences to »

Christine Jorgensen was the first person in the US to transition, in the early 1950s. In later life, she spoke extensively on gender issues. Pictured here in 1970, Jorgensen is at a press reception to launch a film about her life.

> Trans feminism embodies feminist coalition politics in which women from different backgrounds stand up for each other … because if we [don't do it] … nobody will.
> **Emi Koyama**

Non-binary gender

As growing numbers of people begin to articulate their gender as transcending the box of male or female, the concept of non-binary gender has become a crucial part of trans feminism and LGBTQ+ advocacy. People who are non-binary typically use gender-neutral pronouns such as they/them. Like anyone else, they may present themselves as masculine, feminine, both, or neither. They argue that no individual should ever presume they know another's pronouns.

Non-binary genders have existed throughout history and across the globe, such as within First Nations tribal communities in North America, but these indigenous perceptions of gender were actively persecuted by European colonizers.

Important non-binary trans feminists include Canadian musician and writer Rae Spoon, American author and activist Mattilda Bernstein Sycamore, and Indian American spoken-word artist Alok Vaid-Menon.

explore and question society's gender norms around being male and female, drawing on insights from her upbringing as a boy—and being punished and policed for not conforming to masculine norms.

For Bornstein, who was born in 1948, non-binary gender was not an option as she grew up. When she began seriously questioning her gender assigned at birth, she thought she must be a transgender woman. Ultimately, however,

Bornstein identified as neither male nor female. Her writing on this has been key to theorizing non-binary gender, and her stage and reality-show performances have helped bring her ideas to the mainstream.

Scholar, author, and Emmy Award–winning documentary-maker Susan Stryker is another important figure in trans feminism. She has produced many texts that helped shape trans feminism, co-editing *The Transgender*

Studies Reader in 2006, which won a Lambda Literary Award for best LGBTQ book of the year. Stryker's *Transgender History*, covering 150 years of trans history in the US, was published in 2008.

Who has privilege?

In 2001, activist Emi Koyama published "The Transfeminist Manifesto." This essay was crucial for popularizing the term "trans feminism." Writing in response to the feminist critique that trans women are raised with male privilege and therefore do not know the full struggle of what it means to be a woman, Koyama places this argument within a larger context of privilege and oppression. She argues that there are multiple types of privilege and oppression, and that all feminists must take accountability for their forms of privilege while also feeling justified in speaking from their experiences

The Audre Lorde Project was set up in 1994 to raise awareness of issues facing the LGBTQ community in New York City, especially people of color. Its 2016 rally, shown here, focused particularly on justice for trans people.

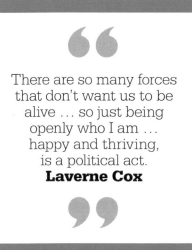
with oppression. She reminds her readership that white cisgender women have privilege. She allows for the possibility that some trans women have experienced male privilege, but she also highlights the forms of oppression trans women face in society—especially poor and working-class trans women of color.

Koyama's manifesto also points out that feminists should recognize trans women's body-image battles and gender dysphoria (distress over assigned gender) as a feminist issue and equate male violence against trans women with violence against cis women. Koyama also highlights the parallels between cis feminists' fights to obtain reproductive justice and control and trans women's campaigns to gain bodily autonomy in health care.

The intersections between gender, race, class, citizenship status, dis/ability, and more have been further explored in 21st-century trans feminist scholarship by Viviane Namaste, Dean Spade, Eli Clare, and others. Spade, for example, a trans feminist American law professor, founded the Sylvia Rivera Law Project (SRLP), which provides free legal services to trans, intersex (having sexual characteristics of both genders), and gender non-conforming people, regardless of income or race, and argues that economic justice is essential to combat gender discrimination. Spade has written extensively about the precarious lives of the most marginalized trans populations, and the grim statistics about the disproportionate rates of abuse and murder inflicted against poor black trans women in the US.

Trans-feminist activists of color in the US—such as *Orange Is the New Black* actress Laverne Cox, prison activist CeCe McDonald, and author and speaker Janet Mock—have been vocal about the need to address the violence affecting trans women of color. Cox used her celebrity status to advocate against the abuses of the US criminal justice system, and engaged in public dialogues with McDonald, a black bisexual trans woman who spent 19 months in prison after fatally stabbing her attacker in self-defence in 2011. In 2014, McDonald was awarded the Bayard Rustin Civil Rights Award by the Harvey Milk LGBT Democratic Club for her activism. ∎

Julia Serano

Born in 1967, Julia Serano is a feminist author, biologist, and LGBTQ+ activist based in Oakland, California. Serano holds a PhD in biochemistry and molecular biophysics, and worked at the University of California, Berkeley, for 17 years, conducting research into genetics, evolution, and developmental biology.

Serano's 2007 book *Whipping Girl*, which is based on her positive and negative experiences as a transgender femme (feminine identity) lesbian woman in feminist and queer spaces, became a key text for 21st-century trans feminism. *Ms.* magazine ranked *Whipping Girl* 16th on its list of 100 best nonfiction books of all time. Serano's accessible writing and scientific insights into gender theory have made her popular both inside and outside of the gender studies classroom.

Key works

2007 *Whipping Girl*
2013 *Excluded*
2016 *Outspoken: A Decade of Transgender Activism and Trans Feminism*

FIGHTING IN THE MO
2010 ONWARD

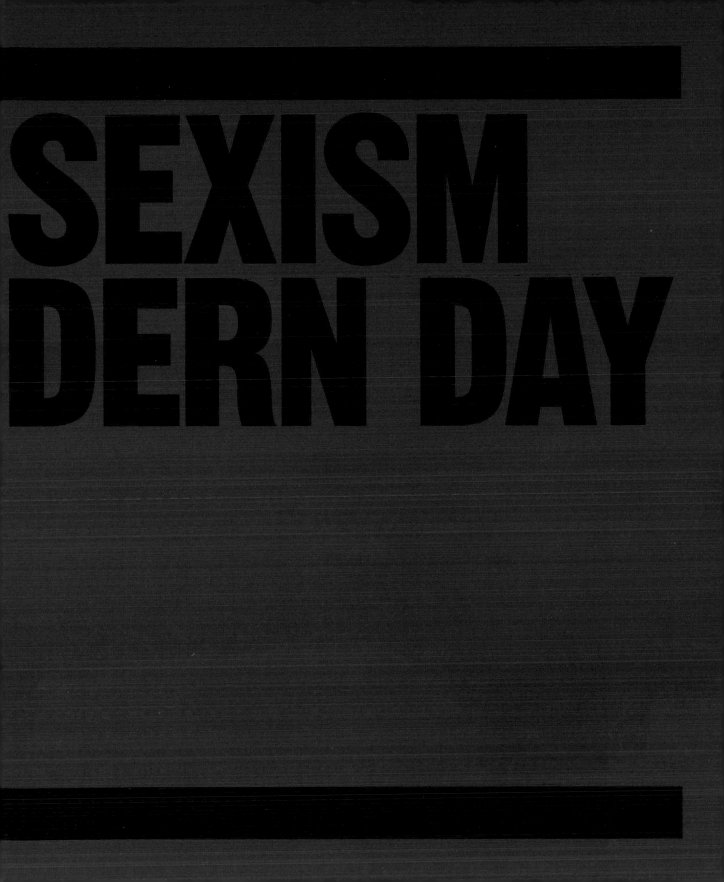

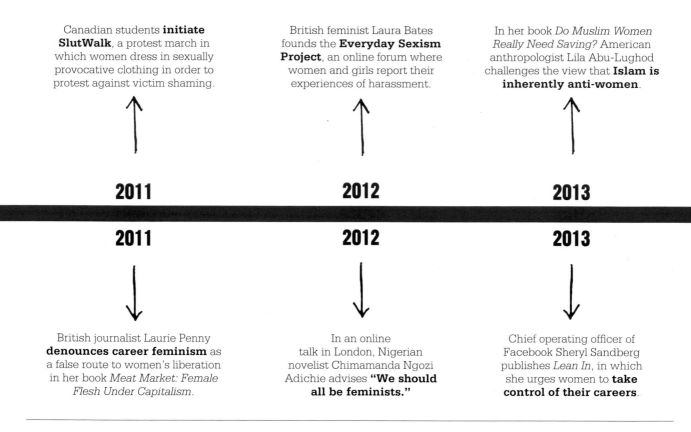

Canadian students **initiate SlutWalk**, a protest march in which women dress in sexually provocative clothing in order to protest against victim shaming.

British feminist Laura Bates founds the **Everyday Sexism Project**, an online forum where women and girls report their experiences of harassment.

In her book *Do Muslim Women Really Need Saving?* American anthropologist Lila Abu-Lughod challenges the view that **Islam is inherently anti-women**.

2011　　　　**2012**　　　　**2013**

2011　　　　**2012**　　　　**2013**

British journalist Laurie Penny **denounces career feminism** as a false route to women's liberation in her book *Meat Market: Female Flesh Under Capitalism*.

In an online talk in London, Nigerian novelist Chimamanda Ngozi Adichie advises **"We should all be feminists."**

Chief operating officer of Facebook Sheryl Sandberg publishes *Lean In*, in which she urges women to **take control of their careers**.

Feminism was re-energized in the second decade of the 21st century. Powerful outcries against sexual abuse, debates around the gender pay gap, and protest marches following the election of US president Donald Trump in 2016 proved that feminism was alive and kicking. Women, many of them millennials, threw themselves into the struggle once more, making full use of social media for publicity and networking.

The fourth wave

By 2012, a fourth wave of feminism was underway. The young women driving it were living in societies where the language of feminism was already well established, but the gender equality they expected did not match their experience and they took to social media and blogging to say so. The proliferation of feminist websites and blogs enabled ideas to spread rapidly. In 2012, British feminist Laura Bates set up the Everyday Sexism Project, an online forum where women could share their daily experiences of sexism. Feminists also turned to "hashtag activism" via Facebook, Twitter, and other social media sites to disseminate information and raise awareness of campaigns such as #BringBackOurGirls, demanding the release of schoolgirls kidnapped by Boko Haram in Northern Nigeria. In 2017 and 2018, the #MeToo and Time's Up movements named and shamed perpetrators of sexual abuse in Hollywood and many other areas of culture, business, and industry.

While younger feminists focused on exposing instances of sexism and sexual abuse on social media, some older women began to question what feminism should mean in the modern age. The British writer and commentator Caitlin Moran and the Nigerian writer Chimamanda Ngozi Adichie argued that in the 21st century feminism is simply common sense. All women and all men should be feminists, they said.

Old issues and inequalities

While some women were proposing a new kind of feminism that favored cooperation between the sexes, it was apparent that age-old problems of double standards and victim blaming were still flourishing. In 2011, when a police officer in Canada advised female students to avoid dressing and behaving like "sluts" if they did not want to be raped, Canadian feminists staged the first

American disability feminist Rosemarie Garland-Thomson publishes "Building a World with Disability in It," an article in which she identifies the **double discrimination** faced by disabled women.

Why I am Not a Feminist: A Feminist Manifesto, a **critique of fourth-wave feminism**, is published by American writer and activist Jessa Crispin.

Women are granted the **right to drive** in Saudi Arabia, the last country in the world to allow them to do so.

2015

2017

2018

2014

2017

#BringBackOurGirls is set up to campaign for the release of schoolgirls kidnapped by the terrorist group Boko Haram in Northern Nigeria.

American actor Alyssa Milano **posts #MeToo on Twitter**, encouraging women to post their experiences of sexual abuse and harassment.

SlutWalk, dressing in sexually provocative outfits to protest against the tendency of courts, police, and others to blame rape on the appearance or behavior of the victims. Similar SlutWalks sprang up in cities across the world.

Feminists in Latin America and Canada campaigned against the murder of indigenous women, introducing the term "femicide" to describe these murders of women by men. They argued that such murders are not isolated incidents as previously maintained, but an expression of patriarchal aggression.

The battle for gender equality continued, particularly in areas of the world where women's rights are still limited. The dangers many women still face for campaigning for equal rights were highlighted in 2012 when Pakistani activist Malala

Yousafzai, then aged 15, was shot in the head on her school bus by a Taliban gunman after writing an anti-Taliban blog. Yousafzai survived the shooting and went on to fight for girls' education worldwide.

In 2018, after nearly 30 years of campaigning, women in Saudi Arabia—the only country where women were still banned from driving—won the right to drive. Meanwhile, in the West, feminists engaged in renewed protest against the continuing gender pay gap, challenging the prevailing view that women had already achieved equal pay. Feminists highlighted not just pay inequalities between men and women, but also among white women and women of color. Other women, such as Facebook's chief operating officer

Sheryl Sandberg urged women in the workplace to "lean in" and seize control if they want to get to the top.

New voices

The inclusiveness of feminism also came under the spotlight. Building on ideas first put forward in the late 1980s, American writer Rosemarie Garland-Thomson argued that disabled women had been excluded from feminist discourse. At the same time, in the ongoing struggle for trans women's rights, trans feminists such as American activist Julia Serano lobbied for trans women to become an integral part of the women's movement. Such initiatives from a variety of social groups have the potential to broaden the scope of the next wave of feminism into a movement for much wider social change. ∎

MAYBE THE FOURTH WAVE IS ONLINE

BRINGING FEMINISM ONLINE

IN CONTEXT

PRIMARY QUOTE
Jessica Valenti, 2009

KEY FIGURE
Jessica Valenti

BEFORE
1750s In the UK, a group of women known as the Blue Stockings meet for intellectual discussions in one another's homes.

1849–1858 America's first feminist magazine, *The Lily*, is an eight-page monthly edited by Amelia Bloomer in Seneca Falls, New York.

1967 Consciousness-raising groups spring up in New York. Women meet in small groups to share their experiences.

AFTER
2018 The #MeToo movement spreads; in the US, #MeTooK12 is founded by the group Stop Sexual Assault in Schools.

The development of the internet during the 1990s exerted a huge impact on the growth, visibility, structure, and tactics of most social movements, including feminism. By the beginning of the 2010s, a new, fourth wave of feminism was said to be developing, and the feminist blogosphere paved the way for a fresh generation of nuanced and savvy feminist discourse and activism.

New needs

Fourth-wave feminists built on the intersectional insights and sex positivity of the third wave, taking them as core tenets of their political

Jessica Valenti

Cofounder of the popular feminist website Feministing and the author of multiple books, Jessica Valenti was born into an Italian American family in New York City in 1978. She holds a bachelor's degree in journalism from the State University of New York at Purchase College and a master's degree in women's and gender studies from Rutgers University.

Two years after graduating from Rutgers, Valenti cofounded the groundbreaking Feministing with her sister while working for the National Organization for Women's legal defense fund.

A columnist at *The Guardian* since 2014, Valenti lives in Brooklyn, New York, with her husband and daughter. In 2016, her book *Sex Object* was a *New York Times* best seller and NPR Best Book winner.

Key works

2007 *Full Frontal Feminism*
2008 *Yes Means Yes!*
2009 *The Purity Myth: How America's Obsession with Virginity is Hurting Young Women*
2016 *Sex Object: A Memoir*

philosophy and practice. Comprised largely of millennials (who came of age in about 2000) and "Generation Z" (born between the mid-1990s and mid-2000s), fourth-wave feminists have often been raised in cultures and families where they were taught gender equality by the beneficiaries of second- and third-wave feminism. When they then find gender relationships to be unequal, fourth-wave feminists are shocked that they should still need

> There are teenage girls today, growing up with Twitter and Tumblr, who have a perfect grasp of feminist language and concepts …
> **Kira Cochrane**
> **British journalist and novelist**

to fight for justice. In response, armed with online feminist articles, as well as Twitter, they live-tweet and livestream the protests they join on Facebook.

Feminism goes viral

In 2004, American feminists Jessica Valenti and her sister Vanessa created the feminist website Feministing with the aim of connecting a diverse range of feminist and women's voices. In line with the Valenti vision, and incorporating all the new tools of the growing blogosphere, it included a blog dedicated to current events and in-depth analysis, a comments section on each article, and discussion forums where members of the site could explore the issues that mattered to them.

Feministing helped make feminist issues visible. The internet allowed for increased accessibility and brought together audiences with disparate backgrounds from different parts of the world. That feminism was still important and needed by young women was

accepted without question by Feministing, and this served as the foundation for all content on the website. According to a profile of Jessica Valenti in UK newspaper *The Guardian*'s Top 100 Women list, Valenti was responsible for bringing feminism online.

Since Feministing, countless examples of feminist activism have materialized across the internet. The anti-street harassment »

Feministing.com subverts a stereotypical image of an attractive young woman in a logo that shows her gesticulating at the sexist beauty standard she is supposed to represent.

> If feminism wasn't powerful, if feminism wasn't influential, people wouldn't spend so much time putting it down.
> **Jessica Valenti**

platform Hollaback!, founded in New York City in 2005, has allowed women who were sexually harassed to publicly expose the incident by uploading their stories and photos of those who harassed them.

In 2011, a Facebook post by American black queer feminist Sonya Renee Taylor, in which the 230 lb (104 kg) Taylor wears a black corset and proclaims her power and desirability, went viral. Afterward, Taylor created The Body Is Not An Apology, an online movement for empowerment and self-love in the face of what she terms "body terrorism" against marginalized people. A key part of this movement is the online feminist magazine of the same name, which features the work of writers from across the globe. In 2018, Taylor also published a book, *The Body Is Not An Apology: The Power of Radical Self-Love*.

The magazine *Teen Vogue* made headlines in 2015 when it announced it was shifting its focus to become an overtly feminist, pro-social justice venue for young women and people of marginalized genders. It added a news and politics subsection, which received more views than the entertainment section by 2017. Its readership has responded enthusiastically: online traffic rose 226 percent between 2015 and 2017.

Hashtag activism

The backdrop to fourth-wave feminism has been the rapidly changing political and cultural milieu of the post-2008 financial crash, the effect of government austerity measures on marginalized populations, and the multiple social movements that have sprung up during the rise of social media— from the hopes of the Arab Spring in 2010 to the US-based Occupy Wall Street of 2011. The rise of "hashtag activism" (a term coined in a 2011 article in *The Guardian*) has been strongly incorporated into fourth-wave feminism. Hashtag activism involves the use of hashtags with identifiable phrases that drive digital activism. This way, an activist group's audience can find minute-by-minute Twitter updates aggregating all posts that use that phrase. Groups use their hashtags to spread information, to share photos of a protest, or to livestream an act of injustice in "real time" and encourage their audience to share the videos. These tactics have been successful in promoting social justice issues, as tweets, videos, and images are viewed and shared on the internet thousands or even millions of times.

Examples of hashtag activism abound. After Neda Agha-Soltan was shot dead after protesting against the government during the Iranian elections in 2009, the hashtag #Neda began trending as a "most-viewed" hashtag. In Nigeria, feminists used #BringBackOurGirls to highlight the kidnapping of 276 schoolgirls by the Boko Haram terrorist group in 2014. In the US, #BlackLivesMatter calls attention to the plight of black people facing racist police brutality. The hashtag #BlackTransLivesMatter has been used by supporters of Black Lives Matter to bring awareness to the murder of black trans people (especially low-income black trans

Women in the US protest against the 2017 inauguration of President Trump, who faces allegations of sexual misconduct. The march formed part of a worldwide protest.

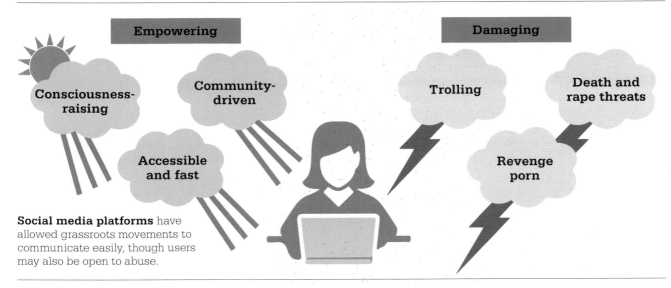

Empowering

Damaging

Consciousness-raising

Community-driven

Accessible and fast

Trolling

Death and rape threats

Revenge porn

Social media platforms have allowed grassroots movements to communicate easily, though users may also be open to abuse.

women), while #SayHerName focuses on black women who have died during encounters with police.

#MeToo

The #MeToo movement is another prominent example of fourth-wave feminism using hashtag activism. Originally set up in the US as a movement for underprivileged sexual assault survivors by black feminist Tarana Burke in 2006, the Twitter manifestation of #MeToo brought public awareness of the extent of sexual assault and demanded that perpetrators of sexual violence be held to account. Since 2017, the #MeToo movement has become global and the phrase has been translated into multiple languages.

The #MeToo movement became so influential in popular culture that *Time* magazine chose "the silence breakers: the voices that launched a movement" as its 2017 "Person of the Year." Multiple women's stories were highlighted in the article, from prominent and vocal supporters such as Burke and US actresses Rose McGowan and Alyssa Milano, to "everyday" women fighting sexual harassment and violence. This increased visibility also

means that claims of sexual assault are taken more seriously by society. Convicted and alleged perpetrators across the arts, media, sports, and politics have had to face serious repercussions for their behavior.

Internet harassment

There are also downsides to the #MeToo era. Women on the internet, especially marginalized women such as women of color, are subjected to trolling (the posting of incendiary messages designed to stir up hatred), rape and death threats, and doxxing, in which hackers release someone's

> "
>
> The worst thing you can call a guy is a girl. Being a woman is the ultimate insult.
> **Jessica Valenti**
>
> "

private information to the public and encourage bullying and harassment.

Revenge porn, in which hackers gain access to women's nude photos or video footage and post them on the internet for a public audience without the subject's knowledge or consent, is another harassment tactic. This has been used by abusive men to exploit and shame ex-girlfriends, and by misogynists seeking revenge on feminist public figures, such as against British actress Emma Watson in 2017.

Danish-Swedish lecturer and magazine editor Emma Holten became an activist against revenge porn in 2011 after having nude photos stolen and posted on the internet. In response, she published her own series of nude photos in a project called "Consent." Holten has subsequently created other activist projects and given lectures on revenge porn and online rights.

Governments are gradually waking up to the impact revenge porn has on people's lives. Most US states and several countries, including the UK, Canada, New Zealand, and Japan have now introduced laws to criminalize it. ∎

FEMINISM NEEDS SEX WORKERS AND SEX WORKERS NEED FEMINISM

SUPPORTING SEX WORKERS

IN CONTEXT

PRIMARY QUOTE
Feministfightback.org.uk

KEY FIGURE
Carol Leigh

BEFORE
1915 In Canada, ex-prostitute Maimie Pinzer opens Montreal Mission for Friendless Girls, an apartment where sex workers can gather and socialize.

1972 Sex workers in Lyon, France, start a European sex workers' rights movement.

2001 The Sex Workers' Rights Movement introduce the red umbrella as a worldwide symbol of sex workers' rights.

AFTER
2016 Amnesty International publishes its policy and research on the protection of sex workers' rights, which recommends that consensual sex work be decriminalized.

When Carol Leigh first used the term "sex work" at a conference in the 1970s, she hoped it would give sex workers more dignity than the term prostitute and mark the start of a movement. The American sex workers' rights activist wanted to define the role of the sex provider as an agent in a business transaction.

Thanks in part to Leigh, the concept of sex work as a valid form of labor that gives workers economic opportunities and financial independence is gaining mainstream acceptance. Yet people voluntarily engaged in sex work still face stigma and struggle to access the same entitlements—such as safe working conditions—held by workers in other sectors. A cohort of feminist activists want to end the culture of slut shaming and victim blaming, and promote the idea of the emancipated person reclaiming bodily autonomy and making choices that suit them.

While third- and fourth-wave and sex-positive feminists are largely supportive and advocate sex workers' rights, some radical feminists believe feminism and sex work are mutually exclusive. Abolitionists, such as Kathleen Barry in the US and Julie Bindel in the UK, define sex work as abuse that amounts to "paid rape" and campaign to end it. In contrast, sex-worker inclusionary feminists, such as Margo St. James and Norma Jean Almodovar in the US, campaign to empower sex workers and give them a legitimate status in the labor market rather than end sex work altogether. ■

> ❝
> 'Sex work' acknowledges the work we do rather than defines us by our status.
> **Carol Leigh**
> ❞

See also: Sexual double standards 78–79 ▪ Rape as abuse of power 166–171 ▪ Antipornography feminism 196–199 ▪ Sex positivity 234–237

MY CLOTHES ARE NOT MY CONSENT
ENDING VICTIM BLAMING

IN CONTEXT

PRIMARY QUOTE
SlutWalk Toronto, 2011

KEY ORGANIZATION
SlutWalk

BEFORE
1971 American psychologist William Ryan coins the term "blaming the victim" to describe the way African Americans are being blamed for their own racial oppression.

1982 Canada passes a rape shield law that prevents defendants in sexual misconduct cases from using the victim's past sexual history as evidence.

AFTER
2012 The fatal gang rape and torture of 23-year-old Jyoti Singh Pandey on a bus in Delhi sparks protests across India and the world.

Feminists have long critiqued the way women are blamed for the sexual violence committed against them. In the US, journalist Leora Tanenbaum's 1999 book *Slut! Growing Up Female with a Bad Reputation* details how female survivors of sexual violence are placed into a binary of "good victims" and "bad victims." Survivors seen as "bad victims" are those said to have "slutty" clothes, or who did not fight back "enough," or who are highly sexually active and therefore "not rape victims at all."

SlutWalk

Founded in Canada in 2011 by Sonya Barnett, Heather Jarvis, and others, SlutWalk is a protest march against victim blaming and slut-shaming of sexual assault survivors. It reclaims the word "slut" to declare women's right to sexual freedom without being judged. Protesters hold sex-positive signs, conduct workshops, and speak out about being survivors. However, some feminists are critical of SlutWalk's reclamation of the term "slut" as well

Demonstrators take part in a SlutWalk march in Glasgow, Scotland, in 2011. Protesting that how a woman dresses is no excuse for rape, SlutWalk is now an international movement.

as the revealing outfits worn by marchers. For example, African American feminists complain that the movement does not take account of their history of sexualization under slavery and the unease they consequently feel about the term "slut." Women often targeted by police violence—including black women, immigrant women, trans women, and sex workers— are also sceptical about the white privilege inherent in a movement that seeks to regain a positive relationship with the police. ∎

See also: Sexual double standards 78–79 ▪ Rape as abuse of power 166–171 ▪ Black feminism and womanism 208–215 ▪ Fighting campus sexual assault 320

FEMININITY HAS BECOME A BRAND
ANTICAPITALIST FEMINISM

IN CONTEXT

PRIMARY QUOTE
Laurie Penny, 2011

KEY FIGURES
**Laurie Penny,
Kathi Weeks,
Jessa Crispin**

BEFORE
1867 German philosopher and
economist Karl Marx publishes
Das Kapital: Volume 1, in
which he argues that
capitalism will eventually
collapse, benefiting no one.

AFTER
2013 Facebook executive
Sheryl Sandberg publishes
Lean In, advising women on
how to be successful in the
business world.

2017 The bronze sculpture
"Fearless Girl" is installed
on Wall Street in New York
City to celebrate women's
corporate leadership, an
initiative criticized by
anticapitalist feminists.

A woman produces leather goods
for sale in her own business. "Career
feminists" see such autonomy, free
from patriarchal interference, as the
route to women's equality.

W hile liberal feminists
tend to seek women's
empowerment through
economic advancement ("career
feminism"), anticapitalist feminists
argue that capitalism is a failed
economic system that leads to vast
inequality in income and reinforces
the subordinate status of women.

In her 2011 book *Meat Market:
Female Flesh Under Capitalism*,
British journalist Laurie Penny
attacks liberal feminism, career

feminism, and consumerism as
false routes to women's liberation.
Drawing on Marxist theory, Ariel
Levy's critique of raunch culture,
and analysis by feminists ranging
from Shulamith Firestone to Julia
Serano, Penny highlights the way

> **... women are alienated
> from their sexual bodies
> and required to purchase
> the fundamentals of
> their own gender.**
> **Laurie Penny**

capitalism turns women's bodies into commodities—in particular through the reinforcement of gender stereotypes—and influences the domestic sphere, where an unequal division of labor between women and men persists. The capitalist commodification of femininity is shown by the "pink tax," whereby products that are essential to women are more expensive than essential products for men—an imbalance exacerbated by the gender pay gap that leaves women with less money to spend than men.

New approaches
The American scholar Kathi Weeks went further than Penny in her 2011 book *The Problem with Work*. She argues that Marxist and feminist movements have wrongly accepted paid work as the main method of distributing income. Instead, she boldly calls for a "postwork" society in which state-supported men and women produce and create for themselves, resulting in a richer culture. Work, according to Weeks, is an institution whose existence can and should be questioned.

Fellow American writer Jessa Crispin's 2017 book *Why I Am Not a Feminist: A Feminist Manifesto* takes aim at what she calls "lifestyle feminism," a type of feminism more concerned with individual choices than radical collective struggle. The conflict between this liberal feminism and anticapitalism was evident during the Democratic primary season before the 2016 US presidential election. The liberal feminist agenda of Hillary Clinton was pitched against what many viewed as the stirring socialism of Bernie Sanders.

Other feminists reject capitalism by working to create alternative, non-corporate structures. In the US, the Chicago-based, nonprofit group Woman Made Gallery supports female artists in a field that continues to be dominated by men. In Seneca Falls, New York, WomanMade Products specializes in selling goods made by women, with profits helping to fund socially responsible groups.

Renewed activism
Since the global financial crisis of 2008 and subsequent governmental austerity measures, anticapitalist feminism has gained fresh momentum. During the 2011 Occupy Wall Street movement, in which anticapitalists set up camp in New York City's financial quarter, women's working groups sprung up in cities across the US, demanding the dismantling of capitalism. Within a year, such sentiments had become global, with Occupy movements in more than 82 countries. Yet there were also complaints that Occupy had been commandeered by men and its camps were unsafe for women. ▪

The pink tax
Women tend to be charged more than men for the "women's" version of the same goods. This is known as the pink tax, or the pink premium. A 2015 report from the Department of Consumer Affairs (DCA) in New York City entitled "From Cradle to Cane: The Cost of Being a Female Consumer" found that on average, women were charged 7 percent more than men for similar products. In particular, they paid 7 percent more for toys, 8 percent more for clothing, 13 percent more for personal care products, and 8 percent more for senior home care products.

Women in Australia, Britain, Canada, and the US have campaigned against the so-called "tampon tax," in which tampons are taxed as a luxury item despite being an essential health item. So far, only Canada has removed this tax (in 2015).

Pink products aimed at women, from razors to scooters, tend to be more expensive than identical items in darker colors designed for men.

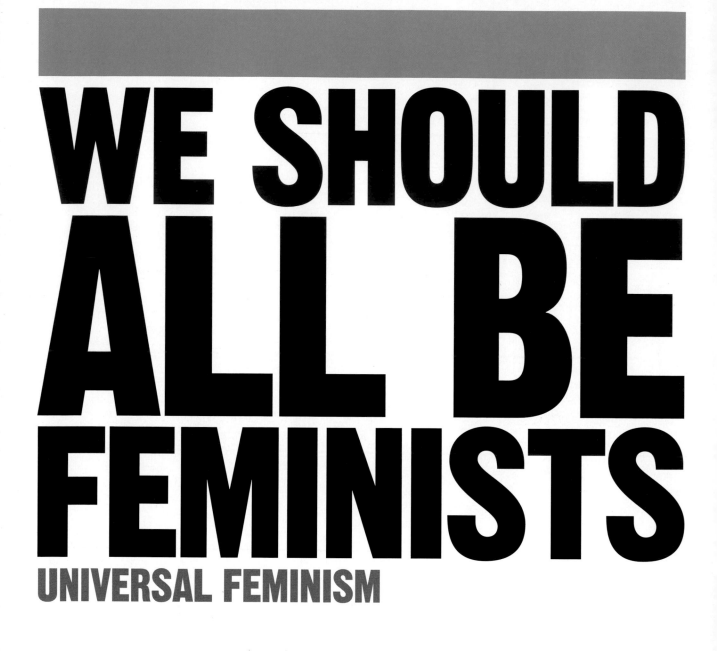

WE SHOULD ALL BE FEMINISTS

UNIVERSAL FEMINISM

IN CONTEXT

PRIMARY QUOTE
**Chimamanda Ngozi
Adichie, 2012**

KEY FIGURES
**Caitlin Moran,
Chimamanda Ngozi
Adichie, Jessa Crispin**

BEFORE
2000 American feminist icon
bell hooks publishes *Feminism
Is for Everybody: Passionate
Politics*, in which she argues
that feminism is good for
women and men.

2004 In the US, Jessica
Valenti sets up the website
Feministing.com produced by
and for young feminists.

AFTER
2016 American entertainment
magazine *Billboard* describes
Beyoncé's album *Lemonade*
as a "revolutionary work of
black feminism."

2017 *Good Night Stories
for Rebel Girls,* stories that
challenge gender stereotypes,
is published in the US.

We need to reclaim the
word 'feminism.' We need
the word 'feminism' back …
Caitlin Moran

What makes a feminist?

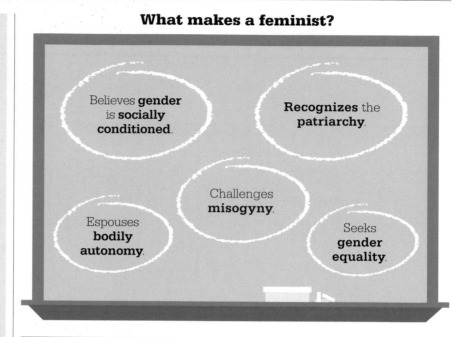

Believes **gender**
is **socially
conditioned**.

Recognizes the
patriarchy.

Challenges
misogyny.

Espouses
**bodily
autonomy**.

Seeks
**gender
equality**.

At the end of the first
decade of the 21st century,
there was a huge surge in
feminist discourse across the
internet, particularly in the feminist
blogosphere. Some women held the
"postfeminist" view that the battle
for women's liberation had been
fought and won and women could
now choose their own destiny. They
argued that feminism was too
hostile to men and irrelevant to most
women's lives. Other feminists
denounced such views as selfish,
ignoring the needs of women who
were still struggling. They urged
women to remember the radicalism
of second-wave feminists and unite
to dismantle the patriarchy, the
cause of women's oppression across
the world. At the same time,
entrenched critics of feminism
expressed the view, as they had for
decades, that feminism was nothing
more than an attempt by women to
assert their supremacy over men.

In the midst of these online
storms, some high-profile women
began to promote feminism as a
matter of common sense. Distilling
their notions of feminism into a
basic liberal motto of equality
between the sexes, they posed
the question: "Who would not
be a feminist?" They proclaimed
that they were feminists and that
everyone else should be, too.
Adherents of this type of feminism
included British writer and cultural
critic Caitlin Moran, actor Emma
Watson, US First Lady Michelle
Obama, and the Nigerian writer
Chimamanda Ngozi Adichie.

A matter of common sense
Caitlin Moran's 2011 memoir
How to Be a Woman uses humor
to advance the idea of feminism
being basic common sense. In
contrast to many books on
feminism written by academics,
which could often be theoretical
and abstruse, Moran's book set out
to make feminist ideas accessible
and relatable. She tells stories from
her own life, from the naming of
body parts by her family and the
pressure she felt as a teenager to

See also: The roots of oppression 114–117 ▪ The beauty myth 264–267 ▪ Bringing feminism online 294–297 ▪ Sexism is everywhere 308–309 ▪ Leaning in 312–313 ▪ Sexual abuse awareness 322–327

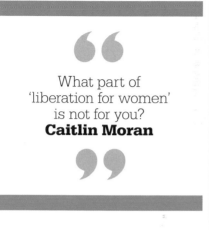

> What part of
> 'liberation for women'
> is not for you?
> **Caitlin Moran**

remove body hair and wear high heels to undergoing an abortion as an adult.

Moran argues that life for women in the 21st century is inextricably tied to feminism's historical gains. Without feminism, writes Moran, women would not even be able to read a book, let alone open a bank account or vote. Moran disputes the idea that feminism is only for a subset of women, arguing that even women who live their lives in ways not understood as traditionally feminist have a place in feminism.

Celebrities, such as British actor Emma Watson, have also advocated common-sense feminism. In 2014, Watson launched her HeForShe initiative as part of her work as a goodwill ambassador for UN Women. The campaign seeks to enlist the active support of men in the prevention of violence against women. After emphasizing the right of women and men to be equal,

A leading proponent of a new approach to feminism, Caitlin Moran uses her blog and her newspaper column to share her often quirky views on women and society.

Watson added that perceptions of feminism as man-hating had to stop and reiterated the view, expressed by Hillary Clinton in a speech in 1995, that feminism was not a women's issue but a matter of human rights, in which men also had a stake. Men, too, deserved to be freed from gender stereotypes.

Former US First Lady Michelle Obama focuses on the practical application of common sense feminism to effect meaningful change. She is an active supporter of girls' education worldwide, and declared her allegiance to the #BringBackOurGirls campaign in support of the schoolgirls abducted by terrorist group Boko Haram in northern Nigeria in 2014. She also stresses the importance of women's leadership and called out Donald Trump's disrespect for women during the 2016 US presidential election campaign. Obama's efforts to incorporate such

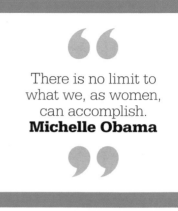

> There is no limit to
> what we, as women,
> can accomplish.
> **Michelle Obama**

issues in her role as First Lady contributed to her image as a role model for women, particularly young black girls.

Feminists unite
It is not just Western feminists who champion feminism for men and women everywhere. Nigerian writer Chimamanda Ngozi Adichie—whose first novel *Purple Hibiscus*, about a girl growing up in a violent patriarchal family in Nigeria, was published in 2003—delivered one of the most eloquent arguments for a more collaborative form of feminism in a 2012 TED Talk (online talks about "ideas worth spreading") called "We Should All Be Feminists." Adichie said that she got the idea for the talk when a male friend called her a feminist in the same tone one would use to call someone a terrorist. The talk was not a rallying cry for Nigerian feminism, or an attack on Nigerian men, but a plea for change in Nigerian society, and in the wider world.

Adichie condemned the different standards that were applied to acceptable behavior in girls and boys in Nigeria. Girls and women in Nigerian society, **»**

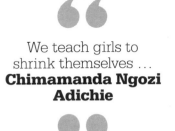

> We teach girls to shrink themselves …
> **Chimamanda Ngozi Adichie**

Adichie declared, were expected to do housework, to put men first in order to spare men's egos, and to self-regulate their own sexuality. Unmarried women, she said, were seen as having "failed" simply because they had no husband.

The Bring Back Our Girls
campaign of 2014 demanded the release of hundreds of schoolgirls kidnapped by Islamic terrorists in northeastern Nigeria. The campaign united women all over the world.

Men, meanwhile, continued to be seen as the "standard" humans. The fact that men do not recognize this, asserted Adichie, was part of the problem. She emphasized that men can and should be feminists, too, and that men and women must unlearn gender stereotyping in order for everyone to fulfil their potential. Part of this work, Adichie argued, involves raising children differently so that the next generation has more equitable ideas about gender, a view she expanded upon in her 2017 work *Dear Ijeawele, or A Feminist Manifesto in Fifteen Suggestions*— 15 ideas on how to bring up a daughter in a gender-neutral way that is rooted in Nigerian and (her own) Igbo culture.

Although Adichie was accused of being "un-African" by some critics, "We Should All Be Feminists" seemed to strike a chord, not just in Nigeria but around the world. In 2013, the American singer and feminist Beyoncé sampled these words in the track "Flawless" on the

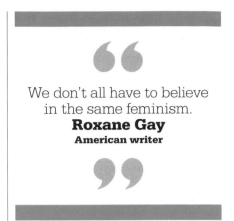

> We don't all have to believe in the same feminism.
> **Roxane Gay**
> **American writer**

album *Beyoncé*; Dior put the slogan We Should All Be Feminists on T-shirts; and when the talk was published as a book in 2014, it was given to all 16-year-olds in Sweden, in the hope that it would spark debate within schools and make boys think about gender equality.

The critiques
Distilling feminism down to the fundamental message of gender equality has the advantage of being easily understood. As such,

Chimamanda Ngozi Adichie

Born in Enugu, Nigeria, in 1977, Chimamanda Ngozi Adichie spent her early life in the university town of Nsukka, where her father was a professor of statistics and her mother the registrar. After studying medicine and pharmacy, she traveled to the US to study communication, and later graduated in communication and political science at Eastern Connecticut State University.

Adichie began her first novel *Purple Hibiscus* while studying in Connecticut. The book was shortlisted for the Orange Prize for fiction in 2004 and won the Commonwealth Writers' Prize in 2005. Adichie has held a number of posts in American universities and splits her time between the US and Nigeria.

Key works

2003 *Purple Hibiscus*
2006 *Half of a Yellow Sun*
2009 *The Thing Around Your Neck*
2013 *Americanah*
2014 *We Should All Be Feminists*
2017 *Dear Ijeawele, or A Feminist Manifesto in Fifteen Suggestions*

it has the potential to reach a wide audience, encouraging people with different perspectives to all look upon themselves as feminists. However, not all feminists are comfortable with this universal approach. Moran's brand of feminism, for example, has been criticized by some women for not taking into account the issues faced by those who do not share her advantages in life as a well-paid writer and commentator.

Above all, common-sense feminism is critiqued for not being radical enough and for leaving behind its revolutionary roots. Simply wanting equality with men, and wearing a T-shirt that says so, critics argue, does not offer a serious challenge to existing male-dominated power structures.

In her 2017 book *Why I am Not a Feminist: a Feminist Manifesto*, American feminist writer Jessa Crispin explains that she does not call herself a feminist because the term has been rendered banal and "toothless"—something that everyone can support while ignoring the fundamental disparities in the world. In her book, Crispin—who began her career as an abortion counselor for the birth control organization Planned Parenthood—criticizes what she calls "lifestyle feminism," created by patriarchal corporate culture and often reduced to slogans. She argues that there is no point in having more women in power if the system of patriarchy remains the same, and is critical of the individualistic "lean in" type of feminism promoted by Facebook's Sheryl Sandberg, who advises women to work harder and adopt male strategies for getting to the top. Instead, Crispin calls for sustained struggle against the capitalist economic system in order to effect profound social change. She insists that achieving minor adjustments to the status quo will do nothing to help the multitudes of poor and oppressed women of the world.

Meeting challenges

In some ways, feminism has never seemed more powerful than it is now, with women from different marginalized backgrounds across the world, aided by the internet, standing up to the myriad political and economic threats to their well-being and safety. The spread of feminist ideas across social media has had an impact on women everywhere, from teenage girls in remote corners of Africa to celebrities in Hollywood.

In order to harness this power, and achieve change, many women argue that it is valuable to have successful female role models who stress that they do not hate men. Yet, while some of the "superstar feminists" are inspirational, their influence may be limited if they decline to back up their slogans with their actions and challenge the dominant structures of power in society head-on. ∎

> **"**
> I'm a feminist …
> It'd be stupid not to
> be on my own side.
> **Maya Angelou**
> **"**

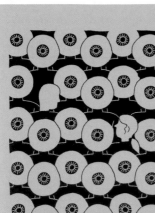

NOT A MEN VS WOMEN ISSUE

SEXISM IS EVERYWHERE

IN CONTEXT

PRIMARY QUOTE
Laura Bates, 2015

KEY FIGURE
Laura Bates

BEFORE
1969 Carol Hanisch of New York Radical Women writes the paper "The Personal is Political," advocating consciousness-raising as a form of activism.

1970 Harvard professor Chester M. Pierce coins the term "microaggression" for the small insults experienced by African Americans.

AFTER
2017 The #MeToo campaign is launched in response to allegations of sexual misconduct against film producer Harvey Weinstein.

2018 Women in the entertainment industry found Time's Up to campaign for the elimination of sexual harassment in all workplaces.

When British feminist Laura Bates began her acting career, she did not anticipate the sexual objectification she experienced during auditions. Being thought "sexy," she found, was more important than talent. This led her to reflect on the sexism and harassment she faced in other areas of her life and to ask other women about their experiences. She discovered that sexism in some form was routine for most women.

"Sexism sells? Not with us!" says a banner from the German feminist group Terre des Femme (Women's Earth) at a protest in Berlin in 2013 against the insidious use of sexism in advertising.

In 2012, Bates set up the Everyday Sexism Project, inviting women to share their experiences of sexism, which she then posted online. This call for submissions was extended to Twitter, with women posting under the hashtag #EverydaySexism.

See also: Sexual double standards 78–79 ■ Consciousness-raising 134–135 ■ Intersectionality 240–245 ■ Bringing feminism online 294–297

> To be a feminist is to be accused of oversensitivity, hysteria, and crying wolf.
> **Laura Bates**

The response was immediate and overwhelming, coming from women of all ages, classes, and races. They wrote about rape and sexual assault, sexualized comments at places of education, and sexual harassment at work. Girls also reported being put down by family members because of their gender. Examples included male work colleagues constantly commenting on a woman's physical appearance or relationship status; male gropers telling women they should be grateful for the attention; women being threatened physically for their opinions on social media; and strangers making sexual comments in public places that girls were too young to even understand.

Reflecting misogyny
The cumulative effect of the responses was to validate women's sense of grievance; in the past, they had often been told they lacked a sense of humor, could not take a compliment, or were taking things too seriously. It also showed that sexism was ubiquitous and that the normalization of its more minor forms, which are often deemed too trivial to mention, allows the misogyny underlying the most serious abuse and oppression to

flourish. Fighting sexism in the modern day, Bates says, is "not about men against women, but people against prejudice."

Entries to the Everyday Sexism Project continue to come from many countries. In the wake of its early success, however, Bates was subject to extensive online trolling, including rape and death threats, and faced relentless criticism in person, later writing about the overwhelming levels of hatred directed toward her.

Deeply entrenched
The 2016 US presidential campaign showed sexism exists in the highest levels of power. Donald Trump, whose contemptuous comments about women had been publicized over many decades, was caught on tape describing his experiences of assaulting women. Yet 41 percent of all women (52 percent of white women) voted for him. Many powerful men are profoundly sexist; as yet, this does not stop women (and others) from supporting them. ■

> If your compliments are making women feel uncomfortable, scared, anxious, annoyed, or harassed, you're probably not doing them right.
> **Laura Bates**

Laura Bates

Born in Oxford, UK, in 1986, Bates grew up in London and Somerset. After earning a degree in English literature at St. John's College, Cambridge, Bates worked as a nanny and also as a researcher for psychologist Susan Quilliam, who was rewriting the 1970s classic guide to lovemaking, *The Joy of Sex*.

In 2012, motivated by her own experience of sexual harassment, Bates set up the Everyday Sexism Project, inviting other women to share their stories of sexism. In 2014, she published a book about her findings, setting the respondents' experiences in the context of legal and social inequalities. Bates' research is used to lobby members of parliament and helps train British police officers. Bates also gives talks to schools and universities and is a contributor to the New York–based Women Under Siege, campaigning against sexual violence in war.

Key works

2014 *Everyday Sexism*
2016 *Girl Up*
2018 *Misogynation*

WE CANNOT ALL SUCCEED WHEN HALF OF US ARE HELD BACK
GLOBAL EDUCATION FOR GIRLS

IN CONTEXT

PRIMARY QUOTE
Malala Yousafzai, 2013

KEY FIGURE
Malala Yousafzai

BEFORE
1981 REPEM (Red de Educación Popular entre Mujeres) is set up to further education for women and girls in Latin America.

1993 The World Conference on Human Rights asserts women's right to "equal access to education at all levels."

AFTER
2030 World leaders vow in 2016 to deliver free access for all girls (and boys) to primary and secondary education by 2030, and affordable tertiary education or training.

2100 By this date, all children in low-income countries should complete primary education, based on economic trends cited by UNESCO in 2016.

The third item on the United Nations' millennial list of development goals was to promote gender equality and empower women. One specific target on the list was to have as many girls as boys enrolled in primary and secondary education by 2005. By 2006, progress had been made—more girls than boys enrolled at primary level in all developing regions—yet by 2013, 31 million girls still had no access to primary education. UN Women, which works for gender equality, reports that two thirds of the world's 796 million illiterate people are female.

Feminist advocacy groups support the UN goals, but feel they focus too narrowly on the economic benefits of learning. They emphasize that education is both a right and a means of shaping future women, building their confidence and meeting their aspirations. They suggest other issues should be questioned, such as how girls are taught, whether school curriculums

In Swaziland, two sisters walk to school. The Swazi government introduced free primary education in 2009, but many school principals require extra fees from parents.

See also: Education for Islamic women 38–39 ▪ Intellectual freedom 106–107 ▪ Fighting campus sexual assault 320

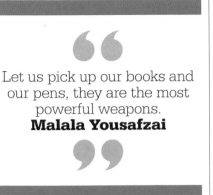

> Let us pick up our books and our pens, they are the most powerful weapons.
> **Malala Yousafzai**

should be more inclusive, and what forms of further education are available to meet local needs.

Local activists

In many countries, women's groups are working at local and national levels to educate girls and women—sometimes against the odds. The Revolutionary Association of the Women of Afghanistan (RAWA), founded in 1977, ran underground schools for girls and boys during the Taliban era (1996–2001), when education for girls was banned. It was resistance to a similar ban in Pakistan's Swat Valley, occupied by the Taliban in 2009, that set Malala Yousafzai, then a schoolgirl, on the path to becoming a world-famous activist for girls' education.

Local women's groups also advocate adult education. In Mexico and Central America, for example, they are working with the global advocacy organization Women Deliver to implement Personal Advancement and Career Enhancement (PACE) programs in their communities.

The Forum of African Women Educationalists (FAWE) promotes female education at both child and adult levels in sub-Saharan Africa.

Founded in 1992 by five women ministers of education, FAWE now has 35 national chapters. It campaigns for policies that treat girls and boys equally and programs to help adult women return to education. Its network of mothers' clubs in Zambia, Gambia, Liberia, and Malawi offers adult literacy classes as well as activities that generate income. The mothers, in turn, raise awareness of the benefits of girls' education.

A global concern

Gender disparities in educational access are not confined to the developing world. In the US, while more women than men gained doctoral degrees in 2016 for the eighth year running, it is still clear that African American and Hispanic girls perform less well than white girls educationally, though the gap is narrowing. They are, for instance, five times more likely to be suspended. The racial education gap remains a challenge in the developed world, while global target dates for gender parity in education and lifelong learning lie well into the future. ∎

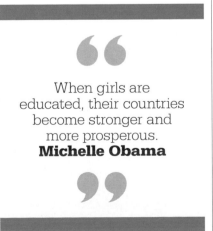

> When girls are educated, their countries become stronger and more prosperous.
> **Michelle Obama**

Malala Yousafzai

Yousafzai was born in the Swat Valley of Pakistan in 1997. She grew up there under the Taliban occupation, which banned girls from education. Defying the ban, she attended school and wrote anti-Taliban blogs that promoted the importance of education for girls. In 2012, while returning home on a bus after taking an exam, she was shot in the head; two girls beside her were also injured. Flown to the UK for a life-saving operation, she has since campaigned tirelessly for the rights of girls' education and also campaigned against Taliban extremism. In 2014, she won the Nobel Peace Prize, becoming the youngest Nobel Laureate. She set up the Malala Fund which finances various schools in war-torn areas. She is currently studying at the University of Oxford while continuing her advocacy for education.

Key works

2013 *I Am Malala: The Story of the Girl Who Stood Up for Education and Was Shot by the Taliban* (co-authored with Christine Lamb)

NO FEMALE LEADERS, JUST LEADERS

LEANING IN

IN CONTEXT

PRIMARY QUOTE
Sheryl Sandberg, 2013

KEY FIGURE
Sheryl Sandberg

BEFORE
1963 Betty Friedan writes
The Feminine Mystique,
chronicling the boredom of
American housewives.

1983 US feminist Gloria
Steinem's collection of essays,
*Outrageous Acts and Everyday
Rebellions*, includes an essay
on "The Importance of Work."

AFTER
2016 American journalist
Jessica Bennett receives
enthusiastic reviews for her
book *Feminist Fight Club*,
which urges women to support
each other in the workplace.

2017 After the sudden death
of her husband, Sheryl
Sandberg writes *Option B*, in
which she calls for a more
compassionate workplace.

In her 2013 international best seller *Lean In: Women, Work and the Will to Lead*, Sheryl Sandberg, Chief Operating Officer of Facebook, urges women to reach for the highest ranks of every institution of power. Instead of focusing on the "glass ceiling" of systemic barriers stopping women from getting to the top, as many feminists had, she tells women who have made it to demand more for women lower down the ladder.

When Sandberg was heavily pregnant and working for Google, for example, she asked for reserved parking, a policy that remained in place for pregnant women after she left. As a top executive, she argues, she had the power to put policies in place that benefited other women.

Trickle-down feminism

Critics questioned whether the trickle-down feminism Sandberg advocates would work, pointing out that earlier female leaders, such as the UK's former prime minister Margaret Thatcher, were not known to fight for the feminist cause. They also disagreed with Sandberg's assertion that the onus should be on women to believe more in themselves, and berated her for ignoring intersectional discrimination, such as the racism experienced by women of color.

Some critics commented that Sandberg said little that women of earlier generations had not heard before, but she was credited with

A mother wheels her child to a day care on her way to work. Childcare is still primarily seen as a woman's responsibility, even when she also has a demanding career.

raising important issues, such as encouraging women to negotiate their salary; use assertive body language to feel more powerful; and watch against negative, gendered connotations of words such as "bossy." Her appeal was also in being a rich, white woman at the top of the corporate ladder, someone to whom corporate America aspired.

Adapt to the system

Sandberg laments the absence of paid maternity leave in the US and the persistent gender discrimination women face when trying to balance work and homelife, but her solution is to adapt to the system and persevere in unfavorable work environments. She also advocates that women devise strategies for survival at work before and after pregnancy: "The months and years leading up to having children," she says, "are not the time to lean back, but the critical time to lean in." Citing the example of a female investment banker, she says that dedication to her job during the busy child-rearing years paid off

later. When the children had left home, a woman who had "leaned in" would still have a fulfilling career.

Sandberg acknowledges that not everyone wants to reach the top, and is not insensitive to the emotional demands of motherhood. Citing her own experience at the top of the corporate ladder in 2013, she describes "running" back to her laptop after spending time with her children in the evening and secretly breast-pumping in a bathroom stall while taking conference calls. Stating that the days when she could disconnect from work on vacation or over the weekend had "long gone," Sandberg describes extended working hours as "the new normal for many of us."

The book's critics

High-profile fans of *Lean In* included Chelsea Clinton and Oprah Winfrey, but many feminists criticized the book. Shortly after its publication, the American feminist and scholar bell hooks dismissed Sandberg's strategy and said that it would not liberate women. Instead,

hooks, who described Sandberg as a "lovable younger sister who just wants to play on the big brother's team," maintained that "leaning in" only served the interests of the patriarchal power structure of white, middle-class men. ▪

Sheryl Sandberg, whom *Fortune* magazine ranks as one of the five most powerful women in business, publicizes *Lean In* in Germany. The book became an international best seller.

Women are leaders everywhere you look … Our country was built by strong women and we will continue to break down walls.
Nancy Pelosi
American politician

Women CEOs

In 2013, when *Lean In* was published, Sandberg wrote that just 5 percent of CEOs at the top 500 companies trading on the US stock exchange were women, while only 25 percent of the senior executive positions and 19 percent of board seats were held by women. As Sandberg said, the numbers had barely budged in a decade.

In 2018, five years after *Lean In* was published, the number of women CEOs in the US was still at 5 percent, according to the Glass Ceiling Index published in the UK by *The Economist* magazine.

Studies have found that having more women and generally more diversity on boards leads to better decisions, more creative problem-solving, improved profits, and less damaging risk-taking. In 2018, 27 global investors, including major pension funds, joined the 30% Club, a UK initiative started in 2010 to get more women onto the boards of top companies. It aims for women to occupy 30 percent of such roles by 2020.

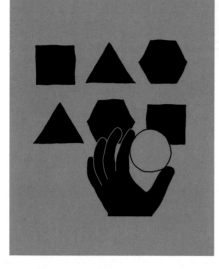

WHEN YOU EXPOSE A PROBLEM YOU POSE A PROBLEM
THE FEMINIST KILLJOY

Feminists have long been portrayed as irrationally angry, humorless people, who are only drawn to feminism because they are unhappy and wedded to victimhood. For women of color, the combination of sexism and racism has resulted in demeaning stereotypes, such as the "angry Black woman," the "spicy Latina," and the "Asian dragon lady." In response, feminists point out how these depictions are deliberate strategies used to undermine women's anger about discrimination, violence, and other forms of mistreatment.

Ignoring the roots of feminists' anger while painting feminists themselves as the problem is nothing new. Detractors of the suffragettes in the late 19th and early 20th centuries accused them of being ugly and "mannish," and in the 1970s and '80s, those hostile to feminists berated them as combative, man-hating lesbians. More recently in the US, right-wing commentators have characterized young feminists as navel-gazing "special snowflakes"—millennials who have been raised to think of themselves as beautiful and unique but who are not resilient (hence snowflakes) and feel entitled to privileged treatment.

Becoming the killjoy
In 2010, British-Australian feminist and writer Sara Ahmed published an essay called "Feminist Killjoys (and Other Willful Subjects)," in which she explores feminism and emotion, in particular the ways in which feminists' refusal to be happy in the face of women's oppression violates social norms.

In her essay, Ahmed uses a table as a simple metaphor for emotional oppression experienced by feminists. When a family is gathered around a table, sharing polite, and supposedly safe, conversation, states Ahmed,

> Feminism is not a dirty word.
> **Kate Nash**
> **British singer**

See also: Political lesbianism 180–181 ▪ Anger as an activist tool 216 ▪ Antifeminist backlash 270–271 ▪ Bringing feminism online 294–297

A self-professed Feminist Killjoy takes part in the 2017 Amber Rose SlutWalk in Los Angeles. The event promotes gender equality and combats sexual violence and body-shaming.

working out how to respond to offensive statements from a family member can be traumatic. A person may start to feel "wound up" from the emotional injury of the discriminatory words, yet if she questions those words she risks being construed as the "killjoy," who has ruined the gathering. By bringing something up as a problem, an individual creates a problem and becomes the problem she has created.

In the context of discussing racism, states Ahmed, people of color responding to white people's racism are often painted as the killjoy in the room, effectively viewed as the source of the tension in a group gathering (or in society) rather than recognized as legitimately targeting racism.

Angry and proud

Ahmed's discussion about the figure of the "feminist killjoy" resonated with many feminists, and in 2013 she started the blog "Feminist Killjoys" to connect with readers about these issues in an accessible forum outside academia. The blog's motto was "killing joy as a world making project."

Through her academic and online work on "feminist killjoys," Ahmed counters the idea that feminists and other maligned people from marginalized backgrounds should suppress their anger. Systems of power, Ahmed argues, require those who are marginalized and oppressed to maintain a veneer of happiness to perpetuate the illusion that the status quo is acceptable. Rather than asking women to "lean in" to, or work within, the dominant power structure, Ahmed reminds women that the wilfulness and anger of marginalized people throughout history have been necessary to create social change. To become conscious of oppression, she says, is to throw off a shallow sense of happiness and security. This, in turn, requires those committed to justice to grapple deeply with the emotionally disturbing realities of power.

The need to cultivate wilfulness as a feminist killjoy, argues Ahmed, also means questioning oppressive tendencies within feminism itself. As an example, Ahmed cites the work of feminists of color who reject the false notion of a happy feminist "sisterhood" to deliver difficult but honest truths about white feminists' racism.

Through her analysis, Ahmed emphasizes how feminists should embrace being killjoys and form supportive networks to face up to sexism and racism. More precisely, she suggests, it is often necessary to speak out and bring up negative feelings for others as part of coming to terms with and dismantling oppression. Ahmed's concept of the feminist killjoy asks women to rethink what constitutes joy and whose pain that joy is built on. As Ahmed has written, there can be joy in killing joy. ▪

Sara Ahmed

Born in Salford, UK, in 1969, Sara Ahmed moved with her Pakistani father and English mother to Adelaide, Australia, in the early 1970s. Since earning her PhD from Cardiff University, Wales, in 1994, Ahmed has held senior academic positions in Australia, the UK, and the US. She resigned as Director of the Centre for Feminist Research at Goldsmiths, University of London, in 2016, in protest at the university's failure to challenge and deal with sexual harassment. Ahmed lives with her sociologist partner Sarah Franklin and continues to write, research, and lecture on feminist, queer, and race issues.

Key works

2004 *The Cultural Politics of Emotion*
2010 *The Promise of Happiness*
2010 "Feminist Killjoys (and Other Willful Subjects)"
2017 *Living a Feminist Life*

WOMEN ARE A COMMUNITY AND OUR COMMUNITY IS NOT SAFE

MEN HURT WOMEN

Violence against women, argues feminists, is not simply an issue of individual men abusing individual women. Rather, it is symptomatic of larger power structures that normalize men's contempt for women. In its most extreme form, men murder women.

Fighting femicide
First coined in 1801 but politicized by feminists in the 1970s, the term "femicide" refers to men's murder of girls and women due to their gender. The most marginalized women in society are at the highest risk of femicide. In the US, for example, this equates to low-income transgender women of color.

Latin America has some of the highest rates of femicide, which academics attribute to the complex historical interplay between

A 2016 protest in the Mexican city of Ecatepec, where some 600 women were murdered over the previous four years, includes a pair of high-heeled shoes that belonged to one of the victims.

See also: Protection from domestic violence 162–163 ■ Rape as abuse of power 166–171

Ni putes ni soumises

Founded in 2002, Ni putes ni soumises (NPNS, "Neither Whores Nor Doormats") is a French feminist group dedicated to fighting violence against women. The group was created by Samira Bellil, Fadela Amara, and others in response to misogynist violence in the public housing complexes of the immigrant-concentrated French suburbs, or *banlieues*.

In particular, NPNS decries the organized gang rapes known as *tournantes*, or "pass-arounds." They also protest against the increase in Islamic extremism in the banlieues and the treatment of Muslim women there, especially the pressure for women to veil, drop out of school, and marry at an early age. In addition, NPNS fights against poverty more broadly.

Critics of NPNS argue that in focusing on the misogyny of Muslim immigrant culture, the group risks glossing over the misogyny of the wider French society and also feeding the Islamophobia of right-wing groups in France.

Supporters of the group Ni putes ni soumises (Neither Whores Nor Doormats) protest on the streets of Paris in 2005.

colonization, genocide of indigenous peoples, misogynist interpretations of religion, rigid gender roles, and economic problems. El Salvador, for example, is said to have the highest rate of femicide in the world, with 468 deaths in 2017 equating to 12 per 100,000 people. Movements such as #NiUnaMenos (#NotOneLess) in Argentina and #NiUnaMas (#NotOneMore) in Mexico stage regular rallies to protest against femicide as well as police inaction in response to it. #NiUnaMenos, formed in 2015, has spread to other countries across Latin America and Europe, indicative of the transnational and cross-cultural relevance of the movement. More than a dozen Latin American countries have passed laws against femicide in recent years.

Male entitlement

In the US, the rise online of the "incel" movement—a shortening of "involuntary celibates," a term first used on the internet in 1993—has alarmed commentators. Its adherents (generally white,

heterosexual men) lament their inability to find sexual partners, a failure they blame on women, especially feminists. Posters in the incel online community have advocated rape as a method of procuring sex.

Such incitements are not merely intimidatory. Self-identified incel Elliot Rodger was driven by his hatred of women and jealousy of others' sexual relationships. He murdered six people and wounded

> "
> Men are afraid that women will laugh at them. Women are afraid that men will kill them.
> **Margaret Atwood**
> **Canadian novelist**
> "

14 more in Isla Vista, California, in 2014, and is hailed as a hero among many incels. His murder spree was reportedly referenced by the mass shooter at Umpqua Community College in Roseburg, Oregon, in 2015. Likewise, in 2017, a man posted online that "Elliot Rodger will not be forgotten" before later murdering 17 people and wounding others at his high school in Parkland, Florida. In April 2018, a man suspected of killing 10 people and injuring 14 others in Toronto, Canada, was also found to have praised Rodger online.

In response to this crisis, many scholars have turned to the work of American sociologist Michael Kimmel; in his 2013 book *Angry White Men: American Masculinity at the End of an Era*, he attributes such violence to the shrinking of male privilege. The solution, according to Kimmel, must be the creation of a masculinity that rejects violence and the hierarchical "othering" of disfavored groups—namely women, people of color, and LGBTQ+ people. ■

EQUAL PAY IS NOT YET EQUAL
THE PAY GAP

IN CONTEXT

PRIMARY QUOTE
Hillary Clinton, 2016

KEY ORGANIZATIONS
American Association of University Women, Fawcett Society

BEFORE
1963 In the US, the Equal Pay Act amending Fair Labor Standards Act is signed.

1970 The UK's Equal Pay Act bans favoring men over women in pay and employment conditions.

2002 In the US, Equal Pay Day moves to a Tuesday each April, to show the extra time women need to work to earn what men earned in the previous year.

2014 The UK's Equality Act permits tribunals to order equal pay audits.

AFTER
2018 British companies with over 250 staff are required by law to publish their pay gap.

The term "gender pay gap" refers to the difference between what men and women earn, implying the extent to which women earn less than men. The data, compiled by company and government statisticians, is either "adjusted"—taking differences in jobs, hours, education, age, marital status, and parenthood into account—or "unadjusted," which

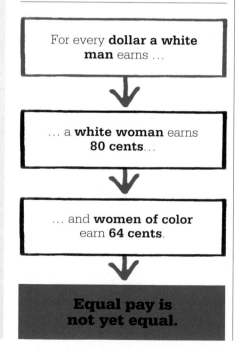

For every **dollar a white man** earns …

… a **white woman** earns **80 cents**…

… and **women of color** earn **64 cents**.

Equal pay is not yet equal.

leads to a wider gap as figures are weighted by highly paid CEOs, who tend to be men. Either way, the pay gap narrowed between the 1960s and '90s, due to progress made in women's rights in many countries, as well as unionization and improved employment rights, but progress has since slowed in the developed world.

Data in 2018 reveals that women in the US earn, on average, around 80 percent of a man's salary. The European Union has an average gender pay gap of around 16 percent. In the UK, women in their twenties have begun to outearn men of the same age, but the UK's gender pay gap is still around 21 percent.

Myths and motherhood
The reasons for pay disparity broadly divide into two categories: voluntary (for example, working part-time) and involuntary (socially mandated discrimination). There are many myths that attempt to explain or justify the pay gap, the most widespread being that it is a matter of career choice: women do not want to take on managerial roles, and men are more likely to choose higher-paid industries such as construction while women

See also: Marriage and work 70–71 ▪ Socialization of childcare 81 ▪ Pink-collar feminism 228–229 ▪ Privilege 239 ▪ Leaning in 312–313

> If fighting for equal pay and paid family leave is playing the gender card, then deal me in!
> **Hillary Clinton**

Women trade on the Thai Stock Exchange in 1989 prior to the industry's computerization. The financial sector still has one of the widest pay gaps, especially when it comes to bonuses.

choose caring or service roles that are poorly paid. However, almost all data suggests that discrimination, not choice, is the real reason for the pay gap.

The workplace discrimination theory holds that women are seen as less capable than men. Socially ingrained bias may give rise to assumptions that a female boss will lack leadership qualities. In some cases, men are simply presumed to be the main breadwinner, and therefore in need of a bigger salary.

Women's pay is also impacted by having young children, due to perceived lower productivity and commitment, disruption of training, and a lack of state-funded child care that leads to women working fewer hours. Many cite the US's lack of paid maternity leave as the biggest problem. Yet in Denmark, where this is mandatory, a similar wage gap persists, with evidence of the "motherhood penalty," including a hiring bias against mothers and women of childbearing age.

Another myth is that women are less capable of negotiating higher salaries. Studies have found that women were unsuccessful when they did try to negotiate, or were penalized. Education also plays a part, particularly as fewer women study science, technology, and mathematics, which tend to lead to higher paid work. However, in Brazil, women tend to be better educated and work longer hours than their male counterparts, yet still earn 24 percent less.

Fighting for pay parity

Since 2000, the narrowing of the gender pay gap has slowed, and progress in the US has stalled. At this rate, women will not reach pay parity with men until 2119, but the fight against the pay gap has now intensified. Organizations such as the American Association of University Women in the US and the Fawcett Society in the UK campaign for change, while social media campaigns and the publication of controversial pay gaps are bringing widespread attention to the issue. ▪

The racial pay gap

There is a significant racial as well as gender pay gap in many developed countries. In the US, for example, black women generally earn around 64 percent of white men's salaries, despite the fact that 80 percent of black women are the family's main breadwinners. Native American women earn around 57 percent, and Hispanic and Latina women fare the worst at 54 percent, with the lowest median weekly pay. Asian American women have the closest average pay to men, but there is significant variation between different Asian nationalities.

All ethnic groups, apart from Asian men, and all women earn less than white American men: black and Hispanic men earn around 73 percent and 69 percent respectively. Women of color tend to be paid less than white women, even when they are educated to the same level.

SURVIVORS ARE GUILTY UNTIL PROVEN INNOCENT
FIGHTING CAMPUS SEXUAL ASSAULT

IN CONTEXT

PRIMARY QUOTE
Emma Sulkowicz, 2014

KEY FIGURES
Annie E. Clark, Andrea Pino

BEFORE
1972 In the US, the Title IX civil rights law prohibits discrimination based on sex, including sexual harassment.

1987 An American survey claims one in four women are sexually victimized on campus.

AFTER
2017 Education Secretary Betsy DeVos says the US government will take into account the rights of those accused of sexual assault as well as their accusers.

2017 The Sexual Health Initiative to Foster Transformation (SHIFT) at Columbia University, New York, publishes a landmark study into sexual violence and health among undergraduates.

For many young women, the campus experience has involved sexual violence. Surveys have suggested that across American campuses, up to one in four women students are sexually assaulted while in college.

Student campaigns against sexual violence and abuse on campus gathered momentum from 2010, with some survivors demanding more direct change. This new activism found voice in the documentary film *The Hunting Ground*, released in 2015, which recorded the experiences of women (and people of other genders) trying to report sexual assault on campus. Their efforts to report the attacks had been greeted by college authorities and by police with victim-blaming, disbelief, and pleas to consider the perpetrator's future.

The film focused particularly on two survivors of sexual violence—Annie E. Clark and Andrea Pino. They had founded the campaigning group End Rape on Campus in 2013 and traveled around campuses in the US, giving talks and meeting other survivors. As a result of their campaign, colleges across the US were investigated for Title IX civil rights violations.

In a controversial protest that made headlines in 2014, Emma Sulkowicz—an art student at Columbia University in New York—created a work called "Mattress Performance (Carry That Weight)." This involved Sulkowicz carrying a mattress everywhere she went until Columbia agreed to expel the man accused of raping her. The university found him "not responsible." ∎

Every student has the civil right to an education: rape should not stand in our way.
Andrea Pino

See also: Rape as abuse of power 166–171 ▪ Survivor, not victim 238 ▪ Ending victim blaming 299 ▪ Sexual abuse awareness 322–327

DRIVING WHILE FEMALE
THE RIGHT TO DRIVE

IN CONTEXT

PRIMARY QUOTE
Manal al-Sharif, 2017

KEY FIGURES
**Manal al-Sharif,
Loujain al-Hathloul**

BEFORE
1990 Sheik Abdelaziz bin Baz, the official grand mufti of Saudi Arabia, passes a fatwa (religious edict) upholding the ban on women drivers.

2015 Saudi Arabia proposes hosting the Olympic Games with only male competitors. Joint bidders Bahrain would host the women's events.

AFTER
2018 After Saudi Arabia's driving ban is lifted, doubts remain as to whether any women will still be charged for "immoral behavior" crimes, and whether women will remain free to drive without a male relative in the vehicle.

Throughout the Muslim world, women drive. Until 2018, Saudi Arabia was the one Muslim country that withheld their right to drive. According to Saudi law, a woman caught driving could be arrested, fined, and even publicly flogged. In 1990, 50 women activists protested against the driving restrictions and were all arrested. Most lost their jobs and had their passports confiscated.

Forward and reverse
Manal al-Sharif, an activist for women's rights in Saudi Arabia, led the campaign for women to drive, using YouTube in 2011 to post videos of her driving a car. She was arrested and imprisoned for three months. In 2017, al-Sharif wrote of her experiences in *Daring To Drive*. The same year, as part of a modernization program, Saudi Crown Prince Mohammed bin Salman declared that by June 2018 women would be allowed to drive. Seven feminist activists took to their cars immediately but were arrested. One activist, Loujain

A Saudi woman drives legally for the first time on June 24, 2018. Other recent reforms have seen Saudi women able to join the military and visit sports arenas and cinemas.

al-Hathloul, who had been arrested before for speaking out against the monarchy, was still in prison when the driving ban was lifted.

Despite the new right to drive, campaigners fear that the ultra-conservative Saudi monarchy will stall on further reform. Above all, they want to end the system of male guardianship that prevents women from taking many actions without male permission, such as marrying or traveling. ∎

See also: Female autonomy in a male-dominated world 40–41 ∎ Early Arab feminism 104–105 ∎ Modern Islamic feminism 284–285

#METOO
SEXUAL ABUSE AWARENESS

IN CONTEXT

PRIMARY QUOTE
Tarana Burke, 2006

KEY FIGURES
Tarana Burke, Ashley Judd, Alyssa Milano

BEFORE
1977 Film director Roman Polanski flees California after being indicted for drugging and raping a 13-year-old girl.

1991 Attorney Anita Hill testifies against her ex-boss, US Supreme Court nominee Clarence Thomas, accusing him of sexual harassment—claims which he denied.

AFTER
2018 Hollywood's Time's Up campaign launches a $13m legal fund for women taking action against sexual abuse.

2018 The International Labour Organization conference considers a treaty to protect people at work from violence and harassment.

At the time they happen, certain events are thought to constitute a tipping point, after which nothing will ever again be the same. Some believe the 2017 #MeToo campaign against sexual violence and abuse is an example, marking a global transformation in public awareness of practices that were previously commonplace, but rarely exposed.

The term "Me Too" is not new. It was first used to promote solidarity for survivors of sexual abuse by African American activist Tarana Burke in 2006. While working at the youth organization Just Be Inc. in Alabama, Burke ran workshops for young survivors of sexual violence. If they needed help, but felt unable to ask for it directly, they were asked to write "Me too" on their worksheets. Around 20 of the 30 girls present—far more than Burke had expected—simply wrote "Me too." This was the beginning of the Me Too movement, which was

Tarana Burke speaks out in Beverly Hills, California, during a Take Back the Workplace and #MeToo march and rally in November 2017 at the Producers Guild of America.

I have no tolerance for discrimination, harassment, abuse, or inequality. I'm done.
Alyssa Milano

originally made up of young women of color coming together to find solidarity and support. The message for those women was that they were not alone.

From 2006 onward, awareness of sexual harassment, and activism to counter it, continued to grow. In 2015, a cover of *New York* magazine featured photos of 35 women who had accused American comedian Bill Cosby of sexual assault; he was convicted on three counts in April 2018. During the US presidential campaign of 2016, an audio tape from 2005 came to light, in which Donald Trump boasted of groping women without their consent; he

We need a global cultural change in the workplace, from the Hollywood Hills, to the corridors of Westminster, to the factory floors of Dhaka …
Helen Pankhurst
Granddaughter of Sylvia Pankhurst

See also: Survivor, not victim 238 ▪ Antifeminist backlash 270–271 ▪ Bringing feminism online 294–297 ▪ Sexism is everywhere 308–309

In 2017, the phrase "Me too" went viral as millions of women across the world responded to the MeToo hashtag on Twitter to indicate their experience of sexual harassment and abuse.

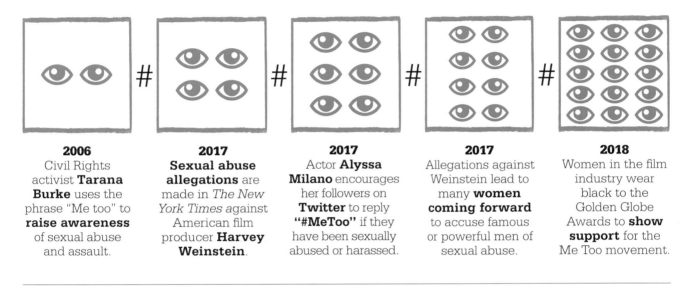

2006
Civil Rights activist **Tarana Burke** uses the phrase "Me too" to **raise awareness** of sexual abuse and assault.

2017
Sexual abuse allegations are made in *The New York Times* against American film producer **Harvey Weinstein**.

2017
Actor **Alyssa Milano** encourages her followers on **Twitter** to reply **"#MeToo"** if they have been sexually abused or harassed.

2017
Allegations against Weinstein lead to many **women coming forward** to accuse famous or powerful men of sexual abuse.

2018
Women in the film industry wear black to the Golden Globe Awards to **show support** for the Me Too movement.

used the phrase "grab them by the pussy." Many attending the 2017 Women's Marches wore "pussy hats" to mark their disgust at the new president's words.

A landmark case

On October 5, 2017, *The New York Times* published an account of its long investigation into allegations of sexual harassment by Hollywood film producer Harvey Weinstein. It covered alleged incidents in several cities and countries over almost three decades, and reported that Weinstein had paid off women who lodged complaints against him. More women quickly came forward, Weinstein was fired from his own company, and eventually charged with rape and sexual abuse. He has denied these and many further accusations of sexual misconduct.

Increasing numbers of women now began to talk publicly about harassment by Weinstein and other powerful men in Hollywood and elsewhere. They had tried to speak out before, they said, but their complaints were dismissed, and some women had been silenced by threats and lawyers. It was claimed that Weinstein's sexual predation was an open secret in Hollywood, yet, before the *New York Times* report, no one had effectively challenged him. Some said they had stayed silent because they feared the effect on their careers of opposing such a powerful man.

Ashley Judd was the first actor to publicly accuse Weinstein, and she later filed a lawsuit against him in April 2018. In it, she claimed that he had spread false statements about her, sabotaging her career, after she had rejected his sexual advances, claims which he denied. Other actors and former employees also described their own experiences. The high profiles of accused and accusers attracted considerable publicity, soon prompting further allegations of sexual misconduct against other men in the entertainment business.

Social media

Ten days after the *New York Times* feature, prompted by a friend, actor Alyssa Milano put up a post on Twitter calling on women who had been sexually harassed or assaulted to write "Me too" as a reply. Milano's post was the first "Me too" online.

Thousands of "Me too" responses followed within a matter of hours, with one woman using the #MeToo to describe her experience of rape and harassment. After that, millions posted their own #MeToo accounts on Twitter and across social media. Their revelations, showing the ubiquity of sexual harassment and worse, were also widely discussed in mainstream media. Women who until then had been too afraid or ashamed to reveal experiences » suddenly began to tell their stories, encouraged by the atmosphere of heightened understanding.

Impossible to ignore

As #MeToo gathered strength, some men and many trans people also began to post reports of their experiences of sexual misconduct in the workplace. The actor and director Kevin Spacey was among those accused by young men, although he denies allegations.

It also became apparent that sexual harassment was prevalent across many kinds of industries. In December 2017, the *Financial Times* charted the "Weinstein effect" on reports of sexual abuse. In February, there had been the lone voice of Susan Fowler, an American software engineer, who had written a blog outlining alleged harassment at Uber in California. There was a media case in April, two further tech cases in July, and another some weeks later. Then,

after the Weinstein allegations, *Financial Times* research found more than 40 instances in the US and UK of high-profile men in politics, finance, the media, and the music, tech, and entertainment industries who had been accused of sexual misconduct. A number of those men lost their jobs.

A global response

The realization that even powerful men might now be punished for what, in some cases, had been decades of sexual harassment, has emboldened victims. The #MeToo campaign has also helped to remove the stigma from reporting such incidents. It has sparked a wider public discussion about sexual misconduct, compelling employers and employees to consider what is and is not acceptable behavior.

While the highest profile #MeToo accusers have come from the entertainment industry,

> We want perpetrators to be held accountable and we want strategies implemented to sustain long term, systemic change.
> **Tarana Burke**

working women from professions and industries in the US and other English-speaking countries were quick to follow the lead and air similar experiences.

The #MeToo movement spread rapidly to the rest of the world. In October 2017, in less than a month, the hashtag had been shared on Twitter in 85 countries via 1.7 million tweets. Hashtags in other languages helped spread the word. Italian director Asia Argento launched #QuellaVoltaChe ("that time when"), explaining that a director had exposed himself to her when she was just 16 years old. #YoTambien ("me too" in Spanish) and #balancetonporc ("squeal on your pig" in French), followed, as did hashtags in Arabic and Hebrew. Muslim women customized the hashtag, creating #MosqueMeToo to detail a catalogue of incidents, including some at the holy city of Mecca in Saudi Arabia.

Actors and other women in the film industry wore black at the 2018 Golden Globes celebrations in Beverly Hills, California, to signify their support for the #MeToo campaign. Some men also wore black in support.

The backlash

The backlash against the #MeToo movement was swift. What about the men now too fearful to ask a woman out, critics asked; must all men's behavior change? One complaint, in the French newspaper *Le Monde* in January 2018, took the form of an open letter signed by 100 prominent women, including the actress Catherine Deneuve. They argued that the #MeToo movement was too extreme and endangered sexual freedom. While deploring abuse, they said that seduction was not a crime. They felt that #MeToo was both tyrannical and puritanical, that it risked casting women as perpetual victims, and that men accused of sexual abuse had been subjected to a "media lynching" without right of reply.

Deneuve later defended her stance, apologizing only to victims offended by the *Le Monde* article. One solution, she felt, lay in education and tougher measures to target sexual abuse at work as soon as it occurred.

Catherine Deneuve, here at a Paris fashion show, was one of a number of prominent women who accused the #MeToo movement of going too far.

The women affected have also described how sexual harassment wrecks personal lives and careers, causing loss of confidence and emotional damage, and stalling promotion opportunities.

High risk

To a world that seemed shocked by #MeToo revelations, it soon became clear that sexual misconduct at work remains a debilitating everyday experience in too many women's lives—in the developed and developing world. Labor rights activists have highlighted the plight of the world's poorest women, such as the millions working for minimal wages in factories or on the land, who are at significant risk of sexual abuse. Undocumented migrants, wherever they live, are also especially vulnerable. The activists explain that the less control individuals have, the greater the likelihood that employers or others in a position of power will abuse that power, often sexually. In the US the Bandana Project, founded by Southern Poverty Law Center (SPLC) in 2007, campaigns against the sexual exploitation of low-paid female farm workers in the American South—the farm workers, many of them migrants, cover their faces with a bandana in order to deflect unwanted sexual attention.

When "MeToo" was first used as a hashtag to signify a movement against sexual abuse, Tarana Burke—its instigator—was not well known. Now recognized as both a longtime activist and woman of color campaigning against sexual abuse, she has helped to expose the multiracial nature of sexual misconduct. Burke was one of eight female activists invited to the 2018 Golden Globe Awards as guests of stars such as Michelle Williams, Emma Watson, and Meryl Streep,

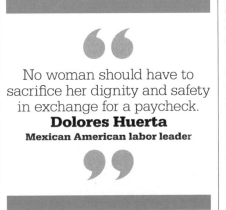

> No woman should have to sacrifice her dignity and safety in exchange for a paycheck.
> **Dolores Huerta**
> **Mexican American labor leader**

further helping to publicize the movement. Now a senior director of Girls for Gender Equity in Brooklyn, New York City, she has, however, kept away from much of the current debate. While aware that the #MeToo discussion has expanded far beyond its original focus on young women of color, she has pointed out that the movement was being built steadily from 2006 onward; it did not happen as quickly as the media made out. Under the banner You Are Not Alone, the Me Too website states that, since 1998, more than 17 million women have reported a sexual assault.

Zero tolerance

Few would dispute the sudden and significant impact of the Weinstein case and #MeToo campaign on sexual abuse awareness. As a 2018 directive from an American law firm with offices worldwide stated: "If it's unwanted, it's harassment." However the issue evolves in decades to come, #MeToo is a sign that campaigns that respond to suffering and fight for women's rights are as relevant today as they ever were. ∎

DIRECTORY

In addition to the feminists and feminist organizations contained in the main section of this book, countless other individuals and groups have challenged the subordination of women, contributed to the development of feminist theory, or helped improve the everyday lives of women across the globe. Their fields of endeavor range from politics, education, law, and workers' rights to birth control, consciousness-raising, and improving female representation in business, the arts, and historical records. Many of these women faced fierce opposition or ridicule from the male-dominated institutions they sought to change, sometimes from women themselves. Over time, however, many of their views were not only acknowledged but integrated into the very definition of a modern society.

FEMINISTS

CHRISTINE DE PIZAN
1364–1430

Italian author, political thinker, and women's rights advocate Christine de Pizan was born in Venice, Italy, to Thomas de Pizan, physician and court astrologer to King Charles V of France. She first began writing to support her family after her husband died from the plague. She then found success writing love ballads, attracting many wealthy patrons in the French court. Her 1402 book *Le Dit de la Rose (The Tale of the Rose)* critiques French author Jean de Meun's popular *Le Roman de la Rose (Romance of the Rose*, c. 1275), which de Pizan argues is a misogynist attack on women that unfairly paints them as seductresses. In 1405, she wrote *Le tresor de la cité des dames de degré en degré (The Book of the City of Ladies)*, which illustrates women's contributions to society and argues for their education. Portuguese and Dutch translations of *The Book of the*

City of Ladies soon followed, and an English version was completed in 1521. De Pizan is thought to have been the first professional female writer in the Western world.
See also: Female autonomy in a male-dominated world 40–41 ▪ Intellectual freedom 106–107

MARY WARD
1585–1645

Nun and early women's rights proponent Mary Ward was born into an English Catholic family in North Yorkshire that was attacked by anti-Catholic mobs during the reign of Queen Elizabeth I. When she was 15, she joined the Poor Clares Franciscan convent in northern France, but deciding she wanted a more active life, she left in 1609 to found a new order—the Institute of the Blessed Virgin Mary (known now as the Sisters of Loreto), committed to educating women. Rather than pursuing the route of cloistered contemplation

insisted upon by Church authorities for women in the Church, Ward stipulated that the sisters in her order should work on behalf of the poor and create and teach in Catholic schools across Europe. Ward walked more than 1,500 miles (2,400 km) to ask Pope Urban VIII for Vatican approval of the Institute, fighting for its right to exist despite the fact that the Vatican had previously imprisoned her and ordered the suppression of her movement. Ward's two orders, Loreto and the Congregation of Jesus, founded in 1609, went on to establish schools around the world.
See also: Institutions as oppressors 80

ANNE HUTCHINSON
1591–1643

Born in Lincolnshire, England, Anne Hutchinson was a midwife, herbalist, and preacher, best known for challenging male religious authority through her preaching and unconventional ideas. After she married William Hutchinson in 1612, the couple became followers of Puritan minister John Cotton. When Cotton was persecuted by the Anglican Church and fled to the Massachusetts Bay colony, in North America, the Hutchinson family followed with their 10 children in 1634. As Anne Hutchinson continued to preach doctrine contrary to established Puritan belief, the male Puritan leaders, including Cotton, turned on her, and Massachusetts governor John Winthrop called her an "American Jezebel". Declared heretics and banished from the colony, she and the family moved to Rhode Island, and then, after William's death, to what is now New York City. She is honored today as one of the earliest proponents of civil liberties and religious tolerance in colonial New England.

See also: Institutions as oppressors 80 ▪ Feminist theology 124–125

SOR JUANA INÉS DE LA CRUZ
1648–1695

Known as the first feminist of the Americas, Sor (Sister) Juana Inés de la Cruz was a writer, poet, dramatist, composer, philosopher, and nun. Born Juana Ramirez, the illegitimate daughter of a Creole mother and Spanish father, she was a self-taught scholar who contributed to early Mexican literature and to the Spanish Golden Age of literature (early 16th–late 17th century). Fluent in Latin, she also wrote in the Aztec language of Nuatl. In order to avoid marriage and pursue her studies, Cruz joined a convent in 1667, where she wrote about love,

religion, and women's rights. Her letter *La Respuesta* (*The Answer*) was written to a priest who hoped to silence her and other women and deny them an education. Scholars have drawn on Cruz's romantic poetry to other women to argue that she may have been what would today be understood as lesbian. Now recognized as a national icon, she is featured on Mexican currency.

See also: Female autonomy in a male-dominated world 40–41 ▪ Intellectual freedom 106–107

MARGARET FULLER
1810–1850

Author of *Women in the Nineteenth Century* (1845), the first major American feminist text, Margaret Fuller was a teacher, writer, editor, and social reformer from Cambridge, Massachusetts. Her father gave her an education equal to that of a boy. Fuller went on to become an advocate for women's education and employment, the abolition of slavery, and prison reform. In 1839, she began hosting "conversations" for women to discuss intellectual topics. When Ralph Waldo Emerson invited her to edit his Transcendentalist journal *The Dial* the same year, Fuller accepted but resigned after two years. She moved to New York City in 1844 to become the first full-time book reviewer in American journalism at the *New-York Tribune*. She was also the *Tribune*'s first female international correspondent, traveling to Europe during the 1848 revolutions in Italy. Fuller died in a shipwreck with her husband and son while returning to the US.

See also: Collective action in the 18th century 24–27 ▪ Intellectual freedom 106–107

TÁHIRIH
1814–1852

The poet and women's rights champion Táhirih was a Persian theologian who organized women to speak out against their inferior status in society. Táhirih, which means "The Pure One," was born Fatimah Baraghani and was educated by her father. She became an adherent of the Bábi faith, an Abrahamic monotheistic religion that departed from Islam and was a precursor to Bahá'í. Speaking of women's rights during a conference of Bábi leaders, Táhirih took off her veil as a challenge to the men present, some of whom were appalled by this action. She was ultimately executed in secret at the age of 38, an act that turned her into a martyr for the Bahá'í community. Her last words were reported to be: "You can kill me as soon as you like, but you will never stop the emancipation of women." The national US organization Táhirih Justice Center, founded in 1997 to fight for an end to violence against women and girls, is dedicated to Táhirih's legacy.

See also: Education for Islamic women 38–39

CONCEPCIÓN ARENAL
1820–1893

The writer Concepción Arenal was a major feminist luminary in Spain, an activist in what was then a very traditional country. She was the first woman to attend a Spanish university, where the authorities required her to dress as a man in classes. Her first writing on women's rights was her 1869 text *La Mujer del Porvenir* (*The Woman*

of the Future). She championed women's access to education and critiqued the notion that women were biologically inferior to men. However, she did not advocate women's access to all occupations because she did not think women were skilled at leadership. Nor did she want women to be diverted from their roles as wives and mothers by politics. Arenal was also dedicated to prison reform, the abolition of slavery, and helping the poor. In 1859, she founded the Conference of Saint Vincent de Paul, a feminist group that aided the poor. In 1871, she began a 14-year involvement with *The Voice of Charity* magazine in Madrid, and in 1872 founded Construction Beneficiary, a group committed to building low-cost housing for the poor.
See also: The global suffrage movement 94–97 ▪ Anarcha-feminism 108–109

ANNA HASLAM
1829–1922

Influential Irish suffragist Anna Haslam was born into a Quaker family in County Cork, Ireland. She was raised to believe in pacifism, the abolition of slavery, the temperance movement, and equality between men and women. Haslam and her husband Thomas were founding members of the Dublin Women's Suffrage Association (DWSA) in the 1870s. After campaigning for 18 years against the 1864 Contagious Diseases Act—which subjected women suspected of prostitution to forced medical examinations and possible arrest—Anna's activism helped repeal the Act. Haslam also saw incremental victories for the right of women to vote in Ireland,

culminating in the 1922 victory that resulted in all Irish women over 21 finally being given suffrage.
See also: The global suffrage movement 94–97

KATE SHEPPARD
1847–1934

Born in Liverpool, UK, Kate Sheppard immigrated to New Zealand with her family in 1868, where she became involved with the Christchurch chapter of the Woman's Christian Temperance Union. Sheppard went on to become the most prominent suffragette in the country. She became the editor of *The White Ribbon*, the first newspaper in New Zealand to be run by women, and ultimately helped the country become the first in the world to establish suffrage for all white adult citizens in 1893. Indigenous Maori people, however, were not allowed to vote until the Commonwealth Franchise Act was passed in 1902. Sheppard was elected as the first president of the National Council of Women of New Zealand, an organization founded in 1896 to achieve gender equality. In later life, she traveled to the UK to assist with the fight for women's suffrage there. In 1991, New Zealand honoured her by replacing Queen Elizabeth II with Sheppard on the 10-dollar bill.
See also: The global suffrage movement 94–97

CARRIE CHAPMAN CATT
1859–1947

American teacher, journalist, and women's suffrage leader Carrie Chapman Catt grew up in Charles City, Iowa. She attended Iowa State

Agricultural College, where she was the valedictorian and only female graduate of her class. Catt became interested in women's suffrage as a teenager when she realized her mother didn't have the same rights as her father, and was a suffragist from 1880 onward. In 1900, she served as president of the National American Woman Suffrage Association (NAWSA), and two years later, she founded the International Woman Suffrage Alliance. She also cofounded the Woman's Peace Party in 1915. Her "Winning Plan," which combined securing women's suffrage on a state-by-state basis while pushing for a constitutional amendment, succeeded in passing the 19th Amendment in 1920, guaranteeing women the right to vote. That same year, Catt founded the League of Women Voters, which still exists today, to help women take a larger role in public life.
See also: The birth of the suffrage movement 56–63

EDITH COWAN
1861–1932

The first woman member of parliament in Australia and a prominent social reformer for the rights of women and children, Edith Cowan was born on a sheep station in Western Australia. Orphaned when her father was executed for the murder of her stepmother, she lived with her grandmother until she married at the age of 18. In 1894, Cowan cofounded the Karrakatta Club—the first social club for women in Australia—and she became a prominent member of the women's suffrage movement. Western Australian women were granted the right to vote in 1899, five years after South Australia but before any other state. Elected to parliament in 1921, Cowan served only one term but in that time she secured legislation that enabled women to enter into the legal profession. She also advocated sex education in schools.

See also: The global suffrage movement 94–97

HANNA SHEEHY-SKEFFINGTON
1877–1946

Born Johanna Mary Sheehy in County Cork, Ireland, suffragette and nationalist Hanna Sheehy-Skeffington cofounded the Irish Women's Franchise League in 1908 and the Irish Women Workers' Union in 1911. She grew up in a family of Irish nationalists, yet her father opposed women's suffrage, a contradiction that shaped her views on both Irish independence and Irish women's oppression. She later remarked, "Until the women of Ireland are free, the men will not achieve emancipation."

After her marriage to Francis Skeffington in 1903, Hanna and her husband adopted the surname Sheehy-Skeffington. In 1912, they cofounded the *Irish Citizen* feminist newspaper. Hanna also took part in militant action together with other suffragettes and served time in prison for smashing the windows at Dublin Castle. In 1913, she was fired from her teaching job for her activism. After her husband was killed during the 1916 Easter Rising against British rule, she lectured extensively in Ireland and the US on Irish nationalism.

See also: The birth of the suffrage movement 56–63 ▪ The global suffrage movement 94–97

KARTINI
1879–1904

Indonesian activist Kartini, whose full name was Raden Adjeng Kartini, was an advocate for girls' education and Indonesian women's rights. Born in Java in what was then the Dutch East Indies, she was educated at a Dutch-speaking school until the age of 12. She was then confined to her parents' house until she was married—a practice that was common at the time. During her seclusion, Kartini continued her studies, including reading Dutch texts, which fueled her interest in Western feminism. As someone whose parents pressured her into an arranged marriage with a man who had multiple wives, she wrote letters against polygamy, and opened a primary school for indigenous girls in 1903 that taught a Western-based curriculum. She also hoped to write a book, but died at the age of 25 after giving birth to her son. Kartini Schools—Dutch schools for indigenous girls—were opened in her memory from 1912.

See also: Education for Islamic women 38–39 ▪ Intellectual freedom 106–107

ANNIE KENNEY
1879–1953

Working-class English suffragette Annie Kenney, who worked in a Lancashire cotton mill between the ages of 10 and 25, is known for helping to escalate the women's suffrage movement into a militant phase. She was arrested and jailed 13 times for disrupting political meetings and, on one occasion, spitting at a police officer. She was a committed member of the leading militant suffragette organization in the UK, the Women's Social and Political Union (WSPU). Kenney and WSPU cofounder Christabel Pankhurst were reportedly lovers, and Kenney was romantically linked to at least 10 WSPU members. In 1912, she was put in charge of the WSPU in London and organized its illegal activities from her home at night until she was jailed in 1913. She published an autobiography, *Memories of a Militant*, in 1924.

See also: Political equality in Britain 84–91

MARGARITA NELKEN
1894–1968

A Spanish intellectual and socialist, Margarita Nelken was born into a well-to-do Jewish family in Madrid. Educated in Paris, she grew up to be a translator, art critic, and novelist. An interest in politics and feminism led her to publish "The Social Condition of Women in Spain" in 1922, and in 1926, she was appointed by the government to investigate the working conditions of women. In 1931, Nelken became a member of the Socialist Party and she was elected to parliament later that year, even though Spanish women did not have the vote. Controversially, she did not support women's suffrage in Spain at that time, because she thought Spanish women would support conservative Catholic forces. When the Spanish Civil War broke out in 1936, Nelken stayed in Madrid to work for the resistance. After the Nationalists' victory in 1939, she went to Mexico, where she pursued her earlier career as an art critic.

See also: The global suffrage movement 94–97 ▪ Women's union organizing 160–161

BELLA ABZUG
1920–1998

Known as "Battling Bella," Bella Abzug was a lawyer, member of Congress, and a leader of second-wave feminism in the US. Her first campaign slogan in 1970 was "This woman's place is in the House—the House of Representatives." Born to Jewish immigrants in the Bronx, New York City, Abzug challenged the sexism of her Orthodox Jewish congregation as a teenager and went on to earn a law degree from Columbia University in 1947. As a lawyer, she championed the Equal Rights Amendment, fought for due process for Willie McGee—her black male client who had been sentenced to death—and opposed the Vietnam war. Elected to the US House of Representatives, Abzug was one of the first members of Congress to advocate gay rights; in 1974, she introduced the Equality Act with New York Representative Ed Koch.
See also: The birth of the suffrage movement 56–63 ▪ Racial and gender equality 64–69

CORETTA SCOTT KING
1927–2006

Born in Marion, Alabama, American civil rights campaigner Coretta Scott King married civil rights leader Martin Luther King, Jr., in 1953. After her husband's assassination in 1968, Coretta Scott King continued in civil rights leadership roles, founding the Martin Luther King, Jr. Center for Nonviolent Social Change in Atlanta, Georgia, in 1968. Scott King also became involved in the women's movement, LGBTQ rights, pacifism, and ending apartheid in South Africa. In 1966, she stated that "women have been the backbone of the whole Civil Rights Movement," and she hosted the National Organization for Women's second convention. She also campaigned for the Equal Rights Amendment and participated in the National Congress of Black Women. In 1983, she advocated the addition of sexuality as a "protected class" to the Civil Rights Amendment, lobbying for LGBTQ equality until her death.
See also: Racial and gender equality 64–69 ▪ Black feminism and womanism 208–215

ROSEMARY BROWN
1930–2003

The first black woman elected to the Canadian government, Rosemary Brown was born in Kingston, Jamaica. She moved to Canada in 1951 to study social work at McGill University, where she experienced both racism and sexism. After graduating, Brown became involved with the British Columbia Association for the Advancement of Coloured People as well as Voice of Women, a Canadian pacifist group founded in 1960. Serving in the British Columbia legislature as a member of the left-wing New Democratic Party from 1972 to 1986, Brown fought to remove sexist bias from textbooks, pushed for female representation on public boards, and worked to ban discrimination based on sex or marital status. Her autobiography, *Being Brown: A Very Public Life*, was published in 1989.
See also: Racial and gender equality 64–69 ▪ Anger as an activist tool 216

JOKE SMIT
1933–81

Born in Vianen, Netherlands, Joke Smit was a feminist, journalist, and politician. In 1967, she published "Het onbehagen bij de vrouw" ("The Discomfort of Women"), an essay that describes Dutch women's frustrations with being confined to roles as wives and mothers and is credited with starting the second-wave feminist movement in the Netherlands. In 1968, Smit went on to cofound the anti-hierarchical feminist action group Man Vrouw Maatschappij (MVM, Man Woman Society), with Dutch politician Hedwig "Hedy" d'Ancona. In the 1970s, Smit wrote about feminism and socialism, the importance of education for girls and women, the division of labor between men and women, the liberation of lesbians, and many other feminist topics.
See also: The roots of oppression 114–117 ▪ Family structures 138–139

FRANÇOISE HÉRITIER
1933–2017

French feminist anthropologist Françoise Héritier explored society's hierarchical division of the sexes in her first and second volumes of *Masculin/Féminin*, published in 1996 and 2002. Mentored by the anthropologist Claude Lévi-Strauss at the Collège de France, Héritier applied structural analysis to the field of anthropology, showing why it was useful for understanding gender- and kinship-based relationships in West Africa as well as in France. Héritier later succeeded Lévi-Strauss at the Collège de France, becoming the first Chair of the

Comparative Study of African Societies. Héritier served as the president of the National AIDS Council from 1989 to 1995.

See also: The roots of opposition 114–117 ▪ The problem with no name 118–123

RUTH BADER GINSBURG
1933–

The second female justice of the US Supreme Court, Ruth Bader Ginsburg was born to Jewish parents in Brooklyn, New York City. She studied first at Harvard Law School then at Columbia Law School. In 1972, Ginsburg cofounded the American Civil Liberties Union (ACLU) Women's Rights Project, becoming the ACLU's general counsel in 1973 and the Director of the Women's Rights Project in 1974. She won five of six gender discrimination cases she argued before the US Supreme Court from 1973 to 1976. After serving as a judge in the Washington, D.C., Circuit Court of Appeals for 13 years, in 1993 she was nominated by President Bill Clinton to the Supreme Court, where she has been a champion of women's rights. Describing herself as a flaming feminist, she announced at the age of 85 that she had no plans to retire until she was at least 90.

See also: Achieving the right to legal abortion 156–159

MARGARET ATWOOD
1939–

A writer of plays and poems from the age of six, novelist Margaret Atwood was born in Ottawa, Canada. After earning a master's degree from Radcliffe College in the US in 1962, Atwood taught writing at universities across Canada. She began publishing award-winning poetry in 1961, and in 1969 published her first novel, *The Edible Woman*. This was the first of several books that would be described as feminist by both fans and critics, although she has rejected the label of feminism. Nevertheless, much of Atwood's work highlights women's oppression, most famously in her acclaimed 1985 dystopian novel *The Handmaid's Tale*, which has been adapted as a film, opera, and television series.

See also: The roots of oppression 114–117

OMOLARA OGUNDIPE-LESLIE
1940–

Nigerian feminist writer, poet, editor, and activist Omolara Ogundipe-Leslie is considered one of the most important contemporary writers on African women and African feminism. She was born in Lagos to a family of educators who believed in the importance of teaching their children African history and language, despite the fact that Nigeria was then a British colony. Her mother also taught her progressive ideas about gender. In her 1994 book *Re-Creating Ourselves: African Women & Critical Transformations*, she coined the term "stiwanism" (Social Transformation in Africa Including Women) to advocate the overthrow of institutionalized structures in African society that oppress women. Ogundipe-Leslie's work explores the impact of colonialism and neocolonialism on African cultures as well as African women's internalization of patriarchy. At the same time, she also stresses the importance of understanding the complexities of precolonial, indigenous African cultures, and the impact they have had on African women's lives.

See also: Anticolonialism 218–219 ▪ Postcolonialism feminism 220–223

ALICE SCHWARZER
1942–

German feminist Alice Schwarzer began her journalism career in 1969. While working in Paris, she signed the Manifesto of the 343, a public declaration by 343 women that they had undergone an abortion—a campaign that led to the legalization of abortion in France. She later admitted that she had never had an abortion. One of the cofounders of the Mouvement de Libération des Femmes (MLF, the French Women's Liberation Movement), Schwarzer helped spread their ideas to Germany. In 1975, she published a book called *Der kleine Unterschied und seine grosse Folgen* (*The Little Difference and Its Huge Consequences*), in which 17 German women told of their experiences of sexual oppression. The book triggered fierce debate in Germany and was widely translated, bringing Schwarzer international recognition. She went on to found the German feminist journal *EMMA* in 1977, which took its inspiration from the American liberal feminist magazine *Ms*. Schwarzer has advocated for women's economic independence as well as bans on pornography and wearing the *hijab* in public.

See also: Achieving the right to legal abortion 156-159

DONNA HARAWAY
1944–

Born in Denver, Colorado, Donna Haraway is an emerita professor at the University of California, Santa Cruz. She is best known for her 1985 essay "A Cyborg Manifesto" and her 1988 essay "Situated Knowledges: The Science Question in Feminism and the Privilege of Partial Perspective." Haraway's early work questioned male bias in the construction of scientific knowledge labeled "objective." She explored how assumptions about human gender and race influence (white male) scientists' interpretation of the behavior of non-human species, a topic she expands on in her 1989 book *Primate Visions: Gender, Race, and Nature in the World of Modern Science*. In "A Cyborg Manifesto," Haraway argues for replacing the idea of identity politics with what she calls "affinity politics." More broadly, her work challenges anthropocentrism, or the centering of humans over other species, and considers how humans incorporate cyborg technology into their lives.

ANNE SUMMERS
1945–

The Australian feminist Anne Summers was born to Catholic parents in Deniliquin, New South Wales, in 1945. After becoming pregnant while studying politics and history at the University of Adelaide in 1965, Summers underwent a botched abortion, an experience that fueled her growing interest in feminism. After marrying and then leaving a fellow student, she founded a Women's Liberation Movement group in Adelaide in 1969, and the following year set up a refuge for victims of domestic violence in Sydney. In the early 1970s, Summers began to write, publishing *Damned Whores and God's Police* in 1975, a book about the roles of women in Australian society. After a stint as editor of the feminist magazine *Ms.* in New York City, she returned to Australia and became a political adviser on women's affairs. She continues to write, broadcast, and organize conferences on feminism.
See also: Modern feminist publishing 142–143 ▪ Achieving the right to legal abortion 156–159

JULIA GILLARD
1961–

The first female prime minister of Australia (2010–2013) and the first female leader of a major Australian political party (the Labour Party), Julia Gillard immigrated to Australia from her birthplace in Wales as a child. As prime minister, Gillard faced relentless sexism from the opposition. In 2012, she delivered a speech to parliament that became known as the "Misogyny Speech." In this rebuttal to opposition leader Tony Abbott—who had been calling on Gillard to end her support for House Speaker Peter Slipper after he had sent sexist texts to an aide—Gillard accused Abbott of being hypocritical and consistently misogynistic. Her speech went viral and was hailed by feminist blogs and many political leaders. Since leaving office in 2013, Gillard has fulfilled various roles on public bodies, including chairing the Global Institute for Women's Leadership.
See also: Sexism is everywhere 308–309

ROXANE GAY
1974–

Born in Omaha, Nebraska, to Haitian parents, Roxane Gay is a best-selling feminist author and creative writing professor at Purdue University in Indiana. Gay first began writing essays when she was a teenager. Her writing explores themes of gender, race, sexuality, and body size and includes works of fiction and non-fiction, such as her 2014 book of essays *Bad Feminist* and her 2017 collection of short stories *Difficult Women*. Gay's memoir *Hunger,* also published in 2017, explores her navigation of a fat-hating society as a woman of size.
See also: Fat positivity 174–175 ▪ Intersectionality 240–245

KAT BANYARD
1982–

Called "the UK's most influential young feminist" by the *Guardian's* Kira Cochrane in 2013, Kat Banyard came to feminism after encountering sexism at college. Growing up, Banyard had assumed that feminism was a bygone issue from an earlier era. Her growing interest in feminism led her to cofound and direct UK Feminista, which lobbies politicians to enact feminist legislation, conducts classroom workshops in schools on sex equality, and coordinates feminist campaigns against "lads' mags" and sexual harassment in school. It also focuses on fighting sexual objectification. Banyard is the author of *The Equality Illusion: The Truth About Women and Men Today* (2010) and *Pimp State: Sex, Money and the Future of Equality*

(2016). She argues that men must be active partners with women in the fight against gender inequality.
See also: Fighting campus sexual assault 320

PATRISSE CULLORS
1984–

Born in Los Angeles, California, Patrisse Cullors is the cofounder of the Black Lives Matter movement and a queer activist.

Cullors entered into political activism as a teenager and went on to found Dignity and Power Now, an anti-police brutality coalition that focuses on the conduct of sheriffs in county jails. She has attributed her early commitment to fighting for racial justice to her own experience of growing up in a low-income black family in Los Angeles, as well as grappling with police brutality against her brother in LA county jails. In 2013, Cullors, together with friends Alicia Garza and Opal Tometi, founded Black Lives Matter as a response to the acquittal of George Zimmerman for the murder of unarmed black teenager Trayvon Martin in Florida. Cullors has won multiple awards for her activism and is a board member of the Ella Baker Center for Human Rights, an action group set up to prevent cycles of urban violence.
See also: Anger as an activist tool 216 ▪ Queer theory 262–263

ORGANIZATIONS

DANISH WOMEN'S SOCIETY
1871

The world's oldest women's rights organization, the Dansk Kvindesamfund (Danish Women's Society) was cofounded in 1871 by Matilde Bajer and her husband Frederik Bajer. Matilde had been active in the Swiss-based Comité locale de l'association internationale des femmes (Local Committee of the International Women's Association), and Frederik was a politician and a prominent supporter of the Women's Emancipation movement. The Danish Women's Society advocated women's rights to paid employment and independence in the family. It later agitated for women's right to vote in Denmark (achieved in 1915) and the legalization of abortion (achieved in 1973). Today, the Danish Women's Society operates as a women's rights NGO and publishes *Kvinden & Samfundet* (*Women and Society*), the world's oldest women's magazine.
See also: Early Scandinavian feminism 22–23

SEKIRANKAI
1921

The women's rights group Sekirankai (Red Wave Society in Japanese) was the first women's socialist organization in Japan. Founded by anarchist activists Sakai Magara, Kutsumi Fusako, Hashiura Haruno, and Akizuki Shizue, Sekirankai was active for eight short but explosive months in 1921. Its members argued that capitalism must be overthrown in order to achieve a socialist society, and claimed that capitalism turns women into slaves and prostitutes. On May Day, known also as International Workers' Day to socialists and communists, Sekirankai distributed copies of their "Manifesto to Women" in Tokyo. Written by socialist Yamakawa Kikue, it critiqued capitalism from a feminist perspective and denounced it for enabling imperialism. About 20 members marched through the streets, and all were arrested. Government legislation curtailing freedom of speech and assembly, especially for women, combined with social disapproval effectively dissolved Sekirankai, but its members went on to create other Japanese socialist feminist groups.
See also: Feminism in Japan 82–83

GULABI GANG
2002–

Founded by social activist Sampat Pal Devi in the Banda District of Uttar Pradesh, northern India, Gulabi Gang is a team of mostly women from India's lowest caste, the Dalits ("untouchables") who fight male violence, poverty, and child marriage. The Gulabi Gang focuses on training women in self-defense, equipping them with long bamboo sticks known as *lathis*. The group provides women with resources to achieve financial security and thus less dependence on men. "Gulabi" means "pink" in Hindi and refers to the members' distinctive pink saris. Women in the group range from ages 18 to 60. Gulabi Gang takes justice into their own hands in the face of the widespread failure of the police to protect them from male violence, and members use tactics such as dialogue, confronting abusers, public shaming, and martial arts. Indian filmmaker Nishtha Jain's documentary about the group, *Gulabi Gang*, premiered in 2012.

See also: Indian feminism 176–177

FEMEN
2008–

Founded in Ukraine by Anna Hutsol, FEMEN is headquartered in Paris and has branches across the world. The radical feminist group is dedicated to fighting the sexual exploitation of women, the oppression of women under dictatorship, and patriarchal religion, and is committed to atheism. The group is known for its controversial topless protests and defines its deliberately provocative tactics as "sextremism." FEMEN's slogan is "My Body Is My Weapon!" Its members view toplessness as an important part of women reclaiming their bodies from patriarchal control, writing on their website, "Manifestation of the right to her body by the woman is the first and most important step to her liberation." FEMEN targets theocratic Islamic states practicing Sharia law, a focus that some critics claim is Islamophobic. FEMEN is also committed to ending prostitution and the "sex-industry," which the group calls "genocide."

See also: Popularizing women's liberation 132–133 ▪ Sex positivity 234–237 ▪ Raunch culture 282–283

PUSSY RIOT
2011–

Russian feminist punk rock group Pussy Riot, based in Moscow, stages public guerrilla performances to oppose President Vladimir Putin and his crackdown on freedom of speech, women's rights, and LGBTQ rights. The group started with around a dozen members and now has a rotating cast of musicians and artists. Since their arrest in 2012 for playing anti-Putin songs inside a Russian Orthodox church, members Nadezhda Tolokonnikova, Maria Alyokhina, and Yekaterina Samutsevich have become visible representatives of the group in the global media. All three were convicted of religious "hooliganism," and while Samutsevich's sentence was suspended on appeal, Tolokonnikova and Alyokhina were forced to spend two years in prison. Upon release, Tolokonnikova and Alyokhina became campaigners for prison reform, in addition to their other activist work. Pussy Riot's songs include "Kill the Sexist," "Death to Prison, Freedom to Protests," and "Mother of God, Drive Putin Away." During the final of the 2018 football World Cup in Moscow, four Pussy Riot activists in police uniform ran onto the pitch calling for an end to illegal detention. They received 15-day jail sentences.

See also: Guerrilla protesting 246–247 ▪ The Riot Grrrl movement 272–273

MOVEMENTS

PRESIDENTIAL COMMISSION ON THE STATUS OF WOMEN
1961–1963

The Presidential Commission on the Status of Women (PCSW) was commissioned by US President John F. Kennedy. It was a political compromise by Kennedy to investigate women's inequality while retaining support from the labor movement, who had been instrumental in his electoral victory and largely opposed ratification of the Equal Rights Amendment (ERA). Former US First Lady, diplomat, and activist Eleanor Roosevelt served as the PCSW's Chair. The PCSW found that women in the US were not as well educated as men, nor did they take part in economics or politics at the same rate. In its final 1963 report entitled "American Women," it stopped short of endorsing the ERA, advocating instead for a Supreme Court decision that would find women entitled to equal protection of civil rights under the 14th Amendment to the US Constitution. Still, the PCSW's creation led to the founding of the National Organization for Women (NOW) in 1966, and to commissions in all 50 US states by 1967 to study women's status at a local level.

See also: The birth of the suffrage movement 56–63 ▪ Racial and gender equality 64–69

MANIFESTO OF THE 343
1971

Written by French feminist philosopher Simone de Beauvoir, the Manifesto of the 343 (ridiculed as the Manifesto of the 343 Sluts or 343 Bitches) was a petition signed

by 343 French women declaring they had illegal abortions and demanding reproductive rights. Because of the illegal status of abortion in France at that time, the women's declaration exposed them to the risk of criminal prosecution. In the Manifesto, which was published in *Le Nouvel Observateur* magazine, de Beauvoir highlighted the fact that each year a million French women had abortions in dangerous conditions, and declared that she, too, had an abortion. The Manifesto inspired 331 French doctors to pen a 1973 manifesto on behalf of a woman's right to abortion. In January 1975, abortion during the first 10 weeks of pregnancy was legalized in France.
See also: The roots of oppression 114–117 ▪ Achieving the right to legal abortion 156–159

CONTRACEPTIVE TRAIN
1971

On May 22, 1971, members of the Irish Women's Liberation Movement (IWLM) took direct action to provide contraceptives to Irish women. Because contraception had been illegal in the Republic of Ireland since the 1935 Criminal Law (Amendment) Act, IWLM cofounder Nell McCafferty, along with other women in the IWLM, took a train to Belfast in Northern Ireland. They attempted to buy birth control pills but were unable to obtain them, as Northern Irish women were required to present a doctor's prescription. Instead the women purchased condoms and spermicidal jelly as well as hundreds of packets of aspirin to fool customs officials into thinking they were contraceptive pills. International media crews followed them on their journey. The

women flaunted the contraceptives at customs officials, risking arrest. The event helped break the taboo against discussing birth control. Contraception was fully legalized in the Republic of Ireland in 1993.
See also: Birth control 98–103 ▪ The Pill 136

#BRINGBACKOURGIRLS
2014–

In April 2014, 276 female students were kidnapped from Chibok, Nigeria, by the Islamic terrorist group Boko Haram. Days after the kidnapping, Obiageli "Oby" Ezekwesili—a Nigerian accountant and former vice president of the World Bank's Africa division—said in a speech that Nigerians must take tangible action to "bring back our girls." Later that month, Ibrahim Abdullahi, a corporate lawyer in Abuja, Nigeria, referenced Ezekwesili on Twitter, writing in a tweet, "Yes BringBackOurDaughters #BringBackOurGirls." This was the first use of the BringBackOurGirls hashtag on social media. It soon became a global call, attracting supporters such as US First Lady Michelle Obama. Since then, 57 girls escaped in 2014, and dozens were later found or rescued. As of 2018, however, more than 100 girls remain missing, several are presumed dead, and kidnappings continue.
See also: Bringing feminism online 294–297 ▪ Universal feminism 302–307

HEFORSHE
2014–

A solidarity campaign for gender equality, HeForShe asks boys and men to get involved by taking the

HFS pledge to tackle gender bias, discrimination, and violence. Initiated by the United Nations Entity for Gender Equality and the Empowerment of Women, also known as UN Women, the campaign was launched in 2014 with a speech by British actor Emma Watson, who is also a UN Women Goodwill Ambassador. In her speech, which quickly went viral, Watson explained how she came to identify as a feminist and the importance of boys and men becoming involved in the fight against gender inequality. High-profile men involved in the HeForShe movement include former UN Secretary-General Ban Ki-Moon, former US President Barack Obama, and American actor Matt Damon.
See also: Bringing feminism online 294–297 ▪ Universal feminism 302–307

TIME'S UP
2018–

In the wake of the #MeToo movement against rape culture and serial sexual abuse, Hollywood celebrities formed the Time's Up movement, announcing its creation in *The New York Times* on January 1, 2018. The announcement included several initiatives, such as calling for women at the Golden Globe Awards to wear black and speak out about sexual harassment, as well as setting up a legal defense fund of $13 million to help non-celebrity women's lawsuits against workplace sexual harassment and assault. On its website, Time's Up features an open letter against sexual violence and workplace inequality signed by almost 400 women.
See also: Bringing feminism online 294–297 ▪ Universal feminism 302–307

GLOSSARY

Anarcha-feminism
A combination of anarchism and feminism based on the belief that patriarchy and hierarchies result in oppression. Anarcha-feminists strive for a community-based society, in which individuals are able to control their own lives.

Androcentric An ideological focus on men as the primary sex, where the default human being is male, and women are viewed as subordinate to men.

Antipornography feminism Activism informed by the belief that pornography sexualizes and normalizes violence against women.

Biological determinism The idea that men's and women's behaviors and personalities are innate and determined by physical rather than cultural factors.

Black feminism A feminism informed by the experiences of women of color that maintains that sexism, racism, and class oppression are inextricably linked.

Bluestockings A group of educated women who attended intellectual social gatherings in each other's homes in mid-18th-century London.

Capitalism The economic system in which a society's trade, industry, and profits are based on private ownership, rather than industries owned by the state or by the individuals who work in them on a profit-sharing basis.

Cisgender A person whose gender identity matches the one they were assigned at birth. It is often abbreviated to "cis."

Cishet Referring to a person, a situation, or group, that is both cisgender and heterosexual.

Civil Rights Movement
A political movement in the US in the 1950s and '60s, led by and for African Americans. Its supporters fought for equal opportunities with white Americans and the end to legalized racial discrimination.

Compulsory heterosexuality
The idea that patriarchal society enforces heterosexuality as the default sexual orientation.

Consciousness-raising A form of activism originating in 1960s New York that came out of the concept "the personal is political." Women gathered in small groups to discuss the realities of their lives and thus find common experiences of oppression that would inform their activism.

Coverture A legal framework that prevailed in many English-speaking countries before the end of the 19th century, by which a married couple were treated as one entity and the woman was under the man's protection and authority.

Domestic labor Unpaid work carried out in the home, mainly by women. The performance of this essential work is often considered key to women's inequality.

Dress reform A movement in the middle to late Victorian era that promoted practical and comfortable clothing. This was in contrast to the uncomfortable and over-elaborate women's clothing such as corsets that were worn at that time. Dress reformers were often treated with disbelief and ridicule.

Dyke Previously a derogatory term, this word was "reclaimed" by lesbian feminists in the 1970s and is an important identity to some lesbians. However, many people still believe it to be a slur and it is often used to insult masculine women.

Emotional labor A requirement of some jobs, especially those often done by women, where workers must manage their own feelings and show enthusiasm or caring. It is also used in relation to women's unacknowledged role of organizing and maintaining emotional and social connections.

Empowerment Measures to improve the lives of oppressed people, particularly legal and social changes, such as improving girls' education in the developing world. It also describes a feeling of strength experienced by individual women when they make changes in their work or relationships with themselves and others.

Equality feminism A strand of feminism, sometimes deployed by conservatives in the US, that focuses on legal equality between women and men.

Essentialism The belief that there are profound differences between men and women that are essential to their identity and that cannot be changed.

Eve teasing A euphemism, used in South Asia, meaning the sexual harassment and abuse of women in public places.

Fat positivity An acceptance of people of all sizes, recognizing that it is not necessary to be thin in order to be healthy or happy; a movement to combat anti-fat bias.

Feminism A wide range of social movements and ideologies based on asserting women's rights; collective activism for legal, economic, and social equality between the sexes; and the belief that women should have rights and opportunities equal to those of men.

Feminist theology Examining the history, practices, beliefs, and scriptures of religions from a feminist perspective.

First-wave feminism A period of feminism from 1848 until around 1918–1920. It focused on women's right to vote, rights within marriage, and the ending of legal barriers to education and work.

Gender The state of being male or female; socially constructed behaviors, roles, and activities that are connected to masculinity or femininity; someone's deeply held internal perception that they are male or female.

Gender fluid Relating to a person who considers their identity or gender expression as not fixed or including both male and female.

Gender gap The differences between men and women on a range of variables, such as education, income, and politics.

Herstory A second-wave feminist word for "history," which emphasizes women's lives, and removes the prefix "his."

Heteronormativity The strong belief that heterosexuality is the only normal sexual orientation, and that differences between men and women are also distinct, natural, and complementary.

Incel A man who considers himself "involuntarily celibate" because he cannot attract the sort of woman he wants. Incels are often aggressively anti-women, blaming them for their lack of sex and love.

Internalized sexism When women themselves believe mainstream society's perceptions of female inferiority.

Intersectionality An important strand of modern feminism that explains how different aspects of an individual's identity, such as race, gender, and age, create intersecting systems of discrimination.

Intersex People born with a mixture of male and female sexual characteristics, including chromosomes and sex hormones.

Kyriarchy An idea that encompasses multiple systems of oppression, including patriarchy, and considers how each person fits within that. For example, a white working-class lesbian woman has simultaneously more and less power than a black upper-class heterosexual man.

Lesbian feminism Feminists for whom lesbianism was an intrinsic part of their feminism, and vice-versa. This strand of feminism began in the late 1960s due to the exclusion of lesbians from mainstream feminism in the US.

LGBT/LGBTQ/LGBTQ+ Initials that stand for lesbian, gay, bisexual, transgender, and, post-1990, queer. The term encompasses different groups within sexual and gender cultures. A "plus" sign indicates the inclusion of people who are uncertain of their sexuality and intersex and asexual people.

Liberal feminism The focus on women's ability to choose the lives they want and achieve gender equality through individual actions, rather than collectively.

Male chauvinism A patronizing and degrading attitude by males toward females, coming from the belief that men are superior.

Male chauvinist pig A second-wave feminist slang term for a man who believes in male superiority and acts unpleasantly toward women as a result.

Male gaze The way in which the visual arts portray women as passive objects to be viewed by heterosexual men.

Marxist feminism A strand of feminism that believes that women's oppression is mainly or exclusively an effect of capitalism.

Matriarchy A family, group, or state that is governed by a woman or women; a form of social relationship in which the mother or eldest female is head of the household; a situation in which family descent and inheritance comes through the female, rather than male, line.

Microaggression The regular small acts of invalidation that are directed toward members of marginalized groups.

Misogyny Men's hatred of and contempt for women; entrenched prejudice against women.

Non-binary A general term for something that comprises more than two elements. In feminism and gender studies, it is an umbrella term for people who do not identify as either male or female, or who identify as both.

Objectification In the context of feminism, treating women as sexual objects in relation to male desire, and not as individuals with thoughts or rights of their own.

Oppression The exercise of power and authority over one group of people by another, or by the state, in a cruel or unjust manner.

Other, the A term used to describe how a group views anyone outside the group in terms of its own standards.

Patriarchy The social system in which men are assigned most or all of the power, privilege, and value, and women are largely or completely excluded from this power; a system in which the father or eldest male is head of the household, and descent is determined through the male line.

Pay gap The difference in pay received by different people doing the same job. It often refers to the

gender pay gap, by which men are paid more than women, but it can also refer to earning differentials due to race or class.

Performativity The way in which individuals "perform" masculinity or femininity, encompassing the way they feel, look, or act; this itself constructs both what masculinity or femininity means to that person and how they are perceived by others, indicating that gender is not necessarily fixed or stable.

Phallocentric An emphasis on the phallus—the symbolic, rather than actual, male sexual organ—as a sign of male dominance.

Political lesbianism The idea that lesbianism is a political choice and that women should give up men to combat male oppression, whether or not they desire other women.

Positive discrimination Explicitly favoring members of a group that has experienced, or does experience, oppression.

Postcolonialism The study of the aftermath of colonialism and imperialism—whether this was as a method of government or a way of seeing the world—and its effects on social and political power.

Postfeminism A term that gained prominence in the 1980s, positing that feminism was no longer necessary because its goals had been achieved.

Privilege The idea that members of one group are advantaged in comparison with members of another group. White women, for instance, have privilege compared to women of color, regardless of

other aspects of their lives such as class or education. According to this theory, some people are more oppressed than others.

Queer An umbrella term used from around 1990 for gender- and sexual-minority individuals or groups; members of the LGBT community who are not interested in the political goals of the gay movement; a way of disrupting conventional norms of gender and sexuality.

Queer theory A range of academic ideas that question, among other things, whether identities are fixed, whether gender or sexuality are binary, and whether any behavior is really normal.

Radical feminism The belief that women will only be free from oppression when a male-controlled society—patriarchy—ends; women's collective activism to achieve these aims.

Rape culture An environment in which sexual assault and abuse is normalized or trivialized.

Reproductive freedom A woman's right to abortion and birth control and the freedom to make these choices without judgement or pressure.

Revolutionary feminism The most extreme version of second-wave feminism, in which men were viewed as "the enemy" of women.

Riot grrrl A grassroots movement of young feminists, most popular in the early to mid-1990s. Its followers expressed themselves through punk music and other forms of creativity such as zines.

Second-wave feminism A period of feminism from the mid 1960s to early '80s, especially in North America and Europe, but with an impact on many other countries around the world. It focused on women's experiences within the family, in sexual relationships, and at work.

Separatism The idea that one group (in this instance, women) should remove themselves from opposing groups (such as men) as much as possible in their political, social, domestic, and working lives.

Sex positivity A philosophy that promotes sexuality and sexual expression, and considers them to form part of women's freedom.

Sexism The use of stereotypes to advantage or disadvantage one gender over another; systemic discrimination against women; lack of respect for women.

Sexual politics The power relationships between one group of people (men) and another (women).

Sisterhood A strong bond of solidarity among women based around collective action to improve women's rights.

Slut-shaming Criticism leveled at women whose sexual behavior or revealing clothing transgress codes of conventionally acceptable behavior, which has the effect of placing the blame for sexual violence upon the victim.

Subaltern A person or group that is ascribed a lower status in a hierarchy, or placed outside of political power structures in any given society.

Suffragette A woman, especially from early 20th century Britain, who sought the right to vote through organized, sometimes violent, protest.

Suffragist A first-wave feminist who campaigned for the extension of voting rights to those, especially women, who did not have them, through the use of peaceful, constitutional means.

SWERF A "sex worker exclusionary radical feminist" claims women engaging in sex work are doing something that oppresses women in general and harms individuals within it. They believe that sex workers' opinions about their experiences should be discounted.

TERF A "trans-exclusionary radical feminist" believes that trans women are not "real women" and therefore have no place within feminism, as expressed by the "womyn-born-womyn" policy of some TERF events.

Third-wave feminism A period of feminism that began in the 1990s and ended around 2012. Its strongest focus was on personal choice and the empowerment of women as individuals.

Trans (transgender) A person whose gender identity differs from that assigned at birth.

Trans feminism A movement by and for trans women, promoting their involvement within feminism as a whole and pushing for issues specific to trans women.

Transnational feminism Theory and activism looking at the ways globalization and capitalism affect and disempower people across genders, sexualities, nations, races, and classes.

Transphobia Prejudice against, and fear of, trans people.

Victim-blaming When the victim of a wrongful act or crime is held fully or partially responsible for it.

White feminism Feminism that focuses primarily on issues that affect white women.

Womanism A term coined by writer Alice Walker in the 1980s to refer to the history and experiences of women of color that mainstream, second-wave feminism did not address.

Women of color A political term that encompasses women of African, Asian, Latin, or indigenous heritage.

Women's Liberation Movement An important part of second-wave feminism, the WLM came out of the radical movements of the late 1960s. "Women's Lib" was based on collective activism across many of the world's industrialized societies. It rejected the idea that piecemeal political and social reform would lead to profound or rapid change, and held that a more deep-rooted transformation was needed.

Womyn/Wombyn/Wimmin Alternative spellings of the word "women" which were used by some second-wave feminists to avoid the suffix "-men."

Zines Hand-made magazines produced in small numbers, often for fans, by the punk bands of the Riot Grrrl movement of the 1990s.

INDEX

Page numbers in **bold** refer to main entries; those in *italics* refer to captions

D

E

F

G

H